HITLER'S THIRD REICH OF THE MOVIES AND THE AFTERMATH

Rolf Giesen

Orlando, Florida

Hitler's Third Reich of the Movies and the Aftermath

Published in the USA by
BearManor Media
1317 Edgewater Dr. #110
Orlando, FL 32804
www.BearManorMedia.com

Softcover Edition
ISBN: 978-1-62933-629-9

Printed in the United States of America

Table of Contents

ACKNOWLEDGEMENTS

Grateful thanks are due to the late émigré writer Curt Siodmak who created ***The Wolf Man*** (and to Siodmak's charming wife, Henrietta). He once told a German TV interviewer who asked him to please comment in front of the camera about the Nazis in one minute and a half: ***This you can't tell in one and a half minute.***

Thanks to the late cinematographers Gerhard Huttula (who worked on some of the biggest Ufa films, ***The Great Love, Münchhausen*** and ***Kolberg***), H. O. Schulze (who photographed the light rings around the machine-woman in Fritz Lang's ***Metropolis*** and collaborated with Leni Riefenstahl on her ***Olympia*** films), Ewald Krause, Karl-Ludwig Ruppel, Heinz Pehlke, the late art director Fritz Maurischat, the late trickfilm animators Gerhard Fieber, Dr. Werner Kruse, Ferdinand Diehl, Heinz Kaskeline, and Lester Novros, to the late actor Ferdy Mayne, the late Hollywood legends Hal Roach, Ray Harryhausen and Forrest J Ackerman, the late Fischinger biographer Dr. William Moritz. Witnesses of the past have died in the meantime. Still with us are Jörg Jannings (nephew of Emil), director Roland Emmerich, VFX experts Volker Engel, Dennis Muren and Robert Blalack, distributor Hanns Eckelkamp, actor Rinaldo Talamonti who over the years supplied first-hand information.

More thanks to fellow historians William Gillespie, an expert on Karl Ritter, who read the manuscript written in words that are not part of my native language, color film specialist Gert Koshofer, J. P. Storm, Jens Geutebrück, Frank Noack, Rolf Aurich, Whitney Grace, and the staff members of Deutsche Kinemathek Berlin and Filmmuseum Dusseldorf.

Images courtesy of
Christian Doerge (Apex Verlag)
Jens Geutebrück, Coronaretro Archives, www.gotha-wiki.org
J. P. Storm Collection
Dr. Ralf Bülow
and
Collection Rolf Giesen / Deutsche Kinemathek Berlin

In the age of a diversified, marginalizing and atomizing internet, film books seem to be a dying species. Even more so I must thank brave publishers like Ben Ohmart of Bear Manor Media who still give us film historians a chance.

RG

PRELIMINARY NOTE

DON'T EXPECT

one of the contemporary film books written by scholars and theorists who transfer their literary tools to the film medium and devote their spare time to Nazi film semiotics excavating allegedly unknown movie subtexts.

Most film historians despise the work of Curt Riess (a.k.a. Curt Martin Steinam, 1902-1993), a journalist and critic well-known in Germany, exiled in 1933, who published 60 books. In the United States he worked for *The Saturday Evening Post* and *Collier's Weekly*. Returning to post-war Germany he wrote a popular book about German films: ***Das gibt's nur einmal: Das Buch der schönsten Filme unseres Lebens*** (***It Only Happens Once: The Book of the Loveliest Movies of Our Life***) that reads like a first-hand report. Even if parts were invented by this clever mind, one enjoyed reading because Riess, dealing with National Socialist films, told of both entertainment and political propaganda, in an entertaining way. This questionable but lively quality is missing from most of today's dusty research. Riess knew that the film production of the so-called Third Reich was in most cases ordinary entertainment with an "icing" of propaganda.

Our book shouldn't rely on invented parts, but nevertheless it too should read like an experience report and refer to the entertainment aspect. Not the

National Socialist propaganda, of course not, but this entertainment had a stunning afterlife in post-war German cinema to this day.

SO DON'T EXPECT

a book that covers only movies made from 1933 till the end of WW2. ***Nosferatu*** or ***Metropolis*** (made years before the Nazis seized power) are toying with elements that were familiar to Nazis, including anti-Semitism. Post-war science fiction films such as ***Star Wars*** and ***Independence Day***, the latter directed by a German in Hollywood, rely on images familiar from WW2.

It is also a story about family entertainment in Nazi times, about animated films that were supposed to fulfill the Nazis' dream of creating a cartoon film industry that would rival Disney and make Europe's children happy, while the little captives of a children's barrack in Auschwitz who dreamed of Disney's ***Snow White***, too, thanks to murals painted by a Jewish artist, ended in burning fiery furnaces.

And this is a story of those who were lucky enough to leave Nazi Germany in time and tried to seek work in the U.S. film industry, such as Joe May (who sadly failed) and writer Curt Siodmak (who made a living writing horror stories).

It is a story of contemporary filmmakers who are still intrigued with National Socialism in an odd way and fascinated by the power of the dark side.

The Nazis were no Indo-Germanic tribe that all of a sudden overran Germany and miraculously vanished in 1945, as Henryk M. Broder, a journalist, once wrote: They were and are part of German nationalist identity. The Nazis were monstrosities that grew out of the well-wooded Germanic spirit. Fascism and fascist fundamentalism didn't start with Mussolini and Hitler - and didn't end with their deaths. In a global world the danger of dictatorship (in the West) and despotism (in the East) seems to be bigger than ever. Democracy is at stake.

So, in a way, this book turns out to be a critical review of hundred years of German filmmaking (and some of the filmmaking abroad that was heavily influenced by Germans), from the end of World War 1 up to recent productions.

Karl Neumann.

Courtesy of J. P. Storm Collection

INTRODUCTION

Weesow/Werneuchen near Berlin. In May 1945 a man who was arrested and interned by the Soviets was found dead. He had hanged himself in a toilet. His crime: He had produced cartoon films, no propaganda like the Americans did with ***Der Führer's Face*** or ***Education for Death***, just peaceful bee-and-honey shit. No, you won't find his guilt in the two short Agfacolor subjects he supervised and that since have become part of German entertainment.

The search for traces what happened behind the screen of the National Socialist film industry is like a crime story. If only my colleagues and I would be better investigators ...

The name of the suicide victim was Karl Neumann.

His personal data sheet identifies him as employee of a meat factory, an expert in sausages:

- Bank accountant, *Deutsche Überseeische Bank*, Berlin

- Clerk in a meat factory in Cologne

- Floor manager, *Rügenwalder Wurst- und Fleischwarenfabrik/Ostsee* (Baltic Sea), another meat factory

But then - aha!

- Member of NSDAP since 1931

- Member of SA, later SS

- Full-time head of propaganda NSDAP Gau [County] Pommerania
- Personal assistant, Reich Ministry of Enlightenment and Propaganda
- In Charge of Enforcement, Memorial Day 1935
- Chairman *Reichsarbeitsgemeinschaft* [Working Pool] Safety Measures etc.

But that certainly didn't qualify him to produce cartoons like Disney did. He was neither an artist nor was he what we might call a person with a creative mind. So he was an average Nazi.

But wait a minute: Some of this animation was produced in Dachau!

The very first American soldier at the liberation of the Dachau concentration camp near Munich on April 29, 1945, was a man by the name of Robert B. Sherman. He and his brother Richard, the legendary team of the Sherman Brothers, were the sons of Russian-Jewish composer Al Sherman and became Walt Disney's favorite songwriters working on ***Mary Poppins*** and ***The Jungle Book,*** the latter probably the most popular animated film ever screened in Germany. Back then Robert couldn't possibly know that round the corner the Nazis had produced cartoon films to rival Disney's output and failed miserably.

The Third Reich produced 1,350 feature films but no more than 219 of them were termed after WW2 *Vorbehaltsfilme*, restricted movies because of militaristic, history-falsifying, revisionist content. Today only 40 NS films are still banned. Apart from that Nazi filmdom seemed to have been suspiciously peaceful like that animation they ground out in Dachau next to a concentration camp: pure run-of-the-mill romanticism, a lovely clean idyll invented by the same petite bourgeoisie that had elected Hitler (and he was the greatest petit bourgeois), all - to quote one of Disney's cartoons - flowers and trees, woods and meadows if...yes, if there were not these ugly brown spots, the dark side of wartime propaganda: 'blood and soil' and anti-Semitism.

PRELUDE:

Jewish Vampires Demonize German Cinemas and Minds

In 1940, the "Final Solution of the Jewish Question", the Holocaust, was prepared on the screen by one of the most infamous propaganda efforts of all time: a 65-minute semi-"documentary" titled ***Der ewige Jude*** (***The Eternal Jew***). In one exposing sequence the "director", SS Hauptsturmführer Fritz Hippler, who was later sidelined by his boss, Dr. Joseph Goebbels, due to alcoholism, interjected images of rats:

In the Polish and Russian sections of Eastern Europe, the nineteenth century, with its muddled ideas about human quality and freedom, gave the Jews a great lift. From Eastern Europe they spread across the entire continent during the nineteenth and twentieth centuries, and then across the world. Parallel to these Jewish wanderings throughout the world, is the migration of a similarly restless animal [sic!], *the rat. Rats have been parasites on mankind from the very beginning. Their home is Asia, from where they migrated in gigantic hordes over Russia and the Balkans into Europe. By the middle of the eighteenth century, with the growing shipping traffic, they took possession of America as well, and eventually Africa and the Far East. Wherever rats turn up, they carry destruction to the land, by destroying mankind's goods and nourishment and spreading diseases and plagues such as cholera, dysentery, leprosy, and typhoid fever. They are cunning, cowardly and cruel, and usually appear in massive hordes. They represent the elements of sneakiness and subterranean destruction among animals. Just as the Jews do among mankind.*

The Jew as disease-causing agent, louse, germ, poison, abcess, ulcer, parasite and flagellum; the Jew as incarnation of an apocalyptic plague is an image used quite often by anti-Semites: The National Socialist response gave the impression as being required under the pretext "pest control".

This kind of imagery was not new to the way Germans think. Anti-Semitism has a long, unfortunate history in Europe and in what is now Germany. It is not what Alexander Gauland, one of the leaders of far-right German AfD party, by downplaying the crimes of the Nazis, called "just a speck of bird shit in over 1,000 years of successful German history" [1]. In the Middle-Ages, the Black Death was blamed on the Jews which resulted in a wave of systematic mass murder in 1348-1350:

When the Black Death struck in Europe, it caused a demographic catastrophe without precedent. Between 30% and 70% of the population died. No disease within living memory had spread so quickly causing such massive numbers of deaths. As populations searched for an explanation for this sudden epidemic, their attention turned to the Jews. After one tortured Jew "confessed" to poisoning the wells, pogroms occured in many towns in Northern Europe. Switzerland, Northern France, Germany, and the Low Countries witnessed attacks, often before the Black Death reached them. [2]

This became one of the cornerstones, a fatal episode in history that burned its way into the collective memory. In 1881 over 200,000 Germans signed a petition that urged the government to restrict the immigration of Jews. What lit anti-Semitism again in 1918 was the lost war.

And so a deliberately overlooked pinch of anti-Semitism made it into German silent films. Siegfried Kracauer called a famous film book he published in 1947 ***From Caligari to Hitler***. It could have been titled ***From Nosferatu to Hitler*** as well, because films like ***Caligari*** and even more so,

1 Kongress der Jungen Alternative, June 2, 2018.

2 Nico Voigtländer, Hans Joachim Voth, *The geography of hate: How anti-Semitism in interwar Germany was influenced by the medieval mass murder of Jews.* VOX CEPR Policy Portal.

Nosferatu, directed by Friedrich Wilhelm Murnau, revealed a war-wounded nation.

The shadow of *Nosferatu* looms over his victim, horrified Gustav von Wangenheim.
Courtesy of Christian Doerge

Nosferatu - Eine Symphonie des Grauens (***Nosferatu: A Symphony of Horror***) was sparsely released in 1922 and otherwise seemed to have been either a case of and pretense for money laundering or a case of a production company (Prana Film, Heinrich "Enrico" Dieckmann and Albin Grau, an occultist who, under the name "Frater Pacitius", sympathized for a brief time even with Aleister Crowley) that didn't fit in with the corporate policy of the big ones like Ufa. Nevertheless the picture and its anti-Semitic ideas of a vampire who brings in his wake an army of rats and the plague survived the bankruptcy of Prana Film.

The parallels between vampirism and European anti-semitism go back much further than **Nosferatu**, *and were in fact part of the continental zeitgeist for centuries. Jews – as well as gypsies, another popular scapegoat target of post-World War I Germany – were often depicted as bloodsuckers, and some have even traced the vampire's aversion to Christian imagery to this parallel. There was also* *a popular myth that circulated for centuries regarding the alleged Jewish practice of drinking the blood of Christian children.* [3]

This practice, the so-called "blood libel", refers to a centuries-old false allegation that Jews take a liking to murdering Christians and their children to use their blood for ritual purposes:

The blood libel spread throughout the Christian world in the Middle Ages. When a Christian child went missing, it was not uncommon for local Jews to be blamed. Even when there was no evidence that any Jew had anything to do with the missing child, Jews were tortured until they confessed to heinous crimes. Some Christians believed that the four cups of wine that Jews drink at the Passover Seder celebrations were actually blood, or that Jews mixed blood into hamantaschen, *sweet pastries eaten on the Jewish holiday of Purim. Others claimed that Jews used Christian blood as a medicine or even as an aphrodisiac. Scholars have documented about 100 blood libels that took place from the twelfth to sixteenth centuries. Many of them resulted in massacres of Jews.* [4]

Nosferatu is no explicit anti-Semitic movie, certainly not, but it is a piece of a jigsaw that surely is a sad part of Teutonic culture and xenophobia. [5]

The image of the Jew as a proto-vampire is found on cathedral walls and in sculptures, paintings, frescoes and literature dating back to the Middle Ages. [...]

The metaphor of the vampire Jew was not forged in a cultural vacuum but rather was derived from a new anti-Semitic gene, the hateful and terribly efficient trope of the blood libel. [6]

Nosferatu features prominently in this category: *As many have pointed out, Murnau's version of* **"Dracula",** *a.k.a. the repulsive Count Orlok, possesses many physical features commonly found in stereotypical caricatures of Jews at the time: A*

3 Ibid.

4 *Blood Libel: A False, Incendiary Claim Against Jews.* https://www.adl.org > resources > glossary-terms > blood libel.

5 See: Marie Mulvey-Roberts, *Dangerous Bodies: Historicising the Gothic Corporeal.* Published to University Press Scholarship Online: September 2016: *In chapter 4, the vampire theme continues with a discussion of* Dracula, *Jewishness and blood. It will be argued that the early film version of Stoker's novel,* Nosferatu, *encrypts the ostensibly dangerous vampire body as metaphor for the crypto-Jew.*

6 Ushi Derman, *The Myth of the Vampire Jew and Blood Libels.* https://www.bh.org.il > blog-items > myth-vampire-jew-blood-libels/.

long hooked nose, long claw-like fingernails, bushy eyebrows, a large forehead with bald head, and a general feminization of his appearance which was also common. His appearance is not only comparable to anti-semitic imagery, but he is also made to look something like a rat, in accordance with the disgusting rodents he brings with him. This, in turn, ties back into the Jewish stereotype, as Jews were often equated with rats as well. [7]

***Nosferatu* (Max Schreck) leaves the ship accompanied by a rat.**
Courtesy of Jens Geutebrück, Coronaretro Archives

When, right before the liquidation of the Prana Film Company, an article appeared in *Lichtbild-Bühne*, criticizing the financial misconduct of its management, the editor, Karl Wolffsohn, a Jew, received an insulting card filled with anti-Semitic remarks. Another movie magazine, *Film-Hölle* (*Film Hell*), used this incident to publish a satirical poem titled **Der Nosferatutunichtgut (The Nosferatu Scalawag):**

---

7 *Nosferatu at 90: The Jew as a Vampire.* thevaultofhorror.blogspot.com/.../nosferatu-at-90-jew-as-vampir... An anti-Semitic attitude is to be found in Bram Stoker's novel as well.

Die Symphonie des Grauens
Hielt uns noch lange wach.
Zur Symphonie des Kl – – agens
Ward sie dann allgemach.
Doch ward ihr ein Verleger,
Der nicht verlegen war,
Zum Ärgerniserreger;
Der sagte nämlich wahr.
Und einzig, weil vermeintlich
Der Hieb zu heftig traf,
Ward man jetzt judenfeindlich
Als Ansichtkartograph.
So kleinlich war, und nichtig
Der Inhalt des Gemurrs.
Prana, dein Kurs war richtig.
Jetzt ist es dein Kon-Kurs!

Not easy to translate but we'll try:

The Symphony of Horror
Kept us awake a bit.
Turned into a Symphony of Lawsuits
Gradually.
A publisher, however,
Who wasn't intimidated,
Became an irritation
Because he spoke the truth.
And as this hit massively,
Their response was anti-Semitic
By sending a picture-postcard.
Nit-picking and futile
The Content of the Grumbling was.

Prana, your course (Kurs) was proper,
Now it led to your bankruptcy (Kon-Kurs)! [8]

An early draft of the most notorious picture, ***Jud Süss*** (***Jew Suss***), almost two decades later, had an organ-grinding singer of street ballads appear on the market place of Stuttgart and warn the population against the "Vampire Jew":

Dear friends and godfathers,
listen to the song of the great vampire,
wolves, rats, vipers are bad,
but the worst of all predators is:
the Jew, the Jew, the Jew;
he reigns in the country,
sucking our blood,
takes away house and farm and shirt.
To the Devil with the Jew!
Taxes, fire and plague are shameful,
war and discord are dreadful, too;
these things are nothing yet against
the beneficiary of it all:
the Jew, the Jew, the Jew;
he reigns in the country,
sucking our blood,
takes away house and farm and shirt.
To the Devil with the Jew! [9]

No wonder that Julius Streicher saw ***Nosferatu*** several times at the time of its release. One year later, in 1923, Streicher, Hitler's early vassal, became the editor of *Der Stürmer,* a vulgar anti-semitic hate sheet. [10]

8 Film-Hölle, No. 8, 1922, p. 10.
9 Collection of Deutsche Kinemathek Berlin.
10 Ushi Derman.

Nosferatu (Max Schreck), at the bedside of Greta Schröder, is caught by the first shaft of sunlight.
Courtesy of Jens Geutebrück, Coronaretro Archives

Nosferatu not killed by daylight - but by a crude camera effect.
Courtesy of Christian Doerge

By tragic coincidence, a number of Jewish artists were involved in the making of ***Nosferatu:***

The screenwriter, Henrik Galeen (Heinrich Wiesenberg), left Germany after Hitler's rise to power. He died of cancer in 1949 in Randolph, Vermont. His brother-in-law, actor John Gottowt (Isidor Gesang) who played Professor Bulwer, was murdered in Wieliczka (Poland) by an SS officer. Alexander Granach (Jessaja Gronach), the Jewish real-estate agent Knock, escaped and lived in exile under similar dangerous circumstances, in Stalin's Soviet Union. Thanks to Lion Feuchtwanger, the author of a ***Jew Suss*** book, he got out of there and became a versatile supporting actor in Hollywood films (***Ninotchka***; ***For Whom the Bell Tolls***; Fritz Lang's ***Hangmen Also Die***). He died in New York City from an embolism after an appendectomy in March 1945, a few weeks before the "Führer's" suicide.

Jewish Magic versus a Christian Madonna

According to director Fritz Lang, Goebbels told him that he and Hitler had seen ***Metropolis***, one of the most expensive (and least successful) of all German silents, somewhere in the village in 1927. Back then Hitler, Goebbels claimed, recognized in Fritz Lang the much needed cinematic megalomaniac, a soulmate so to speak.

Like all megalomaniacs, Fritz Lang, at heart an architect who was said to have been a true dictator on the set of his films, a pharaonic slave driver, dreamed of creating his own monument. In the case of ***Metropolis***, a monument of apocalyptic and eschatological elements turned into film. Under the roof of a New Tower of Babel we encounter the protagonists: Maria the Woman – *Hail Mary, full of Grace, the Lord is with thee* – and The Savior from the Skies, Freder Fredersen, the son of the bosses, son of arch capitalist John Fredersen. Their enemy – reading the anti-Semitic subtext – is a Jewish inventor, C. A. Rotwang, disguised in the monk's cowl of the alchemist, who abuses saintly Maria and – pure blasphemy, pure evil - transforms her into the robotic whore of a soulless future, modeled after Anita Berber (1899-1928), a drug-addicted dancer and actress who needed scandal like her daily bread.

Lang was raised a Roman Catholic by his mother: *Lang had learned about love and sex from Catholicism, and his outlook remained intrinsically Catholic throughout his life. There were Madonnas, like his own mother, pure and saintly (Kriemhild before the vengeful transformation; one-half of [actress] Brigitte Helm in* ***Metropolis***). *And there were whores, who possessed the tempting inducements of sin. Sins could always be forgiven, and like Mary Magdalene, prostitutes could be uplifted. Prostitutes in the end were for Lang* [...] *a shrine at which to prostrate and worship.* [11]

Rotwang is nothing less than an evil version of Rabbi Loew, who in 19th century literature became associated with a Frankenstein-type Golem, the man of clay. Finally Rotwang is killed on the roof of an underground cathedral by the Christian Savior, Freder:

---

11 Patrick McGilligan, *Fritz Lang: The Nature of the Beast.* New York: St. Martin's Press, 1997.

In the ultra-modern city of Metropolis, Rotwang is an anachronism, a figure out of an earlier time and age. He lives in a house of medieaval design and dresses and acts like a figure out of earlier Expressionist films. His associations with medieaval images of the Jew, which would be reinstitutionalized in Nazi propaganda – the scientist, the magician, the alchemist – bring forth associations of radicalized conflict, further impacted both by the use of the robot Maria and the Orientalism of the setting in which she first appears. [...] *The Robot Maria, Rotwang's most fearsome creation, is introduced to an intra-diegetic audience in a nightclub of 'Oriental splendour', the Yoshiwara (the name of the traditional pleasure quarter of Japan's Edo, now Tokyo). This association between an overly sexualized female and the decadence associated with the Orient also feature in anti-Semitic images of the Jew as 'Oriental'.* [12]

Although the movie was butchered by the time of its American release, the ideological, racist background remained but even English-speaking trades ignored it and just hailed the technology that was set in motion to produce a movie termed the EIGHTH WONDER OF THE UNIVERSE:

An ultramodern film spectacle set in the city of the future – Metropolis the awe-inspiring, machine-managed, machine-brained city of 100 years from now. Only a genius could conceive such a theme – only a master technician such as Fritz Lang, the great U.F.A. producer, could visualize the conception. There is no make-believe – the futurist city is there on the screen before your amazed eyes! Buildings towering thousands of feet into space, elevated railroads and roadways, aeroplanes whisking down those steel canyons in the heavens – and, marvel of marvels, the Robot Woman, the mechanical thing science dreams of – a living, walking, working being – minus a soul! IMAGINE A GREAT DRAMATIC ROMANCE IN SUCH A SETTING! NO WONDER THIS 10 REEL MARVEL HAS THE ATTENTION OF THE WHOLE WORLD TO-DAY! [13]

This return of magic and alchemy is set in the year 2026, in the illogically

12 David Desser, *Race, Space, and Class: The Politics of Cityscapes in Science-Fiction Films*. In: Annette Kuhn (ed.), *Alien Zone II: The Spaces of Science-Fiction Cinema*. London and New York: Verso, 1999, pp. 82-83.

13 Sydney newspaper advertisement announcing the screening of *Metropolis* in April 1928.

Gothic skyscrapers of a corporate city-state, the Metropolis of the title. Society has been divided into two rigid groups: one of planners or thinkers, people of the mind, who live high above the earth in luxury, and another of workers who live underground toiling to sustain the lives of the privileged. The city is run by Johann 'John' Fredersen, a man of mind and money, who took Hel, the woman that Rotwang loved. Consequently the American version names him Masterman, obviously a member of a master race envisioned by Hitler. Hel died when she gave birth to Fredersen's son Freder. In the meantime, beautiful, altruistic and evangelical Samaritan Maria (or Mary) takes up the cause of the slave laborers. The peace-loving young woman advises the desperate men not to start a revolution but to continue suffering and pray for the advent of a Christ-like mediator who turns out to be Freder. Rotwang the Jew hates Freder the Siegfried-like hero, who was the cause of Hel's death, and therefore wants to destroy his ancient rival, Freder's father John, by going to kill two birds with one stone.

As he realized that he had nothing more than a cheap, trashy novelette in his hands instead of true utopian content, Fritz Lang pushed just for form and visuals. He asked his art directors Otto Hunte, Erich Kettelhut and Karl Vollbrecht to build the expensive sets and the scenery for a huge model of the city, complete with tiny airplanes flying above the skyscrapers, ground vehicles and even pedestrians to be animated frame-by-frame, all of which had nothing to do with future reality! It took weeks to accomplish the task. It is almost certain that Hitler particularly liked that biblical monument of architecture that anticipated his dream project of a gigantic domed building, the People's Hall, in a future German captial named Germania, formerly Berlin. (Hunte and Vollbrecht, by the way, would later work on ***Jew Suss***. At least Hunte was called by a colleague a "little Nazi".)

Today some scholars, such as Elly Hoffman, deny the close relationship of the ***Metropolis*** story to National Socialist thinking but their arguments are weak:

Metropolis *certainly contains elements that would seemingly go along with the pro-worker yet anti-communist message of the Nazi Party.* [...]

However, while **Metropolis** *might posit some ideas with regard to cooperation between the classes for the 'greater good', and while Joseph Goebbels and Adolf Hitler might have claimed that such ideals fell within the Nazi Party line, in practice Nazism, as an ideology, not only failed to live up to this ideal, but in fact did not hold this ideal* [...]

Nazism was built upon several principles, principles that **Metropolis** *alternatively completely ignores or firmly contrasts in its narrative.* [...]

When speaking of the principles of Nazi ideology, it can be generally divided into three 'pillars': the Führerprinzip, *the* Volksgemeinschaft, *and* Judenkampf.

Of course, the author agrees, old man Fredersen is the Führer, the unquestionable leader of the Modern Babylon Metropolis which is essentially a fascist dictatorship. But he also acts as a redeemable figure that, upon being filled with fear for his own son, and at last learns to empathize with the citizens of Metropolis, with the people below him: *This promotion of leadership accountability to the people, this promotion of a flawed but not intrinsically evil figurehead who can do better and ultimately does, certainly goes against the* Führerprinzip.

Certainly not. The principle of leadership is quite intact in ***Metropolis*** although Fredersen needs to be built up as a strong Führer.

Metropolis may initially appear to promote the *Volksgemeinschaft*, Hoffman says, where the workers constituted a key social group that Hitler appealed to during his rise to power: *However, if one breaks through the Nazi propaganda and takes a view of the situation that had developed in Germany objectively, it becomes clear that Hitler had far more in common with John Fredersen than with his son. What the Nazis said and what the Nazis did, after all, were often two different things.*

Sure they were. But ***Metropolis*** depicted the *Volksgemeinschaft* as Nazi propaganda liked to portray it. And the Savior of *Volksgemeinschaft* on screen was Freder, the Son of "God", as Hitler saw himself as Savior of the *Volksgemeinschaft* in real life.

Third, we have the notion of the Judenkampf*: the supposedly eternal and intrinsic struggle of the German* volk *against the 'cancer' of the Jews. The Jews were* *viewed as the ultimate foe of the German people* [...] *This notion of a race war, a struggle for survival, was more important to the Nazi ideology than any other, and this, of course, is absent from the film as well.*

The author realizes the fact that Rotwang the inventor *might* be Jewish. But according to Nazi ideology he might not be a real Jew because he is much too creative: *Goebbels often proclaimed that, "The Jews lack creative abilities", and Rotwang is, if nothing else, certainly creative.* [14]

Other writers disagree with Hoffman's sometimes difficult to understand explanation: *They are all brothers in* **Metropolis**, *only one is not: "Rotwang". The bug-eyed, hook-nosed scientist with Albert Einstein frise wears a strange coat that reminds one of a caftan, he has a strange star in the laboratory which - in this context - strongly reminds of the Star of David and, not in vain, his strange name is "Rotwang". The scientist epitomizes a colorful bunch of anti-semitic clichés which had summed up until 1927. He lies ("the Jews and their lies"), he is revengeful ("the Jewish God of Wrath") and he drives the masses to almost execute the good "Maria" on a quasi cross ("Jesus murderer"). But Fritz Lang also incorporates stereotypes of his time. "Rotwang" is éminence grise to Johann Fredersen, the factory owner ("Behind the capital there is the Jew") as well as creator of a female robot that calls for revolution ("Behind Marxism there is the Jew").* [15]

Hitler and Goebbels loved not only ***Metropolis.*** They were awestruck when they saw another epic, the monumental Wagnerian two-part film version ***Die Nibelungen*** by Lang and his screenwriting wife Thea von Harbou that had been released three years earlier: a pathetic screen rendering of the Teutonic epic poem written around AD 1200, clearly a Nazi favorite featuring a blond, blue-eyed "Aryan" hero, Siegfried, the forerunner of Freder, and the blind Nibelung loyalty until death brought to them by the Eastern hordes of the barbaric Huns.

14 Elly Hoffman, *Fritz Lang's Monster: Was Metropolis a Pro-Nazi Film.* https://medium.com/science-technoculture-in-film/fritz-langs-monster-was-metropolis-a-pro-nazi-film-f9cbeoff5fd5.

15 *Metropolis - die Rehabilitation eines deutschen Propagandastreifens.* schlamassel.blogsport.de/2010/06/08/metropolis-die-rehabilitation-propagandastreifens/

Paul Richter as Siegfried holds hands with Margarete Schön as Kriemhild in Fritz Lang's *Die Nibelungen* Courtesy of Jens Geutebrück, Coronaretro Archives

The film was destined to restore the nation's damaged self-awareness by recalling its medieval glory. The contemporary reviews were as pathetic as the movie itself:

Like Volker von Alzey the bard once played his fiddle to spread the epic of the Nibelungs all over the world, Fritz Lang today grabs the silent chords of the film to present to the demanding eye what rested in the dark womb of an ominous past. He resurrects the Germanic heroic ballad and confesses himself to a deed whose audacity most Germans will not grasp. A defeated people poetizes its belligerent heroes in an epic of pictures like the world has never seen before – this is a powerful achievement!

Fritz Lang accomplished it and a whole people remains steadfastly at his side. A whole people because he grabs its innermost heart. [...]

This masterpiece will be carried in Germany by the national consciousness of our people, and so this achievement will bear fruit. [...]

This great, unique cinematic work shall bestow us hours of solemn emotion, it may make a contribution to awake the noble mind and to declare unrelenting war to evil! It may be a shining weapon of German faith which wields undauntedly and unconqueredly through the world with the bell ringing of pure, free humanity. It may be an enlightened symbol, the flaming torch of a new day, it may be like Balmung, Siegfried's sword, and prevail where it strikes. [16]

Siegfried enters the Magic Forest.
Courtesy of Jens Geutebrück, Coronaretro Archives

16 Die Filmwoche No. 7, 1924, Special issue *Die Nibelungen*.

Siegfried confronts the dragon.
Courtesy of Jens Geutebrück, Coronaretro Archives

By the way, the costumes were designed by the late Paul Gerd Guderian, the brother of Hitler's future general and tank expert Heinz Guderian.

Nevertheless, young audiences of today witnessing a revival of the ***Nibelungs*** might laugh about the völkisch masquerade directed by the monocled Lang:

The girl maybe is only fifteen. Out of her headphones the rhythm of a drum machine penetrates into the wagon of Berlin subway line 2. "You got a ticket for the opera?" the girlfriend sitting next to her asks. The girl pulls the plugs out of her ears. "No, it isn't exactly an opera." Would be awkward, wouldn't it? "No, it's a black-and-white movie from the twenties and an orchestra plays live."

The detail most uncool she withholds. It's not only black and white, it's silent too. And it deals with people who in primordial days plodded through Germania wearing fur boots on their feet and helmets with horns on their heads. In some schools they molest you with such crap still today, but the German of the Nibelung Ballad is even more hermetic than Kanak Sprak, the ghetto slang of the dagos. [...]

And above that Lang's **Nibelungen** *inhere the national, the pre-fascist. When*

Alberich the dwarf with his spinach chin grovels in front of Siegfried and embraces the Nibelung treasure, Werner Krauss' anti-Semitic performance in **Jew Suss** *reaping gold and jewelry immediately comes to one's mind.*

The actor who played tricky, sneaky Alberich, guardian of the Nibelung hoard who is killed by Siegfried in self-defense, was Georg John (born Georg Jacobsohn). John was later deported to the ghetto Lodz where he died in November 1941.

Till the death of the Nibelungs time feels like it's just creeping by. Who thought John Wayne's last stand in **The Alamo** *to be heroic hasn't seen the* **Nibelungs**. *Never before and after there was so much desperate somberness on the screen. The applause that six hours after the first sound sinks on the radio symphony orchestra conducted by Frank Strobel signals more relief that it's over than excitement.* [17]

Fritz Lang's monumental film architecture impressed even Hitler. Courtesy of Jens Geutebrück, Coronaretro Archives

Speaking of Fritz Lang we have to mention his first talkie, ***M***, produced in 1931. It was voted by cineastes the best German film of all time in a 1994 poll,

17 Hanns-Georg Rodek, *Nibelungen bestehen auch gegen Metropolis*. In: Die Welt, April 28, 2010.

with 306 votes out of 324. But one shouldn't forget (and the Nazis didn't!) that the child murderer Hans Beckert was played by a Jewish actor, Peter Lorre a.k.a. László Loewenstein, born in Rosenberg, Hungary. Goebbels liked that movie for a special reason, *Saw* **M** *by Fritz Lang. Fabulous. Against humanist stupidity. For the death penalty. Well made.*

Westdeutscher Beobachter, a regional newspaper published by NSDAP, understood the maniacal child murderer's cry being incapable of struggling against the evil that a curse put inside him, as only Nazis could understand it:

Concurrently, this cry is a Jewish confession of guilt, a self-disclosure begging for downright extermination. This Jewish begging must be fulfilled...

No wonder that this scene with Peter Lorre made it right into ***The Eternal Jew***:

Before the clip, the narrator claims that the film exonerates the murderer while blaming the children for their own deaths. Reinterpreted in such a way, **M** *becomes a film made by Jews, portraying the Nazi version of Jewish values, and starring a Jew. And, Lorre's part in* **M** *becomes documentary proof of Jewish criminality and immorality, themes already introduced in* **Der ewige Jude.** *That is, the film implies that "Lorre the Jew" is not just an actor playing a part; he* is *a child murderer.*

This reinterpretation of Lorre as an actual Jewish murderer of children plays upon the viewers' emotions, evoking a visceral rejection of Lorre's character, of the film itself, and of Weimar film and Jews in general. In this instance, **Der ewige Jude** *also tacitly but powerfully evokes an age-old prejudice that existed well beyond the confines of both Weimar- and Nazi-era films. That is the filmmakers intended the* **M** *clip to remind viewers of the familiar charge of blood libel, the fictional Jewish sacrifice of Christian children.* [18]

But surprisingly Fritz Lang who had made three movies that impressed the Nazis decided against working in Germany. So why did he turn down Goebbels' purported lucrative offer to promote him to the position of the leading director of the German film industry, as he later wouldn't get tired to

18 Robert C. Reimer (ed.), *Cultural History through a National Socialist Lens: Essays on the Cinema of the Third Reich.*Rochester, New York: Camden House Inc., p. 146.

emphasize? Why did he leave a country that would bestow an honor he longed for many years? Was it only because Goebbels decided to ban Lang's latest entry, the third ***Mabuse*** film: ***Das Testament des Dr. Mabuse*** (***The Testament of Dr. Mabuse***)? Was this movie meant as an accusation of Nazism as Lang would later assert? Lang was no leftist in those days. He was still married, at least on paper, to screenwriter Thea von Harbou, a member of Hitler's party since 1932.

Apparently, Lang lived at least politically in friendly unison with his nationally spirited wife. Actor Willy Fritsch says in his memoir that Fritz Lang at that time was "more patriotic than a German national Junker". "When he learned that I drove a Cadillac, he blew his top. Fritz Lang took the view that it was every good German's duty to drive a Mercedes." [...]

Fritz Lang too tried to come to terms with the new situation. Conrad von Molo, who worked as editor on the final Reich German **Mabuse**, *said about Lang: "He was wavering; he would have loved to go with the Nazis."*

According to Molo, Lang did everything to "play a key role" in the German film industry. Two days before his movie was banned, on 27 March 1933, together with directors Carl Boese, Viktor Janson and an aspiring natural talent by the name of Luis Trenker, Lang had founded the Directors' Group of the National Socialist company organization (NSBO). [...]

Before 1933 Fritz Lang, in spite of different offers from Hollywood, would have never thought to leave Germany for political reasons. [19]

According to Lang, Goebbels had summoned him to the offices of the newly-created Ministry of Enlightenment and Propaganda: "The Führer and I have seen your films, and the Führer has made clear that this [Lang] is the man who will give us the National Socialist film."[20] There only was one small obstacle: Fritz Lang was raised Catholic, but his mother had *converted* to Catholicism. Actually, she was Jewish. But Goebbels reassured the nervous Lang that in his case, considering his artistic merits and the fact that he was

19 *Ein Schlafwandler bei Goebbels.* In: DER SPIEGEL, November 26, 1990.

20 Patrick McGilligan, *Fritz Lang: The Nature of the Beast.* University of Minnesota Press, 1997.

a World War combat veteran, they would make an exception and do without an Aryan certificate.

Lang claimed that his only goal was to talk Goebbels out of the ban of ***Testament des Dr. Mabuse*** - to no avail.

Checking Goebbels' diaries, such a meeting never took place. The offer of being promoted Germany's star director maybe was just fabricated by the self-absorbed Lang. And it isn't true that he immediately after this "meeting" boarded a night train and left Germany (as his passport, filed at the German Cinematheque, proves).

No, there were other reasons: It was Thea von Harbou who had separated from her half-Jewish husband in 1932 in favor of Indian student Ayi Ganpat Tendulkar (1904-1975), whom she called a "true Aryan". Besides that, Lang's favorite producer, Erich Pommer, had left Germany and worked in Paris. Pommer was a Jew as was Seymour Nebenzal, the producer of ***M*** and ***Testament***. Right now, there was no producer at hand in Berlin. And, fortunately for Lang, he had a second conscience that prevented him from walking into the Nazi trap. This conscience was personified by his little-known secretary, confident and final wife Lilly Latté who sympathized with the Socialists. So Lang slowly prepared his exile and transferred money and belongings out of the country to Paris where Erich Pommer, on behalf of Les Productions Fox Europa, produced, with him as director and with actor Charles Boyer, the film ***Liliom*** from a play by Ferenc Molnár.

Goebbels screened a re-cut version of ***The Testament of Dr. Mabuse*** at his home in October 1933 following a birthday party but still wasn't satisfied:

For quite a while there is silence after the film ended. All the guests watch Goebbels. But he keeps silence too. "That's a fancy movie," the minister's 13-year-old stepson, Harald Quandt, pipes up. Some guests smile. Nobody answers. "I am going to ban the movie," Goebbels says all of a sudden. "I am going to ban it because it proves that a group of serious men with a do-or-die attitude is capable to set the world on fire." He makes a thoughful pause. A great director has to stoop to such things if he isn't offered better topics." [21]

21 Heinrich Fraenkel/Roger Manvell, *Goebbels. Eine Biographie*. Cologne/Berlin:

On March 4, 1938 (Lang had become a Hollywood director in the meantime), Goebbels mentioned the movie again in a speech at the Reich Chamber of Film [Reichsfilmkammer]:

A few days ago I have seen again a film that was made end of year 1932 and was finished beginning of year 1933. This movie was banned back then for political reasons. But this is not what should interest us in this context. More interesting is another fact. In the circles of experts this film was regarded as technical and visual sensation. It conquered new ground. But when we set eyes on it today, 5 years later, we are startled about the triviality of the presentation, the roughness of the means and the shortcomings of the acting. [22]

Above all, Goebbels had to pick a bone with ***Testament's*** releasing company, the German division of a U.S. major, Universal Pictures.

Although the Nazis liked Fritz Lang his film *The Testament of Dr. Mabuse* was banned.

Courtesy of Jens Geutebrück, Coronaretro Archives

Molden, 1960, pp. 204.

22 Dr. Joseph Goebbels, Speech at Reichsfilmkammer, March 4, 1938. In: *Jahrbuch der Reichsfilmkammer* 1938, p. 7

All Quiet on the Western Front

Julius Streicher, Goebbels and others had a cunning archenemy born in Laupheim, Germany, who in their eyes had betrayed his German homeland. Carl Laemmle had become a movie mogul in the United States and head of Universal Pictures. They hated Carl Laemmle not only for being a "Film Jew" but for releasing Rupert Julian's ***The Kaiser, the Beast of Berlin*** in 1918: *A story of mad, ruthless ambitions, a shocking expose of the secret instincts of the wickedest human being in all history."* They called Laemmle a denigrator of his native country.

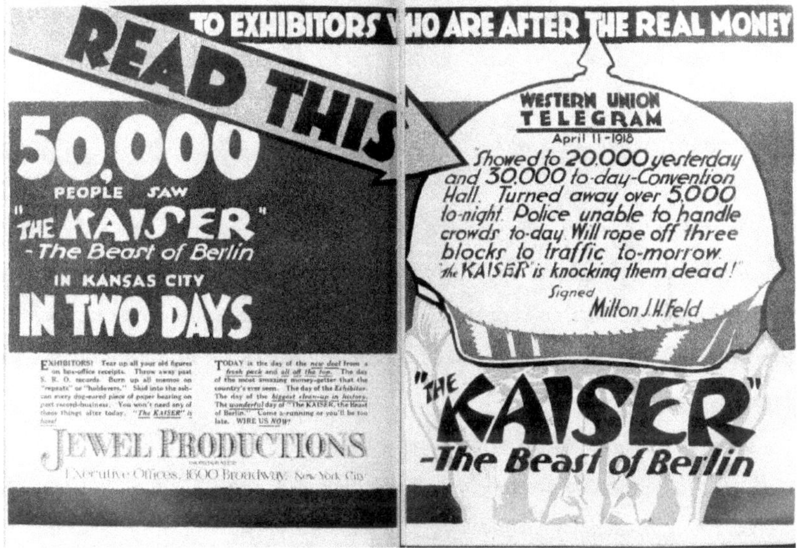

The Kaiser - The Beast of Berlin
Rolf Giesen Collection

The final straw was Universal's film version of Erich Maria Remarque's anti-war novel ***All Quiet on the Western Front.*** The German-dubbed version opened at the Mozartsaal (Mozart Hall), a Berlin cinema at Nollendorfplatz, on

December 4, 1930. Seldom was a Hollywood movie expected with such anticipation in Berlin since the pros and cons of this film had been debated so lively. Three former German Reich chancellors were seen in the audience: Philipp Scheidemann, Hermann Müller, and Wilhelm Marx. There were authors like Alfred Döblin (***Berlin Alexanderplatz***) and Carl Zuckmayer, artists like George Grosz and journalists like Egon Erwin Kisch.

First serialized in 1928 in the German newspaper Vossische Zeitung, *the book was published on January 31, 1929, and instantly became a literary juggernaut. In Germany, the initial print run sold out on release day, and some 20,000 copies moved off the shelves in the first few weeks on its way to more than a million books sold by year's end. Abroad,* **All Quiet on the Western Front** *was a big hit as well, selling 600,000 copies in both Britain and France, and 200,000 in America. The film rights were snatched up by Universal Pictures for a record $40,000...*

It's a gritty pull-no-punches look at the horrors of war. Limbs are lost, horses are destroyed, starving soldiers root through garbage for food, the troops are ravaged by poison gas and artillery bombs, and few make it out alive. [23]

Remarque's novel and the film were in stark contrast to the war-glorifying diaries *In Stahlgewittern* (*Storm of Steel*) and *Der Kampf als inneres Erlebnis* (*The Inner Experience of Battle*), two books quite popular with nationalists and Hitler cohorts:

In 1920 a relatively unknown member of the Reichswehr published an account of World War I that soon became a bestseller. The book was In Stahlgewittern, *its author Ernst Jünger. It was followed two years later by* Der Kampf als inneres Erlebnis. *Their common subject was war.* [...]

At the time that Jünger published these books which show war as a positive experience, the general literary feeling in Europe was still strongly anti-war. [...]

Even though Ernst Jünger does not deny the horrors and atrocities of war, his books are an apotheosis of the subject. Paradoxically, war to him is the one thing that will serve to perpetuate the human race. This is achieved in a way that is

23 *The Most Loved and Hated Novel About World War I.* https://www.smithsonian.com > history.

vaguely reminiscent of Darwin's theory of the survival of the fittest. In war a new elite or new "race" is born. Just as war has fathered it, it in turn will be responsible for the following generations. Race, in Jünger's sense, is not a biological term, rather than a philosophical experience. To survive, and to create the new man, the soldier has again to be made aware of his past. Only by linking his prehistoric existence with modern man and modern man's accomplishments, will he be able to form this new race.

Blood, i.e. instinct rather than reasoning, originality rather than the stiftling process of learning, is modern man's only means for survival. [24]

Such writing was more to the liking of the Nazis than Remarque's book.

Goebbels assumed correctly that right after ***Western Front***'s premiere the Nollendorfplatz cinema would let its guard down. So enough tickets were bought at the box office to let the Brownshirts in the following day, December 5, 1930, to cause a riot that would bring the Nazis into the headlines of the German papers.

7:00 p.m.: The lights went off in a cinema hall that was filled to capacity. The curtain rose. On the screen the main title flashed. The names of Carl Laemmle, President Universal Pictures, and Erich Maria Remarque, author, appeared.

Suddenly, people began shouting. The projectionist cranked up the sound but the angry screams drowned out the movie soundtrack. There they were standing on their seats and in the corridors, the rowdies assembled by Dr. Goebbels, Hitler's Gauleiter (and deputy) in the German capital.

After a while, the screening was interrupted. The lights went on. The theater manager went to the stage. His name was Hanns Brodnitz. Since 1928 he was in charge of Ufa's premiere theaters in Berlin. He raised his hands to calm the audience, "May I ask you, ladies and gentlemen, to stop interrupting the screening. Otherwise, we would be forced to stop the film.

---

24 Sabine Schroeder-Sherwin, *Leben heisst Töten; die Kriegsdeutung Ernst Jüngers dargestellt an In Stahlgewittern und Der Kampf als inneres Erlebnis.* Thesis: Portland State University, May 10, 1972, pp. 1-3.

So please, shift your protest to the streets where it belongs. The majority of the audience wants to see this movie."

Shrill whistles:

"Get down off your soapbox! Down from the stage, Jew! Berlin Awake!! Germany Awake!!!"

In chorus:

Deutschland erwache!!! Germany Awake!!!

The National Socialist members of the Reichstag, among them Goebbels and Pastor Ludwig Münchmeyer, encouraged their followers. Brodnitz left. Applause. Fourteen years later, Brodnitz would lose his life in Auschwitz. The screening continued, the sound amplification as loud as possible. But still the machine gun fire on screen could not drown the yelling and screaming of the Nazis:

"We weren't such wimps and sissies. We fought for Germany. A foul movie is this: Sudelfilm! Sudelfilm!! Sudelfilm!!!"

"Judenfilm! Judenfilm!! Judenfilm!!! Jewish film!!!!"

White mice were released.

"Juda verrecke!! Juda drop dead!!!"

Other patrons were molested. Suddenly someone threw a stench bomb, then a second.

Shrewd Joseph Goebbels succeeded in turning this riot into a triumph for the Nazi propaganda machine. They called ***All Quiet on the Western Front*** a Jewish smear-film (*Juden-Schmutzfilm*).

In its issue of December 7, *Völkischer Beobachter*, the propaganda paper of the Nazi Party, described the pandemonium with relish:

The screening of this production of the Jewish-Bolshevist underworld had to be stopped. Already during the first scenes of this scandalous movie, there were shouts of protest. Especially disgusting scenes with German soldiers repulsively portrayed resulted in outraged shouts: "Enough", "Such Jewish sass we don't have to put up with." Thereupon, the Marxists present in the audience tried to lash into the National Socialists. It came to a fight, and stink-bombs were thrown, white mice were released. In front of the Mozartsaal large crowds had come together, among them many Communists who tried to attack the National Socialists.

The Nazis' triumph was perfect when the Superior Board of Censors under the Cabinet Council, Dr. Ernst Seeger, banned Laemmle's pacifist production for being anti-German.

With the cancellation of **All Quiet on the Western Front**, the *Nazis had won victories real and symbolic - over the Weimar Republic, exposed as a paper tiger cowed by street violence; over the cultural memory of the Great War, redefined as a patriotic cause sabotaged by enemies within; and over American cinema, branded as an infection spread by Hollywood Jews.* [25]

That didn't prevent Hitler from liking another Universal release and praise it to the skies, Paul Kohner's production of ***Der Rebell*** (***The Rebel***)*;* showing the resistance of a South Tyrolean partisan fighting Napoleon's troops. In August 1933, the co-director and star, Luis Trenker, was invited by Hitler to his Berchtesgaden residency:

Hitler's county house at the Salzberg in Berchtesgaden is a 'beautiful place', Trenker reports with a smile. The Führer's taste, his understanding of the countryside, his urge for wideness, and the big line manifest in his residency which is located in a classic lovely area.

Four times Hitler saw **The Rebel** *and each time he enjoyed this cinematic work. 'By the way,' the Führer remarked, 'they run it these days in the Luitpold Cinema in Munich.' Trenker was most amazed about the Führer's knowledge. Trenker himself didn't know this.* [26]

Carl Laemmle was aware that Trenker sympathized with the Nazis. But if he had hoped that a man like him could reconcile the Nazis with his German division he was wrong. Universal was one of the first U.S. film companies to shut down offices in Berlin. And until his death in 1939 Laemmle took the side of German émigrés.

---

25 Thomas Doherty, *Hollywood and Hitler 1933-1939*. New York: University of Columbia Press, 2013, p. 8.

26 *Trenkers Besuch beim Führer: Reichskanzler Adolf Hitler über den deutschen Film.* In: Film-Kurier, August 23, 1933, p. 197.

Image 12: Luis Trenker (center) as *The Rebel*.
Courtesy of Jens Geutebrück, Coronaretro Archives

Edge of Darkness: The Hollywood Tomb of Joe May

In 1941, film composer Friedrich Hollaender published an outstanding, unfortunately - except for a friendly review in the *New York Times* - largely overlooked and forgotten book (with a preface by Thomas Mann): ***Those Torn from Earth***. Besides the portrayal of other émigrés the author focuses on the rise and tragic fall of particularly one prominent "Film Jew" who appears in the novel as Jacques Mando. Without this Jacques Mando or actually Julius Otto Mandl, born in 1880 in Vienna as son of a Jewish merchant, there would have been no Thea von Harbou and no Fritz Lang. Mandl made a few films in Hollywood like ***Confession*** (for Warner Bros.) and a handful films for Universal: ***The Invisible Man Returns, The House of Fear***, ***The House of Seven Gables,*** but he seemed to be unable to adjust to Hollywood, planning his hopes on a madman's whim. His life ended in an inferno. He died dead broke - after a Viennese restaurant he and his wife, a brilliant cook, had opened in Los Angeles, the Blue Danube, closed down after a few weeks.

In his prime, critic Willy Haas called him a *Super monumental director.* But originally Mandl started out as a playboy who slathered his money around. His father was associated with the Hirtenberger Defence and Ammunition factory, his uncle they called the "Krupp of Austria". Mandl could have lived easily from the interest rates until he made the mistake of a wrong investment. In 1902 he had married Hermine "Minna" Pfleger, an operetta singer and with her help he now sought out the field of entertainment as future profession. Pfleger's stage name was Mia May, and henceforth Mandl called himself Joe May.

In 1911, thanks to Mia, he got in touch with the flickers and one year later, in Berlin, started his career as a film director at Continental Artfilm with ***In der Tiefe des Schachtes*** (***In the Depth of the Shaft***), a tragedy of love. Mia was the star. Together with actor Ernst Reicher, the brother of Frank Reicher (Captain Englehorn in ***King Kong***), May made a name for himself by directing a series of detective films modelled on Conan Doyle's Sherlock Holmes:

In 1913, director Joe May made a film that employed a number of aspiring actors. One of them was Ernst Reicher. Reicher, who had studied in England in the criminal neighborhood of Whitechapel where he had met a criminalist whose astuteness he admired, one day suggested to make a film about the adventures of a private eye. He christened him **Stuart Webbs**, *and so the first detective picture* **Die geheimnisvolle Villa (The Mysterious Villa)** *was produced. What nobody had expected happened. Until then this film was the biggest business one could imagine. Everywhere it was shown, domestically and abroad, the audience lined up at the box office of the cinemas. It didn't last long until the second* **Stuart Webbs** *picture was produced, then the third, the fourth, the twentieth. Ernst Reicher maybe made 40-50 films as* **Stuart Webbs**, *that gentle, chivalric, highly intellectual, athletic detective who saw his exclusive task in relentless service for justice.* [1]

In May 1915, Joe May founded his own production company, May Film GmbH, and as ***Stuart Webbs*** belonged to Reicher, who committed suicide in Prague exile in 1936, he created a new gentleman detective hero: ***Joe Deebs***, played by Max Landa and later by Harry Liedtke.

Detective films were trendy in those days. Even members of the Imperial Family, August Wilhelm, Friedrich Sigismund and Friedrich Karl, attended in June 1914 a screening of ***Der Hund von Baskerville*** (***The Hound of the Baskervilles***); this one, however, not by May but by his competitor Richard Oswald, another later expatriate who wasn't able to establish himself in Hollywood.

During World War I, Friedrich Hollaender writes in his novel, May suggested a not that absurd idea to the Austrian Ministry of War to rout the Russian army by projecting a huge picture of the Madonna into the sky. The Russians would think that the Blessed Mother was on the side of the Austrians. Billy Wilder recalls and confirms this weird project in his memoirs. [2]

---

1 Oskar Kalbus, *Vom Werden deutscher Filmkunst, Part 1: The Silent Film.* Altona-Bahrenfeld: Cigaretten Bilderdienst, 1935, p. 38.

2 *Billy Wilder. Eine Nahaufnahme von Hellmuth Karasek.* Hamburg: Hoffmann und Campe, 1992, pp. 100-101.

From success to success May became Germany's leading director, and his movies starring his wife Mia became bigger and bigger. His company May Film was controlled by Ufa.

Die Herrin der Welt (***The Mistress of the World***), made in 1919 and loosely based on a novel by Karl Figdor, was an 8-part serial (but with each episode an individual story, so no cliffhanger situation) that cost 8 million Reichsmark and was shot on the May Film backlot in Berlin-Woltersdorf:

In the center of the action is a young Danish woman, Maud Gregaards, played by Mia May. The heroine of this film (who belongs to the middle-class) struggles through manifold hardships and dangers and becomes the richest woman on earth, the **Mistress of the World.** *The story of Maud Gregaards takes place in all countries. The fate of this woman leads us through the deserts of Africa and into the honky-tonks of Canton [Guangzhou, China] which were built in Woltersdorf under the supervision of [Martin] Jacoby-Boy. Whole streets and temples were constructed to give an authentic image of the life and activities in this city. A hundred steamboats and other boats and lavishly decorated houses gave the background of the harbor. A Central African Temple Mount and a gigantic temple were erected as palatial background for another part of the movie and on wide areas Negroes were dwelling in a real kraal on the May lot.* [3]

May's serial that was released as a condensed version (4 sequels, each 5 reels) in the United States by Famous Players Lasky was not only a hopeful dream for a colonialist future of defeated Germany, it was also a utopian, cosmopolitan vision of what we call today Global Village. (*Variety*, however, called it in its review "infantile fiction".)

One of May's collaborators on these series was Fritz Lang who inhaled every bit of his Austrian compatriot's cinematic megalomania. During the preproduction of May's next epic, the 2-part ***Indian Tomb*** starring Mia and Conrad Veidt (who due to other conflicting schedules was unable to appear as F. W. Murnau's ***Nosferatu***), Lang met writer Thea von Harbou and collaborated with her on the script.

3 Lichtbild-Bühne, November 15, 1919.

A story of Indian love and obsession: Ayan, the Maharajah of Bengal, awakens Yogi Ramigani from his holy sleep. The Yogi has the power to transcend space and time, read people's minds and readily grant their wishes. Asked by the Maharajah to fetch a renowned English architect, he rematerializes in Herbert Rowland's living room in England and commissions him to build the most lavish and most beautiful tomb in the world for the Maharajah's wife. But Princess Savitri, the Maharajah's wife, is still alive and has no intention to die for the sake of the building.

As he knew that May wouldn't tolerate another god besides him, Lang decided to try and go out on his own. He took May's best architects Hunte, Kettelhut and Vollbrecht (except Jacoby-Boy who was a Jew) and some of May's best actors: Bernhard Goetzke, Paul Richter (Lang's future Siegfried) and Georg John. And he took Thea von Harbou. She became his second wife.

Mia May would quit acting in 1924 after the suicide of their daughter Eva.

When May drowned in Hollywood's sewers 20 years later, Lang extended no helping hand to get him out of the dilemma. In 1930 May visited America to study the changing production methods of sound films. "What we can learn from Hollywood," he said upon his return, "is optimism."

When he later sought exile in this city of optimism, May lost all hope. Friedrich Hollaender has him (as Jacques Mando) complain that everything here is seen through film glasses: "Life is transformed into a film strip." The artificiality of Hollywood became Joe May's Tomb: "I observe already that all emotional reactions in daily life have been standardized. Constrained and underplayed."

In 1943, May co-wrote one of Hollywood's anti-Nazi films, his final film for Universal, ***The Strange Death of Adolf Hitler***, with émigré actor Fritz Kortner whose name also appeared in a cast that consisted of a Who's Who of other expatriates: Ludwig Stössel, William Trenk (a.k.a. Willy Trenk-Trebitsch), Rudolph Anders (a.k.a. Rudolf Amendt), Kurt Katch (a.k.a. Kurt Katsch), Frederick Gierman (a.k.a. Friedrich Giermann) as Heinrich Himmler, Richard Révy, John Mylong-Münz (a.k.a. Adolf Heinrich Münz),

Trude Berliner, Martin Berliner, Hans Heinrich von Twardowski, Wolfgang Zilzer, Ilka Grüning, Lotte Stein, Elisabeth Neumann-Viertel, Fritz Brunn, Louis V. Arco (a.k.a. Lutz Altschul), Otto Reichow, Frank Alten, and Irene Seidner. Ludwig Donath who, like May, was born in Vienna, best known to movie lovers as supporting actor in ***Gilda*** and Hitchcock's ***Torn Curtain*** (as GDR Professor Lindt), plays a Chaplin-inspired dual role as gifted voice imitator Franz Huber who, thanks to plastic surgery (and the makeup services of ***Frankenstein*** creator Jack P. Pierce), is supposed to act as the double of the murdered Hitler and tries his best to sabotage war. But May wasn't allowed to direct it. James P. Hogan, a hack director known for ***Bulldog Drummond*** and ***The Mad Ghoul***, took over what should have been a Joe May production. Another director, Frank Tuttle, remade the story in 1951 in Austria as ***The Magic Face*** with Luther Adler taking over Donath's part.

The King Brothers, Frank and Maurice, were on their way up as May was on his way down when they met. They assigned him to direct ***Johnny Doesn't Live Here Any More*** in 1944, his last official picture [4], a Monogram comedy-fantasy with Simone Simon of ***Cat People*** fame who is pursued not by Robert Mitchum (in a minor part) but by a (optically superimposed) mischievous Gremlin with a cartoon voice (supplied by "Bug Bunny" Mel Blanc) whom only she can see: *The Gremlins are little people who live somewhere above the clouds. They spend most of their time annoying aviators but occasionally one of them comes down to earth and settles upon a poor pedestrian.*

This spirit is a Bad Luck Gremlin who hands Simone his name card introducing himself as B. O. Rumpelstilzken, licensed gremlin: *Once he gets on your trail, he will follow you to the ends of the earth. So if you want to avoid bad luck, keep clear of Rumpelstilzken.*

Rumpelstilzken augurs Simone Simon seven years of bad luck. But the bad luck was more to Joe May who struggled until his death. In my collection I've got some of the meagre checks he received from Universal as royalties for his work: a few hundred dollars that didn't even pay the rent. At the bitter end

4 May would do a few TV pilots that were not accepted and contributed to the story of Universal's ***Buccaneer's Girl***.

the once so successful May was forced to write begging letters. He had sold Mia's jewelry to keep the car, "I simply don't see how to keep going... I am at a loss." May passed away after a long illness on April 29, 1954, in Hollywood, poor as dirt.

In 1995, Stefan Weidle translated Hollaender's book about Mando-Mandl-May and published it under a thoughtful German title: ***Menschliches Treibgut - Human Driftwood***.

MAIN PART:

Joseph Goebbels' Keynote Speech

Although screenwriter Walter Reisch had to leave Germany in 1933 and work in Austria, in a late interview with Thomas Elsaesser he seemed to have forgotten this and claimed that until 1934 the Nazis didn't exactly know what to do with the film industry: *There was not the slightest hint of anti-semitism in Berlin and not a single hint in the film industry.* [27]

On March 28, 1933, Goebbels, a "passionate lover of film art", talked at Berlin's Kaiserhof hotel in front of the beer-drinking members of the *Dacho*, the Umbrella Organization of German filmmakers, in length about his cinematic likes and dislikes. Curt Siodmak, later to be the writer of some of the most successful horror films of the 1940s, was present and recalls the event. After promising that they, the Nazis, wouldn't leave power as soon as some might expect but were determined to stay Goebbels said:

"I can further add in my favor that I have seen most films made at home and abroad. Therefore I have a certain fund of knowledge and experience, so that I am in a position to give a judgment on things that are in any case of substance."

In his speech he highlighted Fritz Lang's ***Nibelungen***, ***Der Rebell*** (***The Rebel***) by Kurt Bernhardt and Luis Trenker, Kurt Bernhardt's ***Last Compagnie***, the 1928 silent melodrama ***Anna Karenina*** starring Hitler's favorite actress Greta Garbo who had made a single movie in Germany (G. W. Pabst's ***Die freudlose Gasse***) before she was hired away to Hollywood by Louis B. Mayer.

Goebbels even mentioned Sergei M. Eisenstein's ***Battleship Potemkin*** which was quoted in his diaries as early as June 30, 1928: *In the evening we saw* **Potemkin**. *I have to say that this film is fabulously made. With quite magnificent crowd scenes. Technical and landscape details of succinct power. And the hard-hitting slogans are formulated so skillfully that it is impossible to contradict them. That is what is actually dangerous about this film.* Who isn't firm in his *weltanschauung* could be transformed into a Bolshevist.

---

27 Thomas Elsaesser, *Flieger, grüss mir die Sonne: Österreich und Walter Reisch.* In: Beckermann, Ruth and Blümlinger, Christa (ed.), *Ohne Untertitel: Fragmente einer Geschichte des österreichischen Kinos.* Vienna: Sonderzahl Verlag, 1996, p. 340.

To Curt Siodmak's surprise (and relief) Goebbels also mentioned ***F.P. 1 antwortet nicht*** (***F.P. 1 Doesn't Answer***), based on a book written by Siodmak that told of a huge floating platform in the Atlantic Ocean which is supposed to make long-distance flights viable, adapted for the screen by Walter Reisch.

At that occasion at the Kaiserhof the Nazis could have collected, among the 300 persons present, all Jews who still worked in the German film industry, Siodmak wrote in his memoirs: producer Erich Pommer, directors Hanns Schwarz and William Thiele, the famous actors' agent Elizabeth Blumann, and dozens of writers: *Our lives could have been extinguished on this very day but the Nazi movement hadn't still won their strike capability - which gave us a chance to escape the holocaust.*

When Siodmak left, he overheard an actor behind him, Louis Ralph, talking to a an acquaintance: *Now we are going to take over* - as if the Jews would have prevented him from becoming a good actor.

The day after Goebbels' speech Ufa's board of directors obliged, clicked their heels and passed the following resolution:

With regard to the question raised by Germany's national revolution concerning Ufa's further engagement of Jewish workers and staff, the board of directors has resolved to revoke as far as possible its contracts with Jewish personnel.

Immediately they laid off a number of their most prominent filmmakers, including producer Erich Pommer and director Erik Charell, both responsible for one of Ufa's biggest sound film hits, ***Der Kongress tanzt*** (***The Congress Dances***). Pommer had already received an invitation to supervise Fox' European production from offices in Paris and would be able to hire Fritz Lang. The Nazis offered to allow him to work in Germany provided Fox would install the branch office in Berlin but both, Pommer and Fox, turned them down.

Goebbels' warning, almost casually expressed at his Kaiserhof speech, echoed in Siodmak's mind:

We will not even entertain the idea of tolerating a re-appearance in some disguised or open form by ideas that are being eradicated root and branch in the New Germany.

Siodmak wasn't sure. What about *his* ideas?

Preventively, Curt Siodmak went to see Ufa production chief Ernst Hugo Correll to try and ask for pending fees from ***F.P. 1***. Correll told him that he had received instruction to dismiss "certain" directors, scriptwriters, and employees and that their contracts had been terminated: So, sorry, no money. The production head didn't utter the word *Jew*. But Siodmak realized that Goebbels' warning did include him. So, on the advice of his wise Swiss wife Henrietta, he didn't hesitate a moment (like Fritz Lang did) and left Germany.

Horst Wessel vs. Hans Westmar

The crisis of movies, Goebbels had said at the Kaiserhof, was a spiritual one. Nevertheless, he despised some of the 1933 films that tried to chum up with the victorious Nazi movement. The Nazis themselves canceled the premiere of a ***Horst Wessel*** martyr film that was produced by Volksdeutsche Film GmbH.

The ***Wessel*** movie, which was destined by its makers to become the flagship of National Socialist filmmaking, was adapted from his own novel by fantasist-turned-occultist Hanns Heinz Ewers. In 1913 Ewers had scripted and supervised Paul Wegener's dual role in ***Der Student von Prag*** (***The Student of Prague***). Ewers' anti-feminist nightmare novel ***Alraune*** was filmed three times, twice with Brigitte Helm (of ***Metropolis*** fame) and once, post-war, with Hildegard Knef and Erich von Stroheim. Allegedly, Hitler had asked the writer in the Brown House in Munich to write a novel about the death of SA man Horst Wessel, who was killed in 1930. In the foreword to the book we read:

Grateful thanks to the Führer of the German liberty movement, Adolf Hitler. It was he who one year ago suggested and assigned me to write about the "fight for the street", a chapter of German history whose true nature remains completely unknown to wide sections of our people in spite of daily reports in all newspapers. [28]

A contemporary reviewer couldn't help than to make fun of Ewers' trashy literature:

Horst Wessel? Why, it's just our little Alraune! Fashions change. But obscene or nationalist, it's the same bloodlust of the weak and impotent. [29]

Another critic, Bert Brecht, called Ewers a successful pornographer who, among others, had written a book in which a dead body is exhumed and raped. Brecht hinted at a story that was published in Ewers' 1922 book ***Nachtmahr: Der schlimme Verrat.***

Klaus Mann, Thomas Mann's son, was aghast when he read the novel:

---

28 Hanns Heinz Ewers, *Horst Wessel. Ein deutsches Schicksal.* Stuttgart/Berlin: Cotta'sche Buchhandlung Nachfolger, 1932.

29 Walter Mehring, *Marriage! Horst Wessel. Alraune, née Ewers.* In: Die Weltbühne, January 10, 1933.

A horrendously *written book, beyond the pale of literature.*

An almost unbearable read. But you have to know your enemies. What a guttersnipe, this Ewers - but perhaps he is typical of this Germany with his indescribable *mediocrity, mendacity, and meanness.* [30]

According to National Socialist legend, the original Horst Wessel (1907-1930), son of a parson, student and leader of an SA sturm in Berlin Friedrichshain (who, by the way, was an extra in Henrik Galeen's 1926 remake of ***The Student of Prague***), was shot by communists, but actually the murder was not politically motivated. In fact, Wessel, sort of a pimp, was killed by a con man, the lover of his landlady.

In Ewers' novel he is transformed into a saint, the Christ-like hero of a Passion, with his mother filling in for the Blessed Virgin Mary:

Again the mother dreamed: Highly erected a gigantic cross, the crossbars pleached with a swastika. Beneath stood Horst in his brown storm trooper uniform, looking up stony-faced. Never ever this image would leave her. And she knew: If a people's misery is calling for a victim - then always there are the bravest, the noblest and best of men who are predestinated. And always, always the end comes like this: Beneath the cross there is a mother. [31]

In a few weeks 30,000 copies were sold.

In Ewers' novel and film version young Korps student Horst Wessel, coming from waltz-loving Vienna, on screen played by Emil Lohkamp (1902-1993), is shocked at the decadence of Weimar Republic's nightlife with Negro bands and all that jazz. Giving up his studies, he devotes himself exclusively to SA activities against the "Jewish-Bolshevist" Communist Party: "I'm telling you, all Germany is at stake down there on the streets. And that is why we must get closer to the people; we cannot stand aloof anymore. We must fight, side by side, with the workers - it's all or nothing!" Paul Wegener joined his friend Ewers in the ***Wessel*** film project and loaned his almost Slavic features to the Muscovite wire puller Kuprikoff, who decrees Wessel's martyr

30 Klaus Mann, Diary, August 1-2, 1933.

31 Hanns Heinz Ewers, *Horst Wessel. Ein deutsches Schicksal.*

death. Betrayed by a neighbor and riddled with bullets, Wessel passes away at a hospital. His final word is *Deutschland - Germany.*

Involved in the making of the film was Dr. Ernst ("Putzi") Hanfstaengl, an early associate of Adolf Hitler and then the party's foreign relations press officer:

"I showed Hitler and [photographer] Heinrich Hoffmann the rough cut and they seemed to like it well," Hanfstaengl said, "but I had reckoned without Goebbels... The premiere was arranged. The invitations were sent out. Everyone in Berlin society from the Crown Prince down was to be present and suddenly Goebbels banned the film from screening.

"This was too much. A lot of money had been tied up in the project and now ruin stared us in the face. I stormed in to see Hitler and then Goebbels, but the little man had invented a thousand excuses why it was not to be shown, although his real reason was jealousy. It was too bourgeois in approach, emphasized Wessel's Christian background too much, was not full of the National Socialist spirit, it was trite - everything was wrong."

In a communiqué it was stated that the movie "neither does Horst Wessel and the National Socialist movement, foundation of this state, justice, nor is his [Wessel's] historic personality adequately portrayed. So the film endangers the life interests of this state and the reputation of Germany".

Two months later, with only a section about the origin of the *Horst Wessel Song* (with lyrics scripted by Wessel before his death) removed, the film finally opened under a different title: ***Hans Westmar - Einer von vielen. Ein deutsches Schicksal aus dem Jahre 1929*** (***Hans Westmar, One of Many: A German Fate from Year 1929***) and was poorly received by Berlin audiences although the reviewers pretended some sympathy not regarding the (missing) cinematic qualities but the political background.

<u>Völkischer Beobachter</u>

You, Hans Westmar, we suppose, will have an enormous and necessary political task even outside the Reich: to mediate an objective knowledge what was happening in Germany, why Adolf Hitler simply had to win.

Der Deutsche

The great propaganda value of the film - it will be shown abroad too - is that it shows bluntly how much Berlin was already seized by the Soviets and international cultures.

Much to his surprise, of all people, Hanns Heinz Ewers, who would have liked to be a Nazi, witnessed that on 10 May 1933 some of his books became part of the Nazi book burnings. And that, on June 30, 1934, in the Night of the Long Knives, Hitler would "purge" the SA whose hymn of praise he had sung.

Emil Lohkamp as Horst Wessel a.k.a. Hans Westmar (1933)
Author's collection

Mickey Mouse Meets Hitler Youth Quex

While Jews, communists, and "exaggarated intellectuals" were scaled down and exiled, others were raised. One of them was Karl Ritter, who became one of the leading film directors and producers of the Third Reich.

Not many people, however, know that Ritter (1888-1977), a personal friend of Bayreuth's new first lady Winifred Wagner, was the graphic artist and copy-writer behind the German ***Mickey Mouse*** campaign of the early 1930s. This is how Ritter saw the cartoon Mouse:

Mickey is born in the country of Black Bottom, Slow Fox, Nigger Songs, in the country of jazz, in a word: the U.S.A. Mickey is the sound film mouse. Father: Walt Disney, an American artist and cartoonist. A marvelous, ingenious, extremely witty, splendid guy! A whiz par excellence, a virtuoso of humor up to date, a universal genius in all things technical, obsessed by the sense of motion and rhythm as only few of his contemporaries are.

Mother: the animated drawing, like the **Silly Symphonies**, *crazy jazz compositions from a strange, enlivened fairy tale nature! There are crickets and grasshoppers dancing, spiders playing dreamlike harp melodies on their webs, flowers and trees, birds and insects begin to live like human children, even clouds, lightning and rain begin to behave like people of today.*

Godfather: the sound film. One cannot imagine Mickey without sound. Everything Mickey does makes noise, tuneful or else. Mickey plays xylophone on the teeth of a cow, transforms a squeaking mother pig into a concertina, misuses cattails as singing saws, dances to the tunes of the newest hit songs on piano keys, plays the harp on macaroni noodles, hairs of the beard, spider webs. Even when Mickey hangs on a railroad car and thumps with his bottom on the railroad ties, it sounds like clownish chimes that move your legs. [...]

Mickey's language is international: Old and young, Chinese or Eskimo and Nigger, white or red, everybody understands him: a new Esperanto [...] *the divine language of the laughing human heart!* [32]

---

32 Filmwoche No. 12, 1930.

German Merchandising of a Mickey Mouse Egg (1931)
Courtesy of J. P. Storm Collection

Karl Hermann Josef Ritter himself was born on November 7, 1888, in Würzburg as son of a professor at the Music Conservatorium and an opera singer. His mother lost her singing voice as a consequence of his birth. In 1907 Ritter entered the Bavarian War Academy; the next year he joined the Bavarian Army. In 1909, as a young lieutenant, he became interested in aviation. A year later he constructed a single-decker plane. In 1911 he passed his flying certification and married Erika, daughter of fanatical anti-Semite Carl Ritter (same name, no relation), cousin of Siegfried Wagner, Richard's son. This brought him to Bayreuth. Ritter was a participant in World War I, a personal friend of aviator and WWI combat flyer Ernst Udet and met Hitler in Wagnerian circles in the early 1920s. On October 19, 1925, Ritter and his wife joined NSDAP.

Beginning to work for Disney's future German distributor Südfilm in

Berlin in 1926, he met Joseph Goebbels whose career had started as Gauleiter in the German capital the same year. But being a member of NSDAP, Ritter feared problems because Südfilm, due to financial difficulties, was absorbed by Heros Filmgesellschaft. Heros had a Jewish executive by the name of Isidor Goldschmidt, who also controlled British International Pictures Ltd. London. For that reason, on 28 April 1928, fearing that "too many Jews" were associated with the film industry, the Ritters dropped out of Hitler's party for good measure. Karl Ritter built himself quite a career: working with young Alfred Hitchcock on the German versions of his films, producing the German version of Charles Chaplin's ***City Lights*** and consulting on ***Berlin Alexanderplatz***, the Alfred Döblin novel filmed with Heinrich George, working in Paris, Vienna and Prague. He even co-authored, with Dr. M. Paul Block, a 70-page children's book ***Micky Maus. Ein lustiges Filmbildbuch***, the first-ever Mickey book to be published in Germany.

Soon after, in 1931, Ritter's career as a film director began as a substitute for Carl Lamač who had become ill, supervising Edgar Wallace's ***Der Zinker*** (***The Squeaker***) with Lissy Arna, Karl Ludwig Diehl, Fritz Rasp, Paul Hörbiger, Szöke Szakall and Ernst Reicher: Stuart Webbs himself.

But then, bad news: In December 1932 Emelka and Südfilm had to declare bankruptcy. Ritter was suddenly without a job, like millions of his fellow countrymen. William Gillespie, an Australian film historian, checked Ritter's diaries. In January 1933 the aspiring director's situation was quite desperate:

Our furniture was removed. Only the piano we would not give up. Do not know how long we can manage. In any case, we cannot pay the rent, and stand before a fiendishly hostile hopeless situation.

A consolation is the political situation, which we instinctively hope for.

Then, on 30 January, the change: Hindenburg declared Hitler Reich Chancellor.

On Erika's 46th birthday, came a turning point - the takeover of the N.S.D.A.P. A.H. is Reichskanzler, Germany bursts forth.

With the 30th of January 1933 our fate should take a decisive turn for the better. It was high time. We were up to our necks in water. [33]

In February, another streak of luck: Ritter signed a probationary three-year contract with Ufa's general manager Ludwig Klitzsch and was offered his own production group on a silver tray. Immediately he joined forces with director Hans Steinhoff, like Fritz Lang known as a firm dictator on the set, and together they made Ufa's first bow to Adolf Hitler: ***Hitlerjunge Quex*** (***Hitler Youth Quex***) adapted from a book by Karl Aloys Schenzinger, a made up biography of a killed Hitler Youth named Herbert Norkus, in the film renamed Heini Völker and played by Jürgen Ohlsen. With this movie Heinrich George, as Heini's choleric Communist father, got the "chance" to move from the left-wing side of artists and establish himself as a leading right-wing actor of the Third Reich.

Hitler Youth Quex, *a blend of historical fact and myth, contains all the elements of a passion play: an innocent blond child; a desperate mother who attempts a joint suicide with her son; a drunken father drawn to communism for reasons beyond his control; the dark slums of starving Beusselkiez* [a Berlin workers' district]; *German communists as tools of a foreign power; idealistic and heroic Hitler Youth; the redemptive death of a lamb of the Volk; and the promise of regeneration of the nation through Adolf Hitler.* [34]

From the pressbook Ufa released with the movie:

Ufa considers it one of the finest tasks of German film to tell our national comrades and beyond that the whole world of the spiritual groundwork of the huge movement that expressed itself in the fact of the national revolution. It is not the duty of the film, this most modern of all art forms, to give lectures on social and political questions. The film's duty is to process ideas in the colorful reflection of a dramatically inspired, many times amusing, upraising and agitating plot, ideas that - and this is important for cinemas - engage the people of today far beyond the borders of the Reich. How did German youth merge with this movement? This

33 William Gillespie, *Karl Ritter: His Life and Zeitfilms under National Socialism.* Potts Point, Australia, 2014, pp. 13-14.

34 Jay W. Baird, *To Die for Germany: Heroes in the Nazi Pantheon.* Bloomington,. IN: Indiana University Press, 1990, p. 121.

movie tries to answer the question telling us about the life and fate of a German boy: the story of Hitler Youth Quex.

There are off-site circumstances that push the little Communist boy Heini Völker towards the Hitler Youth: Father workless, marriage broken, the whole neighborhood held under red terror. Only ever hatred, hetz, ire - and no friends! No clean outfit, no fun playing and wandering. Against this other boys: they were wandering, they didn't bandy blows constantly, they don't consider 'Klauen' [stealing] and dirty jokes for the greatest achievements, they sing songs, strange, whipping, marching songs, friends marching alongside friends. In good spirits and with shining eyes they wear their neat uniforms and - they know about a gorgeous country! Germany is the name - and they told him that it belongs to him too: his Vaterland [home country]. So he becomes a Hitler Youth - but still he feels only hazily that there has to be more than just the outward appearance. Mother who thinks that she cannot protect him from the reenactments of the Commune [Communists] and who doesn't see any meaning in life than him, wants to divest him and herself from the emulations of the world through suicide. She dies, he is saved - and got nothing else on this world than the idea of a new, cleaner, better fatherland that he was chosen to help to create - and slowly he becomes aware that there is something greater than his own fate - as important one may consider it. - This is the fate of all, of the collectivity. Gently, quietly another emotion sprouts in the 16-year-old who falls - touching, hopeless, unacknowledged - in love with a girl who has just come of age and like him is addicted to the great new spring which, timidly and stealthily, begins to blossom in Germany. But this youth was created for fight, with the guideline: Common good comes before self. Both young people who aren't aware what links them print leaflets at night. He, Quex, volunteers to distribute the leaflets where red terror dominates, the very district where he grew up. That's the most beautiful day for them! And when he - conscious that his girlfriend fears for him in proud anxiety - tears down the red flag from the tavern where the Commune meets and sets up the swastika, black on white ground in a red field - he feels that life cannot give him a better day. And fate proves him right. Hunted down and caught by the Communists, he dies the martyr death of German youth that a generation ahead had died at Langemarck [in 1914 the location of the Battle of Flanders], the death for the new fatherland. Away from her dead friend, the girl he loved marches on and with her the youth - towards Endsieg [final victory] - roaring around the battle song of the Hitler Youth.

We are the children
of this German soil.
We are
the divine seed
of the German future!
In our hearts one word is burning:
Let there be!
We are the fight,
the hope and the exploit!

Ufa was offered many stories that dealt with the ideas of what's going on today. Selected was this one because the cinema owner should get what truly belongs into his theater: a film that will make hundreds of thousands laugh and cry.

The eulogy of Nazi poet Eberhard Wolfgang Möller commenting the death of the real Heini Völker, Herbert Norkus, by the hands of the fiendish, satanic Reds illustrated the almost religious symbolism that colors, uniforms, and flags had for this movement and how all this melted with the cult of death: *Herbert Norkus was murdered while wearing a white shirt. When the shirt was examined later, however, the blood had turned brown. So the boy was wearing a brown shirt after all when he died. How unbelievably marvelous for such a thing to happen!*

The end of the movie with Heini substituting for Herbert is a final ecstatic apotheosis: *As Heini lies dying, a vision grows with him of an army of brown-shirted Hitler Youth and behind them the swastika which gradually changes into a monumental emblem of salvation engulfing the entire screen. In a series of dissolves, the marching columns, flags, and the dead Quex with the sound track taking up the Hitler Youth's marching song, merge into a single heroic image. The masterly use of fade-overs and editing heighten the mythical effect of this vision of a collective identity, which was supposed to leap from the screen to the audience below and capture the psyche of the spectators. The doctrine of salvation through the sacrifice of one's life was linked to the flag in an effort to provide the Nazi movement with the requisite energy to achieve its goals.* [35]

Illustrierter Film-Kurier
The brave little soldier has died the hero's death, for his cause, for his comrades, for the ardently loved banner and for the Führer. But other German boys set up the flag again which is consecrated with the blood of one of their best.

The premiere took place on September 11, 1933, at the Ufa Phoebus Palace in Munich. Long columns of Hitler Youth stood guard outside the cinema. Guests of honor were Hermann Göring, Rudolf Hess, Robert Ley, Ernst Röhm, Vice Chancellor Franz von Papen, General Werner von Blomberg and above all - the Führer himself.

When at the premiere the last image faded away, a Hitler Youth and a Hitler Girl stood on the stage like two little wanderers in a big world. They extend their arms up to the Führer. He approached them and thanked them likewise. He looked down approvingly with a benign smile at the two unknown players and speakers of the great German Hitler Youth who were chosen by fate to bear witness for hundreds of thousands of a gesinnung, a cast of mind which stands worthy besides the great days of the pioneers of the movement.

The Führer's greetings was directed at the inviolability of a spirit that defends the Fatherland for better or worse and that again and again decently ascends from the depths of the movie. [36]

In October Ritter was issued membership no. 12 in the Reichsfachschaft (Association) of the Reichsfilmkammer. Asked which political parties he had joined since 1918, he answered that he was National Socialist: always! "In our cinemas we want to see nothing else than convinced National Socialists," Ritter said. "The path of German films will lead without any compromise to

35 Hilmar Hoffmann, *The Triumph of Propaganda: Film and National Socialism 1933-1945*. Providence and Oxford: Berghahn Books, Inc., 1996, pp. 51-52.

36 Reichsfilmblatt.

the conclusion that every movie must stay in the service of our community, of nation and our Führer."

Original movie poster *Hitlerjunge Quex*
Courtesy of Rolf Giesen Collection

The Ruler and the Laugh Doctor

The bloodletting of the German film industry was fateful for the reputation of German films in foreign countries. The Nazi film industry desperately needed luminous figures and was willing to roll out the red carpet for them.

One of Hitler's favorite films in this time was ***Der zerbrochene Krug*** (***The Broken Jug***), which was the dream project of Emil Jannings: a good and proper comedy written by Heinrich von Kleist, with Jannings as lazy village judge Adam who is going to solve the case of a broken jug that nobody else has broken than the judge himself. The original play was premiered in Weimar in March 1808, the movie in October 1937. Jannings, having won the very first Academy Award as male actor in 1928, became the big cheese of German films. For Goebbels and Hitler, Emil Jannings meant prestige. And Jannings would cooperate because he was interested in what he gently called *pinkus*, money which he usually transferred abroad to his account in the Netherlands. While Charles Laughton, an equally gifted actor, had sold his talent to Hollywood, Emil Jannings sold his soul to the Nazis. (In 1926, he had been Mephistopheles in F. W. Murnau's ***Faust*** film, towering mountainously over a medieval village, certainly the role model of the mountainous demon Chernabog in Disney's ***Fantasia***, but obviously Jannings didn't learn from the saying: *Who wants to eat with the devil must have a long spoon.*)

The Broken Jug was sort of a bonus, since Jannings had repeatedly demonstrated his willingness to accept roles not only in classics but in political prestige pictures:

In 1935 he was Friedrich Wilhelm I (the Old King), father of Fridericus (the Young King played by Werner Hinz), in Hans Steinhoff's historical drama ***Der alte und der junge König*** (***The Old and the Young King***): "Make Prussia great!"

Völkischer Beobachter:

The triumph of German film!

This is film: German film. Finally. A gargantuan work of creative power that blows with mighty force the tight boundaries... It is an epiphany of the German soul as it can't be thought more monumental and upsetting. The phenomenal impression becomes an experience... Outstanding: Emil Jannings.

Emil Jannings and Angela Salloker in *The Broken Jug (Der zerbrochene Krug)*
Courtesy of Jens Geutebrück, Coronaretro Archives

Der Angriff:
We are surprised and overwhelmed... This film provides the political, the sole great fateful drama of the state... Prussian spirit has Germany presented with a movie which will sweep away forever all previous celluloid onto the scrap heap. In it we see Prussia's heroic march through the centuries.

And even bigger than ***The Old King*** that was made in 1934 and released in '35 was the title character that Jannings portrayed in ***Der Herrscher*** (***The Ruler*** a.k.a. ***The Sovereign***, 1936-37), loosely adapted from Gerhart Hauptmann's play ***Vor Sonnenuntergang*** by Thea von Harbou and Curt J. Braun, the very movie that made Veit Harlan the big hope among Nazi film directors: *Emil Jannings appears as a responsible entrepreneur running an enormous steelworks, which he finally leaves to the state rather than his money-grubbing family. The inefficient directors of the company are supposed to justify the 'Führer principle' in commercial life.* [37]

37 Felix Moeller, *The Film Minister: Goebbels and the Cinema in the Third Reich.*

The Old King (Emil Jannings) admires his Potsdam Giants. Man with mustache right behind him: Rudolf Klein-Rogge, Fritz Lang's favorite villain.

Courtesy of Jens Geutebrück, Coronaretro Archives

Emil Jannings as *The Ruler* (*Der Herrscher*)

Courtesy of Jens Geutebrück, Coronaretro Archives

Stuttgart and Fellbach: Edition Axel Menges, 2001, p. 71.

As Krupp-like industrialist Matthias Clausen (Jannings) goes for strong leadership:

We are here to work for the Volksgemeinschaft [people's community]. The objective of every industrial leader who is aware of his own responsibility must be to serve the Volksgemeinschaft. This will of mine is the supreme law which governs my work! Everything else must be subordinated to this will, without opposition, even if in doing so I would lead the whole company into the abyss!

Such words fascinated Hitler who was going to lead German people into an abyss.

In slightly modified version: **He who does not submit himself to Hitler's supreme law has no place Germany!**

Jannings' final speech was the greatest credo for the National Socialist Volksgemeinschaft one could imagine: *I break with my children and in-laws. They are not worthy to inherit my legacy. They are unable to maintain it. So I herewith bestow the factory I have created after my death upon the state, the Volksgemeinschaft. I am certain that from the ranks of its workers and clerks who have helped me to build the factory the man will emerge who is called to continue my work, may he come from the smelting furnace or the plotting board, from the laboratory or from the bench vise. I will teach him the few things that an outgoing president is able to teach the newcomer because who is born to lead doesn't need another teacher than his own genius.*

That was music to Hitler's ears. He didn't attend a university or academy and in WW1 was no more than a simple private but believed himself a born genius. Goebbels was present when Hitler saw the film for the first time and made a respective entry in his diary: *Tonight to the Führer. We palaver a long time. See Jannings film* **Der Herrscher**. *The Führer is totally moved and embraced. It [the picture] leaves the deepest impression. Especially in its background description. I grant it the highest ratings. Call Jannings and tell him. He is deliriously happy.* [38]

38 March 13, 1937.

Emil Jannings, the *Ruler*, meets with his Board of Directors. Courtesy of Jens Geutebrück, Coronaretro Archives

Exiled writer-director Berthold Viertel was justifiably disappointed to no end when he saw Jannings again on the screen in such pathetic effort:

He had grown by inches, and every inch a phony prig. An Emil, diluted to fit into line, groomed as though Goebbels had been at his beard with a cat's paws, claws retracted. He has been really preened for glory, a fat goody-goody, a royal merchant, an industrial magnate. [39]

The Nazi press, however, was enthusiastic and hailed it as the greatest achievement of German film so far.

Hamburger Tageblatt:

This film is a contemporary one, a genuine National Socialist one... It pressures merits and crimes of the German past remorselessly in front of the [camera] lens.

Producer on behalf of Tobis-Magna was one Helmut Schreiber of whom we will hear later. In 1938 Jannings assumed, at least nominally, the artistic control of Tobis Filmkunst and was in charge of his own production unit.

39 *Das Neue Tagebuch*, 1937.

From then on Jannings approached Goebbels with a lot of film parts that he thought would fit him: ***Fuhrmann Henschel, Michael Kohlhaas*** and even ***Genghis Khan.*** Goebbels listened patiently, but with him there was no way to make these movies. "It would scarcely be possible to think of a less timely project," he noted about ***Genghis Khan*** at a time when the Germans prepared their fatal attack on Stalingrad. [40]

But when Jannings did appear on screen, one could be sure that it was an expensive picture like ***Ohm Krüger*** (***Uncle Krüger***) in 1941, a biopic about the Boer war leader Paul Kruger (1825-1904). The anti-British propaganda film that accused the English colonial power to be the inventor of concentration camps was considered that important that Hitler himself was asked to approve of Jannings' make-up and mask in the title role.

From 1942 till the end of the war, Jannings made hundreds of thousands of marks, and that was all that mattered to him.

If Jannings, as ***The Sovereign***, was able to present his factory to the German people represented by Hitler, Göring & Co., Goebbels could do likewise concerning the film industry and get it nationalized.

In 1937, the same year ***Der Herrscher*** was released, the Nazis began to swallow German film industry as they had already done with the German press. For their plan they used the discrete offices of Cautio Treuhand, Trust Company which were supervised by former Graudenz mayor Dr. Max Winkler:

As a fiduciary of the government from 1920 on, Winkler had a reputation as a discreet and skillful expert. He had expertise in the media from government work he had done on behalf of the German-language press and for the "preservation of German culture" in neighboring countries. After 1933, Winkler offered his services to the Ministry of Propaganda and the Reich Press Officer of the NSDAP, Max Amann, to help do away with private ownership of newspapers and to bring print under state control. Prohibitions and political chicanery had pushed many newspaper publishers so close to the brink of financial ruin that they had no choice but to sell on terms dictated by the National Socialist "buyers".

40 Joseph Goebbels, *Diary*, July 2, 1942.

This process became the model for the film business. With the first steps toward "nationalization" of Tobis in 1935, a chain of state usurpations began that ended in the early 1940s with the almost total nationalization of Germany's film companies. Working through Cautio Trust Company, which he had formed in 1929, Winkler discreetly negotiated with senior executives to acquire the majority of stock in all major companies. Without himself being a board member or company executive, he could then make them comply with his directives. [41]

Winkler bought Ufa for peanuts and then the other major film companies that suffered from drastically dwindling export numbers. The Nazi state, however, as Goebbels later proudly remarked, earned a fortune when German troops not only invaded half of Europe but with it European cinemas too.

When Winkler met Göring after the coup, the second man in state seemed rather pleased: "The Führer wants you to take over the whole film industry. Goebbels isn't able to do that job properly."

Shortly afterwards Goebbels confirmed that Max Winkler should become *Reichsbeauftragter für die Filmwirtschaft*, Reich Commissioner of the Film Industry. For his services he was offered 180,000 Reichsmark annually, the same sum Ufa chief Ludwig Klitzsch was drawing. He obliged and accepted the job but declined the money. With Winkler having a keen eye on administration, Goebbels proceeded and postulated the primate of art over economics. The first he did was to promote confidents to top positions in the film industry.

Ufa production head Ernst Hugo Correll was forced into premature retirement. He died on 3 September 1942 in Garmisch-Partenkirchen. Alfred Greven lasted only a few months on Correll's chair and was sent to occupied Paris to supervise the production activities of French (but German-controlled) Continental Films S.A. Instead Pg. (Party Comrade) Ernst Leichtenstern was chosen to become Ufa's new head of production. Leichtenstern was as equally qualified for the job as his colleague, cartoon film producer Karl Neumann (the man interned and found hanged in Weesow/Werneuchen right after the

41 Klaus Kreimeier, *The Ufa Story: A History of Gemany's Greatest Film Company, 1918–1945*. Berkeley: University of California Press, 1999, p. 258.

war). In World War I, Leichtenstern was an officer of the Imperial German Navy, in the early 1920s Freikorps member. He joined NSDAP in 1930 and was employed as electrician in the Munich party headquarters, the Brown House, where he established contacts with prominent Nazi figures. (Hitler, Göring, Himmler, Rudolf Hess, Hans Frank, Philipp Bouhler, and Franz Xaver Schwarz maintained offices there.) In 1934 he was promoted Gau Propaganda chief of Munich and Upper Bavaria. Out of the blue, he became chief of the Propaganda Ministry's film department from January 1938 to August 1939 but he certainly didn't know how to run a film company. So he would sit in Ufa's telephone exchange and check who greeted with *Heil Hitler!* and who didn't. Initially, Goebbels wasn't willing to part with this dilettante - until Winkler told him laconically that Ufa was losing millions due to Leichtenstern's incompetence. But that was not exactly Leichtenstern's end. On April 7, 1940, he became mayor of Görlitz and in July 1944 mayor of the "Fortress" Breslau (Wrocław today) where he died in 1945.

Thanks to the war Germany would become Europe's main film manufacturer. Italy wouldn't supply that much, Hungary's output wasn't that important, and the Barrandov Studios in Prague were under German control. Had Ufa ordered 70 prints per film before the war they now had to increase this number to 150 to 160 prints per picture. For German Newsreels (***Siegesfahnen über Deutschland - Victory banners over Germany***) even 1,600 to 1,900 prints had to be struck. In 1942 Ufa, now singled out to represent all of German filmmaking, made 850 million Reichsmark. [42]

In Felix Moeller's book about Film Minister Goebbels there is a very brief remark that sums up the whole tragedy of Jewish emigration for the rest of the humor-loving German nation: *In the field of comedy many must have welcomed the exodus of the more talented Jewish colleagues.* [43]

Jewish humor was witty and intelligent. With the émigrés left, humor fell on hard times in Germany, at least humor that could be considered humanist. Instead German Jews like Ernst Lubitsch and Billy Wilder, actors like Felix

42 *Bei der Ufa machte man das so.* In: DER SPIEGEL 3/1951, January 17, 1951, p. 20.

43 Felix Moeller, *The Film Minister: Goebbels and the Cinema in the Third Reich.*

Bressart, Siegfried Arno, once hailed the German Chaplin, or Curt Bois now enhanced Hollywood comedies, often only in bit parts.

But to say that Hitler and the Nazis didn't have their own sort of humor would be a false statement. The North Germans and citizens of Berlin preferred the malicious glee of *schadenfreude*. Adolf Hitler himself had what we might call a rustic coarse humor. He liked comedians from Bavaria and Austria, including Karl Valentin (who hated him), mumbling Hans Moser (who had to protect his Jewish wife Blanca) and Weiss Ferdl. [44]

Outside of Germany and today not even in Germany people will not have heard the name of Weiss Ferdl, born Ferdinand Weisheitinger on June 28, 1883 in Altötting, a pilgrimage 90 kilometers east of Munich. He was the son of an unwed waitress and was raised by his grandmother; who was going to boost his singing voice by letting him exercise with the Capuchin monks. He even managed to be educated in the cathedral boy's choir in Salzburg. But after his puberty vocal change he reconsidered and began an apprenticeship as typesetter before he returned to the public. Eventually Weisheitinger entered the stage in Regensburg. In 1906 he was seen at the Munich Platzl cabaret right in the center of the Old Town, not far away from Hofbräuhaus. From 1916 until 1944 he was in charge of the little popular theater and helped to discover many a talent.

Weiss Ferdl's humor was unspoiled by education and primitive, therefore congruent with Hitler's. His songs were as popular as the man: *Vom Wunder der Weisswurst* (*The Miracle of the Weisswurst = Bavarian veal sausage*), *Der letzte Münchner Fiaker* (*The Last Munich Carriage*), *Hinterhugldorfer Feuerwehr* (*The Hinterhugldorf Fire Brigade*) and the trolley car hymn *Ein Wagen von der Linie 8* (*A Trolley Car from Line 8*).

As the folk singer and entertainer was known for his singing voice and rude puns he was more qualified for sound films than silents.

He was an early supporter of the NSDAP and Adolf Hitler who was a regular guest at the Platzl, but his denazificiation papers termed him *fellow traveler* (sentenced to pay a fine of 2000 Marks) as he hadn't appeared in

44 There is a documentary devoted to that topic: ***Laughing with Hitler***.

any propaganda films. The list of his film credits includes titles like ***Der Meisterdetektiv*** (***The Master Detective,*** 1933), ***Der Meisterboxer*** (***The Champ,*** 1934), ***Der müde Theodor*** (***Tired Theodore,*** 1936), ***Befehl ist Befehl*** (***Order Is Order,*** 1936), ***Gordian, der Tyrann*** (***Gordian the Tyrant,*** 1937), ***Der Lachdoktor*** (***The Laugh Doctor,*** 1937), ***Der arme Millionär*** (***The Poor Millionaire,*** 1939) as Ignaz Stangelmeier (the Cobbler Nazi) who, coming into an inheritance, denies his petit bourgeois background and curries favor with the aristocracy. Some of these films were even shown, exclusively for German-speaking audiences, in the United States. Unoffending and naive or not, Weiss Ferdl sure had anti-Weimar sentiments and more than slight resentments of Jews.

Weiss Ferdl

Rolf Giesen Collection

Once, on stage, he even portrayed a Jew, Herr Sali Kohn, a merchant who deals with anything, notwithstanding political color:

The hilarity rises at the end of the monologue, as this Jew admits that whereas he formerly sold Hindenburg's picture, "it's not doing so well. Now I'm selling swastikas - they're going great." Feeling superior to Herr Kohn was not difficult; he is an amusing character only because of his utter lack of dignity. Neither sensitive to the ideals for which Germany had gone to war nor principled enough to be outraged over Nazi anti-Semitism, he is wholly absorbed in petty considerations of profit and loss. Moreover, by claiming that the sale of swastikas has been profitable, he embodies the widespread belief that the Jews were continuing to prosper at times when most Germans were beset by economic hardships. [...]

...a character like "Herr Sali Kohn" reflected and gave shape to the popular conception that Jews were self-seeking and unprincipled. In this way, the folksinger's comic treatment of the Jews formed part of the climate of middle-class prejudices that proved so stifling to the Weimar Republic. [45]

Kohn has been baptized, only because of bad people.
He adopts the name of Schmid which delights him.
But he can't keep in mind the name "Julius Schmid".
And if they ask him: What's your name, he says:
"Schmulius Jew".

Scenes like this were the cornerstone of mundane German or Bavarian anti-Semitism. In the 1920s, there were sometimes witty Jewish jokes and dull jokes about Jews.

In 1924, during the Hitler-Ludendorff trial, Weiss Ferdl publicly aligned himself with the indicted coup leaders:

Say, what have they done?
Should it be called a dishonor
If out of humiliation and misery
One is going to save the German fatherland?

---

45 Robert Eben Sackett, *Popular Entertainment, Class, and Politics in Munich, 1900-1923*. Cambridge, Massachusetts and London: Harvard University Press, p. 146.

Hitler invited him as early as 1933 to his Obersalzberg residency. Weiss Ferdl was as deeply impressed when he shook hands with the "Führer" as he was about the handshake of crown prince Rupprecht of Bavaria in WWI. The audience used his tame Nazi jokes as an opportunity to impute him with more radical ones. As Weiss Ferdl often appeared on stage in the outfit of Dachau, people, they quipped, would hint at the concentration camp: *Weiss Ferdl has one foot on the stage, the other in Dachau.*

Weiss Ferdl belonged to the selected few who were tolerated by the regime joking about the party: *Leit, kaufts Häring, dick und fett wie der Gäring! - Folks, buy herring, thick and fett like Gerring* [=Göring]!

More than one year after his denazification Weiss Ferdl received an unfriendly note from the culture department of the American military government. He was called a "patronage child of Nazi functionaries and former party member". Furthermore in the OMGUS report the Bavarian comedian is accused that his occasional criticism of certain state of party affairs was only possible thanks to his good ties with high-ranking party members. After his denazification Weiss Ferdl claimed to be a "victim of a crusade against past and contemporary intolerance". [46]

Weiss Ferdl suffered a heart attack and died four years after his "Führer" on June 19, 1949. Munich honored his memory by placing his fountain figure (created by artist Josef Erber) at Viktualienmarkt, next to Karl Valentin and Liesl Karlstadt.

46 DER SPIEGEL 10/1949.

A Bouquet of Flowers for Marika and Rose-Marie

Actress Romy Schneider (***Sissi***), who had a relationship with Alain Delon, believed that her mother Magda had had an affair with the "Führer". Romy told feminist journalist Alice Schwarzer during an interview in Cologne that her mother Magda Schneider maybe even slept with Hitler. Strictly speaking, it wasn't Romy who told so in Schwarzer's TV documentary ***Ein Abend mit Romy*** (***An Evening with Romy***)[47], but Schwarzer insinuated it herself. Schwarzer's commentary: *Then she said: My mother has slept with Hitler. She had an affair with Hitler. She was convinced that her mother had a sexual relationship with Hitler.* On the spot Schwarzer qualified this statement: Herself … she wouldn't think so. These were only Romy's words. There is no proof, however, that Romy really revealed this. Actually, Romy had asked Schwarzer who taped the interview in Cologne on Sunday, December 12, 1976, to stop the tape recorder while she spoke about it. Fact is that Magda Schneider, the star of Max Ophüls' ***Liebelei,*** lived next to Hitler's residence in Berchtesgaden and was a regular guest at the Berghof. It is almost certain that Magda Schneider worshipped and idolized Hitler.

The Nazis needed those female stars - for the sake of propaganda and glamour: *As the important Nazi figures actually did not constitute a presentable "high society", the stars functioned as a kind of substitute.* [48]

Magdalena Maria "Magda" Schneider and another Hitler favorite, Henny Porten, were exceptions among female German film stars. Schneider was indeed born in Germany, in Augsburg, as was Henny Porten, in Magdeburg; most of the others were not, neither the female stars of WW1 nor those of WW2.

WW1: The great Asta Nielsen was Danish, born in Copenhagen.

Fern Andra (Fern Edna Andrews) was American, born in Watseka, Illinois.

---

47 ARTE, September 16, 2018.

48 Felix Moeller, *The Film Minister: Goebbels and the Cinema in the Third Reich.* Stuttgart and Fellbach: Edition Axel Menges, 2001.

Pola Negri (Apolonia Chalupec) who arrived at the end of the war on German screens was Polish.

WW2 had Ilse Werner (born in Batavia, Dutch East Indies), who passed away, mired in poverty, on August 8, 2005, in Lübeck.

Veit Harlan's third wife Kristina Söderbaum who, after the death of her husband, turned to photography was Swedish - as was Ingrid Bergman who gave a brief ***Intermezzo*** on German screens in 1936 before she departed for Hollywood. Quite popular among Nazis as well as front-line soldiers was Marika Rökk, a Hungarian born in Cairo who grew up in Budapest. Until her death in 2004 in Baden, Lower Austria, she remembered and glamorized the twelve years of the Third Reich as the best years of her life. Hitler sent her roses and she responded by sending him a telegram to chum him up: "If I am able to cheer you up for a few moments, my Führer, and take your mind off your responsibilities, I would be infinitely proud and happy." Although she didn't like Goebbels, another of her admirers, she did her best to put Hitler's Film Minister at ease and have the devil relax for a few hours from the horrors of war. In entertainment Rökk was the Nazis' secret weapon against the American stars like Ginger Rogers. Rökk could dance, sing, was full of spirit, with paprika in her blood.

So it came as a surprise when *BILD-Zeitung* [49] reported (and papers all around the world like *The Telegraph* [50] repeated it) that newly declassified records of Organization Gehlen, the forerunner of German Federal Intelligence Service, had revealed that Rökk and her director-husband Georg Jacoby were suspected of being Soviet spies. They may have been part of a spy ring that worked for the KGB and passed secrets over to Moscow. It is believed that they were recruited by their manager, Heinz Hoffmeister, who indeed worked for Soviet intelligence.

As Reinhard Gehlen's department was a rather doubtful organization, the journalists who eagerly grabbed for it walked on rather thin ice. But it

49 February 19, 2017.

50 *Germany wartime movie star 'was a Russian spy'*. In: The Telegraph, February 21, 2017.

was not only Rökk. Also suspected were two other Nazi film ladies, Olga Tschechowa (Olga Chekhova), the niece of Anton Chekov's wife, and the greatest female star of the Third Reich, Swedish-born Zarah Leander (Sara Stina Hedberg).

Two months after the invasion of Poland in November 1939, Goebbels added a significant note to his diary:

Everyday life may seem to us now greyer and tougher than before. In times like this, it is even more necessary for the State to do its utmost to compensate the situation and provide the people with the entertainment and relaxation that they are entitled now more than ever. Without optimism you cannot win the war, it is as important as the guns and rifles.

Zarah Leander, beautiful and feminine but also very tall, red-haired, with broad shoulders and a deep, breathy masculine voice, belonged to those who provided the vocal guns and rifles in entertainment. She became the highest-paid star in Nazi Germany. Two songs from her most successful 1942 Ufa movie, ***Die grosse Liebe*** (***The Great Love***), underline her importance for the "relaxation" of the German masses: *Davon geht die Welt nicht unter* (*Not for this will sink the world*) and *Ich weiss, es wird einmal ein Wunder gescheh'n* (*I know that one day a miracle will happen*). Music by Michael Jary, lyrics by Bruno Balz.

At the peak of her career, however, and after her mansion in Berlin was bombed, Zarah Leander left the German capital and returned to Sweden. Until this day, some questions concerning her person remain unanswered:

So was Zarah Leander a source of shame for Sweden? Was she a cold-blooded, fame-seeking, profiteering Nazi sympathiser? On paper it would seem so. But who really knows?

Or was she really a source of pride? Was she, as she herself claimed, just an entertainer working to please an enthusiastic audience in a difficult time?

Or was she in fact a spy? Soviet intelligence officer Pavel Sudoplatov claimed, just before his death, that Leander had been a Soviet agent with the codename

"Rose-Marie". He claimed she was a secret member of the Swedish Communist Party and conducted the work for political reasons. [51]

There were rumors already during her lifetime (she died on June 23, 1981, in Stockholm at age 74) but Leander denied any suggestion that she had acted as a spy for any country: "I would not be surprised if they claimed I were spying in Iceland on behalf of the Vatican."

One name is usually omitted from that list but Hanna von Feilitzsch has devoted a biographic novel to a *Mädchen mit Beziehungen,* a girl with connections. The 350 pages of Feilitzsch's book are mainly the work of a hack writer, filled with mistakes except that she turns the reader's attention to an Austrian opera singer, Slovakian-born Kammersängerin Margarete (Gretl) Slezak (1901-1953), daughter of the world-famous Moravian tenor Leo Slezak and a half-Jewish mother, Elsa Wertheim. Contrary to her brother, émigré actor Walter Slezak (who played a Nazi in Hitchcock's ***Lifeboat***), she appeared only in a handful of films but definitely was close to Hitler despite her Jewish roots. Her father warned her that Hitler is the devil in person. Margarete didn't care concerning the devil in Hitler but she did care that her father still got engagements in Nazi Germany and annexed Austria, most notably in Ufa's expensive prestige picture ***Münchhausen*** in 1942.

Hitler had seen her on stage, in a performance of *Goldene Meisterin*, and obviously liked her enough to invite her, prior to the annexation of Austria, to a tea party at the Reich Chancellery, the former city palace of Polish Prince Antoni Henryk Radziwiłł. Hitler loved to talk to actresses and listen to the latest gossip. Gretl in turn invited Hitler to her apartment at Berlin's exclusive Kurfurstendamm, but much to her disappointment Hitler turned up with his secretary, Christa Schroeder, to create a menage-a-trois. Gretl tried to touch and hold Hitler's hand, but he would deny that and tell her that he couldn't possibly allow that as people thought he was married to Germany. And that was it.

51 Neil Shipley, *Sweden's Nazi Sympathiser, secret agent, communist spy, musical diva.* March 30, 2017.

Hitler felt well in the company of actresses but never went too far. Nevertheless, there was the tragic case of alcohol and drug-addicted Renate Müller, the female star of ***Walzerkrieg***, ***Allotria***, and ***Togger***, who was under Gestapo surveillance and suffered a deadly accident. This fed rumors about Hitler's masochistic impulses. Alfred Zeisler who produced one of her most successful films, ***Viktor und Viktoria***, claimed that Hitler had asked her to kick him in the ass. Under the influence of morphine, Renate Müller fell from the first floor of her villa to her death. In a fictitious book, *I was Hitler's Maid* written by Pauline Kohler, another actress, Jenny Jugo, was said to have danced nude in front of the "Führer". Neither the kick in the ass, nor the nude dance are based on facts.

Fact is that Hitler personally lured Pola Negri back from Hollywood to star once again in a German production, but she never met her benefactor, although she found that her "simplest wish" was "granted with the speed of a royal command" and she felt as if she were under the special protection of the "Führer" himself.

The "Führer" also liked heavyweight champion Max Schmeling's Czech actress wife Anny Ondra (Aenny Ondráková), who had worked with Hitchcock in ***Blackmail*** (and was good friends with ***Nosferatu*** Max Schreck up to the actor's premature death in 1936). Hitler was disappointed that director Hans Deppe didn't get more out of Anny in ***Narren im Schnee*** (***Fools in the Snow***, 1938). And he showed interest in another Czech film actress, Lida Baarová (Ludmila Babková):

Hitler became infatuated with her, it is said. But this only lasted for a short while, and their relationship remained platonic. Yet it was Joseph Goebbels, Hitler's second in command, who fell head over heels in love with her and became her lover. He was completely obsessed with her and willing to leave his wife, his family, for her. And as she herself admitted in her memoirs, before she got spooked and started revising them, she herself said that she was enchanted by him. [...]

Their relationship caused such a scandal that she was banned from starring in any more German films. Her career there was over. She was banned at the request of Goebbels' wife, who was a good friend of Hitler. She [Magda Goebbels] went to

Hitler and told him that her husband had gone half crazy over some Czech actress, and Hitler put a quick stop to it. Lida Baarová returned to Prague. [52]

After the war, Baarová was jailed for a year and a half. Upon release from prison, with her mother and sister (who committed suicide) dead, she went to Austria.

The one woman, however, Hitler would have loved to make a star turned him down. He had seen Imperio Argentina (Magdalena Nile del Rio) from Buenos Aires in some Spanish-German co-production by Carl Froelich and the Hispano Company titled ***Carmen*** (***la de Triana***), a version of Prosper Mérimée's classic tale, and was hooked (although otherwise he labeled the movie "bad"). Imperio had arrived from Havana complete with car and chauffeur. She met Hitler in 1938 and revealed the event as a 95-year-old, two years before her death: According to her Hitler made amorous approaches to win her over for the Third Reich: "Hitler wanted to be my lover." She remembered him as extremely restrained and attractive. (Not only did Hitler like her. Among her admirers were Fidel Castro, Eleanor Roosevelt and Tennessee Williams.) Not long after, Goebbels offered her a tempting contract to star in a series of six Spanish-folkloristic song-and-dance movies with interiors shot in Berlin, but only one of them was produced, ***Andalusische Nächte*** (***Nights in Andalusia***). It was not successful and Imperio departed for Italy where she starred in a film version of ***Tosca*** directed by Jean Renoir. She returned to Spain in 1948 and was among a privileged group of artists known as "Franco's Untouchables".

In the end, Hitler contented himself with Eva Braun, assistant to his personal photographer Heinrich Hoffmann, to become his lover and finally Mrs. Hitler for a few days at the end of the Third Reich. Hoffmann arranged it that his assistant sat next to Hitler in a cinema. Eva's secret dream was to become a movie star on screen (she collected all kinds of film journals), but the only achievement which came near to this wish were 16mm black and white and color home movies she filmed of the Berghof and Herr Hitler relaxing in the sunshine on the terrace of the Obersalzberg.

52 www.radio.cz

After Eva's death, the yellow press published excerpts from her (typed) diaries in 1949 allegedly given in trust to actor-director Luis Trenker for safe-keeping until after the war. In this case it was fake news. The forgery started in 1946 with Trenker being asked to write about Eva and so he sat down and finished 15 to 20 pages. Two years later, out of the blue, he was offered a substantial sum for the publishing rights to Eva's memoirs. Trenker could use the money and sat down again and wrote a gross fabicration of pornographic concoction. He denied that he was the faker and claimed that the papers had published it against his will.

When we talk about Trenker, Arnold Fanck's alumnus, another Fanck discovery, a female one, isn't far away.

Penthesilea, Queen of the Amazons

Reinhold Schünzel was what the Nazis called a "half-Jew" and therefore not in the same position as Karl Ritter when he worked in the studios of Neubabelsberg. He was only allowed to work with a limited-term special permit but eventually was commissioned to direct Ufa's great extravaganza of 1935: ***Amphitryon***, a leftover from Erich Pommer's production unit. One of the reasons might have been that Ufa's sales power on foreign markets had faded with the advent of the Nazis. Schünzel was even the more surprised when a special visitor was announced to the ***Amphitryon*** sets: Adolf Hitler. Hitler, accompanied by Goebbels and Ufa general manager Ludwig Klitzsch, revealed himself to be a true movie buff interested in stars and film technology as well. (Besides ***Amphitryon*** he was shown the sets of Gerhard Lamprecht's ***Barcarole*** starring Gustav Fröhlich and - Lída Baarová.)

Later Schünzel went into exile to Hollywood where he would direct a few films for MGM but mainly was reduced to acting in supporting parts. He was seen as Berlin's police chief Kurt Daluege in ***Hostages***, as Gestapo Inspector Ritter in Fritz Lang's ***Hangmen Also Die!***, General Ludendorff in ***The Hitler Gang*** and as Dr. Kurt von Bruecken in ***The Man in Half Moon Street.***

Amphitryon, by the way, was subtitled ***Aus den Wolken kommt das Glück*** (***Happiness from the Clouds***), which many moviegoers understood as reference to ***Triumph des Willens*** which had Hitler descend to Nuremberg in an airplane. This ***Triumph of the Will*** was a cinematic canonization filmed by a woman who would have loved to become the First Lady of the Third Reich: Helene Bertha Amalie "Leni" Riefenstahl (1902-2003).

Most of which Riefenstahl told and said later is to be treated with caution. She was lying when she opened her mouth, some people claim. Above all, she felt guilty in no way, as did at least most of the defendants at the Nuremberg Trials. When Robby Müller, who did a film portrait of her titled ***Die Macht der Bilder*** (***The Power of Images***), mentioned that people might expect an admission of guilt from her, she responded, as if by rote, flying into a rage of self-defense, "What do you mean by that? In what way am I guilty? I regret that I made the film on the Reich Party Convention in 1934. I regret... but I can't regret that I was alive at that time. I never once made an anti-Semitic remark [*not true*] ... I didn't drop an atomic bomb [*true*]. I never slandered anyone [*not true*]. In what way am I guilty?"

There is a photo showing three ladies in 1929. Two of them were already legitimate film stars: Marlene Dietrich (on the verge of being hired by Paramount) and Anna May Wong, who at that time filmed in Berlin. The third lady, however, Riefenstahl, was only known for Arnold Fanck's mountain films that started her career and that of Luis Trenker.

Leni Riefenstahl (as Diotima) and friends during the shooting of Arnold Fanck's *Der heilige Berg* (*The Holy Mountain*, 1926)
Courtesy of Jens Geutebrück, Coronaretro Archives

Leni Riefenstahl's primitive accomodation during the shooting of *S.O.S. Iceberg*.
Courtesy of Jens Geutebrück, Coronaretro Archives

Some of Fanck's alpine movies were produced by Henri Richard Sokal, who belonged to the circle of Leni's numerous lovers (as did Trenker and Fanck) until he left Germany in 1933 and signed (with no great success) with independent Hollywood studio Monogram where he prepared (*sans* screen credit) ***Face of Marble,*** an interesting little horror film directed by William Beaudine, co-written by William Thiele and starring John Carradine. Sokal passed away in 1979 but he left an unpublished (genuine) autobiography. He called Leni's acting abilities limited but found her, in his own words, "mentally and artistically inspiring": *Her nymphomania, if one could term it that way, had élitist features. Her unmistakable instinct for what suited her let her fall in love automatically with the champion most beneficial according to the particular circumstances.*[53] Her ambition was to become an international star,

53 From the files of Deutsche Kinemathek - Museum für Film und Fernsehen

like Marlene, who had "used" Josef von Sternberg as her entrée to Hollywood, like Asian beauty Anna May Wong. To Leni men were *like a tool which has to serve this self-realization.* [54] When Sternberg arrived in Berlin she was around and danced for him. Why was Sternberg courting Marlene and not her? Why didn't he pick her for the part of Lola-Lola in ***Der blaue Engel*** (***The Blue Angel***)? Till the time of her death, she envied and hated Marlene for being the world-renowned star that *she* would have liked to become. As nobody else was willing she convinced Sokal to fund her first directorial attempt. Out of her contempt for ***Der blaue Engel*** grew ***Das blaue Licht*** (***The Blue Light***) for a price of 50,000 Reichsmark to prove her abilities as a filmmaker. Béla Balázs, a renowned film theorist, was recruited to co-write the screenplay, a mystic yarn of a village girl who finds the way to a crystal grotto and the mysterious blue light. The result looked rather amateurish and didn't attract the attention of Hollywood.

Finally Carl Laemmle's Universal took pity and did release one of Leni's movies, but it was not ***The Blue Light*** and was different from her previous entries: Arnold Fanck's ***S.O.S. Iceberg***. When that failed, too, to call upon Hollywood's attention she got in touch with the Nazis and discovered that not only was Laemmle a Jew but Balázs and Sokal too. (Sokal at least what they began to measure a half-Jew.) In 1933 she proposed to Ufa ***Mademoiselle Docteur***, a story idea by Fanck, who had known that lady of German espionage in person. With that project Leni was determined to outdo Greta Garbo as ***Mata Hari***. But even German Ufa didn't realize Leni's star potential. And if the Jews couldn't or wouldn't make her an acclaimed performer on screen and Ufa was too stupid to sign her, maybe the Nazis would.

"But then," she remembers, *"I got a telephone call from the Reich Chancellery asking me to be there at 4 p.m.; the Führer wanted to see me. I didn't have the courage to say no."*

If that would have been so! Actually, it was not Hitler but Leni who put out her feelers. But she had to start at the Ministry of Public Enlightenment

Berlin.

54 Ibid.

and Propaganda before she was allowed to the Reich Chancellery as she knew that the Minister was a womanizer. Now Leni was seen, on an almost daily basis, at Dr. Joseph Goebbels' place and from there she went straight to Herr Hitler. There is an important entry in Goebbels' diary: "p.m. Leni Riefenstahl: she tells me about her plans. I suggest a Hitler film to her. She is very enthusiastic about it."[55] After the war, Riefenstahl claimed that Goebbels was her opponent if not enemy. In truth, at least in the beginning, he was her backer and talked Hitler into meeting her.

Leni Riefenstahl in *S.O.S. Iceberg*

Courtesy of Jens Geutebrück, Coronaretro Archives

55 May 17, 1933.

At that time, however, the Nazis didn't yet own the German film industry. Hitler had no acting job for Leni since he considered himself "Germany's greatest actor". But he assured her that bright prospects lay ahead in the future. Hitler who had liked ***The Blue Light*** (as Leni assured) promised her a gold mountain: "You will have a villa, such as you never even dreamed of. You will have your own film studio. Nothing, neither expense nor lack of money, can obstruct my plans!"

Maybe he said so in her dreams. For, as a first gift, Hitler didn't give the persistent lady either a villa nor the hoped-for film project but a clammy handshake and a deluxe leather edition of ***Mein Kampf***. Perhaps she could help Dr. Goebbels a little in running the artistic side of the film industry?

But Leni wasn't supposed to assist. She wanted a movie rather badly. Unfortunately for her, ***The Blue Light*** was no box office bonanza. And, except for her filming in ice and snow, Leni was considered box office poison. So the Nazis were her last hope. *Finally* - finally, after bothering Hitler long enough, she got an assignment from NSDAP, although it was not what she had hoped for. She was asked to film a Party Rally. The Party Rallies had peculiar names. This one that took place in early September 1933 was called ***Der Sieg des Glaubens*** (***Victory of Faith***). Riefenstahl later claimed that a jealous Goebbels got in her way and prevented her from delivering cinematic art. On screen ***Sieg des Glaubens*** runs just 64 minutes, too long for a short, too short for a feature. And soon the picture would disappear in the poison cabinet because Ernst Röhm, SA chief of staff, was seen standing beside his friend, the Führer. Not a year later that feisty landsknecht had fallen into disgrace and became a victim of the Führer's wrath in the so-called Night of the Long Knives.

Leni was disappointed. But she would stick to her guns and eventually got a bigger assignment, the 1934 party rally ***Triumph des Willens*** that took place without Röhm, who was murdered by his former comrades on July 1, 1934, in Munich Stadelheim Prison. Now it was Hitler - Hitler - and Hitler again. And, to Riefenstahl's satisfaction, Ufa was asked to distribute the film.

At the beginning of the ***Triumph*** "documentary", a Christ-like Hitler - or so it seems - is descending like "a reincarnation of All-Father Odin" to Nuremberg, capital of the Party Rallies, by airplane from the skies: the proverbial ***Happiness from the Clouds***. Actually, it's not even Hitler's plane. The shadow of the plane we see above the medieval town is that of the camera crew's plane.

Triumph of the Will is a male movie, as the Nazi movement was a male one, with women reduced to adore and worship. It is NS pop culture "at its finest". So it seemed to be a proper choice to let a woman compile the picture (because it is a compilation, nothing else).

Not only the female audience, Leni too got ecstatic: *As a matter of fact, the well-known (late) German actress, Hildegard Knef, recalls having heard Riefenstahl say that she had a vision when she first listened to Hitler speak. "I saw the surface of the earth as a semiglobe," Riefenstahl reportedly said. "It opened up, and a huge fountain gushed forth into the sky and fell right back to earth. It was as if the entire surface of the earth was being whipped by a storm."* [56]

On the part of Riefenstahl, ***Triumph of the Will*** was a declaration of love. Later Riefenstahl claimed that the picture fell into her lap. Just like that. But she played hard-to-get and told Hitler about her doubts:

"How am I supposed to know what is politically important or unimportant, what should or shouldn't be shown? If my ignorance makes me leave out some personality or other, I will make a lot of mistakes."

Hitler listened attentively. Then he said, smiling, but in a resolute tone, "You're too sensitive. You're just imagining all these obstacles. Don't worry, and don't force me to keep asking you. It's only six days you'll be giving me."

"Six days?" Again I interrupted him. "It's going to take months. The main work starts in the editing room. But quite apart from the time factor," I pleaded, "I could never take responsibility for such a project."

Then Hitler became insistent, "Fräulein Riefenstahl, you have to have more self-confidence. You can and you will do this project." It sounded almost like an order. [57]

---

56 *Die Zeit,* No. 48, November 24, 1978.

57 Leni Riefenstahl, *A Memoir.* New York: St Martin's Press, 1995, p. 158.

An order: *Ein Befehl*? If she would turn the "Führer" down it would be *Befehlsverweigerung*, a refusal to obey orders. Nobody was present at the meeting, except for Leni's fragile memory. Actually, she didn't play hard-to-get. In fact, she championed for that task and for the reward to stand in the center of attention, besides the "Führer" let it be understood.

With the movie finished, the Party and Ufa staged one of the most pompous premières Germany had ever witnessed: *All the government officials, all the foreign representatives were in the theater. Then, Hitler made an appearance with light-footed nonchalance, on the wide balcony of Germany's largest theater. Before he entered his box he paused. Sitting in the next loge he saw the much-whispered-about mother of Leni Riefenstahl, from Russia. Before 2300 people he went to her seat, bowed, stretched out his arm toward the astonished woman, drew her fingers to his lips and kissed them. Behind 2300 electrified gasps there was but one thought - 'Queen Mother!'"*[58]

On May 1, 1935, Goebbels awarded Leni Riefenstahl the National Film Prize for ***Triumph of Will*** and addressed her in pathetic words: *"This film represents an exceptional achievement in the film production of the past year. It is closely relevant to us because it reflects the present: it describes in unprecedented scenes the gripping events of our political existence. It is a filmed grand vision of our Führer, who is shown here for the first time on the screen in the most impressive manner. The film has successfully overcome the danger of becoming a mere propaganda feature* [sic!]. *It has lifted up the harsh rhythm of our great epoch to eminent heights of artistic achievement. It is a monumental film, thundering with the tempo of marching columns, based on iron principles redhot with creative passion."*

Now Hitler was among the Olympian Gods. He was *the* God, the hopeful founder of a new religion. His admirers went head over heels when they talked about HIM. Hanns Johst, poet and playwright, who wrote only one movie, ***Wilhelm Tell*** (1934), but that one with the future Mrs. Göring

---

58 Ernst Jaeger, *How Leni Riefenstahl Became Hitler's Girlfriend.* Part III. In: *The Hollywood Tribune*, May 12, 1939, p. 13.

(Emmy Sonnemann) in the female lead, wrote about a visit as if entering Valhalla:

The Führer welcomes me!

His room is very large. He sits behind an oblong table. He rises. He makes the demure way to him easier for me. He comes towards me. This man doesn't know any masks. He always has his own face.

This countenance! The whole world knows it. Everybody saw it through thousands upon thousands of prisms and perspectives, from hundreds of photographic, graphic, painted, sculptural endeavors. Millions of human beings saw it, millions gained different impressions.

All interpretations of this face must originate from the eyes - one thinks from the first moment, completely dazzled from the thrill of the counterpart. But longer impression doesn't verify this perception. There is the hair! Neither pictorial nor statuary art have yet expressed its pertinacity and originality. Cheerfulness à la Eichendorff strives against each doctrine. Neither steel helmet nor cap, neither comb nor brush are able to tame what is shaped by wind and weather. Like a cloud it throws a shadow over the face; then it opens the facial expressions by its shine.

The temples are an expression of lithic distance. Like sensitive membranes they rest between ear and eye. These are the loneliest temples I ever saw. They dictate aloofness.

Only heads of great, mental Germans have this outspoken concave form. Here perceptions are monitored adamantly. One looks into the eyes, is welcomed by these eyes but in the meantime these two temples cross-examine you, perceive and check you.

I'm sitting diagonally opposite the Führer. The light from the windows outlines the personality. [59]

Johst won many awards bestowed by the Nazis but after the war he fell into disgrace, was almost unable to publish anything and died in 1978 in a retirement home.

For Leni Riefenstahl the best reward wouldn't be long in coming. First, she was allowed to record the Berlin ***Olympic Games*** in 1936 in a 2-part

59 *Der Dramatiker Hanns Johst beim Führer.* In: Die Bühne, 1939, pp. 190-191.

movie. And eventually it would have been her own film studio in Berlin Zehlendorf and a production of ***Penthesilea.*** Riefenstahl talked at length about this pet project of hers to Herman Weigel, later to write the screenplays for ***Christiane F.*** and Wolfgang Petersen's ***The Neverending Story:***

Penthesilea *was one of my favorite topics.* Originally, ***Penthesilea*** was a play written by Heinrich von Kleist in 1808. But Riefenstahl thought that this rarely staged play about the Queen of the Amazons, telling about a clash of genders, didn't fit the theatrical stage very well: *Either it would be a wonderful radio play or, if you do it right, a great movie.* So she wrote a screenplay and hired Jürgen Fehling as co-director.

What could be told better in images should have been expressed in images. And there I had invented a stylized form. Take for instance the pictures made by [Laurence] Olivier. It had nothing to do with them. And nothing with **Der zerbrochene Krug** *by Jannings. Particulary taking this film as an example I can explain best what I wanted to do. What disturbed me most in* **Zerbrochener Krug** *was that it was filmed theater.* **Der zerbrochene Krug** *suits very well the stage. There is one room and in it a realistic story. But Amazons on stage? Unthinkable, not even in a stylized way I think. Otherwise the reliefs of antique art that depict the Amazons for us are that impressive that I saw a visual direction of the* **Penthesilea** *drama stylistically in form of reliefs. And as the speech of Kleist is irreplaceable in its beauty, I just wanted to shorten here and there. Story and direction I envisioned in a way that the movements of the actors, including the mass scenes, would be stylized. I wanted to shoot in color but the color would have been very thrifty, graphical, like stone.*

And then I wouldn't have shot with clouds in the background but also nature would have been stylized, the sun ten times as big, a tree, much, much bigger and exceptional in its shape. As the words were excessive, so should have been the real elements and the movements and gestures of the actors. I didn't imagine those as for instance in Hamlet, where they act just normally but so as if these characters from antique days, as the heads in the prologue of **Olympia,** *which you have seen, would move and speak that way. And when somebody talks, it should get darker and you* *only hear the sound because it is essential. And then light comes back on heads and figures.* [...]

I thought, however, if you enter a cinema and suddenly they are talking in rhymes, as in **Zerbrochener Krug,** *you see a room and there is a bed and in it lying a man who sleeps and snores. And then he stands up and starts to talk in rhymes, I find that funny. On the stage I am focused right away on poetry: this is stage. But on film one expects, if it isn't animation or an abstract film, reality.*

The screenplay, Riefenstahl said, is lost: *I had withdrawn to Kampen to write the screenplay. And I had to train myself. As Amazon I had to ride splendidly, without saddle and backwards sitting on the horse. After that was done, we got to location scouting. Parts would have been shot in Kampen, others, the big battle scenes, in Libya. Roughly hundred girls were being trained. No girls but real females you would believe to fight a war.*

The battle scenes Riefenstahl wouldn't have done in a way that they looked realistic: *If a warrior grabs a girl and she falls from the horse, she has to fall really. But photography and lighting are handled in a way that it looks like a relief. Nevertheless these are people of flesh and blood. But not as stylized that they would appear like puppets. It is perfectly realistic and sanguine and on the other hand not realistic in light and imagery.* [60]

Verse and images have to unite.

But while she prepared all this, war interrupted and Riefenstahl was asked to produce pictures that were more relevant to the war effort.

On April 10, 1935, Hermann Göring had married Emmy Sonnemann, and although Riefenstahl denied to have had ambitions of marriage, same as Winifred Wagner, people speculated that now he, Hitler, would marry "his Leni". Leni had to console herself with the insight: "Marriage would have brought the Dictator down to the level of the men he ruled. The mysticism of his personality would have been destroyed by marriage and the accompanying brightly-lit living-and-bedroom."

In 1939, when she visited the United States, *Hollywood Tribune* published

60 Herman Weigel, *Interview mit Leni Riefenstahl.* In: Filmkritik No. 188, August 1972.

a series of articles (we already quoted from): *"How Leni Riefenstahl Became Hitler's Girlfriend"* was written by an insider, an ex-lover of Leni's himself, Ernst Jaeger, former editor-in-chief of *Film-Kurier:*

Did Adolf Hitler intend to marry the woman he admired and loved: Leni Riefenstahl? Did the furious tempo of world politics destroy a romance which had already begun before Adolf Hitler became the dictator of Europe?

Jaeger let his readers participate behind the curtains in the second meeting Leni had with Herr Hitler:

'That night ended at dawn,' Leni later told a friend. 'We sat in front of the fireplace. He said he would bring about situations which would cause all the statesmen of the world to come to him to Germany. The new world-order would be determined by him. He has reason to consider himself the greatest statesman in the world, and I, too, believe that of him. I have never seen him so upset and excited. He stood before me as though on an invisible pulpit, his hair flying.' [61]

In 1940, Hitler asked Riefenstahl to contact the Kaiser Wilhelm Institute in Berlin and discuss the possibility of the production of film material that would resist the ravages of time: 'just imagine if, in a thousand years, people could see what we are experiencing today'. [62] This obviously meant seeing HIM still in a thousand years, revived by Riefenstahl's art of imagery.

Around the same time Leni started to document the war efforts of the "greatest statesman" in Poland, but it was too much for her witnessing executions. She quit and convinced Hitler to fund a film version of Eugen d'Albert's opera ***Tiefland*** (***Lowlands***), a project she had begun already in 1934 before ***Triumph*** when she learned that it was the "Führer's" favorite. There wasn't much dialogue: "Only the basic idea remained. The point was that images should express what the opera expressed in music." Leni Riefenstahl portrayed a beggar's dancer who becomes the romantic bone between humble shepherd Pedro (Franz Eichberger) and the imperious Marquès de Roccabruna, Don Sebastian (Bernhard Minetti).

---

61 Ernst Jaeger, *How Leni Riefenstahl Became Hitler's Girlfriend.* Part III. In: *The Hollywood Reporter,* May 12, 1939, p. 12.

62 Bill Niven, *Adolf Hitler, Film Fanatic.* In: History Today, March 14, 2018.

In 1942 large parts of the picture were finished but sickness interrupted postproduction till the end of war. When General Patton and his 7th Army occupied Kitzbühel, the complete Riefenstahl Film GmbH, including the negatives of ***Tiefland***, fell into their hands. When the movie was eventually released on February 11, 1954, in West Germany by Allianz Film, almost nobody took notice.

Bernhard Minetti and Leni Riefenstahl in *Tiefland*.
Courtesy of Jens Geutebrück, Coronaretro Archives

Riefenstahl lied for decades that the Gypsy extras she used in this melodrama all survived the Holocaust:

She has argued that **Tiefland** *was her apology for her involvement with the Nazis, calling it her 'inner emigration' from the regime.*

In Cologne on Friday [August 16, 2002], *however, the pro-Gypsy group, Rome.V, backed by the respected German film-maker Nina Gladitz and writers and academics, alleged that Riefenstahl not only knew most of the extras faced death after filming ended in 1941, but that in some cases she even facilitated the process.* [...]

Rosa Winter, 79, a Sinti who, like most of the extras, was plucked from a Gypsy holding camp at Max Glan in Austria and forced to take part in the film, said Riefenstahl was responsible for sending her to Ravensbrück concentration camp as a punishment for fleeing the film set at Mittenwald in the Bavarian Alps.

Winter ran away after hearing her mother was being sent to that camp, and found her at a police station.

'A very angry Riefenstahl arrived with a high-ranking SS officer and demanded an apology from me. I refused, and she said: "Right, you can go to the concentration camp." My mother went down on her knees to beg Riefenstahl for mercy, but she wouldn't listen,' she told The Observer.

Winter's mother, Maria, was transported to Ravensbrück two days later. Rosa was sent just days later, but never saw her mother again.

'Riefenstahl didn't treat us badly on the set, and we got fed and felt free to a certain extent. But I can never forgive her for the fact that although it was totally in her power to save her extras and knowing the fate they faced, she did nothing,' added Winter, the only member of the 14-strong family to survive the Holocaust, in which 250,000 Gypsies died. [63]

Franz Eichberger and Leni Riefenstahl in *Tiefland.*
Courtesy of Jens Geutebrück, Coronaretro Archives

63 Kate Connolly, *Gypsies' fate haunts film muse of Hitler.* In: The Guardian, August 18, 2002.

In Hitler's Private Cinema

Occasionally Hitler was seen at a film premiere such as ***Morgenrot*** (***Dawn***) together with press czar Alfred Hugenberg, ***Hitlerjunge Quex*** (***Hitler Youth Quex***), ***SA-Mann Brand*** (***Storm Trooper Brand,*** all 1933), ***Stosstrupp 1917*** (***Shock Troop 1917,*** 1934), directed by the infamous Nazi Hans Zöberlein (who commanded a terror raid in Hausham in late April 1945 in which several striking miners were murdered) and actor Ludwig Schmid-Wildy, or ***Pour le Mérite*** (1938) by Karl Ritter and even attending a Heinz Rühmann comedy, ***Der Florentiner Hut*** (***The Florentine Hat***). But what he liked (mainly the entertainment part of movies), he wouldn't watch at a local cinema, of course not.

He had his own cinemas in the Reich Chancellery in Berlin and in the Great Hall at the Obersalzberg Berghof. At Hitler's Berghof residence screen and projectionist's booth were concealed behind a Gobelin tapestry in the Great Hall. Hitler saw everything he got in his clutches. He was an indefatigable film buff. In the evening, after dinner, he watched at least two or more movies, surrounded by his guests. The nightly screenings went often three to four hours. The menu was compiled from films just received from the Propaganda Ministry or on request from film companies. In that way, Goebbels was his master's personal drug dealer concerning illusions of all kind, including movies. If Hitler was in bad mood, he would enjoy a funny movie. Films that pleased him were endlessly repeated; others he didn't like were interrupted after a single reel.

Sources indicate that he considered the films shown to him under three criteria: first, entertainment/distraction function; second, artistic value; and third, ideological conformity. It is clearly confirmed through Goebbels' diaries that the distraction function of entertainment films, even of poor ones, played an essential role to Hitler - as means of recreation especially during critical and stressing political situations. On 16 March 1935, following the announcement of the reintroduction of conscription which was observed critically by neighboring countries, Goebbels and Hitler 'watched a film for relaxation. Nonsense, but it cools us down.' At the peak of the Sudeten crisis, Hitler confided to Goebbels that he wanted to spare his nerves and therefore didn't like to watch any serious films for now. One week before the German invasion of Poland, Goebbels, Hitler and his staff passed 'the dragging time' at the Obersalzberg by watching light entertainment films such as Hans Schweikart's **Fasching** *(Bavaria, 1939).* [64]

Fasching was a forgettable comedy about a Fashion Design student (Karin Hardt) and an architect (Hans Nielsen) who encounter one another in a train on their way to Munich. They decide to explore the Bavarian capital during Fasching (carnival).

Albert Speer, Hitler's chief architect and later minister for armaments and war production, about the "Führer's" likes and dislikes: *Everything featuring [Emil] Jannings and [Heinz] Rühmann, Henny Porten, Lil Dagover, Olga Tschechowa, Zarah Leander and Jenny Jugo, had to be supplied immediately. Revue films with lots of bare legs could be assured of his applause. We often saw foreign pictures, also those that were withheld from the German public. Sports and mountaineering films were almost completely missing, and also animal or landscape documentaries or informative films on foreign countries were never shown. Also, he didn't have any appreciation of Groteskfilme [slapstick comedies] which I loved then, e.g. starring Buster Keaton or even Charlie Chaplin. The German pictures did not suffice to supply the two films required each day. Therefore, many were shown twice or more often, conspicuously never those with tragic plots but mostly lavish productions and those featuring his favorite actors.* [65]

Peter Demetz, a U.S. literature scholar who specialized in German studies, has done some research on dictators' and specially Hitler's fascination with the movies:

He was shocked by one of his first experiences in a movie theater in Linz, at the age of 16 or 17, where he saw a so-called Enlightenment film. It included scenes about syphilis and prostitution. He was still talking about how it shocked him years later, in the middle of the war, in 1943.

---

64 Dirk Alt, *The Dictator as Spectator: Feature Film Screenings before Adolf Hitler, 1933-39*. In: Historical Journal of Film, Radio and Television, 2015, Vol. 35, No. 3, p. 423.

65 Albert Speer, *Erinnerungen*. Frankfurt/Main: Ullstein, 1969, p. 49.

At a conversation at the so-called Führer's Headquarters in January 1942 (not '43), he indeed mentioned the incident.

Enjoying films later, *Hitler had his own motivations. He was looking for himself in films; he had a strong urge to develop his biographical self-awareness. One of his favorite films was, for example, the Hollywood production* **Viva Villa!,** *a movie about the Mexican revolutionary Pancho Villa. Hitler saw himself as the people's revolutionary.* [...]

Hitler was also searching for portayals of father-son conflicts in film, in reaction to his own complicated family background. He also had in mind the Prussian conflict between the old king Frederick William and his son who'd succeed him, Frederick the Great. He found a reflection of such conflicts in British colonial films, in which he recognized conflicts between a conservative father and a less conservative son. [66]

In this regard of special interest to Hitler was Emil Jannings' ***The Old and the Young King: The Youth of Frederick the Great***, the conflict between austere Friedrich Wilhelm I of Prussia, called "The Soldier King", and his son, Crown Prince Friedrich.

Werner Hinz as Crown Prince Friedrich:
The Old and the Young King.
Courtesy of Jens Geutebrück. Coronaretro Archives

66 *Why Hitler watched Hollywood films.* Deutsche Welle, March 26, 2019.

The many gangster films Hitler saw might have confirmed his view of America as a "mongrel nation", decadent and at the same time powerful for its sheer industrial capacity. Interestingly enough, in his play *Der aufhaltsame Aufstieg des Arturo Ui* (written in 1941 in Finnish exile) Brecht saw Ui=Hitler as crime boss.

Occasionally, Hitler would break off screenings when he realized too many Jews were involved in the making, like Louis Friedlander's ***Stormy*** co-written by Ben Grauman Kohn, Charles Vidor's ***The Great Gambini*** starring Akim Tamiroff, an Armenian Jew, or Ernst Lubitsch's ***Bluebeard's Eight Wife*** co-written by Billy Wilder; but at the same time he deeply admired Fred Astaire's dancing skill. Astaire (Frederick Austerlitz) was a Jew too. Particularly between mid-1938 and mid-1939 a number of US releases didn't meet with his applause: ***Shanghai*** (most likely G. W. Pabst's ***Le drame de Shanghaï***, 1938, with a screenplay by Leo Lania, who had written about Hitler as early as 1923), not the American ***Shadows Over Shanghai*** from the same year; ***High, Wide, and Handsome*** (1937) by Rouben Mamoulian; ***Marie Antoinette*** (1938) with Norma Shearer. But at the same time he took a liking in the British colonialist Technicolor production ***The Drum*** (1938) adapted from the book by A. E. W. Mason starring Sabu, Raymond Massey, Valerie Hobson, and Roger Livesey.

Until the eve of WW2, September 1939, when Germany invaded Poland, Hitler spent night after night in his private cinema at the Reich Chancellery or at his residence in the Bavarian Alps watching German, Italian, French, British feature films and newsreels, whatever he could get hold of, starting with films like Willi Forst's ***Maskerade*** (***Masquerade***, 1934), co-written by Walter Reisch and starring Paula Wessely, Olga Tschechowa and the later exiled Adolf Wohlbrück who renamed himself Anton to avoid being confused with Hitler; but even the more American movies, original language with or without subtitles: Frank Lloyd's ***Cavalcade*** by Noel Coward and ***Mutiny on the Bounty*** with Clark Gable and Charles Laughton; ***Broadway Melody of 1936***; Frank Capra's ***Mr. Smith Goes to Washington***; Gregory La Cava's ***Gabriel over the White House***; ***The Lives of a Bengal Lancer***, the most successful film in Germany in 1935, with Gary Cooper (who visited Berlin and the Babelsberg Studios in 1938 where he met Zarah Leander - although he later in Hollywood would cancel a meeting with Leni Riefenstahl) or ***The Charge of the Light Brigade*** with Errol Flynn, the hero star of Warner Bros.-First National Pictures.

Was Errol Flynn, the dashing star of Hollywood swashbucklers, a German spy before and during World War II?

Charles Higham, a Los Angeles writer, contends that Mr. Flynn was a Nazi agent in a biography of the late actor "Errol Flynn The Untold Story," *published by Doubleday & Co. Some friends of the late actor, such as David Niven, have ridiculed the assertion, calling it impossible.*

Documents that Mr. Higham said he used in reaching his conclusion indicate that several of the Australian-born actor's actions before and during the war helped the German cause and that he kept a close friendship with a man who Mr. Flynn had repeatedly been informed was a German spy.

But the documents do not contain conclusive evidence that Mr. Flynn himself was a German agent and they leave open the question whether his behavior was an act of friendship or an act of espionage.

The German mentioned is a Dr. Hermann Erben, an Austrian-born physician.

After the war ended, the American authorities disclosed that Dr. Erben was a member of a large Nazi spy ring that operated in Asia. [...]

Dr. Erben denied last week that Mr. Flynn had worked under him as a German agent.

While many of the actor's friends have assailed the report as implausible, one former employee of Mr. Flynn, Jane Chesis of Los Angeles, said in an interview that she believed that the hypothesis was plausible because of an incident in 1953.

She said that while she was inadvertently looking through a file cabinet in Mr. Flynn's apartment that was normally used only by him she saw a file of letters postmarked in Argentina containing what she took to be the names of Germans. One of the names she noted, she said, was "Hermann Schwinn". [...]

While she was reading the letter, she said, Mr. Flynn entered the room and grabbed her and the file of letters and then flung her to the floor, hurting her enough so that she had to spend the next day at home. When she returned to the apartment a day later, she said, the file was gone. [67]

Be it as it may, Flynn had Nazi sympathies, first noticed for his violently anti-British and pro-Nazi views as early as 1934.

There was indeed a Hermann Schwinn and he was the leader of the Los Angeles German American Bund based directly on the policies of Hitler and determined to underminde Hollywood.

Other Hollywood actors said to have sympathized with the Nazi movement were Wallace Beery (star of ***Viva Villa!***) and Oscar winner Victor McLaglen whose estranged brother Leopold was known as a British fascist. Victor McLaglen himself was heard saying, "Some claim I'm a Nazi, others I'm a Fascist. Once and for all: I'm only a patriot of the good old American kind."

While Warner Bros. were the first to pull out of Germany, Paramount Pictures would stay until 1941 and supply Hitler with prints (eluding Goebbels), asking him for example to lift the ban on William Thiele's ***The Jungle Princess*** and Cecil B. DeMille's ***The Plainsman*** with Gary Cooper.

MGM went so far to buy German bonds that financed rearmament factories in Sudetenland. [68] But on closer examination it was the U.S. commerce department that advised MGM that one way to get blocked currency out of Nazi Germany was to invest in armaments. [69]

In fact, "the moguls who have been castigated for putting business ahead of Jewish identity and loyalty were in fact working behind the scenes to help Jews." [70] Carl Laemmle or Paul Kohner whose agency in Hollywood handled many émigrés belonged to those forces.

Apropos slapstick: Although Speer claimed Hitler wasn't interested in

67 Robert Lindsey, *Errol Flynn Called a Wartime Nazi Spy*. In: New York Times, March 23, 1980.

68 Ben Urwand, *The Collaboration: Hollywood's Pact with Hitler*. Cambridge, Massachusetts: Harvard University Press, 2013.

69 Thomas Doherty, *Hollywood and Hitler, 1933-1939*. New York: Columbia University Press, 2013.

70 Steven Ross, University of Southern California.

slapstick comedies there were two slapstick comedians that appealed to the "Führer". He laughed about ***Way Out West*** (in Germany released as ***Ritter ohne Furcht und Tadel*), *Block-Heads*** - "nice ideas and funny jokes" - and ***Swiss Miss*** with Stan Laurel & Oliver Hardy. In this case his taste corresponded with that of Stalin and Mussolini. It remains to other experts to find out why Hitler liked these two comedians. I met Hal Roach, L&H's producer, at the end of his life in February 1992 when he was flown to Berlin by media mogul Leo Kirch and attended the Berlin International Film Festival and the Babelsberg Studios. He insisted to see the studio where he had met Ernst Lubitsch in the early 1920s but remembered the way to Ufa far shorter. Actually, he hadn't been on the larger Babelsberg lot but in the Ufa Studios in Tempelhof, not that far from the Adlon Hotel. Roach was still excited when he talked about the Duce. He even had a company "RAM Roach and Mussolini" to produce opera films and musicals in Rome but the other studio bosses intervened and the company had to be disbanded. Walter Wanger: "Mussolini? He is great. Sympathetic. Wonderful man. Knows everything."

Not only Roach, but other Hollywood producers and studio chiefs, Walt Disney as well as East European Jewish refugees, worked with Hitler's censors to alter films, such as (thanks to the intervention of German consul Dr. Georg Gyssling) James Whale's sequel to ***All Quiet on the Western Front*** known as ***The Road Back*** (1937), and even cancelled productions. The German branch manager of Metro-Goldwyn-Mayer mentioned in front of the German press the "satisfying collaboration on both sides", and the German branch office of 20th Century-Fox signed a letter *Heil Hitler.*

Among Hitler's favorites were MGM's ***The Wizard of Oz*** directed by Victor Fleming and, last but not least, the exquisite ***Gone with the Wind*** by the same director, both released in 1939. He saw anything Greta Garbo did - no matter in her case if Jews were involved. George Cukor, who was a Jew, directed the Swedish actress in ***Camille*** (Hitler personally intervened in September 1937 to make sure that this movie was shown in German cinemas) and Ernst Lubitsch in the anti-Soviet comedy ***Ninotchka*** (supporting actors were the German émigrés Felix Bressart and Alexander Granach).

Following are the titles of films Hitler wanted to be permanently available in his private film archive at the Berghof: ***Storm Trooper Brand***; Hans Steinhoff's ***Mutter und Kind*** (***Mother and Child***) with Henny Porten; Forst's ***Masquerade***, and surprisingly ***Mädchen in Uniform*** (***Girls in Uniform***); F. W. Murnau's silent ***Faust***, Carl Froelich's ***Traumulus*** (***The Dreamer***) [71], ***Der Herrscher***, ***Der zerbrochene Krug***, all starring Jannings; another F. W. Murnau production: ***Tabu***; Luis Trenker's ***Der Rebell***; ***Triumph des Willens*** (no big surprise); ***Ein toller Einfall*** (***A Mad Idea***) with Willy Fritsch (directed by a Jew, Kurt Gerron) and ***Bomben auf Monte Carlo*** (***The Bombardement of Monte Carlo/Monte Carlo Madness***) with Hans Albers, Heinz Rühmann, and Peter Lorre; Erich Kästner's ***Emil und die Detektive*** (***Emil and the Detectives***) directed by Gerhard Lamprecht and written for the screen by Billy Wilder; Hans Deppe's film version of Theodor Storm's ***Der Schimmelreiter*** (***The Rider on the White Horse***) with Mathias Wieman; Karl Ritter's ***Patrioten*** (***Patriots***) with Lida Baarová; Josef von Báky's ***Menschen vom Varieté*** (***The Stars of Variety***) with La Jana (a.k.a. Henny Hiebel) and Veit Harlan's ***Das unsterbliche Herz*** (***The Immortal Heart***) with Heinrich George; ***Ich liebe dich*** (***I Love You***) with Viktor de Kowa and Luise Ullrich; Franz Peter Buch's comedy ***Umwege zum Glück*** (***Detours to Happiness***) with Lil Dagover; Marika Rökk in ***Hallo Janine***; Alois Johannes Lippl's ***Grenzfeuer*** (***Border Fire***) and Karel Lamač's 1937 version of Arthur Conan Doyle's ***Der Hund von Baskerville*** (***The Hound of the Baskervilles***) with Bruno Güttner as Sherlock Holmes, Fritz Odemar as Dr. Watson and Peter Voss as Lord Henry Baskerville, filmed at Moyland Castle near Kleve. Generally Hitler preferred films that were released from the end of the Great War until about 1932.

If he enjoyed a certain actor, that man or woman was invited to an event as happened to Fritz Odemar's son Erik Ode, who was asked to one of Hitler's receptions in Munich. The actor drove in his car from Berlin to Munich to just being greeted with a handshake. That was all. [72]

71 Goebbels in his diary, January 11, 1936: *Führer very happy. I watch* **Traumulus** *with him again. He is spellbound. Jannings great.*

72 Erik Ode, *Der Kommissar und ich: Die Erik Ode Story.* Starnberg: Verlag R. S. Schulz, 1972.

Hitler's employees and adjutants kept a record about the Führer's likes and dislikes. He disliked, for instance, Johnny Weissmuller's ***Tarzan the Ape Man***, despised (the anti-semitic) ***Konjunkturritter*** (***Prosperity Crooks***) directed by Fritz Kampers (although it starred his favorite, Weiss Ferdl) and ***Frau am Steuer*** (***Woman at the Wheel,*** 1939) starring the former dream couple Lilian Harvey and Willy Fritsch. He dismissed Robert Adolf Stemmle's ***Am seidenen Faden*** (***By a Silken Thread***) starring Willy Fritsch and Gustaf Gründgens in ***Tanz auf dem Vulkan*** (***Dance on the Volcano***). In the latter case we know the reason for Hitler's dislike: Gründgens was a homosexual. If he suspected some homosexual subtext even in an otherwise harmless movie, like ***Abel mit der Mundharmonika*** (***Abel with the Harmonica***) in 1933, he demanded the production to be banned. Fortunately Gründgens was under Göring's protection.

But what caused the rest of his likes or dislikes is left to speculation. In a few cases, to our surprise, we learn that Hitler preferred a total ban over politically imperfect propaganda films that included Jürgen von Alten's military comedy ***Gewehr über!*** (***Shoulder Arms!***), the blood-and-soil semi-documentary ***Ewiger Wald*** (***Eternal Forest***) and the anti-Bolshevist ***Weisse Sklaven*** (***White Slaves***).

During the war, however, Hitler stopped private film screenings, except for watching newsreels and having a say in the edition of ***Deutsche Wochenschau***:

"I can't watch any film in war-time, when the people must make so many sacrifices and I have to make so many hard decisions. Besides, I have to spare my sensitive eyes for the reading of maps and front reports. [73]

But he still took an interest in matters of the film industry. A diary entry by Goebbels dated May 30, 1942, tells about a discussion with Hitler concerning the plan of making the life of ***Ludwig I of Bavaria*** into a film: *The Führer has read the script and found it highly deficient.*

Six years earlier, in December 1936, he suggested what could have become the biggest German movie ever, a ***Nibelungen*** sound film remake: *"entirely*

73 Traudl Junge/Melissa Müller, *Bis zur letzten Stunde. Hitlers Sekretärin erzählt ihr Leben.* Munich: List, 2003, p. 81.

monumental. Syllabus for the schools. A standard reference. Probably already in color."[74]

74 Goebbels diary entry, December 31, 1936.

The "Führer" and his Seven Dwarfs

Hitler loved animation.

In his sketchy, not well researched book *Warum Hitler King Kong liebte, aber den Deutschen Micky Maus verbot (Why Hitler Loved King Kong But Forbade Mickey Mouse to the Germans)* [75] author Volker Koop talks about Hitler's enthusiasm for the 1933 ***King Kong***, that in its time was considered a technical marvel. While the Cooper-Schoedsack production faced problems with the German Board of Censors discussing if the picture might be "an attack on the nerves of the German people", Hitler saw ***King Kong*** at least eighteen times: a record. In the 1990s, before he went nuts about a (never made) ***Metropolis*** remake, German producer Thomas Schühly, besides a ***Riefenstahl*** biopic, contemplated a ***Hitler*** film project that in his mind should transform into something as big as a Shakespearean play. Hitler's love for ***Kong*** was to play a prominent part in Christoph Fromm's screenplay with the Führer identifying with Kong's love interest, Fay Wray. According to Theodor W. Adorno, ***King Kong*** truly was an allegory of the excessive and regressive monster into which the public sphere developed: *the dynamic that exploded in the horror of the Third Reich extended down into the winding-shafts of society as a whole and for that reason was reflected even in the ideology of nations that were spared the political catastrophe.* [76] Adorno saw Hitler as a *composite of King Kong and a suburban barber.* [77]

Even more, Hitler liked ***Snow White and the Seven Dwarfs***. In his private film archive he had three prints of Disney's Grimm adaptation: the original American version, the German-dubbed print, and a Swedish print. Another print, stored at the Ministry for Public Enlightenment and Propaganda, was reserved for screenings for film technicians, artists, and animators.

We once phoned Hitler's projectionist and were told about the Führer's

75 Berlin: be.bra wissenschaft verlag, 2015.

76 Theodor W. Adorno, *Der wunderliche Realist.* In: Noten zur Literatur III, Frankfurt/Main: Suhrkamp, 1965, p. 105.

77 Theodor W. Adorno, *Freudian Theory and the Pattern of Fascist Propaganda.* In: *The Culture Industry: Selected Essays on Mass Culture,* ed. by J. M. Bernstein. London: Routledge, 2001.

enthusiasm for that particular movie. Hitler knew ***Snow White*** almost inside out. William Hakvaag, the director of a war museum in northern Norway, even claimed to have found four watercolor paintings of Disney's dwarfs that were hidden in the frame of a Hitler painting:

He found coloured cartoons of the characters Bashful and Doc from the 1937 Disney film **Snow White and the Seven Dwarfs**, *which were signed A.H., and an unsigned sketch of* **Pinocchio** *as he appeared in the 1940 Disney film.*

Mr Hakvaag, who said he had performed tests on the paintings which suggested that they dated from 1940, said: "I am hundred percent sure that these are drawings by Hitler. If one wanted to make a forgery, one would never hide it in the back of a picture, where it might never be discovered."

The initials on the sketches, and the signature on the painting, matched other copies of Hitler's handwriting, he claimed. [78]

That story, however, was too good to be true and turned out to be a hoax. Nevertheless, papers round the globe published it eagerly.

As a kid Albert Speer, Jr., the son of Hitler's chief architect and Minister of Armaments, was often at the Berghof. Before his death, he was interviewed by Falko Hennig:

Do you remember your childhood on Obersalzberg, for instance Hitler posing with children?

Yes, I sure do.

Your father wrote that Hitler's magic didn't work on children. Can you confirm this?

I don't particularly remember him, just as a nice uncle. But it was great when we were allowed to the mountain without [having to follow the rules of] protocol. That was different from official occasions, such as a birthday. Hitler had a cinema, and there were for instance Mickey Mouse films. This was fascinating stuff for kids of course.

So you have seen Mickey Mouse films with Hitler together?

---

78 *Did Adolf Hitler draw Disney characters?* In: The Telegraph, February 23, 2008.

I would have to lie if I would claim that Hitler was present. But these films belonged to him. [79]

And talking to TV author Heinrich Breloer [80]:

Breloer: Did you see films at the Berghof?

Albert Speer, Jr.: Yes sure, Mickey Mouse.

Breloer: Did the "Führer" see them too?

Albert Speer, Jr.: I don't know if he was present.

Breloer: Fräulein Braun?

Albert Speer, Jr.: Yes, Fräulein Braun and some other people were present.

Frank Schirrmacher, the late co-editor of *Frankfurter Allgemeine Zeitung*, wrote a comment:

Kids who had at times a family relationship with Hitler don't remember him but Mickey Mouse. [81]

I can confirm this. When I worked for Dieter Geissler, the producer of the ***Neverending Story*** film series, he told me that his mother, a sculptor who was commissioned to create a bronze of the "Führer", took him as a kid to the Berghof. He still remembered being there and he even remembered the "Führer's" shepherd dog, but although he was told that he sat on Hitler's lap, he couldn't remember the man.

If one would have expected, however, that Hitler's treasured ***Snow White*** would become as big a success in Germany as everywhere in Europe he was misled. For months, the two most important German distribution companies, Ufa and Bavaria, both state-controlled, competed for the distribution rights. Finally, thanks to Max Winkler's office, Ufa won the bid. Max Schmeling, Anny Ondra's husband, was asked by the Ufa Board of Directors to negotiate with Disney's American distributor, RKO Radio Pictures, the same company that had handled ***King Kong***.

On August 19, 1936, Schmeling had fought Joe Louis in New York City's Yankee Stadium. RKO offered him the exclusive screen rights for the

79 *„In Berlin hatte ich immer Nachteile."* In: taz.de online, May 9, 2006.

80 *Speer und er.* TV mini-series. 2005.

81 Frank Schirrmacher, *Der Engel fährt zur Hölle - Breloers Film über Albert Speer...* In: Frankfurter Allgemeine Zeitung, March 18, 2006.

match, which was only expected to last a few minutes. But when the fight entered the annals of boxing history as "The Fight of the Century", RKO lost millions and sadly realized its mistake. All attempts by RKO to re-acquire the world rights to the picture failed. The movie was successfully launched in German cinemas under the title ***Max Schmelings Sieg, ein deutscher Sieg*** (***Max Schmeling's Victory, a German Victory/Great International Heavyweight Boxing Contest between Joe Louis and Max Schmeling***). In late June 1938, Max Schmeling had a rematch against Joe Louis. This time RKO obtained all rights, but Schmeling was knocked out after only two minutes. Schmeling was not only an internationally renowned boxing champ but also an intelligent businessman who knew how to deal with American companies (after the war, he became a German licensee of Coca-Cola). He agreed to act on behalf of RKO to get ***Snow White*** to the German Reich.

Board meeting of Ufa on January 24, 1939

(TOPIC 5)

Walt Disney color picture

Mr. Zimmermann reports that as a result of negotiations concerning purchase of picture **Snow White** *for German distribution licensee Schmeling is asking 60 % of gross revenues for his shares, deducting the usual costs, with a guarantee sum of RM 500,000. Included in the guarantee, however, are 100 color prints valued at about $50,000 (=RM 125,000). According to German regulations, a German version of an American movie produced in a foreign country is not allowed here. Therefore it shall be re-dubbed. The costs for dubbing exceed to about RM 40,000. This sum, however, can be deducted from gross revenues. The board will get an official confirmation in letter that there is neither objection against purchasing the film, nor against later exhibition. Seller's previous demand to include two Anny Ondra films in the release deal has been dropped.*

Because this is an extraordinary color film, the board approves the above mentioned conditions of sale. [82]

82 Files of Bundesarchiv - Federal Archives.

While the deal was prepared, Leni Riefenstahl visited Hollywood where she was granted no appointments. Only Walt Disney, still interested in releasing ***Snow White*** in Germany, invited her to his studio.

Riefenstahl recalled that meeting in her memoirs (although more than once in her life she seemed to confuse facts with fiction, so her memoirs should be treated with caution):

Walt Disney received us already in the early forenoon in his studios and spent the whole day with us. Patiently, but proudly as well, he showed us how his animated characters were developed and explained his unique technique and let us see the sketches he had made for his new production – **The Sorcerer's Apprentice** [*segment from* **Fantasia**]. *I was fascinated – for me Disney was a genius, a sorcerer himself whose imagination seemed to be unlimited. At lunch he got on to the Biennale [in Venice] where* **Snow White** *and* **Olympia** *were screened in competition. He would have loved to see both parts of* **Olympia**. *No problem. The prints were in the hotel, they only had to be brought here. Disney pondered it for a while, then he said: 'I am afraid that I cannot afford to do that.'*

'Why?' I asked bewildered.

Disney: 'If I would see these films it would be known tomorrow throughout Hollywood.'

'But,' I tossed in, 'you surely have your own screening rooms. So nobody would know it.'

Disney resigned: 'My projectionists are members of the union. They would learn from their gossip. Although I am an independent producer I have no distribution and no cinemas of my own. It could happen that they would boycott me. The risk is too much.'

How powerful the Anti-Nazi League was I could read in the US press three months after I had left America. Walt Disney was forced to give a statement that at my visit he didn't know who I was. [83]

Unbeknownst to Riefenstahl, German émigré artist Oskar Fischinger, a

83 Leni Riefenstahl, *Memoiren 1902-1945*. Berlin: Verlag Ullstein GmbH, Frankfurt/M; Berlin, 1987, pp. 323-327. English edition: *A Memoir*. New York: St. Martin's Press, 1995.

man she certainly had heard about back in Germany because he was one of the best abstract animators, was working on ***Fantasia***. In November 1938, his agent had arranged a job for him at Disney:

I worked on this film for nine months, then through some 'behind the back' talks and intrigue (something very big at the Disney Studios) I was demoted to an entirely different department, and three months later I left Disney again, agreeing to call off the contract. The film "Toccata and Fugue by Bach" is really not my work, though my work may be present at some points; rather it is the most inartistic product of a factory. Many people worked on it, and whenever I put out an idea or suggestion for this film, it was immediately cut to pieces and killed, or often it took two, three or more months until a suggestion took hold in the minds of some people connected with it who had their say. One thing I definitely found out: that no true work of art can be made with that procedure used in the Disney Studio. [84]

Instead, an unhappy Fischinger, whose command of the English language was still weak, became the butt of endless "practical jokes" such as pinning a swastika on Fischinger's office door on September 1, 1939, the day the Germans invaded Poland.

At the end of January 1939, Riefenstahl returned to Europe and was interviewed by a French reporter from *Paris-Midi*:

Three months in America: everywhere lustrous reception except Hollywood where she only was received by Walt Disney, but otherwise was boycotted at the instigation of the Anti-Nazi League. [85]

Film-Kurier reported about Hollywood's Anti-Nazi League under the headline *Filmhetze in Hollywood* (*Film Hetz in Hollywood*):

An Anti-Nazi League has been established in Hollywood which was termed by Vittorio Mussolini [Benito's son] returning home from his research trip a "center of political agitation against the Fascist Idea". [86]

---

84 *Fischinger at Disney, or Oskar in the Mousetrap.* www.centerforvisualmusic.og > OFMousetrap.htm.

85 Film-Kurier January 28, 1939.

86 Film-Kurier January 30, 1939.

According to recent reports, for the time being they [the Anti-Nazi League] want to support needy emigrants before, with might and main, they are going to pursue their true objective of launching film agitation against Germany.

After all, they have worked on a film in which Charlie Chaplin satirizes the Führer and hence wants to make a laughing stock of him. [87]

On February 5, 1939, Joseph Goebbels noted in his diary:

Question if one should remove the American films. I am not quite sure about this matter.

This evening Leni Riefenstahl told me her exhaustive impression which is not pleasant. We have no chance over there. The Jews rule with terror and boycott. But how long?

The Minister responded with a ban on most American films, which included ***Snow White***. Goebbels told one Mr. Peters, who in Berlin did some business for Metro-Goldwyn-Mayer and Twentieth Century-Fox that not only was ***Snow White*** too expensive, but would also demonstrate the superiority of Disney animation compared to German animation. His goal was to establish a German animation industry - but where to find the talent that could compete with Disney's experienced artists?

87 Referring to Chaplin's new production *The Dictator*, later to be called *The Great Dictator.*

Bee Sting Swastika: Cartoons with Aryan Background

One of the most prominent animation producers they had in Germany at that time was Wolfgang Kaskeline who sure would have liked the assignment to create spectacular cartoon features for the Reich.

Each cinemagoer will know the name of Wolfgang Kaskeline because he is credited with most of Ufa's advertising films. When it appears on screen, one will know that now one of those amusing commercials will unreel in which objectivity and humour, farce and fantasy will mix, in which color, form and sound, scene and schematic illustration softly evoke a general impression which will leave, apart from the propaganda effect, a pleasant artistic delight for each receptive eye.

Then Kaskeline is quoted himself, I cannot freely and unconditionally express an artistic idea. The basic idea is always connected with the propaganda object. This is specific, believe me - for a true painter this reference to a subject, this responsibility to the real is a delight. I'm not permitted to interpret something into an object which it doesn't relate to me. Otherwise it will become crooked and forced - not real. [...]

As a painter - and only as a painter - [...] *I am an enthusiastic Don Juan. That is, I love each object. Only the one who loves to explore the final secrets and only if I have put my ear and my eyes to these last secrets, I can reproduce the importance of an advertised object in a way that it will have an impact on the spectator: novel, thrilling, convincing.*

The wish to possess it must be awakened in him for this is the essential thing in all advertising.

And now to the technique of the art of advertising films - no, I better shouldn't begin. It is like a country's government - the better, the less one has to talk about.

I have approximately 20 employees. They transfer my sketches and preproduction art technically with remarkable diligence and - this is the key to the art of animation - accuracy.

Since I have been the first who has created a color sound image, I constantly endeavour to vary the use of sound in all of my advertising films. The expressionist, allegorical film requires different sound, different score than the grotesque cartoon where all objects will become living beings and all living beings will become creatures of magic and juggling. [88]

Cartoonist Gerhard Fieber, who for some time worked with Kaskeline, remembers one particular incident, "Kaskeline made a completely new type of film, he played with colors. Then people from cigarette manufacturer Muratti came, a very dignified lady with her staff, and asked to see the film. So we screened the film for them. Then she said, 'May we see the film again?' She was undecided, 'Can I stay with my family alone?' We had to leave, Kaskeline and myself, and when we returned she said that she will not accept the film, that she didn't like it. One of the directors said, 'Madam, may we put forward a proposal? We will show the film tonight at Ufa Palace at the Zoo, then you will see yourself how the audience will respond to this novel idea in color.' She couldn't deny that of course. We arranged to meet that night, 8:00 p.m., at Ufa Palace. The film received tremendous applause. Why? We had sent all who were available to the cinema to act as clappers and paid 5 marks per person for the service." [89] The applause, however, at least according to Fieber, turned out to be real and spontaneous.

But then, when Kaskeline had reached the peak, problems arose concerning his family background.

On November 1, 1933, the National Socialists revised the *Reichskulturkammer [Reich Chamber of Culture] Law.* According to §4, all artists and technicians involved in the making of advertising and animated films were requested to register their company with Reichsfilmkammer. Their employees had to apply for membership in the section Reichsfachschaft Film [Reich Film Department].

Wolfgang Kaskeline did so on January 25, 1934. [90]

On December 19, 1934, the contingent office of Reichsfachschaft Film reported:

88 *UFA Feuilleton* #8, February 25, 1931.

89 Gerhard Fieber interviewed by Gerd Gockell, 1997.

90 All following documents from Berlin Document Center [BDC], File "Wolfgang Kaskeline."

Re: Wolfgang Kaskeline, Aryan origin

After consulting the Reich Ministry of Interior, Amt für Rasseforschung [Bureau for Racial Investigation], I advise you in the matter of Kaskeline that the Amt für Rasseforschung has sent a questionnaire to Herr Kaskeline on November 22, 1934. This wasn't returned until today (four weeks).

On November 1, 1934, the Contingent Office wrote to Kaskeline:

Regarding your letter dated October 30, 1934, I regret to tell you that a further prolongation is out of question as you had had enough time since Fall of the previous year to provide the necessary documents.

May I indicate that further petitions of Ufa no sooner can be submitted to Reich Ministry of Public Enlightenment and Propaganda until certificate of your Aryan parentage has been received completely.

On November 6, 1934, Kaskeline submitted a petition to Amt für Rasseforschung re: settlement resp. sourcing of the missing documents. Concerning the failure to fulfil obligations and the fact that the questionnaire of the Racial Bureau was not returned by Herr Kaskeline one might recognize at least a protraction.

In fact, Kaskeline had problems to produce such documents and prove a so-called Aryan background.

On September 17, 1935, the Ufa Board of Directors discussed this issue:

Mr. [Hermann] Grieving announces that Reichsfilmkammer has banned animator Kaskeline from continuing work as non-Aryan. The Board assents to pay his fee until end of this month. Also Kaskeline should receive an interest-free loan up to RM 5,000 on October 1, 1935. The loan is not repayable, provided that Kaskeline succeeds in obtaining the renewed accreditation in the next one and a half years. In case of renewed accreditation, the employee's contract with Ufa which now has to be terminated will become valid again. The loan will be immediately payable if Kaskeline would accept animation assignments from third parties. Mr. Grieving is authorized to terminate Kaskeline's employment relationship on that basis.

On September 23, 1935, Reichsfachschaft Film reported to the President of Reichsfilmkammer and denounced Wolfgang Kaskeline:

Subsequent to our letter dated December 19, we are obliged to tell you that it was determined post hoc that Wolfgang Kaskeline (advertising film cartoonist and director) is a non-Aryan.

In the marriage certificate his father is registered as Jew.

Kaskeline has suppressed this fact in his application for Reichsfachschaft Film on January 25, 1934, and indicated parentage as: German Protestant.

We request herewith the expulsion of said person from Reichsfilmkammer/ Reichsfachschaft Film.

On October 1, 1935, Reichsfilmkammer wrote to Wolfgang Kaskeline and asked him for his statement within three days.

Nevertheless, the managing director of Reichskulturkammer, Hans Hinkel, allowed to employ Kaskeline "*bis auf weiteres*" [for the time being] until the fundamental question how to deal in the cases of so-called *Halb- & Vierteljuden* [Half- and Quarter-Jews] had been resolved.

On October 26, 1937, Ufa manager Hermann Grieving had to report to the Board of Directors that Kaskeline had to be dismissed anyway as there was evidence that he had accepted an assignment from third parties:

With letter from December 11, 1937, Reichsfilmkammer asked a number of persons to testify in the expulsion proceedings against Wolfgang Kaskeline, Berlin-Tempelhof, Manfred von Richthofen Str. 34 on Friday, December 17, 1937, 11:00 a.m.: Ufa animators Kurt Blank, Hermann Groth, Bernhard Huth, Georg Leutke, Alfons Ley, Egon von Tresckow, advertising artist Curt Schumann, Mr. [Gerhard] Staab (Tobis Filmkunst), Dr. Kraemer (IMAGOTON Film G.m.b.H.).

With letter dated December 24, 1937, Reichsfilmkammer informed its President:

Re: Wolfgang Kaskeline (non-Aryan)

By decree dated September 25, 1935, it was decided that there are no objections against further employment of war invalid Wolfgang Kaskeline for the time being.

On October 25, 1937, Universum-Film A.G. (Ufa) has filed an application to expel Kaskeline.

It is objected that, contrary to his contract with Ufa, Mr. Kaskeline has recommended an animator known to him, [Edith] Jacobi, for the production of animated titles of the Tobis release **Die Fledermaus** (***The Flittermouse/The Bat***) *to Imagoton-Film G.m.b.H. and that he himself has produced part of the preproduction during his office hours in his Ufa studio or has them produced by subordinated animators and photographers. Furthermore, Ufa complains about the improper demeanour, personal and business, of Mr. Kaskeline.*

The principal result is documented in a file memo dated 20th of this month (p. 91). From this it is certain that Kaskeline is to be blamed for breach of contract and betrayal of confidence as far as Ufa is concerned and that his personal and business manners are not always regarded as impeccable.

The writer, however, concludes that expulsion proceedings are out of question and instead recommends the revocation of the special permit. A special permission like that in the case of Kaskeline, however, is regarded a benefit which doesn't necessitate the same strict requirements. He agrees that Kaskeline's behavior is to be regarded blameworthy, but it doesn't exceed the liberties that prominent artists sometimes presume in business matters.

"There is, however, another issue to be considered," the writer indicated. "I don't know if there are similar cases in point at Reichskulturkammer:

According to our investigations there is no doubt that Kaskeline has an affair with J a c o b i. This is not liable to prosecution according to the *Rassenschutzgesetzgebung* [Law for the Protection of the Race]. However, both would need to contract a marriage according to §3 of the First Regulation on Implementation of the Law for Protection of German Blood and German Honor dated November 14, 1935, and therefore would require the permission by the Deputy of the Führer and the Reich Minister of the Interior. As is known from previous administrative practice, this permission which is necessary for contracting the marriage was always denied."

On February 26, 1938, Reichsfilmkammer wrote Kaskeline that, although he was guilty of breach of faith concerning Universum-Film A.G., the President of Reichskulturkammer had decided to let the matter rest with a one-time but final admonishment.

Nevertheless, Ufa terminated the contract. Kaskeline had to apply for work elsewhere and found a niche with Epoche Gasparcolor-Film A.G.

One year later, on March 4, 1939, the special permission dated September 25, 1935, was cancelled:

You have lost the right to become active in each field that belongs to the domain of Reichskulturkammer.

The decision is final as it is based on a decree by Herr Reich Minister for Public Enlightenment and Propaganda.

I ask immediately to abandon your commitment with company Epoche Gasparcolor-Film A.G. and will report after having done so.

But this time Epoche Gasparcolor intervened on Kaskeline's behalf.

On March 14, 1939, Reichsfilmkammer reported to the Ministry that the company would be damaged if Mr. Kaskeline would be forced to resign immediately:

I endorse the petition that the advertising film assignments will be finished by Mr. Kaskeline and he is allowed an adequate deadline.

Concerning the re-presented issue that Kaskeline is of Jewish birth I ask for decision if an expert report from Reichsstelle für Sippenforschung [Reich Office for Hereditary Research] has to be obtained and if Mr. Kaskeline, until advance of such report of Reichsstelle, should be given a working permit.

On March 22, 1939, Reichkulturkammer informed Epoche Gasparcolor-Film A.G. that the removal of the special permission cannot be revoked: "Regarding the deadline I am prepared to accomodate you..."

Epoche Gasparcolor-Film applied for a deadline of nine months. Only a prolongation of five months (until September 30, 1939) was granted. Simultaneously they tried to file for hereditary and racial investigation at Reichsstelle für Sippenforschung.

On June 5, 1939, Reichsfilmkammer forwarded a petition to Reichsstelle für Sippenforschung (Berlin NW 7, Schiffbauerdamm 26):

Re: Proof of descent of trick film artist Wolfgang Kaskeline, born on September 23, 1892 in Frankfurt/Main, residing in Berlin-Tempfelhof, Manfred-von-Richthofenstrasse 182.

I herewith submit the attached documents:

1. *Petition of Epoche Gasparcolor-Film Aktiengesellschaft, Berlin W 9, Schellingstr. 7, dated May 6, 1939, for a hereditary and racial investigation of above mentioned person,*
2. *Affidavit by Mrs. Katharina Kaskeline dated March 9, 1939 (mother of testee)*
3. *Affidavit by Mrs. Katharina Kaskeline dated March 27, 1939 (mother of testee)*
4. *Affidavit by Bruno von Alt-Stutterheim, Lieutenant in the reserve ret., dated March 27, 1939 (brother-in-law of testee), residing in Berlin-Tempelhof, Thuyring 68,*
5. *Affidavit by Mrs. Olga von Alt-Stutterheim dated March 27, 1939 (sister of testee), née Kaskeline, born on December 14, 1890 in Frankfurt/Main,*
6. *Copy of petition which is addressed to Herr Reich Minister for Public Enlightenment and Propaganda by Mrs. Katharina Kaskeline dated March 9, 1939 (mother of testee),*
7. *Copy of letter from Epoche Gasparcolor-Film Aktiengesellschaft dated March 10, 1939, addressed to Herr President of Reichsfilmkammer, Berlin W 35, Bendlerstr. 35,*
8. *Copy of letter from Epoche Gasparcolor-Film Aktiengesellschaft dated April 22, 1939 to Kanzlei des Führers/Chancellery of the Führer, c/o Mr. von Hegemann (the family name is wrongly recorded; the correct name is: von Hegener), Berlin W 8, Reichskanzlei/Reich Chancellery,*
9. *Questionnaire of Reichsstelle für Sippenforschung (with paternal grandfather and 3 certified photos of testee),*
10. *Questionnaire of Reichsstelle für Sippenforschung with legal paternal grandfather,*
11. *Passport photo of father,*
12. *Passport photo of mother,*
13. *2 passport photos of brother Raimund Kaskeline, engineer, born Frankfurt/Main on March 14, 1888, residing in Rome,*
14. *Passport photo of maternal grandmother,*
15. *Passport photo of daughter Sigrid Kaskeline, born on December 3, 1918, in Berlin,*

16. 2 passport photos of son Horst Kaskeline, born on December 11, 1919, in Berlin,

17. 2 passport photos of son Heinz Kaskeline, born on January 24, 1926, in Berlin,

18. Passport photo of paternal grandmother,

19. 2 passport photos of maternal grandfather,

20. 2 passport photos of maternal grandmother,

21. Folder containing

a) 51 documents

b) 2 document copies,

c) 1 certified copy.

All above mentioned passport photos are not required to be certified by police.

The animation artist Wolfgang Kaskeline made false statements to our office re: his pedigree paper in 1934/35 and tried to conceal the Jewish descent of his father. On November 5, 1934, Universum-Film-Aktiengesellschaft forwarded, inter alia, the copy of a petition by Herr Kaskeline adressed to Reich Minister of Interior, Amt für Rasseforschung [Bureau for Racial Research]. [...]

Wolfgang Kaskeline
Berlin S 19, 11/6/34
Universum-Film
Krausenstr. 38/39
Aktiengesellschaft

To Reich Minstry of Interior,
Bureau for Racial Research, Berlin.

The undersigned asks for recognition of his Aryan descent according to §2 decree for the screening of foreign films dated June 27, 34, next-to-last passage, because he, as he explains below in more detail, is not able to submit documents about the actual Aryan descent of his father and grandfather who both came from Finland.

I was born as German citizen on September 23, 92 [1892], in Frankfurt a.M. and baptized Protestant as son of merchant Viktor Samuel Kaskeline and his wife Katharina née Scherf. My father, who already as a young man had immigrated [to Germany] from Finland and was German citizen, died in 1931 in South Italy. My mother lives in Berlin. I have forwarded the hitherto missing documents concerning the parents of my mother to the contingency office for information.

In spite of all my great efforts, I myself, my brother, who lives in Rome, and my brother-in-law Bruno von Alt-Stutterheim were not successful in collecting any document concerning the birth of my father and grandfather Kaskeline and about the wedding of my parents in Genoa. The Kaskeline family origins, as the name says, from Finland and, as is known to my family, generations ago immigrated from Toscana. Any two generations in Finland were glass painters and glass burners and due to their profession had traveled frequently around the world.

Because of the political change of system in Finland, research regarding the Russian time is extremely difficult, especially as my father, who died in a foreign country, didn't leave any documents since he wasn't interested very much in family history. Certain, however, is only that there is no evidence of Jewish blood in our family. I leave this issue to an expert assessment. My only brother who entered the war as volunteer became a pilot and left as lieutenant, lives in Rome for 8 years. I myself entered Elizabeth Guard Grenadier Regiment on August 1, 14, as war volunteer, came to Jnft. Regt. 203, II. Kpg. and was severely wounded on October 26, 14, in the battle of Dixmuiden. I was made private and received the E.K 2 [Iron Cross 2nd Class]. After a two-year stay in military hospital, I was released as 70% war invalid because of my wound (stiffening of the knee joint, shortenage of the right leg, Peronnaeus paralyzation and Fascialis paralyzation) and received a pension from relief organization.

The past 7 years I worked for Universum Film-Aktiengesellschaft as an artist and now have to attest my Aryan background according to the mentioned contingency decree. Therefore I ask politely to certify that I am of Aryan descent.

I am married to Minna Kaskeline née Berg since 1917. She comes from Buchwald i. Riesengebirge [Giant Mountain range in Silesia] and is of pure Aryan descent.

Mit deutschem Gruss
signed, Wolfgang Kaskeline.

Regarding the origin of his father, the testee explains that he is not able to prove and submit records of the actual Aryan descent of his father and grandfather who both come from Finland. His father (Viktor Samuel Kaskeline) who already as a young man emigrated from Finland and was German citizen died in 1931 in South Italy. In spite of greatest efforts, the testee writes, he, his brother, who lives in Rome, and his brother-in-law, Bruno von Alt-Stutterheim, were not successful in collecting birth certificates of his father and grandfather Kaskeline and the marriage certificate of his parents from Genoa. The Kaskeline family origins, as the name says, from Finland and shall have immigrated, according to a tradition only known to the family, generations ago from Toscana. Any two generations were glass painters in Finland and glass burners and have traveled due to their profession all over the world. "Certain, however, is only that there is no evidence of Jewish blood in our family. I leave this issue to an expert assessment." "Therefore I ask politely to certify that I am of Aryan descent."

These statements of the testee are lies. The same false statements were also made concerning the pedigree paper of Reichsfilmkammer. The father Viktor Emanuel Kaskeline comes not from Finland; he was actually born on December 28, 1858, in Teplitz/Bohemia as son of the J e w i s h couple Ludwig Kaskeline and Linna Schlesinger. The marriage of the testee's parents was not contracted in Genoa but on March 30, 1887, in Frankfurt/Main (according to marriage certificate No. 336 of the register office in Frankfurt/Main, disctrict I, issued on August 3, 1935). This certificate was located by pedigree paper of Reichsfilmkammer without any problems and with it the statements of the testee disproved. The mother of the testee, Mrs. Katharina Kaskeline née Scherf, who lives in Berlin, could have told her son and son-in-law if asked about day and location of their wedding.

The request of Wolfgang Kaskeline (dated November 6, 1934) addressed to the Office for Race Research, to confirm that he is of Aryan descent, is, considering the (false) statements, a manifestation of greatest audacity.

Also the affidavits by the testee's mother, the brother-in-law, Bruno von Alt-Stutterheim, and his sister, Olga von Alt-Stutterheim née Kaskeline, deserve greatest doubt and mistrust. In his affidavits the brother-in-law, Bruno von Alt-Stutterheim, states: "It is known to me for some time that my father-in-law Viktor

Kaskeline, who passed away in 1931, actually is the son of a Teplitz castle owner who was in close contact with his mother (Linna Kaskeline née Schlesinger). This fact was told to me occasionally by my father, forester Wilhelm von Alt-Stutterheim, who was a friend of my father-in-law."

From the letter of Wolfgang Kaskeline dated November 6, 1934, results conclusively that his brother-in-law, Bruno von Alt-Stutterheim, tried to get a pedigree paper for his wife. His father, Wilhelm von Alt-Stutterheim, has died on November 28, 1922, in Rengersdorf district Sagan according to telephone information by Mrs. Olga von Alt-Stutterheim. The testee's father and father-in-law of Mr. Bruno von Alt-Stutterheim, Viktor Kaskeline, died on April 5, 1930, in Riva/Lake Garda. The knowledge of Mr. Bruno von Alt-Stutterheim concerning the misstep of Linna Kaskeline née Schlesinger must stem from the time before the case of death of his father (November 28, 1922). He could have used this knowledge in 1933 or 1934 and not yet on March 27, 1939.

The statements of Wolfgang Kaskeline in the letter from November 6, 1934, are contrary to the statements of Mr. Bruno von Alt-Stutterheim from March 27, 1939. Also the affidavit by the mother, Mrs. Katharina Kaskeline née Scherf, is no proof; on March 27, 1939, she explained: "It was not known to me that my son could be regarded as non-Aryan. I didn't know about such a possibility." This statement seems unreliabale too. At the wedding contracted on March 30, 1887, in Frankfurt/Main, her husband, the merchant Viktor Kaskeline, was of Israelite religion. Mrs. Katharina Kaskeline knew already in the years 1933/34 that her son was obliged to keep a record concerning his parentage. She must have used her affidavit issued on March 9, 1939, back then. This she had omitted.

The pictures submitted by the testee (passport photos) are insufficient. Mrs. Katharina Kaskeline explains under oath: "My husband had no similarity with his siblings who had the Jewish father as documented; he was blond and had glaucous eyes." Mrs. Katharina Kaskeline must have known the brothers of her husband or possess photos of her husband's brothers. There were no photos of her husband's brothers attached, however, which could serve to substantiate her statements.

According to his marriage certificate, the testee is "art teacher and artist" and since 1927 active in the film industry as animation artist. Therefore he has respective knowledge of camera and photography. It is our guess that the testee may have photograped his family (wife and children) and his parents repeatedly. Instead of attaching photos of his father from recent times, however, the testee submits only a passport photo of his father that was made approximately in 1887.

Above we have determined that the attached affidavits in important issues cannot be regarded as well-founded.

You will have to check the petition and decide if regarding the poor and doubtful material the application for hereditary and race file of Wolfgang Kaskeline can be approved. We have refrained from asking the testee to submit more means of evidence as requested.

Heil Hitler!

REICHSFILMKAMMER

Pedigree Paper

signed by proxy, Dr. Jacob.

By special permission of the Reich Minister of Public Enlightenment and Propaganda dated July 25, 1939, at any time revocable, Wolfgang Kaskeline was allowed to continue to work in his profession, until conclusion of the current investigation of his parentage by Reich Office for Hereditary Research.

On February 1, 1940, Reichsfilmkammer reported to Fachschaft Film:

Re: Wolfgang Kaskeline

The Reich Ministry of Public Enlightenment and Propaganda announces by decree from January 27, 1940, as follows:

"After receiving now pedigree paper from Reichsstelle für Sippenforschung which has arranged for a hereditary and race investigation at the Poliklinik für Erb- und Rassenpflege [Polyclinic for Hereditament and Race Cultivation], Berlin-Charlottenburg, in the case of Wolfgang Kaskeline the above mentioned is Vierteljude [One-Quarter Jew].

Thus there are no objections against his registration as fully-valid member of your Chamber."

Nevertheless, Kaskeline's career in the Third Reich, even as "only" a One-Quarter Jew, had virtually come to an end. On February 1944, however, needing experienced animation artists, he was recruited again by Karl Neumann, head of Deutsche Zeichenfilm Company, who desperately needed artists. Kaskeline worked with a team 16 animators and technicians on an unfinished, very ambitious animation feature, ***Walzermärchen*** (***Waltz Tale***), and very likely on military training films for Mars Film.

Concept art from the unfinished *Waltz Tale*.
Courtesy of J. P. Storm Collection

After war had begun, Goebbels and his staff had heard rumors that the Disney Studios in Burbank, California were on the verge of bankruptcy due to a 1940 European export deficit of $1,259,798. The film minister was willing to redeem the reputation of *German* cartoons and one of his associates reinforced him. The name of this associate was Karl Neumann. On May 15, 1941, Goebbels noted in his diary that he had examined a memo the eager, ambitious Neumann had forwarded re: German cartoon film production: "I will support this because it is a good and useful matter." A day later he was prepared to give Neumann free rein in building a production company on a large scale to compete with the obviously struggling Disney and cancel out the ***Snow White*** debacle.

On June 25, 1941, Dr. Max Winkler let the head of Ufa, Ludwig Klitzsch, know:

The Minister of Public Enlightenment and Propaganda has decreed, as I have already announced, the establishment of a German cartoon film production according to the suggestion of ORR Neumann.

It shall be enforced within the framework of a special company, Deutsche Zeichenfilm G.m.b.H. [DZF]

It is necessary to found this company. Cautio Treuhand G.m.b.H. will acquire shares for RM 26,000 and Ufa shares for RM 24,000.

First managing director of this company will be ORR Neumann. A board ad interim will not be appointed.

On August 7, 1941, the entry Deutsche Zeichenfilm Gesellschaft mit beschränkter Haftung was published in the Commercial Register of District Court Berlin-Charlottenburg, Abt. B No. 62 HRB 85 Nz.

Appointing an inexperienced man like Neumann to head such a specialized company was tantamount to doom.

Caricature of Karl Neumann lost in the jungle of German animation. Courtesy of J. P. Storm Collection

Horst Alisch was one of the first trainees of the new company: *Everybody was afraid of Neumann because he was such a radical Nazi. I don't know why he committed suicide later. I only know if he hadn't killed himself the Soviets would have bust him for a number of years. He behaved in a rather nasty way.* [91]

One of the many female employees of Neumann's company was Ingeburg Ammun. She was target of Neumann's wrath because she made disparaging remarks: *If one watches characters like Neumann, they are poor psychopaths.* [...] *Thinking about Neumann, he had only one arm but that arm he hadn't lost in war. He was run over. So he couldn't proudly claim: That arm I have lost for the fatherland.* [...] *He was a phony character and a pretender.* [...] *There were many beautiful girls around, all young and nice to see, who came from fashion schools. So he was surrounded by these beauties and he tried of course to carry on with them. I remember, once I had cut and taken a day off from work.* [...] *Result was a giant farce: If this is going to happen again...! If you don't take your work seriously...! Old man Neumann: I can transfer you to the armament industry anytime and so on.* Eventually Ammun was offered a job as art teacher in some school: *So I went to see Neumann and asked him to get a release from his company that was considered kriegswichtig [essential to the war effort].* But she was told that she was indispensable. She said: *I'm getting crazy if I continue to draw canaries and chickadees for another half a year. My brother had just fallen on the front. And so I began to rail against this useless outfit. There were three of us who from time to time spoke out. One was Christa who was engaged with a Russian, then a half-Dane, Melitta Meinhardt.* [...] *And then we had a faithful German, Sigrid von Weberstedt, who got involved with a Frenchman* [Robert Salvagnac]. *I was summoned to Neumann, and suddenly he wanted to know if I didn't want to make a trip. He patted my hand.* Miss Ammun, however, stood up and told him what she thought: *Herr Neumann, as a man you are finished for me.* So they kept their documents and she was told that she would hear from the labor court. *Four weeks went by. In these four weeks I wasn't allowed to set foot in the company. Nobody was permitted to stay in touch with me: This was a rather depressing time. I couldn't tell my mother what was waiting for me: Armament. Concentration camp.*

91 Transcript from tape-recorded interview with Horst Alisch by J. P. Storm.

I didn't have a clue. And so I left every morning so that my mother wouldn't know and would dally away. When my mother finally learned, she went to see Neumann: He should hold up that misfortune. Her brother had fallen. But Neumann only said: It doesn't interest him. [92]

Animation under the eyes of the "Führer". Courtesy of J. P. Storm Collection

An absolute layman, Neumann failed, although in his best days he had roughly 100 artists and technicians and 151 trainees aboard and was equipped even with crude multiplane technique. On November 17, 1944, the Court of Auditors of Deutsches Reich complained that in a few years almost six million Reichsmark had been spent on the project, with only one (!) 18-minute Agfacolor short finished: ***Armer Hansi*** (***Poor Hansi***), the misadventures of a canary lost in freedom.

92 Transcript from tape-recorded interview with Ingeburg Ammun by J. P. Storm (February 18, 1989).

Original cel from *Poor Hansi*.
Courtesy of J. P. Stom Collection

The original idea of this picture was submitted in October 1941 by Hermann Krause as ***The Story of a Little Canary that Flew into Freedom***. In his cage a canary named Hansi listens to the voice of freedom, love, and adventure. He hears the song of a chickadee and carelessly leaves the birdcage. The canary's wings, however, grow weak, a metaphor that freedom is elusive and dangerous. Hunger, thirst, rain and finally an ugly street cat drive Hansi back to the safety of prison.

The parable of a weak canary, a typical pet bird, feeling safe only in his bird cage prison was outrageously stupid, but it seemed to please the Nazi powers-at-be who had imprisoned a big part of Europe, at least ideologically, and sent millions to the concentration camps. The very thought of freedom, on the other hand, certainly wouldn't appeal to them. It was not part of their brainwashed way of thinking.

Original art from *Poor Hansi*.
Courtesy of J. P. Storm Collection

One of Zeichenfilm's freelance writers, Horst von Möllendorff, tried to warn the company's dramaturge, Frank Leberecht, a close associate of Neumann - to no avail:

I want to comment on two important issues:

The canary who only dreams about the flight into freedom leaves an unsatisfied desire.

The ending leaves an unfree feeling. The cage becomes a prison as the canary returns because he is unable to live in freedom.

Therefore I suggest:

Leave the desire for freedom as core of the plot but give the whole thing another basic idea as follows:

The wish to swap with the life of another

1. This would give a different meaning to beginning as well as the ending.

2. The canary wants to swap his life with a sparrow, and this not in dream but in real life.

After they have lived the life of the other they are happy to become their old selfs and change again. [93]

93 Document made available by J. P. Storm from his collection.

Horst von Möllendorff.
Courtesy of J. P. Storm Collection

In 1944, due to air raids and bomb damage, part of the production had to be transferred to Dachau the same year. Dachau, as is fairly well known, was not only the new home of German animation. Walking through the town, from the other side of the street the trickfilmers noticed some aggravating smell. It was the smell of an old meat factory. Not far away the artists noticed barbed wire fence and living stock wagon drawn by men. A female French artist got to know more when in the so-called Black Express from Munich to Dachau, a distance of roughly 20 kilometers, she got in touch with some SS men in their typical black uniforms who let her see what was going on inside the refinement and that they wore the emblem of the Totenkopf, the death's head, with good reason. None of her colleagues wanted to believe what she had to report when she returned. Actually, the protected area was a concentration camp but they all averted their eyes.

Female animators relaxing in front of Moosschwaige, Dachau. Courtesy of J. P. Storm Collection

Moosschwaige, where the cartoonists were now working, was originally a recreation home for artists. The housekeeper was Carola Freiin von Crailsheim-Rügland, called Carly: *German trickfilm had become homeless. How they learned about the large atelier at Moosschwaige remains an unsolved mystery. Anyway, one day Carly was informed that Munich for a certain time would withdraw from the contract at the discretion of the Ministry of Propaganda to make room for Deutsche Zeichenfilm. Artists who simply wanted to recover didn't count in these days.*

German trickfilm entered with noisy youth. Daily phone calls to Berlin. Many trucks brought animation desks and all the stuff that was needed. Soon architects came to design a studio on a grand scale because the first German cartoon was destined to compete with Walt Disney. [...] *I was worried: Would Dr. Goebbels' hosts produce propaganda films at Moosschwaige? No, that was not the case.*

In charge of the Dachau cartoon factory was Gerhard Fieber, graphic artist and cartoonist, former assistant to Wolfgang Kaskeline. Fieber had helped to design ***Armer Hansi*** and, a true opportunist, had become Neumann's ass-kisser:

When **Poor Hansi** *was finished I wanted to start a project of my own. It was called* **Purzelbaum ins Leben (Somersault into Life)**, *the story of a dog family which sneezes itself into life. I was supposed to make this film in Dachau because in Berlin we were interrupted in our work by bombs. At first* **Maya the Bee** by *[Waldemar] Bonsels was planned. Bonsels lived at Lake Starnberg. But that project was dropped. Maybe he [didn't] like it, and so we began* **Purzelbaum ins Leben.** *I got about 30 artists, inkers and colorists to Dachau.* [94]

Gerhard Fieber framed by artwork from *Purzelbaum ins Leben*

Courtesy of J. P. Storm Collection

94 Fieber interviewed by J. P. Storm.

Fieber put emphasis on receiving screen credit at any price. The finished product of ***Poor Hansi*** hadn't featured his name. The credits read:

DEUTSCHE ZEICHENFILM
G.M.B.H.
presents a short film
in color by Agfacolor

- after which two swallows appeared skywriting the main title ***Armer Hansi***.

On May 25, 1944, Karl Neumann responded favorably to Fieber's request:

Dear Herr Fieber!

With reference to our conversation yesterday, we confirm the following agreement, subject to the approval of Herr Reich film intendant, special department Kulturfilm: In the screen credits of **Purzelbaum ins Leben** *(working title), currently in production at your studio, a full-page title card will record: "Art design by Gerhard Fieber."*

If this title card will appear right after the main title or after the other titles will be decided later on. [95]

Fieber, the Dachau department head, got the impression *that alle male artists were quite happy, basically fit for active service in times of war, not to be conscripted one way or other. That includes me too.* [96]

Fieber supervised a number of employees who were recruited from foreign or occupied countries for service at Deutsche Zeichenfilm: *Jan Coolen was Dutch, Sergei Sesin was Belarusian, a highly intelligent man who was quite popular with his female in betweeners, [Robert] Salvagnac, a Frenchman, was in charge of his own working group but we had to shut that down because, in*

95 Bundesarchiv, Letter Deutsche Zeichenfilm G.m.b.H., Kaiserstrasse 29/30, Berlin C 2 dated May 25, 1944, addressed to Herr Gerhard Fieber, Dachau near Munich. Reference: N/Ul. Signed: Neumann.

96 Notes by Gerhard Fieber. Collection of J. P. Storm.

spite of the advance praise bestowed on him, he came to grips with us. Otherwise, the foreigners were received very well. I had a relationship with them as with colleagues [sic!].

From Wally Feignous, Disney's French representative, the heads of Zeichenfilm GmbH had learned that the Disney Studios allegedly had planned to hire Salvagnac right before German occupation. Even Goebbels was impressed when he heard that: *Exceptionally gifted talent in French film must be hired by us as soon as possible.* [97]

Fieber continues: *In Dachau I had Salvagnac, Mongazon, Fannier, three Frenchmen, to work for me. They were conscripted. Fannier was a man who had some reservations against Hitler and expressed these. Maybe it was foolishness on his part or it was his way, but he used every opportunity to quarrel with a German artist, [Anna-Luise] Subatzus. He always raised trouble, and one day she [Subatzus] turned up in my office and complained about the Frenchman that he would badmouth Hitler and all sort of things and if I wouldn't stop that she would tell her fiancé, an SS officer in the Dachau concentration camp, at least she claimed she was engaged to him, and I certainly would get into trouble. So I asked Fannier to come and see me.* [Laughs] *"Oh brother, can't you shut up, you may have your own thoughts on the matter but if you don't worry about your family, then at least worry about* <u>*mine*</u>*. Listen, if you go haywire, we both run into difficulties." And after the next vacation – they got vacation, the French, they were allowed to go home – he didn't return. Instead he went straight to join the Résistance.* [98]

Anna-Luise Subatzus who later lived in Göttingen added: *Fannier belonged, as far as I know, to the underground movement. He always wore the French lily. He always had that. But nobody cared about that.* [sic!] *The other one, Salvagnac, allowed himself a coup. We had a very beautiful, Madonna-like colorist, and he fell in love with her, and then she got a child from him. Her father was a high-ranked SS officer. I guess Neumann intervened so that Salvagnac escaped unscathed. It must have been Neumann who helped him, somehow.* [99]

97 Joseph Goebbels, diary entry, May 15, 1942.
98 Gerhard Fieber interviewed by J. P. Storm.
99 Anna-Luise Subatzus interviewed by J. P. Storm, March 11, 1989.

Fieber: *Once we got into trouble concerning an artist. We still were in Berlin, right before I went to Dachau. There was a girl - really a very pretty girl, daughter of an SS officer - and this artist fell head over heels in love with her and got a child from him. That was an affair, like the end of the world. I won't forget it. It was a real sensation.* [Laughs] *Hard to work things out. That was Salvagnac.* [100]

Salvagnac got a divorce from his wife who had accompanied him from France so that he could marry the German girl [Sigrid von Weberstedt, the daughter of SS officer Hans von Weberstedt].

They all seemed to be more concerned with their own affairs and hanky-panky than noticing what was going around them. In Dachau, they all tried to ignore the existence of a concentration camp as best they could and blinked at the fact, as so many Germans did, who after the war claimed they couldn't remember or didn't know at all.

Anne-Luise Subatzus: *Once, after the bomb raid on Munich, my friend Cäcilie and I went to a restaurant where we ate sometimes. Many artists frequented the place, there was an old artist too and one of the people who was in charge of the concentration camp. He said the prisoners had cleared bombs and they were entitled to an extra ration. But that was all that we...* [...] *All was fenced off you know. There was a meat factory too where some of the prisoners worked and they whistled when they saw us. We didn't consider that dangerous because we didn't realize what was going on. Later when we learned, we couldn't believe. We didn't see anything. Only this encounter with a whole company of prisoners in a dark tunnel, all with clogs, that was horrifying. There were sheepdogs too. It was horriying I can tell you. A terrible impression.* [101]

While all this was going on, they produced a nice cartoon about a puppy dog.

The picture [**Purzelbaum ins Leben**] *wasn't completely finished. In between came the famed collapse [end of the Third Reich]. I was made part of the so-called Goebbels donation and became soldier end of '44. Then I was told that I should return. Maybe the situation at the front had turned out for the better. Via the High*

100 Gerhard Fieber interviewed by J. P. Storm.

101 Anna-Luise Subatzus interviewed by J. P. Storm.

Command, I received a letter from Deutsche Zeichenfilm signed by Neumann that an application was made for my exemption because they seemed to take a breath of fresh air and believe to come closer to victory again. But that didn't happen. And I was dispatched to join educational and training films and had to make military training films and so on. Antitank barriers and things like that. In animation. But what I worked on wasn't finished yet because the battle front came nearer and nearer, and we knew that what we did was mindless and futile. At that time, we weren't that stupid anymore. We sure realized that the situation was completely desperate and hopeless. [102]

There was, however, one single cartoon in 1944 that at least projected the atmosphere at the end of the Third Reich, but it was not produced by Neumann (although it was offered to his associate, Leberecht). ***Der Schneemann*** (***The Snow Man***) was created by Hans Fischerkoesen from an idea conceived by Horst von Möllendorff, the one who had warned to do ***Armer Hansi*** the way it was done.

One evening, Möllendorff sat in a Berlin beer garden and bothered to find a suitable topic for a cartoon. Eventually he came up with the story of a Snow Man that had a warm spot in his heart. He wakes up in a full moon night on a quiet market place. After some adventures he creeps into a house to rest on a sofa. There he discovers a calendar. The calendar page for January shows a snowman like himself, in a familiar winter landscape. He browses through February, March, April, May, June and stops in July. For the first time he learns about the loveliest of seasons: summer. There is a sentimental feeling in his heart. The Germans have a word for it: *Sehnsucht*. It's difficult to translate: desire, yearning, longing. This Snow Man is sick for the sweet experience of summer. He gets himself frozen in the refrigerator and leaves it with the advent of summer. Everything looks exactly like the promising picture in the calendar. The Snow Man grins from ear to ear and is all smiles when he leaves the house welcoming "the summer of his lifetime".

---

102 Fieber interviewed by J. P. Storm.

Original cel from *The Snow Man*
Courtesy of J. P. Storm Collection

The Snow Man picks flowers and spreads them around. He sticks a red rose into his cold breast. He surprises an excited hen with an egg made of ice and snow. But then the warm July sun begins to burn. Slowly the snowman starts to melt leaving only a top hat and his carrot nose which is picked up by a little rabbit and eaten.

Möllendorff had nothing to do with the filmmaking. His contribution was the basic idea and the writing but that was enough to create an unforgettable character.

Technically, the ***Snow Man*** was surprising because Fischerkoesen's cameraman Kurt Schleicher made use of Max Fleischer's table top process that combined 3D models with 2D animation. But it was not the technique. The color short worked so well because it was a reflection of death. In some odd way, the Snow Man's tragicomic death reflected the millionfold death that had become a firm part of the society of the German aggressor. Now the killing had returned to its breeding ground and transformed into a death wish. So, in a tragic way and not intentionally, the ***Snow Man*** became an image of the society of its day.

The Snow Man

Courtesy of J. P. Storm Collection

March of the Wooden Soldiers

Some other Nazi animators didn't produce 2D animation. They realized that they couldn't beat Disney on his own field. They focused on fairy tale *puppet* films as the Diehl Brothers, Ferdinand and Hermann, did. Particularly front soldiers and Hitler Youth members found something special in these fairy tales that deeply touched them.

This is what a grunt wrote after watching some Diehl films:

In our front cinema which regularly screens cine-films from local film rentals at first we have seen two films from the German fairy tale world: **Tischlein deck dich (Table-Be-Set)** *and* **Stadtmaus und Feldmaus (The Town Mouse and the Country Mouse)**. *At the beginning, my comrades smiled a little bit. But then there was evidence that the fairy-tale pictures had to offer a lot more for the soldier. Not only was it an hour of entertainment, forgetting all sorrows and trouble of our battle. Many thought deeper. Since the days of our childhood, for the first time something rose plastically before our very eyes. We recalled the long forgotten days of our childhood and youth. Our comrades who are family fathers thought about the content of the pictures and at the same time were reminded of their wives and children at home. Because of that, the fairy-tale films moved anybody notwithstanding the deeper meaning behind the plot. We said to ourselves that these too are cultural treasures of our people which we must preserve for a future generation by defending our native country, even by risking our life. War, last not least, is fought not only for material but for cultural goods. And therefore these films have conveyed to the soldiers the meaning of their present life task and have awakened their enthusiasm...* [103]

An eighth grade pupil, who saw the puppet film version of ***Tischlein deck dich*** by the Diehl Brothers, wrote an even more revealing school essay:

Yesterday, to much laughter of the undergraduate class, we saw the picture **Tischlein deck dich (Table-Be-Set)**. *For us grown-ups the fairy tale, however, provided more than entertainment and joy. For in every fairy tale there is a deeper meaning. Today we discussed with our teacher the deeper meaning of this fairy tale.*

103 *Märchenfilme bei den Soldaten.* In: Film und Bild, Reichsanstalt für Film und Bild in Wissenschaft und Unterricht, Issue 4/5, May 1, 1942.

Two tailor's sons acquired, according to the fairy tale, by hard work prosperity and wealth. One got a Table-Be-Set with magic properties: "Tischlein deck dich", the other a Gold Donkey: "Eselein streck dich". Happily they returned home. But the evil and envious landlord robbed them of prosperity and wealth. Luck seemed to have deserted them.

The third brother, however, put an abrupt end to the fraud of the host through the "Knüppel aus dem Sack" (Cudgel-out-of-the-sack). This demonstrates that for the maintenance and security of prosperity and wealth a strong Wehrmacht [German military] is necessary, just a Cudgel-out-of-the-sack. It alone is able to regain for the others the lost treasures.

The three sons of the tailor come, as the fairy tale tells us, from Dingsda (Dingbat). Dingsda, *however, is somewhere in Germany, it can be anywhere. So the three brothers represent our whole German nation which has to master life as the three apprentices do. The little goblin, however, that lives in fairy-tale land and gives the brothers work and pay, represents the luck that everybody needs. For a time it seemed as if luck had abandoned the good three brothers; but then it returns to them forever.*

The treacherous host, who hoped to get rich by employing swindle and meanness, faced the fate of punishment. He resembles the eternal Jew who wants to profit from the work of the diligent and capable without moving a single finger. He is a Schmarotzer [parasite] who only wants to suck the others and exploit them. In spite of his smartness he can't escape punishment; for there is the Cudgel-out-of-the-sack.

So at the end of our review we have come to the conclusion:

1. By work German people acquire prosperity and wealth.

2. The evil Jew wants to rob the German people of prosperity and wealth.

3. German people, however, secures its prosperity and wealth by a strong army.

4. Only a hard-working nation is lucky in the long run.

So this fairy tale strengthens and invigorates us in our unruly belief in the Endsieg [final victory] of Germany in this war. Its "Cudgel-out-of-the-sack" drums heavily on the back of our enemies until all who have called upon the cudgel will buckle like the malicious host did. [104]

104 July 4, 1941 Deutscher Kulturdienst: *"Knüppel aus dem Sack"* School essay - re-

According to Ferdinand Diehl's daughter Monika, the family wrote to Hitler when they were going to draft him and listed his achievements. Hitler then personally spared him from war service.

corded by Ferdinand Josef Holzer. Collection of J. P. Storm.

Snow White in the Children's Barrack of Auschwitz

There were other tales concerning ***Snow White*** and the Nazis' love for animated films, tales about lives that Hitler wouldn't spare like that of Ferdinand Diehl who died peacefully at age 91 in August 1992 in Gräfelfing near Munich. Dina Gottliebová was one of Hitler's victims, a concentration camp prisoner in Auschwitz. Because she had been an art student in Prague, she was sought out by the infamous "Angel of Death" himself, SS garrison physician Dr. Josef Mengele, to do portrait studies. She and her mother Johanna were first sent to Theresienstadt, a camp in northern Czechoslovakia; then, on September 7, 1943 (with 5,000 other victims), they were transferred to Auschwitz-Birkenau in Poland.

Dina and her mother were holed up in the family camp barracks. About a month after being in Auschwitz-Birkenau a capo - the head of the camp - brought her some paints to create a mural in the children's barracks.

Supervisor of the children's block at the Theresienstadt family camp at Auschwitz II-Birkenau was Fredy Hirsch (1916-1944), who was also deported from Theresienstadt. Some say it was Fredy's idea to have Gottliebová paint a mural on one of the walls.

A Swiss landscape poured out: mountains, meadows, cartoon-looking flowers, anything to perk up the kids. There were about 60 of them, ages 6 to 16. They would later go on to meet their deaths in the gas chambers. Perhaps the painting would be a dash of joy in their living hell. A crowd of small ones gathered behind her. The children were transfixed. She asked if they wanted cows or horses on the mural. They said to paint Snow White and her dwarves. Right away she started creating: the fair princess with her raven locks, dancing with the small bearded men. The children loved it, but Dina was worried what the SS guards might think. She would soon find out. A few days later she was called out and a Dr. Lukas [Dr. Franz Lucas] *was waiting for her. This was long before her own camp was gassed, but Dina was sure that day was her last.*

"Immediately my heart was in my pants," she says. "He asked me, 'Did you paint that?'"

She admitted that she was the artist behind the beloved Snow White and the

Seven Dwarves mural. He told her to come with him and then opened the door of the jeep for her - a gesture she found odd.

"I thought it was one of the usual SS ploys, that it was sarcastic," Dina says. "I thought, for absolutely sure, he's taking me to the gas chamber, or I'm going to be shot." [...]

Instead of driving her to a gas chamber, the young artist was taken to a gypsy camp. There, a man was bent over a camera with a black cloth covering his head. Dr. Lukas announced that he had brought "her." Dr. Josef Mengele, the legendary Angel of Death, took off the black cloth and swirled around.

"Can you do portraits?" he asked the young Dina. [105]

Mengele wasn't particularly satisfied with the photographs he took of Roma prisoners. His objective was to prove them "genetically inferior". So he was looking for an artist and summoned Dina to paint the portraits, paying particular attention to their skin tone. In exchange for her and her mother's life, Dina obliged and dipped her brush in watercolors.

In a way, Disney saved her life. As she had seen Disney's ***Snow White and the Seven Dwarfs*** before the *Wehrmacht* occupied Prague Castle, she chose to paint the Princess, the dwarfs, and scenery from the movie for her mural in the children's barrack. In the children's imagination, the characters came alive and gave them a bit of hope in their dire situation.

Ludmila Rutarova, another prisoner at Auschwitz-Birkenau: *Dina was the lover of 'Lagerältester' [camp elder] Willy, thanks to which she saved herself and her mother from the gas. Dina was a swell girl; before the war she'd attended art school in Brno, and could draw beautifully. Mengele hired her to draw Roma in the 'Gypsy camp' for his 'research.'* [...] *It was from Dina Gottliebová that I found out that the Nazis were murdering people in gas chambers in Auschwitz. She told me that she was sure of it, because she'd gotten to see the gas chambers, which she'd also drawn. When I found out about the gas, I cried for three days. I saw huge flames flaring, two meters high.* [106]

105 Dina Babbitt - Good Times Santa Cruz: goodtimes.sc > dina-gottliebova-babbitt.

106 Ludmila Rutarova / centropa.org.

Gottliebová escaped the Death Mills and - a whim of fate - in America married one of ***Snow White's*** animators, Art Babbitt. In 2010 she was interviewed by Rafael Medoff, head of the David S. Wyman Institute for Holocaust Studies:

SZ: *Why did you paint* **Snow White***?*

Babbitt: *I wanted to paint the happiest scene I could imagine. The animated film* **Snow White** *was very popular in Europe in those days. I had seen it in Prague seven times in succession. I was that fascinated by the animation technique. For that time it was very elaborate. While I painted Snow White, the kids stood around me and asked me to paint more, the seven dwarfs and the animals – which I did.* [107]

Dina Gottliebová-Babbitt died on July 29, 2009, in Felton, California.

---

107 Überleben durch Talent - Schneewittchens Albtraum. In: Süddeutsche Zeitung, May 17, 2010.

The Beast with Five Fingers

We have conquered death, John Carradine enthuses in one of his lesser horror pics, ***The Face of Marble***, released in January 1946 by Monogram Pictures. Carradine should have said: *We have escaped death.*

In 1949, in Switzerland, commissioned by producer Lazar Wechsler to write a screenplay (***Swiss Tour***), another émigré writer we already have talked about, Curt Siodmak, met Gustav Ucicky, a declared Nazi director who had directed one of Hitler's favorite Emil Jannings' films, ***Der zerbrochene Krug*** (***The Broken Jug***). "Siodmak, where have you been all these years?" Ucicky, acting the innocent, wanted to know. Siodmak looked him straight in the face, "Luckily, I wasn't invited to spend them in your incineration chambers."

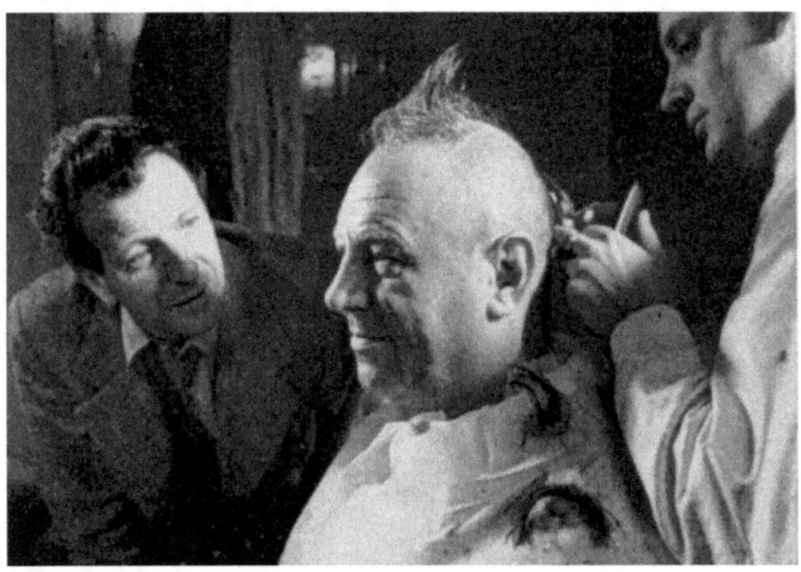

Gustav Ucicky (left) watching Emil Jannings being made up for his part in *The Broken Jug (Der zerbrochene Krug)*.
Courtesy of Jens Geutebrück, Coronaretro Archives

Talented movie émigrés like Siodmak wasted their time with ***Tarzan's Magic Fountain*** starring Lex Barker and horror pictures never to become "mainstream" again. I knew Curt well enough to quote him here extensively.

Grievousness and sarcasm were the constant companions of a writer's broken soul. Curt was one who wanted to make propaganda for Germany, but the Nazis had exiled him. Six decades later, on a trip back to Berlin and the Babelsberg Studios, I asked him why the Germans hated the Jews that much that they killed millions of them. He pondered the question only for a few seconds, then answered, *They were too similar, the Germans and the Jews.* To Curt, that hatred was like the Biblical story of Cain and Abel. Curt was surprised when ***The Shot in the Talker Studio*** (***Der Schuss im Tonfilmatelier***), that he had co-written in 1930 for Ufa and actress Gerda Maurus, Fritz Lang's lover, finally hit him right between the eyes. He had become the target, the prey.

Prior to leaving his London exile because his wife Henrietta wanted their son to be born in the United States, Siodmak received a letter from his former German publisher:

Wilhelm Goldmann Publisher,

Leipzig, January 30, 1937.

To Curt Siodmak in London.

Dear Mr. Siodmak,

Herewith I want to let you know that the complete stock of your book has been confiscated by the Secret State Police.

Sincerely,

Wilhelm Goldmann.

Henceforth, Siodmak was lucky enough to contribute his ideas to pictures that were despised by the cultural elite but that worked so well at the box office that Universal Pictures called them King Midas films: *I wrote many horror films. The fantastic and macabre is a German trait. Look at their fairy tales. Pretty gruesome, aren't they?*

Here he was, Curt Siodmak, writing horror films for Universal while so many others were killed in the real horrors of the holocaust. One day, in 1941,

Siodmak sat in his bungalow at Universal and poetized what later seemed to become part of folklore:

Even a man, who is pure in heart and says his prayers by night,
may become a wolf when the wolfbane blooms and the autumn
moon is bright.

These were memories of his past in Germany:

> *Den Währwolf kannten sie alle. Das war ein Mensch, der nur eine gewisse verzauberte Schnalle an seinem Gürtel zu lösen brauchte, und er nahm die Gestalt eines Wolfes an und fraß Schafe und Füllen, ja vor Hunger sogar Menschen.*
>
> *They all knew the Werewolf* [Man-Wolf]. *That was a man who only had to loosen a bewitched buckle at his belt to change and put on the shape of a wolf. He would feed on sheep and fillies and, when starving, even humans.*
>
> [Karl Gutzkow, ***Der Währwolf***, 1870]

Siodmak got the job from George Waggner, an actor-turned-director. He repeated the story in each interview how he was approached by Waggner: *"We have a title called* **The Wolf Man.** *It comes from Boris Karloff, but Boris has no time to do it. So, we have Lon Chaney, Jr. and we have Madame Ouspenskaya, Warren William, Ralph Bellamy, Bela Lugosi, and Claude Rains. The budget is $180,000 and we start in ten weeks. Good-bye."* One of the sources was a horror novel by Guy Endore: *The Werewolf of Paris*, published in 1933 and turned into a movie by Universal for the first time as ***WereWolf of London*** two years later. But Henry Hull, the star, had refused the hairy Jack P. Pierce make-up and preferred a much simpler solution. Chaney, Jr., however, the unbeloved son of a brutal father, Chaney, Sr., who (according to Siodmak) punished his son by lashing him, was to perform the horror part as envisioned by Pierce. He played the American son of an acting- and storywise domineering Englishman (Rains) who is bitten by a Hungarian werewolf (Lugosi), himself the son of a Russian gypsy (Maria Alekseyevna Ouspenskaya), the story put together by a German writer. This makes ***The Wolf Man*** a truly Cosmopolitan movie.

Siodmak had the luck or, depending on the perspective, bad luck to become typecast and identified with this genre. In an interesting letter to his young German correspondent, Uwe Sommerlad, Robert Bloch (***Psycho***), comparing himself with the established and highly-regarded Roald Dahl, characterized the fate of the horror writer:

The thing about Roald Dahl is that he was accepted as a member of the literary establishment. His work was thus taken seriously, whereas mine is not: I'm a "horror-story writer". Dahl moved in high social circles, and when he mingled with the well-known publishers, critics or journalists at dinner-parties, they regarded him as their equal. This is an important psychological distinction: you would be surprised at the number of books that are published because publishers know the authors socially, on a personal level. We on the outside must "prove" we're worth publication...

Nevertheless, the horror stories relate more of the time and its background than many of the high-class novels by those established authors. The ugly monsters of Universal Pictures looked like the terribly distorted faces of so many unlucky WW1 participants: *Look hard at these men! They gave their lives so that you might live. Feast your eyes on the horror!* [108] Curt Siodmak: *There are no monsters because you can't even define: what is a monster. You only consider a monster according to his looks. There are lots of monsters with pretty faces.* The documentary Siodmak was interviewed for [109] shows a photo of an infamous SS Obergruppenführer who was said to be "as handsome as a Greek

108 ***J'Accuse*** (1938) by Abel Gance.

109 ***Universal Horror.*** Directed & Edited by Kevin Brownlow. A Photoplay Production for Universal Television, 1998.

god": Reinhard Tristan Heydrich, architect of the so-called Final Solution (of the Jewish Question).

Deep in the forests of what today belongs to Poland, in a partly swampland in the Masurian woods, nicknamed "*Mückenloch*" (Mosquito Hole), eight kilometres east of the small town Kętrzyn (back then Rastenburg), Hitler had his "Führerhauptquartier" (Führer Headquarters): *Wolfsschanze,* the *Wolf's Lair.* While the Nazis identified the enemy from the East with vampires, they considered themselves relatives of the wolf. They recalled past glories when men would don the woodland animal's pelts and thus were absorbed by the forests.

The Nazis detested, however, the psychoanalytic theory of the ***Wolf Man***. Four of the five sisters of Sigmund Freud (1856-1939) were murdered in Hitler's concentration camps. In 1910, they brought Freud a patient who had become sort of a wolf man in his nightmares. Sergeï Pankejeff was age 23 at that time and born to a family of aristocrats in St. Petersburg, the younger of two siblings. Pankejeff had a recurring dream that started in his childhood, *"Suddenly, the window opened of its own accord, and I was terrified to see that some white wolves were sitting on a big walnut tree in front of the window. There were six or seven of them. The wolves were quite white, and looked more like foxes or sheep-dogs, for they had big tails like foxes and they had their ears pricked like dogs when they pay attention to something."* This dream intrigued Freud. He analyzed the dream and discovered that it marked a turning point in Pankejeff's childhood, the case of an infantile neurosis.

Curt Siodmak always claimed that his psychoanalysis was his typewriter, *Anything that tortures me I write into it. People say that I have written so many horror stories but it stands to reason that we had to abreact the times we suffered. And these times one cannot abreact by writing a nice love story. These times one can only abreact by making a monster movie like* **The Wolf Man**. *In history, people always wished to be as strong as the strongest animal in the respective country. In India they had the snake man. Then there was the tiger. And the wolf in Europe. And everybody wished to possess such power and transform into such an animal.*

Rudyard Kipling's *Jungle Book* is filled with these beings. There were

Man-Tigers and Ma-Bears in Asia, Man-Hyeanas in Africa, Man-Coyotes in Central America, Man-Lizards in New Zealand.

In 1942, Curt Siodmak got a letter from a Professor Walter Evans, a member of the Augusta College in Georgia, citing the parallels and similarities of construction between ***The Wolf Man*** and the Greek plays. After reconsidering it for a while, Siodmak realized that Evans was right:

In the Greek plays, the gods tell a man his fate, and he cannot escape, in the **Wolf Man**, *when the moon comes up, Lon Chaney knows there's going to be a killing. In the Greek plays, the gods are domineering; in* **The Wolf Man**, *the father of the family is domineering.* [110]

The transformation hits the unfortunate Larry Talbot (Chaney, Jr.) like a curse from the gods. We all are subjugated to *harmatia*, which according to Aristotle lets the tragedy's hero fall from fortune into misfortune.

Siodmak's fee was no more than $3,000 but, so he consoled himself at the end of his life in retrospect, all the others associated with the picture were dead. Eventually, he had survived them all.

To Siodmak, films are the mirror of the human subconscious mind which tries to find means of expression for its own fears. They are an abstract and synthetic medium used by the Id to free itself for some hours from its own fears and anxieties.

But there is more to the myth than pure fantasy or psychology. The myth has become an integral part of Western culture. From an early age, kids are made familiar with the myth of the big bad wolf that has to be killed in fairy tales like *Red Riding Hood* and *The Wolf and the Seven Young Goats*. Herodotus, the ancient Greek historian, tells of an East-European ethnic group, the Neuri, a tribe living beyond the Scythian. Once a year, each of the Neuri was going to transform into a man-wolf. Then there was Lycaon, king of Arcadia, who challenged Zeus and was transformed into a wolf. Augustine, Doctor of the Church, assumed that these animal people were phantasmagorias created

---

110 Siodmak interviewed by Tom Weaver, *Interviews with B Science Fiction and Horror Movie Makers*. Jefferson, North Carolina: McFarland & Company, Inc., Publishers, p. 300.

by demons, and very likely the man-wolves became allies of women who were accused of being in league with the devil.

In Eastern Europe, wolves were considered cunning and evil animals that attacked humans and had a reputation of being almost human themselves, driven by bloody instincts and dark desire and appetite. In Poland, the man-wolf is known as *wilkolak,* in Bulgaria and Slovenia as *vrkolak.* The Slovenian *vurkudlak* translates *wolfskin.* In the area of Gdańsk (Danzig), there are *Unnereerdschkens* (*Untermenschen, subhumans*), the relatives of wolf men and ghouls, who prefer to be where human blood is spilled. They steal pretty human kids to make them Wild Children.

It was none other than Joe May who got Curt his first writing assignment at Universal Studios, Hollywood's main supplier of horror films. In 1939 Siodmak co-wrote ***The Invisible Man Returns*** with May providing starring parts for an invisible Vincent Price and Cedric Hardwicke. May was also supposed to direct the next installment of the ***Invisible*** series from a Siodmak story, ***Invisible Woman*** with Virginia Bruce, Oscar Homolka and a loaded John Barrymore who barely could stand on his feet. But Joe May was on his way down (someone else was chosen by the front office to direct) while Siodmak was on his way up. *Homo homini lupus,* this insight taken from the comedy *Asinaria* by the Roman playwright Titus Maccius Plautus, is not true when it comes to wolves but is eternal truth considering mankind. And it includes Siodmak. He wouldn't lift a finger for Joe May who got him the job in the first place.

His prime time Siodmak had at Universal but, freelancing, he also worked for other studios, for instance RKO where he had a meeting of minds with producer Val Lewton:

I met him in circumstances perfect for a horror picture. My agent made an appointment for me to see him at RKO studios. He sat on Stage 2, watching the shooting of **Cat People.** *The stage was huge, cavernous, the biggest one in Hollywood. In a corner a living room set was built, the rest was dark. Lewton was a big man, an eternal pipe in his mouth. He sat on a chair too small for him. A commotion was going on the set, a noise which had the overtones of panic.*

"Lolita got loose," he said between puffs from his pipe. Lolita was the black panther used in the film. Simone Simon, the French star, convincingly turned into that black cat and committed murder. Lewton seemed to get pleasure out of scaring me, knowing I didn't appreciate a black panther roaming a dark set. He had a streak of sadism in him. He told me later that in school he cherished a game: you put your hand on a wooden desk and the boy next to you tries to stab your hand with a pocket knife. The trick was to withdraw the hand the very last moment possible. Once he nailed a friend's hand on the desk top with dire consequences. I guess that that frame of mind helped him to become a famous motion picture producer. "Just sit quiet and Lolita won't bother you," he said. "But she might eat you." I whispered. There, between his spread fat legs a dark cat's head appeared. The round head turned upwards, the ears folded back, a huge mouth opened, and I looked into a red canyon framed by long white teeth. I heard a growl, deep and menacing. Lewton froze into a statue. I turned into a slab of marble. "She growls," I managed to say. "She purrs," he insisted, but his ruddy complexion had become white. He slowly lifted his hands over his head and signaled like a semaphore. Presently the trainer came along, waving a huge lollipop. The panther slid out from under Lewton's chair. She took a last look at Lewton's fat thighs, undecided if she should take a bite out of them or lick the lollipop. Her sweet tooth made the decision for her. The trainer gave her the lollipop, picked her up, and threw the two hundred pounds of cat over his shoulder. That's how I met Val Lewton. In style!

It's almost certain that Curt invented the story or exaggerated a bit to create a more dramatic effect for his meeting with a well-known producer of horror films, of ***Cat People*** as well as ***I Walked with a Zombie*** based on a short story by Inez Wallace and co-written by Siodmak. Crediting Siodmak only as co-writer of ***Zombie*** means that the rewrite was done by Lewton himself and by Ardel Wray who finished the second draft.

Siodmak: *I found out that he [Lewton] was a frustrated writer. He had ideas that didn't fit my conception. But he had great taste and culture and intelligence, a fact that showed in his pictures. He created the intelligent Lewton horror films. He tried a novel approach to horror pictures, and succeeded. He put recognizable people into fantastic stories.* [111]

While Siodmak wrote his werewolf and voodoo scripts and ***Frankenstein Meets the Wolf Man*** with the wolf man Talbot longing for death and the monster longing for life, all safe with wife and son Geoffrey in Hollywood, the Germans organized their own *Werewolf.* When the Third Reich's downfall was inevitable, Reichsführer SS Heinrich Himmler conscripted a sniper movement: 5,000 "Woad Raiders" who volunteered as terrorists in wolfskin under the name *Werewolf.* The name was borrowed not from Universal's horror films but from a book by Hermann Löns, a regional nature writer born in Culm, West Prussia, today Chełmno. A few years before he died in battle at Reims in September 1914, he published *The Wehrwolf.* He told an episode of the rural Home guard that in 1623 in the Lüneburg Heath, during the bloody Thirty Years' War, resisted the mercenary forces: in terms of today, an asymmetric warfare carried by Werewolf partisans against the superior Allied forces.

Werewolves we were, now we had to become Bite Wolves. [...] *Whoever doesn't bite today will be bitten.* Ruthless violence and bloodlust brand the actions of these werewolves: The German will to resist should cost the enemy streams of blood. SS officer Otto Skorzeny was given orders to train the "packs" of human wolves in this tradition.

While most German civilians were too exhausted by years of war to bother joining this fanatical crusade, holdouts remained across the country. Snipers occasionally fired on Allied occupiers, and citizens kept caches of weapons in forests and near villages. Although General George Patton claimed "this threat of werewolves and murder was bunk," the American media and the military took the threat of partisan fighters seriously. One U.S. intelligence report from May 1945 asserted, "The Werewolf organization is not a myth." Some American authorities saw the bands of guerilla fighters as "one of the greatest threats to security in both

111 *Curt Siodmak:The Black Mask Interview.* Authored by Keith Alan Deutsch. https://blackmaskmagazine.com > blog > curt-siodmak-the-black-mask-interview/.

the American and Allied Zones of Occupation," writes historian Stephen Fritz in Endkampf: Soldiers, Civilians, and the Death of the Third Reich. [112]

Newspapers ran headlines like "Fury of Nazi 'Werewolves' to Be Unleashed on Invaders" and wrote about the army of civilians who would "frighten away the conquerors of the Third Reich before they have time to taste the sweets of victory." An orientation film screened for GIs in 1945 warned against fraternizing with enemy civilians, while the printed "Pocket Guide for Germany" emphasized the need for caution when dealing with teenagers. [...]

While the werewolf propaganda achieved Goebbels' goal of intimidating Allied forces, it did little to help German citizens. "It stoked fears, lied about the situation and lured many to fight for a lost cause," wrote historian Christina von Hodenberg by email. "The Werewolf campaign endangered those German citizens who welcomed the Western occupiers and were active in the local antifascist groups at the war's end." [113]

One of the unofficial centers of the Werewolves was Ústí nad Labem (Aussig an der Elbe): *Number of participants: Per area and training course not exceeding ten participants.* The sad truth: Hitler Youth and BDM Girls were trained by experienced front soldiers in the last weeks of the war in guerilla tactics while their commandant escaped at the end of April '45 with his secretary and the war chest.

The original strategy in 1944-45, however, was not to win the war by such guerilla operations but merely to stem the tide, delaying the enemy long enough to allow for a political settlement with the Western allies that might turn out favorable to Germany. [114] The second attempt, when everything was already lost, was just a propaganda idea. One female broadcaster exclaimed, *I am so savage, I am filled with rage, Lily the Werewolf is my name. I bite, I eat, I am not tame. My werewolf teeth bite the enemy.*

112 Stephen G. Fritz, *Endkampf: Soldiers, Civilians, and the Death of the Third Reich.* Lexington, Kentucky: The University Press of Kentucky, 2004.

113 Lorraine Boissoneault, *The Nazi Werewolves Who Terrorized Allied Soldiers at the End of WWII.* www.smithsonianmag.com./history/nazi-werewolves-who-terrorized-allied-soldiers-end-wwii-180970522/.

114 Perry Biddiscombe: *The Last Nazis: SS Werewolf Guerilla Resistance in Europe 1944-1947.* Stroud, Gloucestershire: The History Press, 2004.

Still grimly determined even after the German surrender, deluded young werewolves fought the 1st U.S. Infantry Division in the lowlands of Karlovy Vary. In the northwestern Erz Mountains, in Vejprty, a Russian field hospital was burned and all patients killed. Grenades exploded in Brournov, Bruntál and in the post office of Děčín. In the very last moment, a unit of werewolves was smashed in the Giant Mountains, home of that mythical creature Rübezahl, which prepared a bomb attack on a government delegation in Pec in the Snow Mountain in Summer (!) 1945. In May and June, in the chasms and ravines of the Lusatia mountains, a strong group of renegade soldiers was assembled by local werewolves. Police and army had to take action against them. In August and September, roughly 200 underaged werewolves were captured and 20 secret weapons stockpiles discovered.

Once the Nazis were overcome, there was no one to extend his or her right arm with a straightened hand saluting *Heil Hitler!* There was no Nazi hand to heil, no hand that returned from the grave, no living, uncontrolled hand like that crawling one that had to be nailed down by a madman played by Peter Lorre:

THE STORY OF THE
EVIL HAND
WHOSE
HARROWING
CRIMES
MADE IT

"THE BEAST
WITH
FIVE FINGERS"

This was the title of a mystery screenplay Siodmak had polished in 1946 for Warner Bros.-First National Pictures from a 1919 short story by William Fryer Harvey to be directed by Robert Florey.

But Siodmak realized that he was wrong when he came back to Germany on several occasions. Below the surface, the evil mind of the Nazis was still active and working. To quote a film title from a Z-picture directed by David Bradley in 1968: ***They Saved Hitler's Brain***.

Criminal brains became a Siodmak specialty. In August 1939 he had finished a screenplay for Universal tentatively titled ***Friday the Thirteenth***, retitled ***Black Friday*** upon its release on February 29, 1940. Boris Karloff as Dr. Ernest Sovac tries to save a friend's life by implanting another man's brain but in doing so causes a split personality. The subject interested Siodmak. In 1942 Henrietta suggested that Curt should withdraw to the desert for a while, like the proverbial Jesus Christ, and try his hand at a novel in which the brain of a megalomaniac millionaire is kept alive by a physician. Out came *Donovan's Brain*, first serialized in a pulp magazine, then published by Alfred A. Knopf. The novel was filmed three times. The first film version was released by Republic Pictures in April 1944 titled ***The Lady and the Monster*** but studio head Herbert J. Yates didn't consider it a wise idea to have the physician doing his research withdrawn in some primitive hut in the desert, like the original writer had done. *Siodmak,* he said, *that scientist wouldn't work in a shabby cottage. He needs to be in a castle.* Consequently, ***Lady and the Monster*** didn't turn out a modern horror film but a relic from the ***Frankenstein*** days. Erich von Stroheim, who since silent days was a specialist in playing sadistic German officers, was one of the stars. Erich von Stroheim was in a similar position like Anton Diffring, an English actor. Diffring's colleague, Ferdy Mayne, once told me what Anton had said: *Now that I had left Germany to escape the Nazis it has become my fate to play the parts of people I disdain, of Nazis.*

Other than Curt Siodmak, one pioneer of German fantasy films, Paul Wegener's associate on ***Der Golem***, the screenwriter of ***Nosferatu*** and ***Das Wachsfigurenkabinett*** (***Waxworks***, directed by Paul Leni), who lived in American exile, was totally forgotten and neglected: Henrik Galeen.

Only once, in 1943, with Fritz Lang's old collaborator Paul Falkenberg, he tried his hand on another scenario that updated the legend of the ***Golem*** and would use his power against the brutal savageness of the Nazis. Alas, it remained unfilmed:

Did Hitler know what he was doing when he deported a helpless crowd of Jews, of all walks of life, from all European nations to Chelm in the district of Lublin?

Did he know at this very spot 350 years ago the holy Rabbi Baalschem had brought to life an image of clay, called the Golem, *in order to save his people from ruthless persecution?*

Did Hitler know that the now lifeless clay figure of this Golem was underneath the narrow streets where modern Jews were thronging this new Ghetto?

With these questions the treatment opened.

The Synagogue is half in ruins. Rabbi Jonah wanders around and prays over the dead, spending comfort to the wounded, listening the living pleading for help. "God will help," the old man promises the suffering. "He will strike the enemy with His Own weapon. He has helped his children in the past… 350 years ago it happened… The Emperor ordered the Jews from his place to exile. Pleading was of no avail. It seemed that the end had come. At this time Rabbi Baalschem, after a long and fervent prayer, created the Golem. The Rabbi was a man of such holiness that God gave him the strength for this task."

According to the magic book Jezirah and following the secrets of the Cabala, the Rabbi formed the image of a man out of rough clay. Then he put the Shem, written on parchment, into the breast of the clay image.

So the Golem came to life, as Rabbi Jonah explained. "Bullets could not hurt it. Swords were powerless against Baalschem's magic… The enemies were smitten by the sign of God and the community was saved… Baalschem took the Schem from the Golem and buried the lifeless figure of clay… here…"

Rabbi Jonah taps the floor with his cane. The crowd demands that he should bring the Golem to life again to save their community. The Rabbi raises his hand and tells them that the time has not come yet.

Then he is going to see Steinhardt, the German district governor. Steinhardt's belief in his Fuehrer is unlimited but otherwise he is dissatisfied with his life, far away from Paris, Brussels or even Warsaw. Life in this Polish town enervates him. His boredom is not likely to be dispelled by the Rabbi's plea for mercy. Steinhardt declares bluntly that all food is to go to the German army. Rabbi Jonah leaves the Governor as a broken man.

In the meantime more Jews, from Norway this time, are deported to the already overcrowded Ghetto. Among them a young woman, Elna, catches Steinhardt's eye. To him, she looks pretty Aryan. He invites her into his car. In a narrow street a bomb hits the automobile. The driver is killed, Steinhardt is uninjured. Elna escapes and is saved by Sholem, a young member of the underground.

Sholem goes to see the Rabbi. There he learns that the Governor has given an ultimatum that if Elna, kidnapped by the Jews, is not brought to him within 24 hours the Ghetto will become another Lidice. Elna is devastated: "Hundreds of human lives against one … can there be any choice?"

German guns are pointing towards the Ghetto.

Rabbi Jonah has no other choice than enter an arched cellar beneath the Synagogue and revive the Golem. Horrified the old man recedes, leaning against the wall. The brickwork gives way and crumbles burying the Rabbi.

Elna, back to Steinhardt, is treated like a queen. Steinhardt sees in her a prototype of the "Nordic race". In the meantime, the Golem haunts the district.

In the midst of a feast a service telegram is handed to the Governor: "Immediate retreat… after destruction of all commodities that might be of value to the enemy."

Before Steinhardt's orders can be carried out a gigantic shadow appears on the wall of Steinhardt's castle, illuminated by the moonlight.

In the distance they hear shots. "What is this? The Russians?" Elna asks. Steinhardt follows Elna to the window: "Not yet… Those are German guns! Their aim… the Ghetto! But before I leave here, you will be mine…"

As Elna rushes towards the door, Steinhardt bars the way. Triumphantly he walks towards her.

The girl tears herself away – flees into a corner…

He laughs… She cannot escape…

Triumphantly he walks towards her… The girl stares at him wide eyed, silent… no tears left… A gust of wind rushes into the room… the door has opened… Steinhardt turns around… In the door stands the Golem… Steinhardt raises his revolver… shoots. But the Golem walks into the room… Steinhardt draws back to the wall… speechless. The Golem, relentless hunter, stalks his quarry… but as he walks on he leaves a trail of blood…

Elna covers her face in her hands… a body thuds to the floor… Elna looks up… the Golem turns…

The Germans are in full retreat. The Ghetto has fought off the attack. The guerillas have led the thrust, now they follow the fleeing Nazis.

Elna bends over Sholem whose head rests on her lap. She dresses his wounded arm… On the floor lies a mask… slanted eyes over mongolic cheekbones, lips frozen in a grin…

The drone of many planes is heard in a distance…

Elna smiles…

"The Russians!" Sholem says.

Frankenstein Made in Germany

Many Germans knew about the concentration camps although no details... and many of them had no sympathy for the Jews who were taken off their streets although nobody thought about them being killed. Just send them, as Hermann Göring once said, to Madagascar. But that Madagascar would translate - Auschwitz... Ralph Giordano, whose mother was Jewish, a piano teacher, survived the Third Reich hidden in a cellar in Hamburg-Alsterdorf and became an acknowledged novelist (***The Bertinis,*** also a TV mini-series). He remembered that after leaving a cinema in 1940 he heard his friend who was accompanying him say, "There sure will be a grain of truth." He meant Ferdinand Marian's Jewish portrayal in Veit Harlan's ***Jew Suss.***

Jew Suss was premiered in Venice. The opening in Berlin's Ufa Palace at the Zoo was a social event, too, before the picture entered general release in the Reich.

A former prisoner of the Sachsenhausen concentration camp recalled the reaction of SS guard detachments to seeing Harlan's film, "One day, it might have been in spring or summer of 1941, all the bearers of the Star of David were called back from the punishment battalion by their commandos and had to gather in front of Block 10. There, Squad Leaders Knippler and Vickert declared that the evening before they had seen the movie ***Jud Süss*** and recognized now that the Jews were even worse than they had thought up to that time. This remark they made with the usual dirty insulting that was reserved for Jews quite regularly. They explained to us that we must receive a *Denkzettel,* an exemplary punishment because of that very movie. All of us, almost 25 men, had to enter the barrack, man by man, and were mistreated separately by Knippler in Vickert's presence. I myself had to lie down on the table and got ten lashes by Knippler with the Ochsenziemer, a strong whip. Others got considerably more lashes."

When war began, Hitler showed discontent with the ideological alignment of German films:

Enraged about insufficient cinematographic war preparations, Hitler in December 1939 leveled devastating criticism against Goebbels in his circle. The propaganda minister reported in his diary Hitler had 'criticized the film harshly, especially the newsreel. I find that not quite justified. He does so in front of all the officers and adjutants. But he has the right to do so, he is a genius'. A much more detailed account of the incident has been delivered to posterity in the diary of Goebbels' rival Alfred Rosenberg who remarked that Hitler repeated on this occasion what he had already stated three days before in Goebbels' absence. Rosenberg's notes reveal that Hitler picked up the allegations that had been raised by the party base against Goebbels throughout the last years. He alleged that cinema did not in the least reflect the National Socialist revolution and the mobilization of the people: 'Nothing is to be seen of it.' [115]

In his defense Goebbels pointed to nationalist pictures as those directed by Karl Ritter, but Hitler refused to accept these as an excuse:

"Yes, some generally patriotic ones but no National Socialist ones," he said.

Marxism was based on the theories of Karl Marx and Friedrich Engels. But what was National Socialism based on? This was the crucial question. There was only Hitler's book ***Mein Kampf*** but that, concerning scientific theory, was not in the league of Marx and Engels. Theory was not Hitler's business.

"The film did not have the courage to get down to the Jewish Bolsheviks," Hitler explained - and that was it. [116]

Goebbels conformed himself to his master's voice with no big difficulty as he was an anti-Semite himself - although not exactly an anti-Stalinist. In a certain way he admired Stalin.

Then he went into action. ***Jud Süss*** was the result. Announcing Veit Harlan's ***Jud Süss*** in 1940, posters showed a bearded, green-faced Ferdinand Marian with yellow eyes, similar to John Barrymore's portrayal of ***Svengali*** (1931), but the film itself was a naïve costume drama: a disgusting falsification of history that led to a miscarriage of justice and to the hanging of Joseph

115 Dirk Alt, *The Dictator as Spectator: Feature Film Screenings before Adolf Hitler, 1933-39.* In: Historical Journal of Film, Radio and Television, 2015, Vol. 35, No. 3, p. 429.

116 Hans-Günther Seraphim, *Das politische Tagebuch Alfred Rosenbergs 1934/35 und 1939/40.* Munich: dtv, 1964, p. 111.

Süss Oppenheimer on February 4, 1738, cast with prominent actors who proverbially rolled their eyes.

Hitler had asked for *Gesinnungsfilme,* and he meant anti-Semitic films, and the film companies delivered what he wanted. Eberhard Ludwig Metzger considered himself an expert in the case of Süss Oppenheimer. He had already written such a film treatment in 1921 but that was never filmed. Now he thought his time had come and suggested to film ***Jew Suss*** to the German film industry.

Ferdinand Marian as *Jew Suss.*
Courtesy of Jens Geutebrück, Coronaretro Archives

For some time Goebbels entertained the opinion that the British ***Jew Suss*** that was filmed in 1934, starring Conrad Veidt, and was admirably faithful to Lion Feuchtwanger's novel could be used by turning the dialogue upside down and distorting it by dubbing in anti-Semitic phrases: the proof that anti-Semitic films were made in foreign countries as well.

Then Eberhard Wolfgang Moeller was hired by Terra Filmkunst to re-write Metzger's script. Möller wanted to show "that the Jew is a totally different being than we are. He is lacking the moral control over his deeds."

Peter Paul Brauer, the new head of Terra, had already a director at hand for Moeller's script: He would direct the picture himself. He started to test actors for the title role (who, secretly, held a competition who might be the worst Jew Suss): Paul Dahlke, René Deltgen, Siegfried Breuer, Richard Häussler and - Ferdinand Marian. They weren't philo-semites but they feared for their career once they had played the Jew.

In Goebbels' eyes, Ferdinand Marian was the ideal cast for the part of the "assimilated" Jew. He was as suave as ***Bel Ami*** Willi Forst who had turned down the part:

At the time, Ferdinand Marian played the title role in Veit Harlan's Terra film **Jud Süss**, *the actor was often asked how it was possible for him to put himself in the Jew Süss Oppenheimer's position. Ferdinand Marian had this answer:*

"Sure, the Jew Süss of this film is a truly unscrupulous criminal man. In the beginning he lives withdrawn, but when the emissary of the Duke of Wurttemberg approaches him and the financial embarrassment of the pleasure-seeking monarch opens up golden horizons for him we recognize him as the Jew, who in fact is a little Jiddchen, *the eternally great enemy who within himself bears the satanic bacillus in a truly demonic manner. When his secretary Levi, played by Werner Krauss, blames him for retiring from the management to get easier into Stuttgart, Süss answers, 'I will open the door for all of you!' This elegant Jew who is able to look like a cavalier desires the daughter of the district consultant Sturm, the beautiful Dorothea, played by Kristina Söderbaum, and when he is rejected and affronted by Sturm (Eugen Klöpfer), Süss, who was given in the meantime a license by the somewhat morbid duke (Heinrich George) for all his exploitative and criminal*

deeds, lures the girl to himself and rapes her who had rejected him. This Süss sports a captivating kindness and the next moment an irresistible impertinence, then again a smart indulgence. He doesn't have the mark of Cain on his forehead. When the duke dies, the outraged Wurttemberg citizens sentence the Jew to the gallows. But even in the hour of death, the Jew curses the city, the country, the people, everybody, and he does so in a mixture of fear of death and an innate despising.

"If an actor would say: I won't play a villain again, then it would almost sound like: From now on I won't move my left arm. In the portrayal of criminals there lies deep sense, too. It serves the beauty, the good by setting off the difference between evil and good. So it is not only the pleasure in a part shimmering with many colors which might stimulate the actor to enthusiastically accept such a role. On the contrary, it is so that 'one isn't only an actor but also forty years of age' and that one must feel what one achieves.

"For myself," Ferdinand Marian resumes, "it was a pleasant moment when Veit Harlan one day said: Nobody else should play the Jew Süss." [117]

But Goebbels wasn't satisfied with Peter Paul Brauer. (Neither was Hitler who disliked Brauer's latest entry, ***Ich bin gleich wieder da/I'll Be Back in a Minute.***) Brauer, in a meeting, had made the mistake of denouncing Goebbels favorite Heinz Rühmann who had told Brauer that he intended to leave the country.

Now the way was free for Veit Harlan. Harlan had directed Emil Jannings in ***Der Herrscher*** and was introduced to Mt. Olympus, to the "Führer" himself: *From Hitler radiated a rather primitive, but absolutely inevitable fakir's effect. Even if one knew clearly that something was wrong with what he said, it was nevertheless right because* he *said it.* [118]

A central element of the film was the rape scene.

Ferdinand Marian [to Söderbaum]:

> *Yes, pray, pray to your God!*
> *But not only the Christians have a God.*

---

117 Ostdeutscher Beobachter.

118 Veit Harlan, *Im Schatten meiner Filme. Selbstbiographie.* Edited by H. C. Opfermann. Gütersloh: Sigbert Mohn Verlag, 1966.

We Jews have a God too.
And this God is the God of Vengeance.
An eye for an eye and a tooth for a tooth.

Left to right: Veit Harlan, Werner Krauss, Ferdinand Marian. Courtesy of Jens Geutebrück, Coronaretro Archives

The raped girl sees no alternative than to drown herself in a nearby river.

To add to the horror aspect, the sequence following her martyrdom seems to have been copied from similar scenes in James Whale's ***Frankenstein***. Here Michael Mark playing a villager carries the dead body of his little daughter Maria, accidentally killed by Boris Karloff's creature, to the towns hall, similar to Malte Jaeger carrying the body of Kristina Söderbaum, raped by the Jew and then drowned, to the community.

After the war, Veit Harlan claimed that he had tried to get out of the project but that Goebbels had forced him into it. Others, like fellow director Josef von Báky, remember it differently: To the contrary, Harlan was proud to have been asked to direct this "prestige" picture. His success as a director went to his head and he turned out being a fanatic, a dictator on the set.

When one talks about ***Jew Suss*** it is mainly in connection with the name of its director. All the others who contributed creatively to the movie escaped from a public verdict. Harlan's assistant director Alfred Braun hadn't any problems to make movies after the war and in 1954 became even intendant of West-Berlin broadcast Sender Freies Berlin. Cinematographer Bruno Mondi returned to Babelsberg and photographed the most beautiful DEFA color fairy tale ***Das kalte Herz*** (***A Heart of Stone***) as well as Romy Schneider's ***Sissi*** films. And former Lang collaborator Paul Falkenberg remembered in a TV interview [119] that he and composer Wolfgang Zeller sat before Hitler came to power in a café at Wittenbergplatz. When Zeller saw a column of Brownshirts, he remarked derogatorily that German history originated just from a few disparaged tribes. After the war, when Falkenberg returned to Germany, they met again but Falkenberg didn't realize that his friend was the composer of Harlan's ***Jew Suss***. And Zeller didn't mention the fact, of course.

The Eternal Jew released the same year as ***Jew Suss*** was even worse because it claims "authenticity". After the invasion of Poland Dr. Fritz Hippler, back then head of the German newsreel service, ordered his camera crew to film a poverty-stricken Jewish community driven into degradation in the ghettos of Lodz, Warsaw, Lublin, and Cracow. In the Nazi press, Hippler stressed the "authenticity" of his work: "No Jew was forced into any kind of action or position during the shooting [of ***The Eternal Jew***]. Moreover, we let the filmed Jews be undisturbed and tried to shoot in moments when they were unaware of the camera's presence. Consequently, we have rendered the ghetto Jews in an unprejudiced manner, real to life as they react in their own surroundings. All who are going to see this film will be convinced that there is never a forced or scared expression in the faces of the Jews who are filmed passing by, trading or attending ritual services." But could these possibly be "their own surroundings" when those surroundings were created by the Nazi occupation forces? ***The Eternal Jew*** is a rather obscene, rotten, infamous

119 Günter Peter Straschek, *Filmemigration in Deutschland.* WDR Cologne, 1975.

propaganda compilation. This "cinematic contribution to the problem of world Jewry" was loosely based on a 1937 exhibition of the same title that was devoted to "degenerate art" and even contained a short "documentary" denouncing Jewish film actors of the Weimar Republic. The 1937 short, however, was rejected by Goebbels: "A bad propaganda film about Jews in films. Made despite my ban. I shall not pass it. Too pushy." By contrast, the 1940 ***Eternal Jew*** provokes the fear and hatred of the "Wandering Jew", of migration and superalienation effectively and distinguishes several categories.

Jews as criminals: White slavery, according to the script to 98 percent in Jewish hands.

Jews as politicians who contributed to the catastrophe of the Treaty of Versailles.

Jews as capitalists and plutocrats: Wall Street and stock market Jews, names like Kahn, Loew, Warburg, Hanauer, Wertheim, Lewisohn, Seligmann, Guggenheim, Wolf, Schiff, Kraus, Stern.

Jews as radical Communist revolutionaries who collaborate secretly with the Jewish plutocrats: Karl Marx, Ferdinand Lassalle-Wolfson, Rosa Luxemburg (a.k.a. Emma Goldmann).

Jews as excessive creative artists: Film Clips with Curt Bois as transvestite and Peter Lorre as child murderer.

The narrator's voice is that of Harry Giese [120], a well-known newsreel speaker and dubbing voice artist who delivered the commentary written by Dr. Eberhard Taubert. The voice pretends to reveal the true face hidden behind the above mentioned character masks: *The war in Poland has given us the opportunity to get to know Jewry at its heart. Nearly four million Jews live here in Poland, although you would seek them in vain among the rural population. Nor have they suffered from the chaos of the war, as has the native population. They squatted indifferently, as non-participants, in the dark streets of the Polish ghetto – and within an hour of the German occupation they had resumed their money*

120 The cynicism of the Adenauer era allowed the same Giese to speak the commentary for the West German release trailer of Ernst Lubitsch's *To Be or Not to Be.*

dealings. The narrator promises that this "documentary" is going to show the Jewish migrants undisguised: without the *"mask of civilized Europeans"*. According to Goebbels, Jews were not human beings: *"Predators equipped with cold intellect that have to be rendered harmless."*

Giese: *These physiognomies refute conclusively the liberal theories of the equality of all men. Jews change their outward appearance when they leave their Polish haunts for the wider world. Hair, beard, skullcap, and caftan make the Eastern Jew recognizable to all. If he appears without his trademarks, only the sharp-eyed can recognize his racial origins. It is an intrinsic trait of the Jew that he always tries to hide his origin when he is among non-Jews.*

Hippler then shows a *bunch of Polish Jews – now wearing caftans – ready to steal into Western civilization.* As these "assimilated" Jews look a little bit awkward in front of the camera, the commentary has to concede that *these ghetto Jews do not yet know how to look at ease in fine European suits.* Berlin Jews, however, we are told, *are more adept. Their fathers and forefathers lived in ghettos, but that's not apparent now. Here in the second and third generation, Aryanization has reached its zenith. Outwardly they try to imitate their hosts. People lacking in intuition let themselves be deceived by this mimicry and think of Jews as just the same as they are. This is a dreadful danger. These assimilated Jews remain forever foreign bodies in the organism of their hosts, no matter how they seem to appear outwardly.*

This story sounds like a record of demonic possession or, in the language of science fiction, like the seed of an alien Fifth Column: a whole stack of extraterrestrial horror stories that ranged from ***It Came from Outer Space*** and ***Invasion of the Body Snatchers*** to ***Alien.***

We recognize the pestherd (center of pestilence) *which threatens the Aryan race,* Giese talks us into believing. *The Jews are a race without farmers and without natural laborers, a race of parasites.*

The Eternal Jew premiered on November 1, 1940:

On Thursday, in the Ufa Palace at Zoo, the festive premiere of the documentary **Der ewige Jude** *took place which, starting on Friday, will be shown in 66 cinema theaters in Greater Berlin. Like never before was a political film started in such a* *wave in Berlin. The enormous success the film enjoyed during its first two screenings at the Ufa Palace justifies the hope that it will dominate the film theaters of the capital over the next weeks.* [...]

Der ewige Jude *is no feature film but a documentary about world Jewry. It portrays, it chronicles soberly, it works in the style of a film report which only wants to impress by the incorruptible image. But in this cold sobriety lies the effect on the spectator. The German spectator has known the Jew mainly as civilized West European who moved in society and in all areas of the public and spiritual life. Little, however, the German knows about the primitive state of the Jew which is conserved in the pure culture of the ghettos in Poland. From these locations, however, the incessant immigration to the cultured countries in the West and especially to Germany ensued.*

Poster for *The Eternal Jew.*
Rolf Giesen Collection

The most horrifying chapter comes at the end: the cruel, inhuman, barbaric slaughter of animals. (This nerve-splitting chapter will be shown in public screenings only selectively.) These are terrifying images of animal torture which couldn't be worse.

When the picture fades away showing German people and images of German nature, the spectator breathes again. From the lowest depths he comes to light again. And he feels the gap between then and now nowhere as deeply, the incredible change since the revolution nowhere that obvious as in the light of these images that speak for themselves without many words. [121]

At 4:00 p.m. screenings the picture was shown at the Ufa Palace *sans* epilogue of animal slaughter for sensitive minds and women, at 6:30 with epilogue for the hardboiled fellow Germans.

The impression given wherever the Nazis ran the movie was that of disgust and menace.

In the Casino Cinema in Lodz: *...here in Litzmannstadt, the former Polish Lodz, was a big part of this picture shot. Here in the ghetto the camera captured those types of Jewry who might represent best world Jewry. In squares, alleys and caves of the Jewish quarters but also in the flamboyant, pompous palaces that today, however, serve different and more worthwhile purposes these characters dwelled. Here these ugly faces were discovered which this film work shows us. Before the regulating hand of German administration intervened and cleared out these Augean stables, the film camera wandered through the ghetto of Litzmannstadt to keep an authentic, an undistorted image of that stinking murky pool from which world Jewry received its continuously floating inflow.*

The characters and faces shown in the film once roamed the streets of the town trading and living as parasites. Here they felt well under the protection of the Polish authorities that let them do and even promoted their moneyed interests. Considering the shockingly high population, they held almost the whole economical as well as cultural life in their hands - if at all one can call it cultural life under Polish leadership.

---

121 Albert Brodbeck, *Der ewige Jude - Uraufführung des grossen Dokumentarfilms.* In: Deutsche Allgemeine Zeitung, November 29, 1940.

The picture left a very strong impression. [122]

In Paris the picture was shown as *Le péril Juif:*

I saw this extraordinary picture in the 'César' on Champs-Élysées. It was shot in Polish ghettos by filmmakers who weren't afraid of bugs, lice or all other pests, of the dirt and chaotic crowd of permanently wandering people. The impressive allegory of the restless migration instinct of the Jews in this picture, these are vast herds of rats. Everywhere these rodents turn up, cumulate to an incredible mass, a relentlessly devastating flood.

Very odd but most impressive in this film is the cruel killing of animals in the slaughterhouses by Jewish ritual slaughterers.

The endless death agony of ox and muttons, lambs that are daggered, according to Jewish law, and, while their executioners laugh nastily, bleating the last sounds of their tormented flesh, to see this is truly a torture. [123]

122 *Der ewige Jude in Litzmannstadt.* In: Film-Kurier, January 20, 1941.

123 *Un film sensationnel: Le péril Juif.* In: Grigoire, July 31, 1942.

Mr. Robot Himself: Harry Piel

In 1945, a U.S. Army jeep rumbles through Biberach an der Riss in Upper Swabia, part of the French-occupied zone. An officer asks for Anton Kutter. To modern astronomers Kutter is known as an optical inventor who developed the *Schiefspiegler*, an obstruction-free reflecting telescope. That, however, is not the reason for the arrival of the Americans. They are more interested in a half-hour feature film that Kutter had produced in 1936 at the Bavaria Studios in Munich Geiselgasteig: ***Weltraumschiff 1 startet*** (***Space Ship 1 Launches***). This film was the third made in Germany that dealt with rocket ships, after the silents ***Wunder der Schöpfung*** and ***Frau im Mond***. It was the story of a spaceship launched from Friedrichshafen on the northern shoreline of Lake Constance (Bodensee) on a gigantic track ramp, similar to George Pal's space ark in ***When Worlds Collide***, on June 13, 1963, for a flyby over the far side of the Moon.

For this ambitious project Kutter helped to install a small special effects department at Bavaria Studios that became the nucleus for later endeavors such as ***Das Spukschloss im Spessart*** (***The Haunted Castle***) and the TV series ***Raumpatrouille*** (***Space Patrol***). Kutter's goal was to promote manned spaceflight. Yet this film had to wait years for its premiere in 1940 because the Germans wanted to avoid too much talk about the rocket-testing establishment that was set up in Peenemünde.

There was not much science fiction in the Third Reich except for Kutter's short film and that floating platform in the Atlantic Ocean that Curt Siodmak imagined in his literary dreams: ***F.P. 1 antwortet nicht*** (***F.P. 1 Doesn't Answer***) had premiered, as an Xmas present, on December 20, 1932, five weeks before the Nazis seized power - and yet Hitler and Goebbels loved the utopistic ***Metropolis***. But why? Why there was no future in the NS media? In the back of their minds, the Nazis were medieval, of course. But at the same time they were technologically interested:

In spite of, and parallel to, the discourse of the archaic and völkisch, National Socialism wanted to be perceived as a future-oriented movement that would be able to realize German hopes to unite a conglomerate of politically contradictory ideas and social myths to shape a German future. Nowhere does this futuristic-utopian orientation find a more glamorous and convincing expression than in the area of technology. When Goebbels spoke about the "steel-like romanticism" of his time, he expressed a central element of National Socialism that Thomas Mann once characterized as "a mix of robust contemporaneity, performance-oriented progress, and dreams of the past - a highly technicized romanticism." These notions were articulated in a variety of cultural settings that all had in common an aestheticization that was part of a political rationale to reconcile modern science and technology with premodern traditions and myths. [124]

And while looking at it, there was indeed a National Socialist film star around, even a member of the party, to fulfill this ambition. His name was Harry Piel and he was a pioneer of sci-fi films. He was the one to consequently produce science fiction films in Germany starting at the time of World War I and continuing at least till the early years of the Third Reich.

Harry Piel in 1926 as *The Black Pierrot (Der schwarze Pierrot)*.
Courtesy of Jens Geutebrück, Coronaretro Archives

124 Florentine Strzelczyk, *Motors and Machines, Robots and Rockets: Harry Piel and Sci-Fi Film in the Third Reich.* In: German Studies Review, Vol. 27, No. 3 (Oct., 2004), p. 543.

When Piel learned that Laemmle's Universal planned a release of H. G. Wells' ***The Invisible Man*** in 1933 that was banned from German distribution, he got cracking and created his own ***Invisible Man*** story: ***Ein Unsichtbarer geht durch die Stadt*** (***An Invisible Man Walks the City***). The working title was ***Mein ist die Welt*** (***Mine is the World***). It was premiered on September 9, 1933. In the mythology of the Nibelungs one of the treasures Siegfried, the hero, collects from a legendary sorcerer, Alberich, King of the Dwarves, is a *Tarnkappe*, a cloak of concealment. This was a myth known to and beloved by all Nazis, and so Piel transferred it to the present day to link it with the grotesque ideas conceived by Wells. A German translation of Wells' novel was published in 1911 by J. Hoffmann in Stuttgart.

Piel plays Harry, a Berlin taxi driver. In a suitcase that was lost in his cab he finds some bizarre gadgetry that renders the carrier invisible. As invisible man Harry fixes a horse race and wins 96,000 Marks. With a fortune at his hand, he indulges himself in a lazy lifestyle but Lotte, his girlfriend, doesn't want to join in. She realizes that something is wrong with Harry: that the man she loves is changing. Instead Lissy, an actress, steps in and gets kept by him. But then Fritz, Harry's new valet, runs away with the "magic box". Hot on the invisible man's track, Harry prevents a bank robbery. He pursues Fritz in a car, riding a motorbike and up into the air aboard a zeppelin. Fighting Fritz, he wakes up and realizes that all was a nightmare. The gadgetry found in his taxi was just a pilot's helmet with blind flight transmitter. The finder's reward pays for Lotte's back rent and for the engagement of the couple.

Piel was that fascinated with Wells' topic that in 1939 he announced another ***Invisible Man***, this time for Tobis release: *This picture will describe the adventures of an invisible man in a funny way.* [125] But that "sequel" was never made.

Hubert August (Harry) Piel, the German equivalent of Douglas Fairbanks, was born on July 12, 1892, in Düsseldorf. After finishing secondary school, he enlisted for seven years as a cadet on the sailing ship *Grossherzogin Elisabeth* and at the age of 19 went to Paris to become a stunt pilot. There

125 Filmwelt, No. 44, November 3, 1939.

he met an innovative film director, Léonce Perret, who arranged for Piel to work at Gaumont. Piel wrote his first script, and the idea of embarking on a future career making films captivated him. In 1912, on his return to Germany, without missing a beat, he founded his own company, the Art Film Publishing House [Kunst-Film Verlags-Gesellschaft]. ***Schwarzes Blut*** **(*Black Blood*)** was the film that started his career as *Dynamite Director*. Exploding bridges and houses became Piel's trademark. These explosions were often real, since Harry was friendly with a demolition expert who let him know when buildings were about to be blown up. Although Piel's first movie was a success, his company went bankrupt. But Piel had tasted blood and stood in business to make movie after movie.

Die grosse Wette **(1915).**
Courtesy of Dr. Ralf Bülow

Piel had been an *Electric Man* as early as 1915 when he produced, directed and starred as a walking Automaton, a robot in the lost ***Die grosse Wette*** **(*The Big Bet*)** that truly can be called Germany's first genuine science fiction movie, long before the term science fiction was invented by editor Hugo Gernsback and Czech writer Karel Čapek coined the term *robot* in his play *R.U.R.*

In July 1916, the Piel-directed ***Das lebende Rätsel*** (***The Living Enigma***) had a premise that was clearly inspired by another H. G. Wells novel: In *When the Sleeper Wakes* (first published in 1899) the protagonist sleeps for two hundred and three years. Harry Piel is a little lowlier and contents himself with one hundred years. Professor Mikett is able to revive Olaf Peer, a millionaire, after a hundred years of deep sleep. Peer is not only staggered by the progress but also falls in love with Mikett's daughter. Marston, however, who is Mikett's assistant, gets jealous and kills Peer with deadly Mars Rays developed by the Professor.

Piel's 1920 production of ***Die Luftpiraten*** (***The Air Pirates***) was most likely based on a pulp series titled *Der Luftpirat und sein lenkbares Luftschiff (The Air Pirate and His Steerable Airship)*, also known as *Captain Mors and the Air Pirate* (modeled after Jules Verne's Robur and Captain Nemo). 165 issues appeared between 1908 and 1912.

In ***Das fliegende Auto*** (***The Flying Car***, 1920), another entry in Piel's sensational detective series, a criminal named Gusson steals the construction plans and prototype of a flying car.

A contemporary reviewer: *Harry Piel works the American way: five somehow connected acts but each with a stunning sensation. Brilliant climbing tours, jewel thefts, man-trained police dogs, breathless chases and original jiu-jitsu, death falls from the roof down to the pavement, leaps into the water from the fourth floor and last not least stunt car driving… in addition to that: horse races, women wrestling… a tiny bit undressing and nudity – and speed – one enjoys it without overworking the brain.*

Piel joined NSDAP in 1933 and became a patron member of the SS. And he went on to produce naive science fiction at a time when some of Hollywood's fantasy films were banned in Germany.

On March 28, 1933, for instance, Rouben Mamoulian's ***Dr. Jekyll and Mr. Hyde*** that Berlin's Paramount branch office was going to release in Germany as ***Das Phantom von London*** (***The Phantom of London***) was banned, as were Alexander Korda's production of H. G. Wells' ***Things to Come*** and ***The Man Who Could Work Miracles***.

Harry Piel in *Menschen, Tiere, Sensationen* (1938).
Courtesy of Jens Geutebrück, Coronaretro Archives

Piel, however, was able to continue sci-fi production with ***Die Welt ohne Maske: Ein Film vom Fernsehen*** (***The World Without a Mask: A Film about Television***).

Dr. Tobias Bern (Kurt Vespermann), an attic room do-it-yourselfer, is going to participate in an international competition for the best wireless image transfer, against the superior power of the big electro groups. His neighbor, Harry Palmer (Piel), is an unemployed victim of the Great Depression but keeps his chin up. Chance brings it about that Harry disarranges some cables, and suddenly they have invented fully fledged television: "We not only teleview, we are looking thoroughly through." All of a sudden, they are able to see through walls and depict whatever lies on the other side of the screen. The invention attracts the interest of South American radio manufacturer E. W. Costa (played by Hubert von Meyerinck, a homosexual) who puts a hit on Tobias Bern and tries to bring the device under his control. During the chase the device gets broken but Tobias and Harry win the first prize for their "ideal combined Peoples Radio Television Set suitable for the mass".

The same year, 1934, Piel produced a second robot film: ***Der Herr der Welt*** (***The Master of the World***) was adapted from a novel by Georg Mühlen-Schulte. Mühlen-Schulte was editor in chief of a Berlin magazine, *Lustige Blätter*. In October 1933 he had signed, together with 87 other authors, among them Gottfried Benn, Max Halbe, Hanns Johst, Walter von Molo, and Will Vesper, the vow of most faithful fellowship of Adolf Hitler:

Peace, work, freedom, and honor are the most sacred possessions of each nation and the precondition of frank coexistence of peoples. The awareness of power and regained union, our sincere willingness to serve unconditionally inner and outer peace, the deep belief in our assignments concerning the rebuilding of the Reich and our determination to not do anything that would be incompatible with our honor and that of our fatherland motivate us in this serious hour to most solemnly plight a troth of most faithful fellowship in front of you, Herr Reichskanzler.

Mühlen-Schulte wrote, by the way, two more film scripts for Harry Piel: ***Der Dschungel ruft*** (***The Jungle Calls,*** 1936) and ***Der unmögliche Herr Pitt*** (***The Impossible Mr. Pitt,*** 1938). In the case of ***Master of the World*** Piel was only producer-director, he didn't star this time.

While Dr. Heller (Walter Janssen) begins a production of working robots in his factory that shall free mankind from the burden of dangerous, health-damaging and deadly dull work, his colleague, Professor Wolf (Walter Franck) develops behind Heller's back a super robot, a fighting machine which shall secure world dominion. Wolf eliminates Heller in order to swallow his factory but Werner Baumann (Siegfried Schürenberg), a mining engineer, stops him. Wolf, trying to keep the unemployed in check with his fighting robots, falls victim to his invention.

Such robots are beneficial - this demonstrates **The Master of the World** -

basically for entrepreneurs who are enabled to throw their workers on the dole. Only when an engineer who falls in love at the right time with the right woman, the widow of the robot manufacturer, takes a stand for his workmates they are regarded: With a share of the profits made from the leasing of the robots they are settled as farmers. While in this half of the story the blessing of technology reaches everybody, the fear of technology prevails in the other half, the horror plot of super robots, a fear that is fed from an experience made in the production process - the experience of the subject being at the mercy of a mechanical object world. As the film allows this everyday horror only in the image of the super robot, it can ban it with the self-destruction of the moloch. Albeit how much this horror resonates in the image of the working robot too, one feels realizing the seriousness of other scenes that are supposed to prove the harmlessness of the sheet metal monsters, for instance when [actor] Otto Wernicke repairs one and talks to it like to a buddy. [126]

Then, in 1939, two German film companies planned big science fiction movies.

In summer, Bavaria Studios commissioned writer-director Robert Adolf Stemmle and announced a huge rocket film ***Zwischenfall im Weltraum*** (***An Incident in Outer Space***), presumably using the technical facility and some of the gadgets built by Anton Kutter: *The eternal wishful dream of mankind culminates in the daring idea to reach the Moon with the support of technically advanced means in order to explore the strangest of all planets* [sic!]. *Not only shall the steel sheeting of the space rocket include delegates of ultramodern sciences, the celebrities of the international press and a choice of the most progressive technology but also bring, in its lightning "fall upwards", to the infinite space between the stars the most important item Earth has to give: love.* [127]

An Incident in Outer Space was designed to compete with an even bigger production announced at the same time by Ufa: ***Weltraumschiff 18*** (***Spaceship 18***). The project budgeted at Reichsmark 1.8 million was based on a novel by Hans Dominik. Dominik was born on November 15, 1872 in

126 Kraft Wetzel, *Liebe, Tod und Technik. Utopie und NS-Ideologie im Phantastischen Kino des Dritten Reiches.* In: *Liebe, Tod und Technik. Kino des Phantastischen 1933-1945.* Berlin: Stiftung Deutsche Kinemathek, 1977, pp. 27-28.

127 Filmwelt, No. 44, November 3, 1939.

Zwickau, Kingdom of Saxony. At the academic high school, the Gymnasium Ernestinum in Gotha, one of his teachers (mathematics and physics) was Kurd Lasswitz, the German H. G. Wells, who inspired Dominik's career as writer of futurist novels. Dominik started as science journalist and specialist for electrical and machine engineering (main area: railway technique) before he turned to writing fiction.

Ufa films that depicted the audacious presentation of technical, future-oriented problems were always the highlights of the annual program, startling, spectacular events that guaranteed success - one should remember **F.P. 1 antwortet nicht** *and* **Gold**. *With* **Weltraumschiff 18** *Ufa continues this tradition by producing a movie that will not only be a worthy sequel of the previous features but even will surpass these in the dynamic order of events, in its adventurousness and the feasibility of the resolving of technical problems, in the modern selection of its location and in the emphasis of human relations. – The most sensational plot requires the existence of large airplanes fast beyond belief - so-called "spaceships" that can perform polar flights in only a few hours and can be stationed for research goals in the Antarctic. During such a flight, they observe the downfall of a giant, earthshaking meteor. As they examine the aerolith, they discover new, unknown elements which spark enormous energies. A fight of science and a battle of nations ensue for these elements, for mysterious powers that could set the world on fire. … Subject, direction and cast point to a film that is great in every respect!* [128]

The cast was to include Willy Birgel and René Deltgen who already were seen in Ufa's spectacular ***Kongo Express*** by the same director, Eduard von Borsody. Brigitte Horney was scheduled for the female lead. But both productions didn't progress beyond the stage of screenplay. Nobody wanted to deal with advanced, most likely war-deciding technology on screen. Interesting, by the way, that the Ufa project mentioned the German Antarctic Expedition of 1938/39 to New Swabia at the behest of Hermann Göring who at that time was in charge of the Four-Year Plan.

128 Ufa Annual Program 1939-40.

Front in the Sky

Spaceships did not dominate the screens in the 1940s, war planes did.

Politically, the film industry was controlled by Goebbels, economically by Dr. Max Winkler, the ex-Mayor of Graudenz. Ritter in a letter written in 1937: "We were not only controlled by the film supervisors, but through Dr. Winkler's organization [Cautio Treuhand]. There sat ancient experts (production managers, heads of production, business managers) so that not the slightest trick was possible. The submitted film calculations were inspected microscopically and had to be relentlessly adhered to, upon approval. Overstepping the approved calculations was severely reprimanded and could threaten one's existence. It was often exasperating with many exterior film shots needed, because of uncertain weather." [129]

Filmwelt magazine devoted a 9-page 3-part series to ***Karl Ritter - Soldier - Graphic Artist - Director***. Ritter was quoted as saying about Hitler, "We must work so that he likes our films. There are no better eyes than his." [130]

Karl Ritter hit it big, of course, with the start of World War 2. Now he could direct in uniform:

Karl Ritter's films are grown in an entirely male mental climate. Comradeship and fight are subjects of **Stukas**, *too. It is a movie with no important roles for women. Background is the days of the German victory in Holland, Belgium, and France. Three squadrons of a Stuka group are brought into action against Liège, Dunkirk, Tirlemont et al. The life between fighting actions following each other in rapid succession is hardly less strained than the hours of flight, the minutes of dogfights, the seconds of nose-diving. Sheer enthusiasm transfigures the danger. Faithful comradeship proves its power when one comrade after another, after an emergency landing has to be bailed out in the middle of the enemy. Out of this comradeship the life of each one continuously receives a stream of power. Faith takes away the fright of death. The emotion becomes more intense in the festive heights of Hölderlin's hymns and Wagnerian music.*

Stukas *is a film about people, not machines - however much the nose-diving*

129 Letter to Peter A. Hagemann, October 18, 1973, Deutsche Kinemathek Berlin.
130 *Karl Ritter Soldat Graphiker Regisseur.* In: Filmwelt #20/1938.

birds of steel themselves are an expression of the will to fight and a daring confidence in victory.

No wonder. In World War 1, Ritter had served in the Luftwaffe and was promoted major: *Young men today,* Ritter wrote in a letter dated July 20, 1971, addressed to film historian Peter Hagemann, *always want to get world-famous immediately with their first attempts at literature and film. I myself became successful on short notice as a* soldier: *in 1909 as lieutenant, in 1910 highly-decorated as life-saver during a flood, then I constructed my own airplane; in 1911 I got a pilot's licence (at the present I am the oldest Bavarian pilot and one of the eight oldest in all Germany) etc. etc.* [131]

Nobody seemed to be more qualified to make military movies than Ritter - and military film meant no paddlefoot drama but Luftwaffe epics: aerial warfare.

To do such films convincingly, Ritter had to rely heavily on special effects - as do sci-fi films nowadays. The lifelike dogfights in the air were the ***Star Wars*** of their days.

Cinematic propaganda efforts of this kind were popular all around the world in those days: the Japanese ***Hawai Marê oki kaisen*** celebrates the bombardement of Pearl Harbor (Toho Production 1942, Special Effects Supervisor: Eiji Tsuburaya); in the United States they had ***A Yank in the R.A.F*** (Twentieth Century-Fox 1941, Special Effects Supervisors: Fred Sersen, Ralph Hammeras) with German cameraman Otto Kanturek who had worked with Fritz Lang on ***Frau im Mond*** dying during production, and ***Thirty Seconds over Tokyo*** (MGM Production 1944, Special Effects Supervisor: A. Arnold "Buddy" Gillespie) which showed an air raid on Tokyo.

In an unpublished working paper [132] Gerhard Huttula, whose career had started as animation cameraman of Wolfgang Kaskeline, his former art teacher, in the 1920s and who was in charge of Ufa's process and trick

131 Collection of Deutsche Kinemathek Berlin.

132 *Zweck und Aufgabe eines Trick-Departments* (*Function and Purpose of a Trick Department).* January 31, 1945. Estate of Gerhard Huttula in the Collection of Rolf Giesen.

department in Babelsberg during the war, outlined his work with scale models and rear screen projection:

As optics record differently than the human eye, it is necessary to construct things according to camera angles. Important is of course the focal length which is determined entirely by the required effects. In many cases it will be needful to enhance the effect of perspective by building model parts in perspective. This has to be done at all time in due consideration of the required focal length.

Huttula's technically most effective shots became part of and enhanced Karl Ritter's films: ***Über alles in der Welt*** (1940/41), ***Stukas*** (1941), and ***Die grosse Liebe*** (1942) with Zarah Leander and Viktor Staal:

The models were made according to exact standards based on construction drawings and photos in due consideration of the special requirements of trick shots. The airplanes for close shots have to be built in great detail, the propeller rotatable with engine drive, while models in the background are simpler and those afar are cut from flat wood because their effect is only that of a silhouette. In the meantime the cloud plates are shot unless there is something in a film library that can be used. It is always appropriate to use real cloud plates so that the impression of the models is equally real. As a rule, the movement of the clouds is, according to the respective scene, more or less overdone to get a good effect.

The airplanes are hanged on hair-thin piano wires that simultaneously supplied the power for the built-in motors. The movement of the airplanes must simulate always the originals to avoid incredibility or impossibleness. This movement is controlled by hand or motor depending on practicability. Artificial fog or smoke will add to the necessary authenticity.

With Huttula working for Ufa and Terra, Karl Ludwig Ruppel and editor Carl Otto Bartning did a semi-documentary at Tobis Studios that relied heavily on model shots, too: ***Front am Himmel*** (***Front in the Sky***). I was able to get hold of a 16mm print and see it together with Ruppel shortly before his death. He explained the dynamics of the shots by pointing out that occasionally they used catapults to shoot airplane models through the stage. The realism of the picture in the face of increasing air raids over Germany was too much. The movie was banned but a goodly portion of the shots ended up in German newsreels.

An important task for modelmakers and animators was the production of picturesque graphics and three-dimensional tabletop shots. In Berlin this task was handled by Mars Film GmbH, a company founded on December 22, 1942, that assumed the assignments of the abandoned Heeresfilmstelle (army film hire service) and Marine Hauptfilmstelle (Navy central film unit). Mars Film was a registered *kriegswichtiger Betrieb* and had its own SS production unit [133].

In January 1945, Mars Film funded by Filmkreditbank GmbH had a staff of 183 employees, 153 of them working in production: 19 directors and dramaturges, 21 cameramen and assistants and 11 trick experts and animators. From the start, however, Mars Film outsourced a bunch of trickfilm assignments to specialized companies: *The former promotional filmmakers who worked now for Mars Film GmbH or better: were ordered to work drew on their long-standing experience with tricks from advertising films, in particular graphics and animation-wise schematizing presentation of technical cycles (such as motors and engines) and chemical (fog and smoke screens) processes.* [134]

Such assignments were handled by Boehner Film Dresden, Technik Film Nar & Polley, Major Hans Ewald (Ewald Film) and Sigma-Film in Berlin, Curt Schumann's small studio in Haynau (today: Chojnów), the animation studio of Dr. Stier in Prague and last but not least Hans Fischerkoesen.

Ludwig G'schrey, a painter, belonged to those artists and technicians who worked anonymously on secret military training films in Fischerkoesen's large studio: *I was released from war service by Ufa, had received a so-called commando at Fischerkoesen. Fischerkoesen at that time worked in Potsdam for the Wehrmacht. I have worked there as regular soldier, in uniform. In between I worked for Dr. Stier. That was a private assignment for training films with*

133 Major Martin Steglich, *Der militärische Lehrfilm*. In: Film-Kurier, September 5, 1944.

134 Günter Agde, *Flimmernde Versprechen. Geschichte des deutschen Werbefilms im Kino seit 1897*. Berlin: Verlag Das Neue Berlin, 1994. p. 137.

machine guns and rifle shooting in high mountains. Finally I was drafted as soldier at Heeresfilmstelle [Mars Film GmbH] in [Berlin] Ruhleben. There I was in the animation department until the bitter end when the Russian tanks arrived. In the Heeresfilmstelle we made films exclusively for the Wehrmacht. It was pointless because the Russians were already near Spandau/Berlin, and yet we still worked on those films. And then all was finished. The last war films we made I still remember: explosion, artillery, very subtle animation films we photographed day and night.

[Hans] Fischerkoesen made three-dimensional films for the army: blue-green [anaglyph processing method]. That was very interesting. Fischerkoesen was very skilled, technically minded too. He was quite inventive. And he had a highly gifted man, [cameraman] Kurt Schleicher. Schleicher was also a mathematician and did all difficult rigging, models and so forth. In Potsdam he rebuilt a former restaurant into a large animation studio where they could make bigger scale models. [135]

Hans Albers as *Münchhausen*.
Courtesy of Jens Geutebrück, Coronaretro Archives

135 G'schrey, Ludwig interviewed by J. P. Storm, November 24, 1989.

Fischerkoesen was forced to accept such assignments because the lucrative production of advertising films was stopped at the end of the war. In the meantime, not far away, Fischerkoesen's colleague Gerhard Huttula feverishly tested Agfacolor film plates used for the transparency projection of Hans Albers riding through the air on a cannonball. The cannonball ride was to be the highlight of Ufa's 25th anniversary film ***Münchhausen. Münchhausen*** was the most lavish production of them all, made to compete with Alexander Korda's ***The Thief of Bagdad.***

Münchhausen was premiered on March 3, 1943:

Berlin. - In a festive company plea held by Ufa on the occasion of its 25th anniversary at Ufa Palace at Zoo and in parallel events in other big Ufa theaters, Reich Minister Dr. Goebbels explained the German film as spiritual power and talked about its organization. Besides the Ufa fellowship and numerous filmmakers, among those who appeared to the ceremony were Reich Minister [Walter] Funk, Reich Organization Leader Dr. [Robert] Ley, state secretary [Leopold] Gutterer, Private Counsillor Dr. [Alfred] Hugenberg and Reich film intendant Dr. Fritz Hippler.

After the Leonore Overture No 3 by Beethoven and a tribute to fallen comrades, the first speaker was general manager Ludwig Klitzsch who talked about the history of Ufa. He said i.a., "When the National Socialist state one year ago put German film under a central leadership it named this leading organ 'Ufa'. This honor satisfies us deeply. Ufa is a foundation of the world war. It was initiated by Generalquartiermeister [chief of the general staff] Ludendorff on behalf of Oberste Heeresleitung [top army command]. We had to abide very painful experiences re: enemy propaganda by photographs and film until it was decided to get down to action. Ludendorff put an end to this dishonorable state with the postulate of combining the economical, artistic, and technical facilities to an influential company under state control. This task was consigned to the former head of the Deutsche Bank, Emil Georg von Stauss [who had died in December 1942]. *On December 18, 1917, it was solved. The Universum Film Aktiengesellschaft was founded. End of February 1918 the company was registered. The following years were under the burden of political and economical instability. They were shaped by the Versailles Treaty. During inflation it was defenselessly exposed to Jewish and economically irresponsible forces. The State withdrew its interests in year 1921 under the influence of leftist circles.*

Eduard von Winterstein and Hans Albers in *Münchhausen*. Courtesy of Jens Geutebrück, Coronaretro Archives

Then, in 1933, it came to that fertile wedlock between time and film. National Socialists struggle for the soul of the German people took this unspent, so highly effective weapon. Reich Minister Dr. Goebbels became the patron of the German film. He taught us to lead the film in a new way. The never expected increase of cinema attendance exceeded already a billion the previous year but is only an exterior expression for today's intrinsic bonds between film and people. When Germany in 1939 was forced again into a world war, there was a completely different picture than 1914. In weekly 32 languages and over 30 prints the reports of our in front line heroically fighting PK men are woven into a thrilling sound film work. More than 50 million people domestically as well as internationally see each week a thrilling image about the fateful struggle of the German people.

In the midst of the increased service of all forces the art of film approaches a new era in its history. It's a convincing signal of the unbroken initiative of German filmmaking that in this time after ten years of laboratory experiments of Ufa and Agfa German color film based on the Agfacolor process was developed. [136]

136 *Im alten Geist zu neuen Zielen.* In: Der Film, March 6, 1943.

Dance on the Volcano: Education for Death

In 2006, at the German cinematheque, we screened ***Jew Suss*** to 150 Berlin pupils. The young people weren't that interested. It was a piece of film from a bygone era. This type of storytelling and acting didn't mean much to them anymore. (Although two of them outed themselves as anti-Semites which later caused lots of useful discussion.) They were more interested in a Disney film released around the same time as the German ***Münchausen*** which, by the way, was written anonymously by Erich Kästner whose books were later filmed by Walt Disney:

Education for Death deeply moved them.

Nineteen forty-three became an important year for the release of ambitious, sophisticated anti-Nazi films. In the middle of World War 2, on January 1, RKO released ***Der Fuehrer's Face***, featuring Oliver Wallace's popular song of the same title. It starred Donald, Disney's popular duck character, having a nightmare forced to do slave labor in an armament factory in Nutziland. The poster for the cartoon showed Donald throwing a tomato right smack dab at the Fuehrer's face. The picture won Disney another Academy Award. Animation director Jack Kinney recalled,

The Russians bought a lot of prints on that. It was a put-down of Hitler, and he was pretty high at that time, you know. It served a damn good purpose, even though it was propaganda, it really did. They had great distribution on it. It went to all the Army camps, and everybody else got to see it. I think it had more [distribution] than things that got a little on the straight side... [137]

(On January 7, RKO followed with a second duck propaganda short. This time Donald starred in ***The Spirit of '43*** and promoted taxes to beat the Axis.)

Along with ***Der Fuehrer's Face***, the Disney people helmed by director Clyde Geronimi adapted ***Education for Death: The Making of the Nazi*** from a book by Gregor Ziemer into what was the peak of their anti-Fascist short films.

Gregor Athalwin Ziemer, who had been headmaster of the American

137 Jack Kinney interviewed by Michael Barrier and Milton Gray. www.michael-barrier.com.

School in Berlin until 1939, had published his story of a German *Pimpf*, or 'Little Fellow', in 1941:

At six, the Party takes him from the National Socialist Welfare Organisation; at ten, he will be promoted to the Jungvolk. He wears a dignified uniform: heavy black shoes, short black stockings, black shorts, a brown shirt with a swastika armband and a trench cap. He receives a number and is given a Leistungsbuch ['performance book'] in which, throughout the years, are registered his physical development and military prowess, his home, school and party activities. If the Pimpf fails to pass the rigid examination for promotion to the Jungvolk, he is made to feel that he would be better off dead. [138]

Disney's short is much better than the RKO live-action feature, ***Hitler's Children***, directed by Edward Dmytryk which was based on the same book. ***Education for Death*** describes, authentically and emotionally, the socialization of Hans, a young, very shy German boy, and his initiation to the Third Reich: *One day, Hans became sick. His mother is praying that her son get well. She knows that the unfit are taken away by the state... and are never heard of again.* But eventually he recovers and finally joins in, like all the others: *Hans is now ready for the higher education as decreed by the Führer.*

Listen to the fanatic cry: "Heute gehört uns Deutschland, morgen die ganze Welt." - *"Today, we own Germany - tomorrow, the whole world."*

We see the youth marching, all armed with torches, burning books by Voltaire and Einstein, scores written by Mendelssohn-Bartholdy, transforming the Holy Bible into Hitler's *Mein Kampf*, substituting the crucifix with a sword and a swastika.

Marching and heiling, heiling and marching, Hans grows up. In him is planted no seed of hope, laughter, tolerance or mercy. For him, only marching and heiling, heiling and marching as the years grind on. Manhood finds him still heiling and marching. But the grim years of regimentation have done their work; now he's a good Nazi. He sees nothing but what the party wants him to see, he says nothing than what the party wants him to say, and he does no more than the party wants

138 *Education for Death: The Making of the Nazi.* London/New York/Toronto: Oxford University Press, 1941.

him to do. And so, he marches on with his millions of comrades, trampling on the rights of others... for now his education is complete. His education for -- death.

We see lines of soldiers, including Hans, chained and muzzled like dogs wandering into war graves.

In an odd way, ***Reason and Emotion***, released on August 27, 1943, the third entry in Disney's series of anti-Nazi cartoons, seems to be the blueprint of Disney-Pixar's ***Inside Out*** (2015). In fact, *Pixar* director Pete Docter had to admit that he was indeed influenced by Disney's anti-Nazi short. ***Reason and Emotion*** tells of two little opposing characters symbolizing thought that live in everyone's head. One thought was brutal and tended to Nazi ideology, while the other thought embodies reason and this was rejecting Nazism. The message is that Americans should control the emotions inside their head, so that the Nazis will never have a chance to infiltrate it by means of brainwashing. In Pixar's new version, five little figures that symbolize basic emotions live in main character Riley's brain, *sans* reason, and get her into trouble.

The 1943 cartoon **Reason and Emotion** *re-established itself in popular consciousness this year, when various media outlets noted that its premise was revived by Pixar's summer release,* **Inside Out**. *When I saw* **Inside Out** [...], **Reason and Emotion** *was the first thing that came to my mind, too.*

The connections between the two films are strong and obvious. The conceit of both movies is the personification of human feelings and thoughts with little characters who live in our heads and govern our actions.

In **Reason and Emotion,** *a little caveman-like guy represents Emotion: the rash, spur-of-the-moment processes that cause us to act without thinking. Reason is represented by a sensible, egghead-type fellow who thinks before he acts. The battle between our instincts and our rationality is dramatized in the film when, for instance, a man passes an attractive woman on the street, and the homunculi inside his head literally do battle. Emotion clobbers Reason over the head with a cudgel to direct the man to make a pass at the woman, who promptly slaps the man in the face.*

That slap occasions a glimpse inside the head of the woman, whose life is governed by similar homunculi. In her case, Emotion is a sassy broad who craves fattening foods, and Reason is a schoolmarm who advocates taking care of one's figure. [...]

Reason and Emotion *is a great film, not just because its animation is remarkable, but because it is so unapologetically plainspoken in its propagandistic message. That clarity is all the more striking because, for the first five minutes of the film, its ultimate message is impossible to discern, though its immediate point is clear: "Uncontrolled emotion can cause you a* lot *of trouble!" Then, after a short scene about the hearsay and rumor that dominate wartime headlines, the film's voiceover narrator says, as Emotion is once again about to clobber Reason, "Go ahead – put Reason out of the way. That's great, fine – for* Hitler!*"*

It's a needle scratcher of a moment, stunning in its bluntness. The film goes on to explain how Hitler preys on the emotions of fear, sympathy, pride and hate in his nefarious attempt to win the war and dominate the world. The only way we're going to win this war, the voiceover states, is to resist these foolish, overemotional entreaties and marshal our own senses of reason and emotion to combat the German Menace with intelligence and passion.

That message is, ultimately, identical to the message of **Inside Out** *– minus the Hitler, of course.* **Inside Out**'s *ultimate point is that we need to strike a balance among all of our emotions, even the ones that can be difficult or troubling. Indeed, the film suggests, it's the balance of emotions that makes us human.* [139]

---

139 Ethan De Seife, *What I'm Watching: "Reason and Emotion"*. In: Vermont's Independent Voice. Live Culture. Saturday, December 12, 2015.

A Glass or Two of Heinz Rühmann's Brandy Punch

While Disney, in between training films for the army (same as Fischerkoesen in Nazi Germany), produced these anti-Nazi films and even funded a feature-length ***Victory Through Air Power***, the Germans faced the debacle of Stalingrad where the 6th Army surrendered on February 2, 1943. Now at German cinemas it was high time for escapist entertainment. Goebbels realized the need for it as early as November 1939, one month after the end of the Polish campaign that started World War 2:

Because everyday life was getting greyer and tougher, the State had to do its utmost to care for entertainment and provide a few hours of distraction to keep people optimistic. Without optimism which Goebbels understood as a weapon you can't possibly win a war.

The more bombs fell, the more entertainment the Nazis delivered to the surviving audience. Rüdiger Suchsland, in his film documentary ***Hitler's Hollywood***,[140] pointed out that entertainment, of course, had a National Socialist background as well. There were musicals, melodramas, romances, costume dramas and even comedies. This seems to appeal to one of the chief characteristics of modern masses: *They do not believe in anything visible, in the reality of their own experience; they do not trust their eyes and ears but only their imaginations, which may be caught by anything that is at once universal and consistent. What convinces masses are not facts, not even invented facts but only the consistency of the system of which they are presumably part.* [141]

The consistency of the system was based on the consistency of illusion. Goebbels knew that as do the entrepreneurs of the digital age.

Among the many stars of Stanley Kramer's screen version of Katherine Ann Porter's ***Ship of Fools***, produced for Columbia release in 1965, was German actor Heinz Rühmann who played a Jewish émigré, Julius Löwenthal. The name Rühmann didn't mean anything to American audiences. In Germany, however, Rühmann was a household name: in early sound films, all the way

140 2016-17.

141 Hannah Arendt, *The Origins of Totalitarinism*. New York: Schocken, 1951.

through Nazi filmmaking, and in post-war Germany as well. But he never made what was to be considered a Nazi film. Most of his Nazi films could be re-released after the war with no cuts. Rühmann was no staunch Nazi, but because he was consistent, he was popular with the Nazis and with the post-war generation.

Heinrich Wilhelm "Heinz" Rühmann was born on March 7, 1902 in Essen and died on October 3, 1994 in Aufkirchen, Bavaria. His parents had leased the station restaurant in Wanne. At evening, Hermann Rühmann put his 5-year old son Heinz out of bed and had him recite poems in front of the customers. Young Heinz enjoyed the applause of the audience. When his family went to Munich, Rühmann realized his ambition to become an actor. His first appearance in a movie was titled ***Das deutsche Mutterherz*** (***The Heart of a German Mother***) and released in 1926, but not before the advent of talkies did Rühmann become a screen star by appearing in Erich Pommer's production of ***Die Drei von der Tankstelle*** (***Three from the Filling Station***) in 1930.

Rühmann was no member of the Nazi Party - but he was always close to the Nazis like so many German citizens. In the manuscript of his memoirs Curt Siodmak called him Hitler's little lapdog. I was the one to omit this remark from the German translation of the book for it wasn't true although there was a strange connection between Rühmann and the leader of the NSDAP even before 1933. Heinz Rühmann took acting lessons by the same Munich actor who, some say, only months later instructed Hitler: Friedrich Basil (1862-1938). A grateful Hitler donated Reichsmark 40,000 to Basil when he became Reich Chancellor. (Still in 1932, Hitler took voice training lessons from a singer, Paul Devrient.) On April 3, 1939, Hitler, styling himself as the ordinary man of the people, watched Wolfgang Liebeneiner's ***Der Florentiner Hut*** (***The Florentine Hat***) starring Heinz Rühmann in the presence of thousand workers. The location was the Strength of Joy ship *Robert Ley.*

And certainly Rühmann was a protégé of Joseph Goebbels. When Goebbels saw Rühmann's ***Wenn wir alle Engel wären*** (***If We All Were Angels***,

1936), he was thrilled to bits: *Really great. The best comedy for a long time. To laugh until one cries. Rühmann surpasses himself. I'm excited.* The story was based on an idea by Heinrich Spoerl, a Düsseldorf lawyer who loved to write and became Rühmann's favorite source of film plots. In April 1936, Spoerl had approached Carl Froelich's production company located at Ufa Studios in Berlin Tempelhof: "In the meantime a little, funny summer novel of mine has been published. Attached please find a copy. As star I could imagine Paul Hörbiger, also Hermann Thimig." Froelich liked the book but decided to cast Heinz Rühmann in the lead and team him with Spoerl for revising the screenplay. In early June, Froelich, Rühmann and Spoerl met for story conferences and location scouting in Beilstein near Cochem, a cute Mosel River town. Location filming began in July. As his female partner Rühmann had asked for his friend Leny Marenbach. The weather was good. So the shooting proceeded smoothly. On October 15, six days after the premiere in Berlin, an excited Spoerl wrote to "Master Froelich":

This morning I read in the Film-Kurier *about the rating* [the picture got]. *I had to clean my eyes but it was really true: Staatspolitisch* - state political. *I was happy threefold. Firstly, at all. Secondly, that your work was acknowledged with the highest possible reward one could receive. And thirdly, that they are beginning to take humor seriously, that they have realized the cultural mission of such a movie.*

Usually, only movies like ***The Ruler, Jew Suss*** or ***Bismarck*** got the predicate *staatspolitisch wertvoll.* State-politically valuable. Why would Goebbels, of all things, distinguish a little comedy? Okay, he was from the Rhine Valley himself, born in Rheydt, but that couldn't be the reason. In ***Wenn wir alle Engel wären*** Rühmann plays a little town clerk named Christian Kempenich who with his wife Hedwig (Marenbach) lives in that small idyllic town in the Mosel Valley. You don't see any Swastikas, no Volksempfänger radio to broadcast Goebbels' propaganda speeches. So what? One day little Kempenich leaves this *urdeutsch*, essentially German and provincial, limited, petit-bourgeois microcosm to attend a christening in Cologne. In the meantime his wife, the same day, enjoys a boat trip on the Mosel River. Due to excessive drinking, the married couple gets (independently of each other) into trouble, suspicious of spouse breaking, but finally exits the adventure innocently. Rühmann doesn't parody, he **is** Kempenich, completely unbiased. He doesn't criticize, he reconciles the audience with this bespectacled, shy type of Boeotian and transforms him into a funny hero: a pencil pusher who has internalized all variants of subalternity. Kempenich's credo at the end of the film was dear to Rühmann's heart. He even quoted in his 1982 autobiography:

If we were all angels, the papers wouldn't have anything to write, the tongues nothing to speak about, the governments nothing to prescribe, prosecutors and poets would be on the dole, and one would die of boredom. It is required that anybody once gets carried away - with all due respect, of course, and only if there is enough space. Then the world is funny and worth living.

Such were the members of the *Volksgemeinschaft,* the people's community the Nazis preferred to see. This is the eternal credo of all the little "apolitical" men who support the respective system in which they live. And the Nazis, of course, considered themselves the "best of all worlds":

Where in all of the world is a government that rewards those who teach to laugh and make the gift of smiling? Where are administrations, authorities, statesmen, and partisans who are not afraid to express this publicly? Three years ago many people in Germany thought the time of laughing was over. Yes, indeed it was over with that kind of laughing! With that slimy, obscene and disgusting grinning that drooled from nude revues, which leaped over from dirty jokes. The jokes of those days were tense, the humor was greasy, the funny caprice was suggestive. In the new Germany one can laugh again!

The reviewer didn't mention whom the Nazis blamed for those nude revues and dirty jokes: the Jews! *Weimar cabaret and revues became one of the prime markers of "Jewish perversion" in Nazi propaganda.* [142]

From now on, Rühmann's motto was: *Kleiner Mann ganz gross,* little man very big.

There was only one slight problem but that was solved soon: Rühmann was not exactly what the Nazis would call, according to one of his film titles,

142 Peter Jelavich, *Berlin Cabaret.* Cambridge, Massachusetts and London, England: Harvard University Press, 1993, p. 252.

a ***Mustergatte*** (***Model Husband***), for he was married since 1924 to Jewish actress Maria Bernheim. In August 1938, a writer of *Der SA-Mann* [143] magazine asked why the actor was still allowed to film in Germany although his wife was Jewish. At that time, Maria Bernheim lived already in Austria but that country was to be annexed soon by the Nazis. The marriage was in danger. Rühmann got in touch with Goebbels. Goebbels in his diary: *Rühmann lamented about his suffering: being married to a Jewish woman. I am going to help him. He deserves it, for he is a really great actor.* Rühmann then approached fellow actor Gustaf Gründgens and asked him to get him an appointment with his even more powerful mentor, Hermann Göring, who once had declared: *I decide who is a Jew!* So Rühmann was invited to Göring's country estate Carinhall outside of Berlin: *I was appointed at 10:30 a.m. but had to wait until I was asked into the reception room where Göring sat behind an enormous desk. On the table surface only a briefcase and two photos: one of his wife, the other of Hitler. The conversation was conducted without stereotypical expressions or phrases. Göring came to the point right away and suggested: 'Make sure that your wife will marry a neutral foreigner. This is the simplest solution. I will give my blessing.' Period, change of subject.*

Rühmann got his divorce, and on May 2, 1939, Maria Bernheim married pro forma actor Rolf von Nauckhoff who had a Swedish passport, while her former husband married a younger actress, Hertha Feiler. Maria was now Swedish and safe, although not working anymore in her profession but in a fashion shop in Stockholm.

The Nazis showed their gratitude. Rühmann's name was removed from the so-called Jews list, and henceforth he would strike bigger than ever. He bought a lovely villa at Wannsee, a lovely, very expensive lake area not far away from Babelsberg Studios, and eventually got his own production unit in the Third Reich within the Terra Film Company. After the war he wrote: *Thanks to my own small production unit which was in political and anti-fascist direction immaculate and consisted of human material that was carefully selected under these principles* [...] *I was able to consequently keep a complete unpolitical and human*

143 Kampfblatt der Obersten SA.-Führung der NSDAP.

position and not in the slightest manner produce a tendencious movie, neither as director nor as actor. [144]

The term *Menschenmaterial = human material*, however, betrays Rühmann's mindset. Mostly, except on a few occasions, Rühmann got along favorably with the Propaganda Minister and even produced a small color birthday film with Goebbels' children. He arrayed them like little soldiers. The same year Hitler granted Rühmann a donation of Reichsmark 40,000, tax-free. While Terra made ***Jew Suss***, Rühmann prepared, under the same roof, his less political pictures that were so highly valued by the regime.

In 1940, he produced Heinrich Spoerl's ***Gasmann***, a term that sounded quite bitter compared to what would happen very soon in the gas chambers of Auschwitz, but Rühmann's ***Gasmann*** is "only" a simple gas meter reader by the name of Hermann Knittel. Maybe not that simple for there were a number of Party officials, including Rudolf Hess, who complained about a scene in which a scantily dressed Gisela Schlüter threatens Hermann Knittel who reads her gas meter quite correctly with her cousin who is member of the Party. Rühmann musters her and says: *All well then, Heil Hitler!* This line was later changed to: *My cousin is a member of the board of directors.* And no *Heil Hitler* anymore. Rühmann answers: *She seems to be in a sore need of it.*

NSDAP member Karl Ritter and the "unpolitical" Heinz Rühmann had one thing in common. They both loved to fly. And they both produced movies devoted to their passion, in close cooperation with Babelsberg's process and model shot coordinator Gerhard Huttula. While Ritter made Luftwaffe propaganda like ***Stukas*** or ***Besatzung Dora*** (that could not be released due to the changed situation of war), Rühmann produced the comedy ***Quax der Bruchpilot***. ***Quax the Crash Pilot*** (1940) was based on a short story by Hermann Grote, published in 1936 and was written for the screen by Robert Adolf Stemmle. Rühmann played awkward trainee pilot Otto Groschenbügel who learns becoming a good pilot the hard way.

Behind the curtain, Göring's Reichsluftfahrtministerium controlled the screenplay and supported the preparation of this so-called innocent film

144 January 24, 1946.

comedy. One of Göring's pilots, an experienced man named Werner Zober, was made available for the film to act as Rühmann's stunt double but crashed and was very seriously injured.

Heinz Rühmann as *Quax the Crash Pilot.*
Courtesy of Jens Geutebrück, Coronaretro Archives

Quax der Bruchpilot *is a war film. The plot follows the standard formula of dozens of war films, German or American: A misfit becomes a hero when he learns to overcome his individuality for the sake of a greater whole. Although the film takes place in 1928 with no overt to war, a military atmosphere pervades the flight academy where the majority of the scenes take place. The instructor declares that pilots form a 'stormy front' that 'fights for the idea'. They fly, he promises, not into the sky but into 'world history'.* [145] The petit bourgeois is being educated to manhood.

145 Cary Nathanson, *Fear of Flying: Education to Manhood in Nazi Film Comedies:* Glückskinder *and* Quax der Bruchpilot. In: Robert C. Reimer, ed., *Cultural History through a National Socialist Lens.* Rochester and Woodbridge, Suffolk: Camden House, 2000, p. 95.

Rühmann later denied all that and pointed out that the plot of that picture took place in 1930. In 1943-44, by the way, Rühmann produced a sequel ***Quax in Afrika*** that wasn't seen on German screens until May 22, 1953. At the same time in post-war Germany, Rühmann's most popular film, ***Die Feuerzangenbowle*** (***The Brandy Punch***, 1944), was re-released again and again, to the present day, and seen by generations of Germans.

Clemens Hasse and Heinz Rühmann in *The Brandy Punch* (*Die Feuerzangenbowle*).
Courtesy of Jens Geutebrück, Coronaretro Archives

Why is this still the most popular film in Germany - although it was made under the reign of the Third Reich? Again: no party badge, no Hitler salute on screen. Instead sheer, innocent escapism. This was exactly how the Germans liked to see themselves: innocent. At least in West Germany, they didn't want to know what had happened. Even in East Germany they considered themselves innocent and claimed that the culprits were to be found in the other part of Germany. And nobody else expressed this innocence, West or East, better than Heinz Rühmann. Everybody knew the picture was made under the Nazi regime but it looked so damned peaceful that everybody wished the Third Reich would have turned out that way (and not in disgraceful defeat).

Again, the story was based on an idea by Heinrich Spoerl who had written it ten years earlier with his (uncredited) colleague Hans Reimann. Rühmann had filmed it immediately under the title ***So ein Flegel*** (***Such a Boor***) in 1934 but that film differed in many ways from the book. In 1943, Rühmann decided to do the author justice.

Rühmann appears as Johannes Pfeiffer (not two but three *fs*: one in front of the *ei* and the other behind). Pfeiffer is introduced as a famous playwright who attends, just for the fun of it, undercover as student a small-town secondary school and proves a true prankster: **The Brandy Punch** *belongs to those schizophrenic films from the late period of National Socialism that serve the regime and at the same time want to look beyond its end, that are filled with outspoken or subliminal Nazi ideologemes and at the same time evoke a yearning for peace and reconciliation, that opens with the repression of fault while it stills happens.* [146]

Ernst Szebedits was chairman of the Friedrich Wilhelm Murnau Foundation that controls most of Germany's pre–1945 "film heritage":

Szebedits struggles to explain why [Karl Ritter's] **Besatzung Dora** *is classified by Murnau Foundation as dangerous but* **Die Feuerzangenbowle** *is presented regularly on TV. The comedy with Heinz Rühmann propagates subliminally ideas of the National Socialist raciology. Young men are compared to trees that have to be pruned to cultivate them for a new time.*

Szebedits has run Murnau Foundation for two-and-a-half years. From the window of his office he looks to the Wiesbaden central station, to a memorial that reminds the deportation of the Jews. He says, 'Whatever film by the Nazis we are going to watch, we can't avoid seeing it in front of the background of the holocaust.' [147]

146 Georg Seeßlen, *Die Feuerzangenbowle.* In: epd film 3/94.

147 Lars-Olav Beier, *Das schizophrene Kino.* In: DER SPIEGEL 10/2014, March 1, 2014.

In 1944, Bernhard Rust, the Nazi Minister of Science, Education and National Culture, a former high-school teacher, tried to stop the release of the movie for its caricatures of Wilhelmine teachers (many of the old ones had to be brought out of retirement as the young ones had to fight and die at the front), but Rühmann travelled with a print to Hitler's headquarters and asked Göring to watch it. Göring put in a good word for Rühmann, and Hitler only wanted to know if the movie was funny. When Göring affirmed, Hitler ordered the release immediately - and to hell with Rust! Nobody was present, not even the "good German" Rühmann, who recalled that he had to wait outside but later described the scene in his memoirs as if he actually was present in the room with Hitler. [148]

For entertainment's sake, the Nazis even made their own ***Titanic***, long before James Cameron.

148 Heinz Rühmann, *Das war's. Erinnerungen*. Berlin; Vienna; Frankfurt/Main: Ullstein, 1982.

The Story of the Nazi Titanic: Suicide or Murder?

In 1940, Tobis Filmkunst launched its ***Titanic*** film, an anti-British drama and disaster picture destined to become a spectacular prestige vehicle of the Nazi film industry. Curt J. Braun and Josef Pelz von Felinau, who had already written about the Titanic and falsely claimed to have been on board of the rescue ship, the Carpathia, were commissioned to write the screenplay but then the project was put on hold. One year later, it was announced again, to be directed by Harald Bratt a.k.a. August Christian Riekel who had written the play ***Der Herrscher*** was based on and was involved with working on Emil Jannings' anti-British ***Ohm Krüger***. Riekel tried to approach Goebbels himself: Britain was on the target list of the Nazis, and the ***Titanic*** was to be an anti-British film too. But Riekel-Bratt was considered an artist not trustworthy to the regime. So Tobis had to look for a Nazi director. Herbert Maisch and Wolfgang Liebeneiner were considered but occupied with other projects. Next in line was Herbert Selpin who was one of the preferred directors of Germany's major star, Hans (***Münchhausen***) Albers. Selpin had recently made a film about a German Africa explorer played by Albers taking on the unscrupulous methods of British colonialists in Africa: ***Carl Peters***. ***Titanic*** was to be his chef d'ouevre, the glorious masterpiece that would him establish in Hitler's eyes as the greatest producer ever. He was assigned a budget of four million Reichsmark.

The villains of the story are the immoral British "plutocrats" of the Titanic's owner, White Star Line, which is on the verge of financial collapse. They ignore safety risks in order to race the vessel across the Atlantic in record time, sailing to New York at full speed along the northern route which is endangered by ice floes. Their goal is to win the 'Blue Ribbon' which would supposedly push up the struggling company's share price to its former level. At first, however, the stock price is falling and J. Bruce Ismay, president of the holding company that controls White Star, gets the idea of buying stock at a low price just before the ship arrives in New York harbor. Ismay goes so far as if to bribe the ship's captain to go faster, in spite of warnings about icebergs. Who is the one who warns everyone? You bet: an incorruptible First Officer named Petersen, cleverly invented by the screenwriters (there was no character of this name in the ship's crew): *Some icebergs are miles long, and 7/8 of them are underwater. There is the danger of colliding with the underwater mass.* Ismay, however, throws caution in the wind and insists that the Titanic is unsinkable. Petersen responds that staying the course at full speed would endanger over 2,000 lives. Ismay has enough of this pessimism. Petersen: *It's not pessimism. It's our duty to consider every possibility.* Ismay: *...as the only German officer on board, you have no interest in the Titanic winning the Blue Ribbon.* Now the cat is let out of the bag. Petersen is a **German** officer. Karl Ludwig Diehl was supposed to play him but was replaced by Hans Nielsen, a good actor but not a good choice as he lacked the necessary "heroic charisma".

Postscript: *The death of 1,500 passengers remains unatoned for, an eternal condemnation of England's quest for profit.*

The Nazi *Titanic*.

Courtesy of Jens Geutebrück, Coronaretro Archives

Nonetheless, a board of inquiry absolves Ismay of all blame. (Some reviewers after the war claimed German cinema audiences might have confused Ismay with their own Führer.)

Although they had an expert opinion by one Professor Schnabel, naval architect and board member of Germanischer Lloyd, that pointed out the many errors of the screenplay, Selpin and the producers would stick to the version they had fabricated.

Titanic was to be Goebbels' first launch of something that would equal some of his favorite American movies. The female lead was to be played by the "German Garbo", Sybille Schmitz. Actually, it was the second time the Germans tried their cinematic hands on the ***Titanic***. In 1912 already, the year of the catastrophe, the sinking of the Titanic was filmed in Berlin by a director from Romania, Mime Misu, using a small model: ***In Nacht und Eis***. This time Selpin requested from his art director, Fritz Maurischat, to sink a more realistic 30ft replica on a nearby lake. A very nervous Ernst Kunstmann who had already worked with Maurischat on the Shuftan process shot the heavily lit scene at night, despite the risk of air raids.

Selpin began to act as a megalomaniac. Not only were at Tobis Studios in Johannisthal nine enormous sets built to recreate the ship's interior, for reasons of authenticity Selpin demanded the use of a real ocean liner for exterior shots. Goebbels obliged and requested the Cap Acona, a luxury vessel finished by Blohm & Voss in Hamburg in 1927 that was only slightly smaller than the Titanic. Now the ship was rusting away in a Polish naval base, used for training submarine crews.

But it was not the expense which brought about Selpin's downfall. Selpin made the mistake of recruiting the services of his screenwriter friend Walter Zerlett-Olfenius, a slim man with the face of a vulture, who was mainly responsible for distorting the facts to emphasize the anti-British tune. Zerlett-Olfenius was sent with a second unit crew to Gdynia (Gotenhafen) for exteriors. When filming was already months behind schedule with the second unit footage still missing, Selpin took the train to Gdynia to find out why his friend was unable to deliver the required shots.

The two men went to the nearby Kurhaus [spa hotel] *at Zoppot, where Selpin demanded to know why his instructions had been ignored. Zerlett-Olfenius told him that the local naval officers, who were under orders from the Propaganda Ministry to cooperate on the production, seemed to be interested only in romancing the girls from Berlin.*

Selpin then asked why Zerlett-Olfenius did not put his foot down, since he had the necessary authority to do so. He answered that those who wore the Ritterkreuz [the Knights' Cross of the Iron Cross, a military decoration] *were supermen, crusaders who could allow themselves what they wanted, and could spend the night with the whole crew of [female] extras if they felt like it. Selpin, who had managed to keep his temper under control during the interview, if not his drinking, snapped back that, as far as he could see, the decoration must certainly be awarded for the number of actresses seduced.*

One has to imagine Selpin's thoughts: *As the rest of Germany hunkered down to rationing and daily bombing, the pampered cast, extras and crew partied every night with unlimited food, alcohol and women.*

A film that tried to mock the imagined depraved behaviour of the Titanic's wealthy British passengers was succumbing to even worse debauchery. [149]

Roaring drunk servicemen kept bursting on to the set during filming - unthinkable, disgusting!

Zerlett-Olfenius still felt the soldier he was in World War 1, initially as a cadet, later as lieutenant, and continued to defend the naval "supermen", particularly a First Lieutenant Redlich.

Selpin grumbled, *"It's your duty to assist during the shooting and care that everything is alright. But of course, if you spot a bearer of the Ritterkreuz, you fall down to your knees. You better care that these rogues don't walk in front of the camera when I'm going to shoot. To become an officer you only have to be that stupid that you cannot choose another trade. And this First Lieutenant Redlich, this jackass, who is he? He arouses himself on his Ritterkreuz. On a set of mine he wouldn't even be allowed to hold a clapperboard but here he acts the big shot to please a few broads. If I could fly I would have dropped three times as many*

149 Tom Leonard, *The Nazi Titanic.* Daily Mail, May 13, 2016.

Englishmen. Anyway, what sort of striplings are they, these phonies. Each idiot can learn how to fly. A bunch of wiseguys and assholes. And these shitheads in their U-boats. They don't even know what work is, what it means to work. What is it after all, this Ritterkreuz? It's no big deal to dump somebody from your boat. I prefer to win with **Titanic** *the Ritterkreuz of movie work. So don't count your chickens before they are hatched. Better care for your work.*

According to witnesses at the post-war trial, Selpin shouted at the top of his voice - and these words may be invented but they perfectly describe the atmosphere, *"Ach du! Mit deinen Scheisssoldaten, du Scheissleutnant überhaupt mit deiner Scheisswehrmacht!"*

This happened in early May 1942. It was an outrageous outburst. Blaming Nazi Germany's "fucking soldiers and fucking army in front of a fucking lieutenant". Zerlett-Olfenius had nothing better to do than to run to his friend, SS Obergruppenführer Hans Hinkel, and denounce Selpin. This was a time when people denounced their close friends, lovers, each other, and kids their parents. Hinkel tried to mediate and on July 27 asked all participants of the table round to his office in Berlin, but the reconciliation between Selpin and Zerlett-Olfenius failed. On July, 30, 1:00 p.m., Selpin was summoned to the Ministry at Wilhelmstrasse.

Goebbels came from behind his desk. David Stewart Hull described the scene: *an unusual procedure as he preferred to hide his deformed foot - and told Selpin that he had a report that the director had made some remarks about the German Navy in Gdynia, but that he was certain the whole incident had been misunderstood. Selpin told him that everything Goebbels had heard was true. Goebbels, making an attempt to control his temper, tried to give Selpin another chance to avoid a charge of treason. Selpin refused to take the bait.*

Finally the propaganda minister shouted: 'Do you really stand by those statements?' Selpin turned white and said, 'Yes, I do.' Goebbels turned to the SS guards and screamed, 'Then arrest this man and take him where he belongs!' [...]

Sometime near midnight of Friday, July 31, 1942, two guards went to Selpin's cell and proceeded to tie his suspenders to the bars of a window high in the ceiling. They brought in a bench, told Selpin to stand on it and grasp the bars, then tied the suspenders around his neck and took the bench away. When the unfortunate man no longer held on, he was strangled to death."

Selpin's widow was informed about her husband's "suicide". To the end of her days she believed that her husband didn't commit suicide. Goebbels promised the informer a new job but nobody working in the film industry wanted anything to do with him: Zerlett-Olfenius was sentenced in August 1946 to four years in a labor camp but the verdict was suspended and Zerlett-Olfenius discharged in 1949. He never worked for the movies again and died in 1975 in Füssen, Bavaria: "I became the gravedigger of my best friend."

Recent research done by Friedemann Beyer [150] contradicts the assumption of cold-blooded murder. Selpin was being brought to the police jail at Berlin Alexanderplatz. In the evening, he received an official letter that he was expelled from the Reichsfilmkammer which meant an employment ban. At late evening, Goebbels noted in his diary that Selpin would presumably have to expect a sentence of long penal servitude. He was accused of treachery against state and party and subversion of the war effort. The next morning at 6:00 the warden found Selpin dead, hanged on his trouser belt. Joseph Wulf in his book about *Theater and Film in the Third Reich* [151] wrote that the strangulation marks of the murderers were still to be seen on Selpin's neck, but all this was legend. Indeed, Selpin did commit suicide.

Titanic was finished by another director, Werner Klingler, but all of a sudden Goebbels felt that the disaster scenes were too depressing to be shown to a German audience in late 1942. So the movie was only screened in occupied Paris.

The Nazi Titanic story was to have one last tragic chapter.

In 1945, the Nazis decided they needed to clear out concentration camps to erase evidence of their terrible crimes. About 5,000 prisoners - Jews, Russians, resistance fighters and some British prisoners - were marched up to the Baltic and packed, in

---

150 *Der Fall Selpin. Chronik einer Denunziation.* Munich: Collection Rolf Heyne, 2011.

151 Joseph Wulf, *Theater und Film im Dritten Reich. Eine Dokumentation.* Gütersloh: Sigbert Mohn Verlag, 1964.

appalling conditions, on to the Cap Arcona, which was lying off the port of Lubeck.

Then, five days before Germany surrendered in May, the ship was sunk by RAF Typhoon fighter bombers. Fire swept through it and those who escaped into the freezing sea faced machine-gun fire from the RAF planes and SS guards. Fewer than 500 people survived. [152]

But German film producers after the war preferred not to make a movie about the destiny of the Cap Arcona but chose instead the *Wilhelm Gustloff*. Karl Ludwig Ruppel was the first to film on the Gustloff, a Kraft durch Freude ship, and after the war, in Munich, they made a movie about the catastrophe: ***Nacht fiel über Gotenhafen*** (***Darkness Fell on Gotenhafen***) produced by Heinz Rühmann's old colleague, Alf Teichs. Carl Otto Bartning who had worked with Ruppel on ***Front in the Sky*** would edit the movie. The Gustloff was sunk by the torpedoes of a Soviet submarine: 9,000 German refugees died, among them 4,000 children. This Russian crime certainly would feed Cold War much better than the fate of the Cap Arcona.

The same was true for the final release of Selpin's ***Titanic*** after the war. In Germany it got a limited release - limited because the Allied High Commission feared the propaganda impact even in 1950:

Seven years after completion it had been passed in the American zone, premiered in Stuttgart. Though the Stuttgart papers recognized the technical perfection of the movie, they called the story Nazi activism. The audience, however, was waiting in front of the cinemas in long lines. Great Britain's high commissioner protested against the screening to the high commissioner of the United States. In Britain's House of Commons a member demanded the movie be banned. [Ernest] Bevin explained according to the 'Daily Telegraph' that **Titanic** *in its present form didn't contain any anti-English tendency but Churchill said such films should be better avoided in the contemporary situation.*

On the other side of the "Iron Curtain", at the same time, ***Titanic*** was passed by the Soviet Film Control section and cleared for screenings throughout East Berlin and East Germany as it fit Cold War quite well. On

152 Tom Leonard, *The Nazi Titanic*. In: The Daily Mail, May 13, 2016.

May 5, 1955, the day of German sovereignty, the film was generally released by Türck Filmverleih in the Western part of Germany, too, under the slogan: *Banned! Banned! Banned!*

Gone With the Wind: Shylock's Shadow

Not one of the highly expensive Nazi propaganda films became really popular with filmgoers. Instead the comedies, melodramas and musicals would win:

Veit Harlan's Agfacolor ***Goldene Stadt*** (***Golden City***) was seen by an audience of 31 million and ***Die grosse Liebe*** in which Zarah Leander fell for the love of Luftwaffe pilot Viktor Staal by 28 million. Géza von Cziffra's ***Der weisse Traum*** drew 26 million to the film theaters.

When it became clear that Germany was going to lose the war, even some outspoken Nazi films recently finished couldn't be possibly released. For instance, Goebbels found Karl Ritter's war film ***Besatzung Dora*** (***The Crew of the Dora***) "very appealing" but thought that it would have been more suitable "for the second than the fourth year of the war", and so, to Ritter's dismay, his picture was banned in November 1943.

The treasure in Goebbels' collection of American films were MGM's ***Mrs. Miniver*** (1942) that he himself considered the best propaganda picture of them all, and Technicolor prints of Darryl F. Zanuck's production ***Swanee River*** and David Selznick's production of ***Gone With the Wind*** (both 1939) that he had screened in front of celebrities like Emil Jannings. For years he dreamed of creating a German counterpart of that successful Selznick International picture:

Great in color and gripping in effect. One gets easily sentimental over it. A great achievement of the Americans. One has to see it repeatedly. We want to follow this example. [153]

On June 1, 1943, two-and-a-half months after Goebbels had addressed a huge audience and announced WW1 general Erich Ludendorff's old formula of *total war* at the Berlin Sportpalast ("*Do you want total war? If necessary, do you want a war more total and radical than anything that we can even imagine today?*"), "Professor" Harlan at Ufastadt Babelsberg received a written order by the Minister of Public Enlightenment and Propaganda confirming an assignment he already had talked about to Goebbels:

153 Elke Fröhlich (ed.), *Die Tagebücher von Joseph Goebbels*, Volume 4, Munich-New York-London-Paris: K.G. Saur, p. 259.

I hereby commission you to make a major film titled **Kolberg**. *The purpose of this film will be to demonstrate by using the example of the Prussian town that gives the film its title, that a policy supported both at home and on the front can overcome every opponent... I authorize you to request whatever help and support you deem necessary from all agencies of the army, state, and party and to point out that the film I have commissioned herewith is being made in the interest of our intellectual war effort.*

According to Goebbels, ***Kolberg*** was approved by the Führer himself. It was clear that Goebbels wanted to have something like a German ***Gone with the Wind***. Harlan made the grade: being promoted to director of Germany's biggest blockbuster-to-be. Sure enough the 5'5" director felt like a little Napoleon, like a general contributing to the "war effort" and commanding an army of extras. Consequently, he turned into a dictator on the set. He certainly was what later was called an *auteur*. Some who had worked with him described him as obsessed, adamant, tender and caring in a way like Fritz Lang. So he is more responsible than, say, a Hollywood studio director at the same time making a propaganda film.

Hitler as well as Goebbels must have been convinced that such a movie could be more useful than a battle won in Russia, Harlan decided: a German town resisting the attack of the Napoleonic forces. In her diary, Kristina Söderbaum, Harlan's wife, called it "terrible news that Veit should do ***Kolberg***" but Veit proceeded with ardor. To his megalomaniacal mind the project was not terrible but terrific and fit his bill with grandeur. Hadn't he made unforgettable mass scenes in the Fridericus picture ***Der grosse König*** (***The Great King***), in which the Prussian ruler (as usually played by Otto Gebühr) became sort of an alter ego of the "Führer"?

Harlan, "*For the movie* ***The Great King*** *I got anything I considered necessary. I received 5,000 horses when I needed them, and I was allowed to shoot battles of each size with real soldiers. Money didn't matter. General Daluege placed almost the whole Berlin police at my disposal.*" [154]

---

154 Frank Noack, *Veit Harlan: The Life and Work of a Nazi Filmmaker*. Lexington, Kentucky: The University Press of Kentucky, 2016, p. 207.

Almost the whole Berlin police? Maybe over some drinks a dead drunk Kurt Daluege might have said so. One shouldn't forget that, according to an ukas issued by Daluege himself dated October 14, 1941, Berlin police had its hands full with supporting the deportation of Jews to the concentration camps. Daluege was a NSDAP member since 1922 and Himmler's deputy in matters of *Ordnungspolizei*, as the regular police force was called in Nazi Germany. In Prague, in 1946, he was sentenced to death by hanging.

To Harlan, making ***Kolberg*** was the most natural thing in the world. Because he had agreed to make ***Jew Suss***, he felt entitled to gratitude and therefore carte blanche producing the most expensive German film ever. For some time, Goebbels had asked him to make a ***Narvik*** picture about the naval battle in the Ofotfjord and the land battle in the mountains surrounding the north Norwegian city of Narvik, starring Hitler's esteemed general, Eduard Dietl. Harlan flew to Norway and demanded "four torpedo boats, at least one battleship, a hundred transport planes out of which, in several waves, 5,000 paratroopers were to jump, and above that six Stukas". [155]

The director began to love power and lived up to his own myth. In some way Harlan dreamed of getting more ships from the Navy than the Navy had at all. In the end the ***Narvik*** picture was never made. ***Kolberg*** was a consolation prize but Harlan was determined to make it as big as ***Narvik*** would have been - or even bigger.

Before shooting of ***Kolberg*** began, he addressed the members of his crew that they were working by personal order of the "Führer". His wife was to play the love interest, in this case a farmer's daughter by the holy name of Maria who urges her two brothers and her boyfriend that it was better to die for the glory of Prussia than to stay alive. The casting happened much to the dismay of Goebbels who feared - no, not the suffering and dying of the townspeople but that Harlan would turn the Gneisenau story into another Kristina Söderbaum picture. In 1807, August Neidhardt von Gneisenau was the commander put in charge of defending Kolberg from the approaching

155 Veit Harlan, *Im Schatten meiner Filme*. Gütersloh: Sigbert Mohn Verlag, 1964, p. 175.

Napoleonic troops. One brother follows Maria's advice while the other, an effeminate cosmopolitan who has attended the Strasborg conservatory, prefers to play violin instead and fraternize with the enemy. Everybody else is keen to die with Gneisenau, played by Horst Caspar, and Nettelbeck, representative of the Kolberg citizens, played by Heinrich George who received a very large payment for his acting.

Veit Harlan's *Kolberg*.
Courtesy of Jens Geutebrück, Coronaretro Archives

There is a dispute over how many extras and soldiers Harlan used for his epic. In his memoirs, he exaggerated the number astronomically and added at least one zero. He claimed all around there were something like 187,000 troops! Heinz Pehlke, then an assistant cameraman, estimated more correctly that they used all in all 5,000 extras. There is a story that Harlan tried to get 4,000 sailors from a U-boat training school in the harbor of Kolberg. A high-ranking navy officer told him that this would be utterly impossible. Harlan produced the proxy signed by Goebbels. An hour later the officer had to give in, "You won, Professor!" Admiral Dönitz' protest came too late. But even here the numbers differ. Curt Riess knows of no more than 2,000 sailors. This seems more likely but certainly there were less, maybe a few hundred. Riess is the one who claimed that five of the extras rounded up by Harlan to storm a hill died during the shooting of the picture [156]. In the spring of 1944, Ufa's process chief Gerhard Huttula, who by the way was also an Agfacolor expert, was invited by his colleague, cinematographer Bruno Mondi, to serve as the film's second cameraman. Huttula didn't forgive me that I mentioned this job in one of my previous books. "***Kolberg*** was the most embarrassing experience of my whole professional career. It was sheer torture. I do not want to talk about it. This man Harlan was a fanatic, really. Didn't care for any of the people who worked with him to get the result he had envisioned. I was lucky not to have been involved that much in his ***Jew Suss***. I remember, while we were going hungry, Harlan and his wife unpacked in the back of my stage packages with delicacies Kristina Söderbaum had received from her Swedish relatives."

According to assistant cameraman Heinz Pehlke, every day something got broken, cables were tearing, something was missing and so on.

On December 12, 1944, while ***Kolberg*** was still in postproduction, being edited and re-edited, Harlan's villa in Berlin-Grunewald, Tannenbergallee 28 was destroyed by bombs. Harlan at this time was offered three projects to choose from: ***Die siebente Grossmacht*** (a Goebbels favorite about the power of a Jewish-influenced fake press); ***Soll und Haben*** from the 1855 book by Gustav Freytag that should include a Jewish caricature, Veitel Itzig; ***The Merchant of Venice***. Harlan decided in favor of ***The Merchant of Venice*** because it was based on a legitimate play by one of the world's greatest writers. We don't know if he did that just to get through the war or if he did it on purpose. After the war, he excused that choice because it offered a chance to tamper with the anti-

156 Curt Riess, *Das gab's nur einmal: Die grosse Zeit des deutschen Films. Band 3.* Frankfurt/Main; Berlin; Wien: Ullstein, 1985.

Semitic tendency: *I realized soon that only with a project* **Merchant of Venice** *there was a chance to elude Goebbels' order* [sic!] *by adhering closely to Shakespeare.* [...] *Above all, it is a comedy. And where there is laughter, in Shakespeare's sense, there couldn't be much mischief. Goebbels made a point remaining faithful to Shakespeare as much as possible.* [157]

The screenplay was written while ***Kolberg*** wrapped shooting. In October 1944, Reichsfilm Dramaturge Eberhard Frowein basically approved of Harlan's screenplay although he and Goebbels had some reservations concerning Shakespeare's stylized dialogue. Goebbels on 12 November 1944: *I study a treatment by Harlan:* **The Merchant of Venice**. *Harlan commits again the mistake to have Shakespeare speak in his original voice. That cannot be made into a movie. We have to translate Shakespeare's lines into a modern, contemporary German.* Goebbels regarded it as impossible to have the actors talk on screen in Shakespeare's language for two hours: *Such experiments we can't afford now that we only produce 42 films per year.* Harlan, however, insisted on his concept and was invited to a meeting with Frowein and Reichsfilm Intendant Hans Hinkel: *Harlan wants to discuss the style of speech used in the screenplay* **The Merchant of Venice** *with the Minister as well. After strong resistance, he agrees with using dialogue in a trimmed contemporary language on the basis of other well-known translations.*

Werner Krauss was supposed to play the title part and repeat his stage "success" at Burgtheater in Vienna in May 1943 directed by Lothar Müthel. Müthel was member of the Nazi party since 1933 and entrusted with the task at the express command of Viennese Gauleiter Baldur von Schirach. Gad Granach, the son of Jewish actor Alexander Granach, commented on Krauss' Shylock interpretation in an interview: *When my father played the part of Shylock, you felt a human touch, but when Werner Krauss entered the stage in this part, you immediately became an anti-Semite.* [158] After seeing Krauss as Shylock,

157 Veit Harlan, *Im Schatten meiner Filme.*

158 *Alexander Granach - Da geht ein Mensch* (2012), a documentary film by Angelika Wittlich.

one critic wrote that with a crash and a weird train of shadows something revoltingly alien and startingly repulsive crawled across the stage.

Another critic, Karl Lahm, agreed:

The mask itself, the pale pink face, surrounded by bright red hair and beard, with its unsteady, cunning little eyes; the greasy caftan with the yellow prayer shawl slung round, the splay-footed, shuffling walk; the foot stamping with rage; the clawlike gestures with the hands; the voice, now bawling, now muttering - all add up to a pathological image of the Eastern European Jewish type, expressing all its inner and outer uncleanliness, emphasizing danger through humor. [159]

Theater critic Herbert Ihering characterized Krauss' racist portrayal of Shylock on the stage as trimmed especially for use in the Third Reich:

With swinging movements and staggering steps, he swept into the arena, an evil, dangerous clown, an eerily comical Ahasver. He stumbled, collapsed and rolled onto the ground. He kicked and was kicked. He scolded and trumpeted. Werner Krauss played an antisemitic Shylock, a red, ugly, joking devil, a ghostly distorted specter. He was spat out of the hell of the Middle Ages, marked with a ghetto's dirt.

Werner Krauss was Shylock not only on stage but was seen in that part already on the silent screen: in Peter Paul Felner's ***Der Kaufmann von Venedig*** (***The Merchant of Venice,*** 1923). The cast included Henny Porten, Albert Steinrück, Frida Richard, and Max Schreck. The *Deutsche Filmkunst 1945 Almanach* announced that it was to be an Agfacolor Film.

The supporting cast of Harlan's version-to-be was to consist of some of the leading German actors: Horst Caspar (fresh from ***Kolberg***), Gustaf Gründgens, Kristina Söderbaum, Bettina Moissi, Ulrich Haupt, Paul Wegener, Hans Brausewetter (who was in the silent version, too), Erich Ponto, and Paul Bildt.

Most important, ***The Merchant of Venice*** wasn't considered proaganda, it had become an all-time classic created by one of the most respected playwrights in history, an artist beyond all blame, William Shakespeare. Who would dare to criticize *him*?

159 Karl Lahm, *Shylock der Ostjude*. In: Deutsche Allgemeine Zeitung, May 19, 1943.

Shylock is meant to be a villain. There can be arguments about his motives and his personality, but there can be no serious argument about his behavior. Given the opportunity - one that he himself has created - he attempts to commit legalized murder.

He is also a Jewish villain. He did not have to be. Christians were moneylenders, too, and the story would have worked perfectly well with a Christian villain. [...] *Jewishness is one of his primary characteristics; he emphasizes it himself, and it is emphasized for him by everyone with whom he has dealings.*

His Jewish villainies, moreover, are strictly traditional. He is a usurer; he is cunning and cruel; he pursues a vendetta against Christians - or against their noblest representative. [...]

As a villain, Shylock was supposed to be a hate figure. As the villain in a comedy, whose designs were thwarted, he was, paradoxically, someone to be taken seriously. Invested with Shakespearean power and, in time, with Shakespearean prestige, Shylock the Jewish villain became part of world mythology. [160]

Nevertheless, Harlan tried to bog the Minister down in a waiting game. He wrote more treatments he hoped the Minister would reject. He even began to talk in Fall 1944 within an intimate circle about a chance of filming the more philo-semitic *Nathan der Weise (Nathan the Wise)* by Gotthold Ephraim Lessing, portraying a human Jew. He claimed that there had been too much interference from Goebbels, and so ***Jud Süss*** (***Jew Suss***) wasn't anymore the picture he had imagined. Harlan was no meathead. He knew that Germany was going to lose the war and that it was high time to cover his ass.

Publicly, however, he mimed the faithful NS believer. *Even in February 1945, he* [Harlan] *trumpeted: the Führer will be victorious. The secret weapons!* as actor Carl Raddatz recalled Veit Harlan's attitude towards the end.

He never did believe in such things. Harlan was a highly intelligent man but very dangerous, as a director. He confused power with brutality - and feeling emotion with sentimentality. That was a great danger. And the biggest danger was

160 John Gross, *Shylock and the Nazis Were a Disastrous Mix*. In: The New York Times, April 4, 1993.

his mania to enact everything himself. With that attitude he could destroy much of the actor's work. By all means, he was obsessed, obsessed by the movies.

In Ufastadt Babelsberg they worked all the time up to the end. According to director Oscar Fritz Schuh, "there was an air-raid almost every day. So we were able to work only in the morning for one or two hours, then the siren howled. Usually it lasted for several hours. Because Ufa didn't have any real air-raid shelters, only splinter trenches, we were driven outside into the greens where it was less dangerous. At 3:00 p.m., we used to return and do some more takes. Often these were a waste because the actresses looked overstressed after the fatigues of an alarm. [161]

Kolberg survived the passage of time. In 1965, Hanns Eckelkamp, Duisburg-based cinema owner and founder of an arthouse distribution company (Atlas Film), had just released Ingmar Bergman's ***Das Schweigen*** (***Tystnaden/The Silence***), which for unknown reasons had been an incredible success at German box offices, but he did own only 50 percent of the grosses. The other half he had to share with Munich media magnate Leo Kirch. Every Monday, a Kirch representative turned up in Duisburg to check Eckelkamp's accounts. Most of Eckelkamp's film program which contained works by Pasolini, Frank Gerry, Polanski, Andrei Tarkovsky and some German silents by Fritz Lang and F. W. Murnau (including ***Nosferatu***) didn't work that well financially. Seeing his company in distress, Eckelkamp, advised by one of his employees, Gert Berghoff, tested a package of Nazi movies at the Oberhausen Film Festival and saw people streaming in. At the same time, a single contested screening of Veit Harlan's ***Kolberg*** took place in the West Berlin Academy of Arts, organized by film historians Gero Gandert and Ulrich Gregor. Gandert remembers that so many people turned up that a big number had to be sent away.

Berghoff persuaded a nervous Eckelkamp, determined to fend off bankruptcy, to purchase the distribution rights and release the Oberhausen Nazi film package starting with ***Kolberg***.

161 Cf. Holger Theuerkauf, *Goebbels' Filmerbe. Das Geschäft mit unveröffentlichten Ufa-Filmen*. Berlin: Ullstein, 1998.

"We had high hopes as we were told that it [***Kolberg***] could easily attract an audience of four million," Eckelkamp says. "That was money that we desperately needed to save our company." But ***Kolberg*** was a *Vorbehaltsfilm*, to be screened due to Allied law only with restrictions. To elude this requirement, Eckelkamp retitled the first entry of his Nazi project ***Der 30. Januar 1945 - Kolberg: January 30, 1945***. This was the date ***Kolberg*** was shown for the first time. He and program advisor Gert Berghoff added a documentary compiled by Erwin Leiser, Raimond Ruehl and TV expert Lothar Kompatzki and a German newsreel (No. 3, 1945) that showed the German troops armed to the teeth. Four clips of Goebbels' Total War speech to hold out were optically inserted to prove the Minister's hand or - his cloven hoof in German film. Otherwise, ***Kolberg*** remained untouched and pristine.

Without wavering, or pretending a scientific approach, Eckelkamp had the film screen-tested by Professors Udo Undeutsch, Josef Hitpass and George Schmitz. In November 1965, previews were organized in Bonn, Duisburg, Kassel, and Kiel. Precisely 2,205 of those who attended were interviewed. According to an Atlas press release, the audience wasn't subliminally affected by the movie. On the contrary, it was stated that they became more critical about fascist tendencies after seeing ***Kolberg*** and the supplement documentary. Immediately, Eckelkamp rushed out and prepared more NS films for post-war release, the second being another Harlan production, ***Der grosse König*** (***The Great King***) with commentary by SPIEGEL columnist Martin Morlock; the third was ***Hitlerjunge Quex*** (***Hitler Youth Quex***).

Eckelkamp, however, hadn't seen ***Kolberg*** yet. When he finally saw it having paid for it, he realized that he had bought the rights to a rather pathetic movie that in scope and grandeur in no way equaled the American evergreen Goebbels loved so much: ***Gone with the Wind***. Even David Stewart Hull who compared it with Selznick's production of 1939 had to concede that ***Kolberg*** was far too talky and that it took an interminable amount of time to get the action going. [162] The prominent cast was theatrical and hammy, and Kristina Söderbaum's naive, amateurish performance ruined part of the movie.

And if that wasn't enough, Eckelkamp was accused of being a revanchist and spitting Nazi venom by critics in West and East. Gleefully *Junge Welt,* an East-Berlin paper, cited West-German cinema attendants:

I served as an officer for Adolf Hitler, in the Third Reich. I must tell you that I admire the courage of this political system [Federal Republic] *to show a movie like this.*

The hold-out movie didn't save the Third Reich and it didn't save Eckelkamp and Atlas. The company was forced to file for bankruptcy at the end of 1966. Instead of four million, "only" 400,000 moviegoers came to see the Veit Harlan/Joseph Goebbels epic.

Harlan didn't live long enough to watch the reissue of his epic (he died on April 13, 1964, on the Isle of Capri), but he survived the war and couldn't be stopped to continue his kind of films. He had met Goebbels for the last time on February 17, 1945, a few days after the massive air raid against Dresden. By this time, Goebbels was already determined to depart this life. Harlan wasn't.

162 *Film in the Third Reich: A Study of the German Cinema 1933-1945*. Berkeley and Los Angeles: University of California Press, 1969.

Even If Everything Shatters: Life Must Go On

While Harlan thought it more wise to turn his back on filmmaking for the final months of the Third Reich, Babelsberg process shot expert Gerhard Huttula worked in the meantime feverishly on the back-projection plates for Ufa's last but unfinished wartime epic. It was to be Karl Ritter's biggest project in the Third Reich. Ufa production chief Wolfgang Liebeneiner welcomed him back at Ufa Babelsberg, and Ritter had high hopes to continue directing but then Liebeneiner took over directorial chores by himself and reduced Ritter to producer of ***Das Leben geht weiter*** (***Life Goes On***). Goebbels had dictated parts of the script. It was a literally bombastic film project that was supposed to issue a general proclamation to hold out and stick together in times of disaster. It was the first *Trümmerfilm*, a production that was filmed in the ruins of destroyed cities. Goebbels, who pushed the project while German cities were smashed to pieces, wanted "to show a Berlin air raid night in a block of flats in the Hansaviertel [in Berlin Tiergarten]. It will involve the whole building, with all its individual floors and families."

The plot according to an Ufa synopsis:

In the Zehlendorf apartment of graduate engineer Ewald Martens, a small circle of friends and cohabitants has gathered to celebrate the birthday of the young housewife Gundel. [...] *For a few happy hours, they forget the burden and seriousness of the war until the little party was stopped dead due to the proclamation of the evacuation of Berlin. Everybody understands that Berlin is a heavily endangered city and the whole population sets to work earnestly and forcefully to support the activities of the government. Not only children and women are dispatched in long extra trains, even furniture and household goods, artwork and cultural artifacts are removed to safe places.*

Martens, too, sends his two little children to the grandparents who live in the countryside. The farewell isn't easy for Gundel but when a few days later the siren boasts once more and the city becomes the target of a nightly air raid she is quite grateful to know that the children are in safety. While the population in all precincts of Berlin joins to build trench shelters, the work and planning in the Ministry of Armaments and War Production [Albert Speer] goes on at full speed. Martens is commissioned to develop and finish a reliable air raid night vision device by the end of November which will indicate the approach of enemy bombers to our night fighters. He plunges into work with a vengeance. Technicians and scientists, laboratories and armament factories he sets in motion. But the difficulties are piling up, problems with transportation, destroyed factories, unsuccessful test series - and time is of the essence, the danger grows from day to day. And again and again new setbacks! Grimly determined, with ultimate tension Martens continues his work. He barely eats and sleeps, for weeks he doesn't come home. Gundel worries about him, and she is concerned about her girlfriend, librarian Lenore Carius, who has completely changed lately. During an air raid, she has met a fighter pilot, Captain Hoesslin. She loves him and feels that he is in love with her. But Hoesslin feels so obliged to his duties as a soldier that he tries to free himself from every relationship of a private nature and doesn't want to see Lenore anymore. Puzzled and desperately, she has to face his decision but cannot grasp it. Gundel understands her girlfriend. She, too, is deeply convinced that beyond fight and death one has to approve of the eternal values of human relationship and has to work up the courage. She talks about it to Martens. [...] *Only a few hours they can spend together but these give new vigor to the worn and burned-out man. Finally, he is able to master the task he was commissioned to solve. The production starts, and the night vision device turns out a valuable asset to the night fighters during the heavy terror attacks in November. The enemy bombers have serious losses although it cannot prevent Berlin from making severe sacrifices. To Martens' unspeakable grief Gundel is among them.*

Life Goes On is a quite surprising project, full of realism and authenticity. Camera assistant Heinz Pehlke remembered that they had a crane to lift the camera towards the bomb bays high above the floor of the stage. Gustav Knuth was cast as engineer Martens, Hilde Krahl as his wife Gundel, Marianne Hoppe as Lenore and Viktor de Kowa as Hoesslin. A stunning number of supporting actors including Heinrich George, Karl Schönböck (who filled in for Willy Fritsch) and Hilde Körber completed the cast. Participating in such an important movie meant to become part of a *Gottbegnadetenliste*, a list of the Divinely Gifted approved by Hitler and Goebbels who wouldn't be drafted at the eleventh hour. In March 1945, the film crew departed for Luneburg Heath, far away from the Soviet troops that slowly approached from the East towards the German capital. Over there, they didn't have to fear bombings and air raids. Liebeneiner not only hoped that film work would prevent him and his crew from serving as Volkssturm men but he got the absurd idea that he could finish it, in some different way, after the war. Ironically, most of the footage was lost during location shooting in the Luneburg Heath, where it was deposited in two zinc caskets to wait for the end of the war. One or two shots survived in a demo reel of trick shots compiled by Gerhard Huttula in late 1944 and are now in the collection of this author.

Götterdämmerung: The Führer's Last Stand

For his end Hitler didn't need a director. He was his own director, with Goebbels promoted to serve as co-director. Hitler had his own blockbuster in mind inspired by Fritz Lang's ***Nibelungen*** and *Götterdämmerung*, the fourth and final part of Richard Wagner's *Ring* cycle. Wagner's *Rienzi*, Hitler once claimed, initiated his quest. *Götterdämmerung* was chosen to draw the curtain. *The Twilight of the Gods*: That was it - as Hitler was the founder of his own religion and hoped that his death would make him sort of immortal:

His idea of the supreme expression of opera was the final scene in Götterdämmerung, *and whenever he witnessed this finale in Bayreuth, he would turn around in his darkened box, seek out the hand of Frau Winifred Wagner, and "breathe a deeply moved Handkuss upon it".* [...] *When the end came for Hitler, he staged his own* Götterdämmerung *in his Berlin bunker. He refused to surrender, preferring the taking of his own life over an unheroic end. By his absolute refusal to even consider capitulation, he ensured vast, horrible destruction of lives and property long after these losses could have had any possible effect upon the outcome of the war. Hitler lived out his fantasy to the end; to the fullest; precipitating the realization of his favorite operatic scene, the final destruction of the gods and Valhalla.* [163]

In Hitler's drug-addicted delirium, Richard Wagner's and Fritz Lang's scenes of mass destruction were transformed into reality in the total destruction of Berlin:

Götterdämmerung ended with Hitler and what remained of his entourage planning the rescue of Berlin. Hitler dreamed up imaginary armies that would fight the Soviet forces to the end. It was clear to many that Hitler had lost all sense of reality but such was his power over those at the top of the Nazi Party that no one challenged him. In his book about the last days of Hitler, Hugh Trevor-Roper described the world Hitler lived in as "cloud cuckoo-land". Some of his orders bordered on the bizarre. [...]

On April 29th – as the Götterdämmerung came to an inevitable conclusion –

163 Reuben D. Ferguson, *An Investigation Into the Effects of the Music of Richard Wagner on the Pseudo-Mysticism of Adolf Hitler and the Third Reich.* April 15, 1994. http://www.arkrat.net/hitwag.htm.

Hitler married Eva Braun and then dictated his last will and testament. He then committed suicide - not quite the ending for one of Wagner's heroes as in his operas the heroes would be expected to fight to the bitter end. [164]

Even today's Marvel and Disney-trained blockbuster audiences know about *Götterdämmerung* and Valhalla - thanks to Mighty Thor as played by Christian Hemsworth but they are not aware of how closely they are watching a Teutonic opera: the Führer's "last stand". Death of love is a motif in Richard Wagner's *Tristan and Isolde*, and even Wagner was once near to suicide. Suicide is a topic in German literature, Goethe's *Die Leiden des jungen Werther (The Sorrows of Young Werther)*, and in the German mind - and Hitler took refuge in this mental state when everything around him collapsed.

The day of his suicide, April 30, was known as Walpurgis Night: Burning of the Witches:

It hasn't escaped the notice of many people, especially in the last 50 or so years, that Hitler's suicide occurred on the old pagan holiday of Walpurgisnacht, the spring festival of Germanic Europe that traditionally celebrates the end of winter. Due to its association with pre-Christian religions of Europe, Walpurgisnacht is sometimes associated with occultism, witchcraft and similar milieu. So, it seems, is the Nazi regime itself, a perceived link that has proven to be very pervasive in popular culture and belief. [...]

Indeed, the mythology of Nazi occultism is a dangerous distortion of history. As argued by Swedish scholar Mattias Gardell, the view that the Third Reich was heavily motivated by or used occult themes and practices tends to paint Hitler and the Nazis as a band of "evil sorcerers" who attained power by casting some sort of mystic spell over the German people, who followed them out of compulsion. This is not what happened at all. Millions of ordinary Germans, the vast majority of them rational and in their right minds, supported the Nazis for years, or at least did not oppose them. Casting Hitler as a sort of Svengali, using witchcraft and black magic to entrance the German people, is utterly false and leads to an "it can't happen

---

164 C N Trueman "Gotterdammerung": historylearningsite.co.uk.

here" kind of complacency. It's a convenient shortcut that absolves us of trying to understand a difficult and dark episode in recent history. [165]

Before he and his wife committed suicide right after their "Führer's" end, taking their children with them to death, Goebbels admonished his last cohorts to behave bravely, *Gentlemen, a hundred years on, a splendid color film will be shown about these terrible times we're living through. And you won't like to be pictured as cowards with audiences whooping and whistling when they see you on the silver screen, won't you? Halten Sie durch! Persevere!*

Other leading Nazis joined the suicide club: Heinrich Himmler, Hermann Göring (before they could hang him at the Nuremberg trials), Robert Ley (in Nuremberg too), Bernhard Rust, or Josef Terboven, the NS Reich Commissioner for Norway, who sat down in a bunker on the Skaugum compound southwest of Oslo and detonated 50 kg of dynamite. But not only the leaders, foot soldiers, too: In Berlin alone, more than 7,000 suicides were reported in 1945, most of them women, fearing the revenge of the Red Army. [166]

The Third Reich itself had become a horror movie.

Oddly enough, the actor who portrayed Hagen von Tronje, the most stubborn but doomed Nibelung hero who had killed Siegfried and found his death at the side of his king in the Castle of the Huns, died the same day as his Führer, on April 30, 1945: Hans Adalbert (von) Schlettow, born Hans Adalbert Droescher. At the Karl May Festival in Werder, he played Santer who killed the noble Apache, *Winnetou*. Hitler and his vassal Schlettow didn't survive the Third Reich. Same is true for an actress named Dora Gerson. It didn't help her that she had dubbed the evil queen in Hitler's favorite Disney picture ***Snow White***. It didn't help that she was the first wife of Veit Harlan. It didn't help that she acted in two early Karl May silents. Hitler adored Karl

165 *A Walpurgisnacht fable: the seductive myth of Nazi occultism.* https://seanmunger.com/2014/04/30/a-walpurgisnacht-fable-the-seductive-myth-of-nazi-occultism/.

166 See Christian Goeschel, *Suicide in Nazi Germany.* Oxford University Press, 2015 and Florian Huber, *Promise Me You'll Shoot Yourself: The Mass Suicide of Ordinary Germans in 1945.*

May but she was Jewish and had to die. So she was murdered in Auschwitz in 1943. But Karl May, his adventure stories survived - and with them some ideals of the “Führer”.

POSTLUDE

Marianne Simson, Queen of Fairy Tales, and Peter Lorre, The Lost One

In 1939, when it became clear that Disney's ***Snow White***, although shown exclusively for Hitler, Goebbels and a selected few, wouldn't be generally released in Nazi Germany, Hubert Schonger, a producer of documentaries and fairy tales, and his distributor Willy Wohlrabe (Jugendfilm) took a chance to rush out a black and white live-action ***Snow White*** of their own. The starring role provided a big chance for 19-year-old Marianne Simson, daughter of a Berlin insurance agent. Marianne started to act on screen the same year, 1935, in a propaganda film titled ***Friesennot,*** as she became, like so many young German girls, a member of BDM Bund Deutscher Mädchen.

In July 1944, she met an athletic battalion commander by the name of Friedrich Goes who was on rest and recuperation in Bansin on the Isle of Usedom, not far from Peenemünde. He had just escaped the reconquest of Crimea Island by the Red Army with some of his soldiers. Casually, he told Simson that the retreat of the Germans wasn't that heroic operation NS propaganda wanted to make people believe. And, concerning the assassination attempt on Hitler, he said, *"Too bad that it didn't work out."* At a celebration of her 24th birthday, Simson mentioned Goes' remark and revealed it to SS officer Otto Skorzeny who had recently liberated Mussolini on Hitler's command.

Marianne Simson's head acts (thanks to camera effects) opposite Hans (*Münchhausen*) Albers in 1942.
Courtesy of Jens Geutebrück, Coronaretro Archives

Goes was arrested but denied that remark. Simson, however, insisted that she had heard him saying exactly that. The court martial discharged Goes because some high-ranked officers put in a good word for him and some movie people bitched about faithless Marianne Simson. Simson, offended in her pride, complained to Goebbels who had Goes arrested a second time. Goes survived just by chance. Right after the war, ***Snow White*** Simson and her parents were interned by the Soviets, due to the Goes affair. Sentenced to eight years in the penitentiary, Simson was released prematurely in 1952 and immediately was hailed by her fans as martyr of Soviet torture.

There had to be some sacrificial lambs - but not too many. And even they escaped like Miss Simson. Or Harry Piel, who was sentenced to six months in prison and prohibited from working until 1949 but finally saved by denazification that enabled him to found a new film company, Ariel Film, in 1950. He was able to produce new and release old films (many of them, however, destroyed in air raids). Harry Piel died on March 27, 1963, in Munich. And not to forget Werner Krauss!

Werner Krauss had to fight his past portrayals on stage (as ***Merchant of***

Venice) and in ***Jew Suss***. In 1948, he had to appear before a de-Nazification court in Stuttgart. In his defense, he produced a letter he had received from George Bernard Shaw, asserting that he thought it "vindictive stupidity" to hold Krauss responsible for the crimes of the regime. Eventually, he was convicted as a "minor offender" and fined. But the audience needed time to accept this until he received honors again. There were some riots when he returned to the Berlin stage in Ibsen's *John Gabriel Borkman*. Survivors of the holocaust held large banners: *Werner Krauss, Go Home!* But after some discussion, he was awarded the Bundesverdienstkreuz (Order of Merit of the Federal Republic) in 1958, made movies, stage plays. Krauss' memory had become weak and had small, sometimes big leaks.

In his autobiography, *Das Schauspiel meines Lebens*, he mentioned ***Jew Suss*** only once: *I refused, no, not refused, I said: I did not feel like doing it.* And: *If I hadn't played it, someone else would have done it.* So he considered it better to pocket the money himself. One cannot please everybody, Krauss claimed: Right-wingers would complain about his portrayals of the Captain of Köpenick or General York; the others, well, about Shylock and ***Jew Suss***... He sure had forgotten that as early as 1920 he talked to colleagues about ideas that in 1933 were in high demand.

His ***Jew Suss*** director, Veit Harlan, faced some problems, too:

It all began when Goebbels' top director needed a license from the Western Allies to continue his work in the film industry, an *Unbedenklichkeitsbescheinigung*, which meant a certificate that there was no objection for political reasons. The commission was basically willing to release Harlan with a clean record as *unbelastet. Tägliche Rundschau,* a Berlin newspaper, called this a scandal. He was still the "devil's director", who later described Goebbels as sort of a charming devil with whom one should have sympathy. In early 1948, Harlan and his wife Kristina attended the première of Kurt Maetzig's (East German) DEFA film ***Ehe im Schatten*** (***Marriage in the Shadows***), modeled after the tragic suicide of actor Joachim Gottschalk, his Jewish wife Meta and their son on November 6, 1941, but the audience regarded the couple's presence as annoying, and the Harlans had to leave before the film started. As a reaction, the commission hesitated to issue the denazification certificate. Then, *Vereinigung der Verfolgten des Nazi-Regimes (VVN, Association of Victims of Nazi Regime Persecution)* and *Notgemeinschaft der durch die Nürnberger Gesetze Betroffenen (Emergency Action Organization of Persons Affected by the Nuremberg Laws)* entered a petition accusing Veit Harlan of crimes against humanity. The petition was supported by the Jewish community in Hamburg and the executive committee of the Social Democratic Party. On March 3, 1949, the Land Court of Hamburg opened a trial and called in 35 witnesses, most of them former colleagues and actors of Harlan. Harlan appeared and exclaimed pathetically, "My party is art. I am a patriot. I love my homeland. I have received fantastic film offers from South America. I have refused all of them. I want to stay here and work here. I am no politician. I am a director." The jury seemed to agree. Harlan even went so far as to quote former Jewish colleagues from the Weimar Republic's stages as involuntary witnesses: Max Reinhardt, Guido Herzfeld, Leopold Jessner, and Fritz Kortner.

After the first trial, which ended on April 23, 1948, Norbert Wollheim, the chairman of the Council of the Jewish Community, wrote:

Veit Harlan, director of the anti-Semitic smear-film **Jud Süss**, *is exonerated of crimes against humanity in Hamburg. With ovations, which started in the courtroom and were not reprimanded by the judge, the former movie hero of the "Thousand-Year Reich" is lifted on the shoulders by his fellow men and with triumphant cheering carried to his vehicle... The legally necessary causal connection between the crimes of the Nazi regime and this shoddy anti-Semitic effort, so the judges have decided, has not been proved.*

Harlan was allowed to return to his beloved profession. He - and even his biographer Frank Noack - regarded his involvement in ***Jew Suss*** as a trap [167] and what they call in German language *Verstrickung*: entanglement, entrapment. He saw himself as the fly that ended up in Dr. Goebbels' spiderweb. In the end, *he* was the victim, not those who ended up in the concentration camps.

167 Frank Noack, *Veit Harlan. Des Teufels Regisseur.* Munich: Belleville, 2000, p. 176.

But there was another adversary for the Harlans to overcome in the person of Erich Lüth, then in charge of the Hamburg State Press Office. In an open letter, Lüth demanded that Germany's reputation shouldn't be ruined by robust money makers, i.e. film producers and distributors like Ilse Kubaschewski of Gloria Film who were going to re-hire the devil's director, creating distrust in Germany's *Wiederaufbau* (rebuilding), but all protests were thrust aside in the appeal proceedings. Lüth was bitter about that, "The Jews came to Auschwitz and Theresienstadt. Nothing happened to Veit Harlan. All that was expected from him was - silence. There was no need for him to become a director again, there would have been other professions open to him. He could have become a film editor, prop master, cabinet-maker or usher in a cinema, door-keeper or 'last man' in the strict sense of Jannings' film (i.e., the toilet man of F. W. Murnau's ***Der letzte Mann/The Last Laugh***) if he would have been reasonable enough to moderate himself." [168]

Not only did Harlan leave the courtroom as a free man in 1949-50. A third trial in 1958 that resulted in a verdict by Germany's highest court, Bundesverfassungsgericht (Federal Constitutional Court), discharged him to the fullest. Harlan proceeded and made mostly unimportant movies as most of his former comrades did: a two-part adventure yarn along the lines of Joe May's ***Indian Tomb*** titled ***Sterne über Colombo*** (***Stars over Colombo***, 1953) and ***Die Gefangene des Maharadscha*** (***Circus Girl***, 1954), a movie about the spy in Tokyo, Doktor Richard Sorge, whose deed was titled an act of treason, disloyalty against the National Socialist State (***Verrat an Deutschland***, 1955), and, in the footsteps of Richard Oswald's silent ***Anders als die anderen*** with Conrad Veidt, a production that Frank Noack called *a homosexual remake of* **Jew Suss: *Anders als du und ich*** (U.S. release title: ***The Third Sex***, 1957) and ***Liebe kann wie Gift sein*** (***Love Can Be Like Poison***, 1958), which in a way opened the path to producer Gero Wecker's Teutonic Enlightenment series written for the screen by Oswalt Kolle, a journalist from BILD Zeitung who stylized himself the West-German Pope of Sex.

---

168 Statement in a radio broadcast, Nord-West-Deutscher Rundfunk NWDR, 22 November 1951.

Harlan complained about German youth that, in his words, was smart but had lost its center. In the end Harlan turned green in the face when a producer dared to offer him, the artsy star director, of all things: a **horror** picture, a stupid, disgusting piece which another director shot with a well-known French actor. The producer was Wolf C. Hartwig, the other director was Russian-Jewish émigré Victor Trivas; the French actor Michel Simon whose head was cut off and, thanks to a mirror shot, rested on a table in nutrition. The title was ***Die Nackte und die Satan*** (1959), known in America as ***The Head***.

In an interview conducted by Günter Peter Straschek for his TV series about ***Film Emigration from Nazi Germany*** [169], Franz Marischka, after the war a director of comedies and soft sex, told that he had asked Jewish émigré actor Fritz Kortner to maybe shake hands with his former friend and colleague Veit Harlan. Basically Kortner who had returned to Germany agreed but then would reconsider and say: *If I would do this I would have to explain for the rest of my life why I did this.*

In the 1960s, while Harlan was still alive, Stanley Kubrick seemed to be obsessed by the curse of Veit Harlan. Christiane Kubrick talked about this obsession after her husband's death with SPIEGEL journalists Urs Jenny and Martin Wolf:

SPIEGEL: *In which way are you, a born Harlan, related to the director of the hate film* **Jew Suss***?*

Kubrick: *He is my uncle.*

SPIEGEL: *Have you met him?*

Kubrick: *Of course. I have introduced Stanley to Veit back then in Munich [when he shot* **Paths to Glory***]. But Stanley was not only just interested in him. He would have loved to make a movie about the absolutely normal life under the aegis of Joseph Goebbels. Alas, the material didn't add up to a screenplay.* [170]

Not only were the old movies of Nazi times re-released: Heinz Rühmann

169 *Filmemigration aus Nazideutschland*, WDR Fernsehen 1975.
170 DER SPIEGEL #35/1999, August 30, 1999.

in ***Die Feuerzangenbowle,*** Hans Albers in ***Münchhausen,*** Kristina Söderbaum in ***Immensee*** and ***Opfergang.*** The postwar film industry - as postwar military - was established by the old forces.

Totally ignored was Peter Lorre who returned to Germany to direct a movie: ***Der Verlorene*** (***The Lost One***), the story of Dr. Karl Rothe, a Nazi scientist murderer, who lives under the name Dr. Neumeister in postwar Hamburg. Brecht would have welcomed Lorre at this East-Berlin theater starring him in a performance of *Herr Puntila und sein Knecht Matti (Herr Puntila and His Servant Matti)* and even wrote a poem to lure his friend back, but Lorre decided in favor of Arnold Pressburger. Pressburger was the producer of Fritz Lang-Bert Brecht's ***Hangmen Also Die***.

This film is not completely fiction. The events are based on factual reports from the past years.

The screenplay was a collaboration of Lorre, Benno Vigny and Axel Eggebrecht. Eggebrecht, "*He consciously connected with* **M**; *that cannot be disputed.*"

What Lorre wanted was another **M**, *a classic film that would put him back at the top of his profession. Eager to trade grease paint for a director's chair, he imagined making a film, free of conditions and restraints, from beginning to end. The actor-director held on to an old dream of creating "a production team that sticks together and can go anywhere and do anything to make a film or a play" without "the responsibility to a company and the weight of departmental overheads."* [171]

Alas, there was an unlucky star looming above this dark *noir* production (Pressburger died during production) that resulted not in a box office bonanza but a box office disaster.

Occasionally, American film companies were seen in Berlin and other German cities. Billy Wilder returned to Berlin with Marlene Dietrich and Jean Arthur in tow to shoot exteriors for Paramount's ***A Foreign Affair*** (1948), while original Nazi stars such as Claus Clausen, Margot Hielscher, Walter Janssen, Sepp Rist, Gertrud Wolle and Otto Gebühr were seen in MGM's

171 Stephen D. Youngkin, *The Lost One: A Life of Peter Lorre.* Lexington, Kentucky: The University Press of Kentucky, 2005.

The Devil Makes Three (1952), directed by Hungarian Andrew Marton and starring Gene Kelly and Italian actress Pier Angeli. The production shot in Munich, elsewhere in Bavaria and in Salzburg:

Appreciation is expressed to the Office of the High Commissioner of Germany, the United States Army Military Police Corps, and the Munich City Police for their cooperation while filming this motion picture in Germany and Austria.

Captain Jeff Elliot, a U.S. Air Force pilot, returns to Germany to find the family which aided in his escape from a prisoner-of-war camp. He finds one member of the family still alive, a 19-year-old girl. All of a sudden, he stumbles upon a secret Nazi group led by Clausen (who had played the former Hitler Youth leader in ***Hitlerjunge Quex***) as a fear-crazed neo-Nazi gold smuggler who is chased into the ruin's of Hitler's Berghof.

One who emerged totally unscathed, just the opposite to Harlan, was surprisingly Wolfgang Liebeneiner. Liebeneiner was entrusted with some of the most successful West German productions of the 1950s: ***Urlaub auf Ehrenwort*** (***Furlough on Word of Honor***), the 1955 remake of a 1938 Nazi film, ***Die Trapp Familie*** (***The Trapp Family,*** 1956), which in the United States became ***The Sound of Music***; ***Auf Wiedersehen, Franziska*** (produced by Artur Brauner's CCC Film Company), the 1957 remake of Helmut Käutner's NS film version of 1941, ***Taiga*** (1958), and ***Die Trapp Familie in Amerika*** (***The Trapp Family in America***, 1958). In the 1960s, he turned to TV and directed a 4-part ***Treasure Island.***

The Minister of Public Enlightenment and Propaganda had called Liebeneiner "young, modern, ambitious, industrious and fanatical" in his diary entry of June 11, 1937, and finally made him production chief of Ufa Studios.

Hitler was also very keen on the actor and director Wolfgang Liebeneiner. He expressly forbade Liebeneiner from being called up into the armed forces. The dictator and his propaganda minister even involved themselves in the marital problems of this creator of important propaganda material. While Goebbels was still discussing 'a number of personal matters that are depressing him very much and that could potentially cause a personal crisis for him' with Liebeneiner and his partner Hilde Krahl (29.11.1942), Hitler had already cleared up 'the matters': he agreed that after Liebeneiner's divorce from the Jewish actress Ruth Hellberg, her son from a previous marriage, who grew up as Andreas Liebeneiner, should not be sent to the extermination camp. [172]

Liebeneiner always felt he didn't need any theory to explain the basics of filmmaking, "You cannot develop art from theory. The example of expressionism was the most recent, striking proof. The German film will get from its *Führung* (leadership) what is within human power regarding innovations in organization, technical improvements, and spiritual direction." [173]

In 1954, Liebeneiner teamed Rühmann and Hans Albers in ***Auf der Reeperbahn nachts um halb eins*** (***Boulevard des plaisirs***, 1954). At that time, Rühmann was briefly considered box office poison because a production company (Comedia Filmgesellschaft) he had founded with Alf Teichs went bankrupt. But Liebeneiner's film and Hans Quest's ***Charley's Tante*** (***Charley's Aunt***, 1956) put him on the map again. Both films were produced by Kurt Ulrich's Berolina Film.

In 1957-58, Ilse Kubaschewski's Gloria film distribution company that successfully released Herbert J. Yates' Republic pictures to post-war German cinemas joined forces with Kurt Ulrich and announced a new picture with the popular actor: ***Ich war ein kleiner PG.*** (***I Only Was a Small Party Member***), the story of a petit-bourgeois who wore a party badge but only was a fellow traveler. Peter Lorre's friend Axel Eggebrecht, a former KPD member and twice interned at the Hainewald Concentration Camp, was asked to cook up a story that would fit the title. But Kurt Ulrich, the producer, found it too harsh to fit Rühmann. Eggebrecht described the little party member as a naive, gullible character, but Kurt Ulrich and Ilse Kubaschewski wanted him innocent so that audiences could easily identify with him. The ballad was finally tailor-made for Rühmann by writers Robert Adolf Stemmle and Herrmann Mostar. With Rühmann cast in the lead, dramaturge Dr. Manfred Barthel speculated, you already see the whole movie. Of course they

172 Felix Moeller, *The Film Minister*, p. 167.

173 Film-Kurier, January 29, 1941.

had to change the story a little: Rühmann was to play a small Pg. who just *accidentally* slided into the NSDAP, so was no real Nazi. Ilse Kubaschewski was enthusiastic: *Millions of former party members will feel addressed.* Gloria's PR department got rolling and knocked out first blurbs: *The man in the street [der Mann aus dem Volke] who has to pay for everything just wants to live an unmolested life. He wants to cultivate his little garden, go to see a movie with his wife... But the march step of world history always scares him out of his modest coziness.* Here is the German word Rühmann was always associated with: coziness - *Gemütlichkeit.* This story certainly would match his character and help his screen image: *A little uninfluential party member. What else could he do? He joined.*

Stemmle was asked to translate this idea into a final draft and, while doing research, he found what he thought would be a reasonable excuse for becoming a Nazi: On January 30, 1933, the little man named Wilhelm Krehlert, a capable agent for wallpaper and member only of a glee club, had mixed up his coat with that of a party member who wore a party badge under the lapel - and from then on couldn't say no and filled the part as most Germans did. Oops! When "all of a sudden" bad things happened and Jews were deported and war started, he would have loved to get out, but now it was too late for that nice family man. After the war, denazified, he got off cheaply and continued to be the nice neighbor as if nothing happened: no war, no holocaust. When critics learned about the project they sneered: *The terror gets cozy, infamy is rendered with homey features.*

We just wanted to describe the Nazi time from a different perspective, Stemmle apologized.

At the last moment, Rühmann got cold feet. Producer Kurt Ulrich remembered the situation: *He simply hadn't the guts back then. Regularly, he received phone calls from people who told him: Heini, let it be, we were always neutral.* But when Rühmann eventually was cast in the film version of Johannes Mario Simmel's ***Der Schulfreund*** (***My School Chum***, 1960), another Gloria/Kubaschewski release, he became such a little guy. Directed by Robert Siodmak, Rühmann starred as Ludwig Fuchs who is declared nuts when he outs himself as Göring's school friend and writes him a letter to please stop the already lost war. After the war, Fuchs has problems to prove that he isn't insane. In the wake of Rühmann's ***Schulfreund***, Ulrich tried to revive ***The Little Party Member***, but now didn't have Rühmann in mind but a different actor, Martin Held, who had played with Rühmann in Helmut Käutner's ***Der Hauptmann von Köpenick*** (***The Captain of Köpenick***). Nothing came of it. The project remained unmade. [174] Stemmle published the story as a novel. [175]

174 *PG: Ballade vom Mitläufer.* In: DER SPIEGEL 12/1960, March 16, 1960.
175 Bertelsmann Books.

Resurrection of the Dead, Part One: The Desert Fox

While Goebbels and family committed suicide, Dr. Winkler and his family escaped with tractor and trailer. But the war didn't end - at least not on the screen.

For many years, war films remained the bread and butter of the film industry in post-war Germany and elsewhere:

In England the hoopla about Rommel exploded anew when American 20th Century-Fox premiered their new Rommel film in London, based on the Rommel biography of British brigadier general Desmond Young. [...]

For this film America refrained from the usual Hollywood pattern of the arrogant German general. In this Rommel picture all German generals are portrayed sympathetically, with the only exception of [Wilhelm] Keitel, who according to reality doesn't appear as militarist but as Hitler's minion. [176]

The reason for the existence of a production like ***The Desert Fox*** (1951) with James Mason in the title role was the Cold War which made the enemy into an ally. All of a sudden, many German elite soldiers turned to heroes, misled by their Führer, but to no fault of their own. Actually, they were needed to build a new German army.

In the movie, Rommel is disgusted by Hitler's command that his armies seek "victory or death". Gradually, he turns against the Führer. Rommel's opposition to Hitler has helped create his image as the Second World War German field marshal it's okay to like. Though he fought for Hitler, he never joined the Nazi party. There is little evidence that he personally held anti–semitic beliefs. On the other hand, he did fight for Hitler - and admired him.

Because the film focuses on the last few months of Rommel's life, it shows much more of Rommel doubting Hitler than loyally serving him - a balance some feel has been pushed too far. When **The Desert Fox** *came out, it was slammed in the New York Times as "a tenderised Hollywood laudation" of "the leader responsible for the deaths of thousands upon thousands of British troops, the crafty general so righteously hated as the dragoman of Hitler". It has been argued by some historians*

176 *Zunehmende Begeisterung*, In: DER SPIEGEL 42/1951, p. 30.

in recent years that Rommel's African war was a less honourable one than many have believed. [177]

The first time Adolf Hitler appeared as star of a German feature film was in 1955 in ***Der letzte Akt***. In the United States it was seen as ***The Last Ten Days:***

It is not a pleasant picture, nor is it a particularly significant or edifying one, as written by Erich Maria Remarque and directed by the German veteran, G. W. Pabst. It is based upon research assembled in M. A. Musmanno's book "Ten Days to Die", *and it conveys no information or speculation that has not already been fully publicized. Hitler, played by Albin Skoda, alternately flames with wild-eyed hope or flares into fits of screaming fury, while his staff generals languish, paralyzed, and the various smaller people in the bunker fearfully or fatalistically await their doom. There is a great deal of military detail about the final deterioration and collapse of the armies and the Luftwaffe, which probably absorbed German audiences when the picture was shown there, but is technical and tiresome here. And there is less than might be fascinating about Hitler's mistress, Eva Braun. What there is of sympathy in the drama mainly centers on a young captain, played by Oskar Werner, who is a courier from one of the hard-pressed army groups. He arrives at the bunker to try to get the Fuehrer to dispatch reinforcements to the corps, and he waits in despair and frustration to witness the macabre goings-on. As played by the blond Herr Werner, who will be remembered from the American film* **Decision Before Dawn**, *in which he appeared as a young Nazi turncoat in the last year of World War II, this captain is a decent, rational fellow. He contrasts sharply to the obvious maniac and the frightened or cynical professional soldiers who swill brandy and bootlick to him. It is evident that this character is included to symbolize the decent Germans who were drawn along by Hitler and had to suffer his Goetterdaemmerung.* [178]

WW2 on screen was more alive in both German states, Federal as well as German Democratic Republic, after than during the war. And in times of Cold War, both German states needed clean militarists, men like Oskar

177 Alex von Tunzelmann, *The Desert Fox: does it capture the real Rommel?* In: The Guardian, October 6, 2011.

178 Bosley Crowther, *'Last Ten Days': German Film Tells of Hitler's Downfall.* In: The New York Times, April 12, 1956.

Werner, to build the Bundeswehr, a name suggested by former Hitler General (and Liberal politician) Hasso von Manteuffel, in the West in 1955 and the National People's Army (NVA Nationale Volksarmee) in the East in 1956.

Hollywood's ***Desert Fox*** encouraged the former editor of Hitler's ***Deutsche Wochenschau***, Heinrich Roellenbleg, to compile a German heroic screen poetry: ***Das war unser Rommel*** (***That Was Our Rommel***). Roellenbleg was supported by composer Norbert Schultze (*Bombs on England, Lilli Marleen,* the ***Kolberg*** film score), former Wehrmacht general Fritz Bayerlein, who later served as consultant on ***The Guns of Navarone***, and Volksbund Deutsche Kriegsgräberfürsorge (German War Graves Commission). The film was premiered by Constantin Film on July 2, 1953, in Würzburg. This film doesn't deal with Rommel's dissatisfaction with Hitler but with the battle that made him a hero among Hitler's generals, the Battle for Africa: *The desert between Tripolis and El Alamein, 2500 km sand, this was the battlefield and the location of a brutal campaign.*

From a contemporary review: *The appraisal brings not so much the film critic or the war historian into the arena than the democratic-minded citizen. The German businessmen, who, aided by some retired officers, examined the newsreel archives, present to the cinema goer a series of German and English war images from the time of the landing of the Africa Corps (February 1941) to the lost battle of Alamein (October 1942). The images may hold certain memories for former Africa soldiers, cinematically they are so uninteresting that the publication of this photo album could be registered with no comment - if there would be silence. Alas, the movie abandons the success of its intended image objectivity by making use for its explanatory notes of the dashing voice of a Prussian petty officer (Hermann Speelmanns): Instead of running a distant commentary from a post-war standpoint, an "adventurous sound" takes place that buys its authenticity by relinquishing the political evaluation of the war today still necessary. One cannot take the battles in Africa - even if they were a campaign without hate - out of the context of the criminal Hitler war; one cannot glorify the field marshal cavalierly as a genius of war without letting you at least feel that in the end he fought his battles for Hitler; one cannot do so because it would tamper with historical truth in a life-*

threatening way if one would enshrine the blind victims of Nazi tyranny only as efficient daredevils without the slightest empathy for real tragedy. This film is in its context of adventurous front and base scenes plus its What-sturdy-guys-we-were commentary designed in a way that in the end one consequently doesn't listen to the hypocritical demand for peace between nations but feels regret over the lost war. [179]

Heroism on all fronts! was what one of these military "documentaries" promised.

And where there was no war, there was what Germans call *Heimat*: *The word* Heimat *is famously untranslatable, holding multiple complementary meanings in German - descendance, heritage, tradition, your culture, your tribe, your family, your language: all make up one's own personal Heimat.* [180] The cities were bombed to ruins but the provinces, the picturesque (mostly southern) rural backdrops were still *Heimat* and turned immediately into a successful wave of films such as ***Schwarzwaldmädel*** (***The Black Forest Girl***, 1950), ***Grün ist die Heide (The Heath is Green***, 1951), ***Wenn am Sonntagabend die Dorfmusik spielt*** (1953), ***Der fröhliche Wanderer*** (***The Happy Wanderer***, 1955*)*, ***Schwarzwaldmelodie*** (***Black Forest Melody***, 1956) or ***Hoch droben auf dem Berg*** (1957), all produced by Berolina and Kurt Ulrich. Here the Germans were still allowed to wear uniforms, but only those of dashing forest rangers (as Rudolf Lenz in ***Der Förster vom Silberwald***, 1954) without thinking about war and surrender. The only enemies here were deer-poachers.

179 KB. in: Film-Dienst, Dusseldorf, July 17, 1953, No. 27, review #2616.

180 *Heimat(film) now: State of the Nation.* https://blog.goethe.de > arthousefilm > archive > 480-Heimatfilm-now-State-of-the-nation.html.

The German Disney

Here we meet Kurt Neumann, the head of Deutsche Zeichenfilm GmbH, again. Alas, we meet him as a corpse.

Werner Kruse, *Herr Neumann was an enthusiastic National Socialist, a sincere National Socialist, absolutely convinced. And he committed suicide in 1945 when the Russians came. A whole world cracked for him. He really was an enthusiastic National Socialist.* [181]

Stefanie Steuer, *When we met him I said, Good morning, Herr Neumann. - Heil Hitler, Frau Steuer. And when it came to an end and we realized already that the war was lost, we heard our dear Herr Neumann greeting for the first time: Good morning, Frau Steuer. I guess he was arrested by the Russians, together with our staff manager, Herr [Fritz] Böhme.* [182]

Anna-Luise Subatzus, *I felt sorry for Neumann. He had family, he had several kids.*

Neumann was after me. We had night watch, my friend Cäcilie, myself and Neumann, we were in one room and we had a campbed for two persons. Neumann called from downstairs that I should come down to him. I considered the situation fatal. I didn't go. And because I didn't, Neumann had a big soft spot for me. He never could have been nicer since the time I didn't go down to him. He had a very nice wife. [183]

Following a denunciation, Karl Neumann was arrested on May 14, 1945, by Soviet Soldiers and interned in a camp in Weesow near Werneuchen. One month later the former head of Deutsche Zeichenfilm GmbH was dead.

Gerhard Fieber, *He lived in Tegel Ort. There, they say, he had brought a few people he disliked into a concentration camp. Somebody denounced him. I can't tell if this is true but the Russians came and collected him. And apparently he has hanged himself in his cell.* [184]

The denunciations now went vice versa. On December 11, 1945, the

---

181 Dr. Kruse, Werner interviewed by J. P. Storm, August 9, 1988.

182 Steuer, Stefanie interviewed by J. P. Storm, September 22, 1988 and March 31, 1989.

183 Subatzus, Anna-Luise interviewed by J. P. Storm, 11 March 1989.

184 Fieber, Gerhard interviewed by J. P. Storm, 25 July 1988 and 10 March 1996.

Magistrat of the City of Berlin, Department for Volksbildung - Presseamt - informed the Political Examination Board of Creative Artists that it had received a letter concerning the well-known cartoonist and animation writer Horst von Möllendorff. The name of the informant was Robert Mewes:

Recently, I read in the Tägliche Rundschau or Deutsche Volkszeitung some articles about Käthe Kollwitz, Heinrich Zille and Otto Nagel. In this issue I read also reports about the caricaturist Herbert Sandberg, a former K.Z. convict, and about the cartoonist Penguin who was a disciple of both, Käthe Kollwitz and Otto Nagel. Now one sees regularly in the Berliner Zeitung (which is published by the city) cartoons drawn by a Mr. von M ö l l e n d o r f f . Pg. [party member] or not, during the Nazi time this Möllendorff published the most delightful Nazi propaganda drawings in the weekly Saxonian magazine Lustige Welt. He idealized Nazism and ridiculed everything that was anti-fascist; he glorified the war and agitated against all enemies of the Nazis. Was this Möllendorff ever a soldier? No, because the Nazis needed him. Just read the old issues of Lustige Welt and you will find Möllendorff again as an extremely active Nazi propagandist. The City of Berlin, however, insists to make this Mantelträger [shabby coat] its in-house cartoonist. With this you render the Antifa [anti-fascist movement] powerless. Ask M. himself or his colleagues, and you will have my word confirmed. [185]

Among the defendants of the German animation scene was also a man by the name of Bernhard Huth who was chief artist at the Ufa trickfilm studio. Regarding denazification, he was cited to the Denazification office of the Spruchkammer.

Bernhard H u t h .

Herr Huth explains that he belonged for a time to a Wehrmannschaft [brigade group]. But when he realized that this was no commando, he left this group.

In the years between 1941 and 1943, he executed the office of deputy Blockwart. The actual block leader was ill and wanted to pass this job on to him. He didn't accept this function voluntarily.

With the Party he didn't sign up himself. One day, the works committee of Ufa

185 Letter dated December 11, 1945.

explained that he would receive the party membership as sort of a gift. He didn't have the courage to reject it, particularly since he didn't have the feeling of doing something wrong. [...]

Answering the question if he felt being National Socialist, Herr Huth explained that an answer wouldn't be that easy; according to party doctrine, one couldn't call him so. Anyway, he never ever was a convinced National Socialist, otherwise he would have signed up to become a party member earlier than 1937 [actually Huth signed in 1933 and it sure didn't come to him as a present]. *Asked if he had regarded himself at any time a Nazi, Herr Huth expressed that the term Nazi today is more or less abused. If one would claim that that man is one of those Nazis, he is not. In his domain he was held in high esteem. There is another point he would make to prove that he didn't act like a Nazi: He always thought autonomously which was not compatible with party discipline. He didn't sympathize with many of the methods the Nazis applied. Yet in his mind the National Socialists took office due to democratic elections and so he had to respect their government and authority [Obrigkeit]. This is still his opinion today. Herr Huth is instructed about this error.*

Furthermore, Herr Huth says that he remains unpolitical to this day. Nobody can blame him for continuing to think this way. Back then, he did believe that National Socialism was a good cause, but later he realized that his opinion was wrong. Only because he did something that was politically stupid, he has to suffer now and live with his wife and two children in a room of 10 square meters. He feels treated today very unjustly. As Herr Huth closes his mind to any objective cautioning, he is expelled and it is left to his discretion to recollect himself and appear again in 8 days for consultation. [186]

Misfortune overshadowed also the life of Germany's most prominent supplier of animation films, Hans Fischerkoesen, before he rose like a phoenix from the ashes of the Third Reich. He was suspected of being a Nazi collaborator and producer of training films for the Wehrmacht, arrested by the Soviets and interned for two-and-a-half years in the former concentration camp Sachsenhausen. While he was in jail, he killed the time by painting the

186 Document Ceter/Bundesarchiv [Ferderal Archive]: Civilian Court Files of Huth, Bernhard. Berlin, March 3, 1948.

walls of the kitchen with allegoric drawings of anthropomorphically walking vegetables. Fischerkoesen was tough enough to bounce back.

I know, Dr. Hans Michael Fischerkoesen, Fischerkoesen's son, remembers, *that he had in mind, even after the war at his re-start, to adapt Wilhelm Busch for a movie. He wanted to do something based on Wilhelm Busch, a longer, almost feature-length film. This didn't happen for two reasons: He didn't find any sponsors and he got lots and lots of assignments from the advertising industry because he had a name that was still in demand after the war. So he had no time for anything else and shelved that project.*

At the end of the war, we were evacuated to a Saxon village. We have been evacuated from the end of '43 until early '44. Mothers with little children were sent to the countryside. My father remained in Potsdam where they still worked feverishly. Of course he had some support from the Netherlands and from Paris. We returned to the studio in some incredible circumstances from Bockelwitz - a village between Dresden and Leipzig - and then came the Russians who billetted on our place.

I was seven years old. My father never talked about this time. One has to understand: The time he spent in the camp, the time before, the whole Nazi time - they have closed the shutter, they didn't want to remember anymore. That was the past, it was dreadful, it was horrible, but now we want to look ahead. You receive a brush off if you ask at all, so you avoid talking about it. Today, I regret that we didn't talk more about the time before '45.

Kurt Schleicher, the cameraman, and Leni Fischer, Fischerkoesen's sister, were the ones who remained when Fischerkoesen was arrested in December 1945: *They were the ones to run the show but there was not much to run, only a few rather odd advertising films.*

Air-raid damages had to be removed: *There were clean-up operations to do, there were bomb craters, the roof as I remember was partly gone. They repaired it. Not all employees were around, only a handful.*

Kurt Schleicher was a tinkerer, a mover and shaker.

Fischerkoesen's studio in Potsdam was located in a former popular restaurant destination that covered an area of 1,000 square meters: *The studio was where they had the dance hall. That was a giant stage.*

I still remember the day they arrested him. It was a day in December. Outside it was dark already. The door bell rang. Two men entered. One remained at the door, he was in uniform, a Russian, and then a little man showed up, in a long black leather coat, with a scar in the face. That was Herr Panzerus. Herr Panzerus was the street umpire and apparently had denounced my father claiming that he had made Nazi films. They took him away saying: We have to bring you to the precinct. We have still some questions. My father who was suspicious wanted to pack some things. But they said: No, no, no, tomorrow morning you will be home again. And that night turned out to last two-and-a-half years. And then, I believe it was July, in midsummer, the evenings were still bright, he suddenly stood in the garden, in front of the door. Once he had smuggled a secret message. That was a New Year's card. A small card he had painted with colored pencils. And this was the only sign of life from the camp. My father got no trial. He was withdrawn from circulation. It was as simple as that, he was silenced: We can't use him, away with him. They didn't need to work. They hung around from dawn till dusk and struggled to survive. My father survived for one reason: Because he was an artist, he got the chance to portray the commandant. They gave him colored pencils and paper. And of course he did portray him as a hero. And after such painting was finished, they dropped some piece of bread in the dirt. The conditions were unthinkable. Once he talked about a theater they had arranged in the camp. Heinrich George was the actor and directed also and my father did all the sets. They have worked together intensely. And my aunt Leni told me when father was still alive: Yes, he worked with Heinrich George who died on the stage. He suffered a heart attack, fell and died in his arms. My father held him. So much for Sachsenhausen. My father was released when they liquidated the camp or were going to liquidate it and they released the people batchwise.

Together with Fischerkoesen [187] his chief artist Rudolf Bär was arrested,

187 Interestingly enough in Fischerkoesen's estate a document turned up that classified him as sympathizing with the resistance:
ERSTE ANTIFASCHISTISCHE KÜNSTLERZELLE (FRÜHER "FREIES DEUTSCHLAND")
FIRST ANTI-FASCIST ARTISTS' CELL (FORMERLY "FREE GERMANY")

too. Dr. Hans Michael Fischerkoesen and animation film historian J. P. Storm directed an inquiry to the Memorial Site and Museum of Sachsenhausen. It was answered as follows:

In Soviet confinement Hans Fischerkösen had the internal prisoner number #99082, Rudolf Bär #99089. [188]

In another statement we read:

As mentioned on the phone, only a few Russian documents still exist from the camp registrar's office of Soviet Special Camp No. 7/No. 1 in Sachsenhausen re: Hans Fischerkoesen and Rudolf Bär. First there are some brief entries about them in the "camp journal" that registered admissions and releases and also the accusations against prisoners in note form. According to it, Hans Fischer was arrested on December 17, 1945, by the operative group Potsdam of NKWD because he was accused to have been defense representative. He was accused of having cooperated with Geheime Staatspolizei (Gestapo), an instrument of the "Third Reich" that served in the combat of political enemies and was found to be in the Nuremberg trials a criminal organization. Concerning the case of Rudolf Bär, it is mentioned that he was deputy defense representative. Both were released as part of the first great discharge action from Soviet camps in Summer 1948. Concerning Fischer and Bär, it is interesting that they were not set at liberty immediately but according to the filing department were transferred on July 19 and 20, 1948, to Operative Sector Brandenburg.

Then there are transfer papers by the operative group of the Potsdam district of

---

MITGLIEDSKARTE NR. 35
MEMBERSHIP CARD NO. 35
HERRN Hans Fischer-Kösen
KÜNSTLERISCHER BERUF: Film-Zeichner
ARTIST PROFESSION: Film Animator
BERLIN, DEN 22. 5. 1943
BERLIN, 22 MAY 1943
Stempel und Unterschrift: Walter [unleserlich]. LEITER UND GRÜNDER
Stamp and signature: Walter [illegible], CHIEF AND FOUNDER
Was it forgery? There shouldn't have been such membership cards in order to protect the resistance from Gestapo.

188 Mail dated June 19, 2014 by Dr. Enrico Heitzer, research associate "Soviet Special Camps", Memorial Site and Museum Sachsenhausen / Foundation Brandenburg Memorials.

NKWD dated December 31, 1945. Mentioned are several persons, in second place Rudolf Bär:

"Beer [sic!], Rudolf, born 1901 in Leipzig, German, Middle school, member of NSDAP since 1933, family background of clerks, married, residing in Potsdam.

From early 1943 to April 1945, he was deputy defense representative of the 'Fischer' company where he exposed cases of sabotage and anti-fascist propaganda."

No. 4 on the list is Hans Fischer:

"Fischer, Hans, born 1896 in Badkesen [sic!], German, no party membership, Middle school, family background of clerks, residing in Potsdam.

He was owner of the 'Fischer' company which edited films for the navy and the army and additionally was defense representative from 1943 until April 1945. [189]

Hans Michael Fischerkoesen, *My father was released and when he came, he immediately whispered to my mother. We children, my sister and I, didn't hear anything. Of course we shouldn't. We had to behave just like normal kids. And then, one morning - or was it in the evening? - the suitcases were packed and we all left. The house was left immediately and we took what we were able to carry. We took a train somewhere - the whole family, 30 persons altogether or even more, Grandma atop. The whole family you have to understand was matriarchy. Father didn't have the say. Grandma was born in 1866 and was nearly 80 and she was atop. We passed Quedlinburg in the Harz district to cross the border. Afoot, in the dead of night - I still remember - we were marching towards the East Harz foothills to cross the then existing border on the way west. Suddenly we heard gunshots. Apparently they had discovered us, I don't know. I was a child. As fast as possible the whole baggage returned to Berlin on adventurous routes. And there we, my father, my mother, my sister and I, found accomodation in Berlin Wilmersdorf with a friendly family, the Groenewalds. And I still remember: We were waiting, waiting. Thanks to an American broadcast, for the first time I heard jazz. The rest of the family split up. Some went to Neuhaus an der Oste, and then we had a relative in Braunschweig who had an express company, Richard Fischer, the youngest brother of my father. They were eight brothers. He succeeded in collecting the little equipment we still owned, two cameras and, most important, an Ufa film editing table, the first sound*

189 Dr. Enrico Heitzer in his mail dated June 19, 2014.

editing table that Ufa had developed in 1934, he had one of those. And with his truck Richard Fischer drove it to Neuhaus an der Oste and stored it there. And then, via Berlin Airlift, we entered a plane, some time in 1948, I remember that the plane was empty, only coalsacks, terribly dirty there. You could touch what you wanted, you got coal-black fingers. Okay, the plane was crowded with refugees, and so we left to Fassberg Airport near Celle. From Fassberg we got to Braunschweig where my uncle Richard had his company. It was a four-story building. The house was a mammoth pile of rubble. They lived in the basement, and this was where we were hosted. And then my father tried to connect with West Germany and found out: If he wanted to produce, there had to be a film laboratory which worked on color film stock, a laboratory that worked at all. At that time there was a proscription by the Allied forces to make advertising films. The only zone where the ban was relaxed was the French zone. And where was the laboratory? He found Remagen where IFU International Film Union was located. They had a laboratory in the urban disctrict of Calmuth but were only equipped for black and white film stock. How to deal with it? So they drove ahead of us, my father and Aunt Leni, in Uncle Richard's truck. [...] *Eventually production could start in late '48. They rented rooms in a hotel. This was Hotel National across from the train station of Bad Neuenahr. I remember this because I arrived there too. My mother and my sister got stuck somewhere in Harz for a few years. But I had to come along because I was supposed to attend a boarding school there. The boy should make something of himself because one day he was supposed to run the company. At that time the rule was: You are only a girl, but the boy - he will make it. Anyway, this was the time. And so I came to Bad Neuenahr, and it was indeed a hotel, several rooms. And bankers came to my father, as he later told proudly, "Fischerkoesen, do you want a loan? We will help you."- "I don't want a loan, I don't want money, I want a* <u>*commission*</u>*." And there were commissions. The first was for a washing powder, Awalan, most likely from Henkel, and the film was titled* **The Six Day Race**. *They built [puppet] bicyclists from wire and fabric remnants which were animated to have a cycle race. This symbolized, so to speak: The laundry was collected for six days and on the seventh day it was washed. Quickly my father relocated to Castle Marienfels. There we were only three years. Soon it became too cramped. At that time, twenty* *relatives were around who joined in: coloring and outlining. Of course there were day girls too. That was from 1949 to '51, '52. Because it became too tight, a lot was purchased in Bad Godesberg, in the urban district of Mehlem, a former banker's mansion. The building had seven-, eight hundred square meters usable floor space. The park around had at that time 40,000 square meters. The mansion, of course, was ransacked and plundered by the townspeople who had extracted the pipes and tubes, everything that was made of copper. They had cut down trees because they needed firewood. The building was rundown. He had it refurbished while he was still in Marienfels and then, in early '52, we moved in and even extended the house sideways. Two, three years later, he had 60 permanently employed staff members who worked there nonstop - back then they had the 48-hours-week - on Saturdays till 2:00 p.m. with added overtime. The housewives were allowed to leave earlier – I think on Thursday afternoon – at 5:00 p.m. because the shops closed at 6:30. That was how they worked in those days. It was real donkeywork I realized. I can tell you: these were golden years.* [190]

The operating capital was a down payment of 8,000 Mark from a soap factory in Düsseldorf. Fischerkoesen once again was on his way up to become Germany's most successful provider of animated films. He was the only animation producer who was granted, in 1956, a title story by the renowned Hamburg news magazine DER SPIEGEL: ***Minnesang auf Markenartikel*** (***Minnesong for Branded Articles***).

A two-minute picture **Durch Nacht zum Licht** (**Through Night to Light**) *entertained last week cinemagoers in several West German cities. [...] The Film opens with a close-up: On the screen a girl appears who tosses and turns asleep, thick drops of sweat on her forehead. Suddenly the blonde girl slips through the bedhead through a gateway into the realm of darkness that opens to her. With waving nightgown, she floats through the room towards the horror of a modern Dante's hell.*

Boney fingers claw at the blank neck of the sleeping one. Daggers point to her breast. The girl whirls into the chasm of skyscrapers, hustles through endless stairs in modern buildings.

Then - at the climax of an inferno of fear - thunderbolts break brightly

190 Dr. Hans-Michael Fischerkoesen interviewed by J. P. Storm, July 29, 2013.

through the gray green of darkness. A voice that resonates redeemingly as if from the otherworld explains to the cinema-goer why he was dispatched for two minutes into the horrors of trickfilm hell. "Nightmares are the result of an upset stomach," the voice thunders. "Best help against indigestion is Underberg." [191]

Hans Fischerkoesen – that's the name of the diminutive stout gentleman, with a cigar authoritatively in the mouth corner – feels strong enough to challenge Walt Disney in his home country. His dominant economical and artistic position as advertising film manufacturer in Germany is assured: With an annual turnover of six million Mark Fischerkoesen ranks far ahead of West German trickfilm producers.

In the previous year, roughly 160 million film-goers in Germany saw his ballads on branded articles in which the warm-hearted, plain Saxon boosted products as different as chocolate and shoe polish, pencils and bras, cigarettes and toothpaste, best butter and stain remover. [...]

Fischerkoesen's general manager Dr. Ulrich Westerkamp, 70, indicates the "healthy humor" he calls "volkstümlich" [simply popular] as background of the success. It is represented best in Hans Fischer himself, the good middle-class son of a cement merchant who obtained for his studio the phone number 12345, who laughs about his own ideas more than one should. Such humor that often expresses itself in banality, platitudes, naturalness seems to have the finger on the pulse of the German audience that – as demonstrated by the million success of the laboriously funny film comedy **Charley's Aunt** *[with Heinz Rühmann] in the previous season – doesn't get tired to laugh about a man who accidentally takes a seat on a bowl filled with ice cream.* [...]

From a contemporary perspective of graphic art, Fischerkoesen's characters are drawn in a surprisingly simple, provincial manner that cannot compete with Walt Disney's urban, strongly outlined and more inventive animation film technique. The characteristics of Fischerkoesen characters could have been developed by a grade schooler: red bulbous nose, round apple cheekies, pointed eyes, potato bellies, legs like matches.

Fischerkoesen keeps to this old-fashioned typing with the same persistence he demonstrates by wearing day for day the same light gray, conservatively cut

191 A herbal digestif bitter produced at Rheinberg in Germany.

Glencheck double-breasted suit and the same tie. All attempts of younger artists working in his studio to enforce a modern graphic style are in vain. [192]

Fischerkoesen hit the nail on the head of the German mindset which was not cosmopolitan and open-minded but narrow-minded and provincial. This is the reason why most of German humor doesn't work in foreign territories. It is way too primitive.

Fischerkoesen's colleague Gerhard Fieber had worked almost till the end of the Third Reich in Dachau for Deutsche Zeichenfilm GmbH but in the final weeks, much to his chagrin, was drafted (luckily for him not as weapon-bearer but animating training films for the army) and spent a few months, until June or July 1945, in war captivity. He looked jaundice-eyed upon Hans Fischerkoesen. Fieber seethed of envy if he talked about the rival:

Fischer made at least ten times as much as I did because he focused on advertising films and didn't make such bullshit as I did, artistic stuff. And so he was able to cash large sums. [...] *At that time, Fischerkoesen earned the earth. Only with advertising films. He'd got his hands full, just incredible. If I had maybe ten customers, he had hundred. Both of us, he and I, were the leading forces in the field. Fischer was ten, fifteen years older than I, we never talked to each other. It never happened.*

In my life as animator I had a soft spot for true artists in this profession and branch of trade.

Fortunately, we German cartoonists were spared largely from politics and were not required to get involved in Party politics. Only the result of our work was what mattered. The best proof was our filmwork: **Poor Hansi** *as well as* **Somersault into Life** *were so-called fairy-tale films, particularly adapted for "big" children, no [political] tendency at all.*

To the best of my knowledge, except for the head of the company, Neumann, and five more employees (Wöhrle in Munich, Böhme, Blümel, Leberecht and Preuss in Berlin), no so-called Party comrades were known in the Deutsche Zeichenfilm Company.

---

192 *FISCHERKOESEN - Minnesang auf Markenartikel.* In: DER SPIEGEL No. 35/1956, August 29, 1956, pp. 34-40.

In war captivity I drew cartoons for the Americans and received much acclaim. A short time later I was released from U.S. captivity unencumbered. [193]

When I think about it today, a lot more would occur to me that should have made me suspicious. This is certain. But frankly speaking: We were that infatuated making animation films that I soaked myself totally in it as much as possible.

The prior requirement [after the war] was to get a film license to work at all. I was asked to go to Omgus in Berlin, there were [German émigré producer] Erich Pommer, Peter van Eyck and Horst [?] and another person, a charming man, I guess he was a Jew, one could see it on a distance of a kilometer [sic!]. Anyway, I had to go there to apply for a so-called clearing trial. This must have been end of '45. And then they told me that I should be at their disposal because they wanted to produce animation films themselves at Kleiststrasse in Berlin, the former America House, for their troops. And Peter van Eyck came to my home - at that time I lived in Lichtenrade - to pick me up and then we began to negotiate, back and forth. A short while later, however, the blockade began and thus the Americans backed away because they've got other problems. But I was already commissioned and had everything outlined and prepared. There were a few other Germans around, they had to edit a film about war criminals that the Americans had made, including the executions. Apparently the Americans didn't have enough of their own craftsmen available. [194]

With no Americans to hire him, Fieber knocked at the door of the other victorious power. In December 1945, he appeared at Zentralverwaltung für Volksbildung [Central Administration for Peoples Education] and introduced himself as "estate trustee" of Deutsche Zeichenfilm GmbH. In a letter dated December 19, 1945, he eagerly offered his services, suggested to finish ***Somersault into Life*** and start some other projects but concealed that the puppy dog story was a product begun in Dachau, so to speak under the Nazis' eyes.

193 Notes by Gerhard Fieber. Collection of J. P. Storm.

194 Gerhard Fieber interviewed by J. P. Storm.

Proposal

=========

Half year work program for "Deutsche Zeichenfilm G.mb.H."
February - July 1946.

1. Completion of color cartoon "Purzelbaum ins Leben,"
Length: ca. 250 m, running time: 9 min. 20 sec.
A funny dog story.
Directed by Gerhard Fieber from his own idea.
Screenplay: Horst von Möllendorff, Fieber.
Music: Friedrich Schröder. (Orchestra: Deutsches Tanzorchester Barnabas von Geczy)
Camera: Kurt Drews.

*This film is near completion. Music and test footage (color and black and white) are available. Funds and resources to complete the production: ca. 30- 40,000 Reichsmark. Work duration until completion: 3 - 4 months. Agfacolor film stock available. Black and white negative film as well. Paper and animation cels: ca. 30,000 sheets available, colors and ink as well. Unit A: Film "***Purzelbaum ins Leben***" ca. 25 people.*

Attached please find treatment and model sheets. Original screenplay will be submitted by mid-January 1946, from present location Bayreuth to Berlin.

2. The production of new black and white animation films, length ca. 30 m per film. Running time: 1 min. 7 sec. each. Possible standard series title ***"Pulsschlag Berlin" Berlin ohne Worte*** (***Pulse Beat Berlin: Berlin Without Words***).

Director: Gerhard Fieber.

Music: (Possibly the radio pulse beat sound)

Camera: Kurt Drews.

Subjects: Recent events glossed in comedy and reality.

1. **"Der U-Bahnschreck" (Ein tägliches Erlebnis) - The Subway Terror (A Daily Experience)**

2. **"Bazillen" (Schwarzhandel unter der Lupe) - Germs (Black Marketing Carefully Examined)**

3. **"Alle ran" (Holzaktion auf vollen Touren) - Go For it (Wood Action in Full Swing)**

Beginning with:

"Purzelbaum ins Leben", *a funny dog story.*

Circle aperture uncovers the inward of a chimney with the flame writing the main title **Purzelbaum ins Leben**. *Tracking shot back, camera captures a basket in which sleeping dog family "Purzel" sways back and forth to the rhythm of music.*

Nies, the droll puppy, rests atop and swings back and forth. Heavy gale pushes the door of the room open, with leaves and rain floated into the room. The draft awakes the sniffy Nies. He tries to climb out of the basket and close the door. He is pushed into the rain and toddles soaking wet back to the basket out of which his mother tries to take him. At this moment the first big sneezer of his life explodes and, driven backwards, he sneezes himself into the world. Handcart, rain gutter and so forth help to move him further away. The family, each member in his own kind, tries to push the runaway back and each of them experiences little nice adventures (gags). Then they get lost in the bag of the dog catcher, a lynx-like creature, except for the yawn who has slept everything away and, perpetually yawning, escapes his fate. He infects the dog catcher with his yawning and puts him to sleep. Then he frees his siblings who struggle inside the bag. And once again it is one of Nies' sneeze explosions that returns them all on the handcart back to where they came from. [195]

The powers of the newly under Soviet umbrella founded Deutsche Film AG (DEFA) seemed to like Gerhard Fieber's pitch and accepted the former Nazi cartoon as their own brainchild:

After six months of work the color cartoon **Purzelbaum ins Leben** *was finished by the DEFA animation department.* [...] *After the collapse of the Hitler regime it is the first animated color film to be produced. Until then only four smaller black and white animation films were made.* [196]

---

195 Letter with letterhead Deutsche Zeichenfilm G.m.b.H., Hankestr. 3, Berlin C 2 signed "p.p. Fieber" dated December 19, 1945, and addressed to Zentralverwaltung f. Volksbildung attention Herr Volkmann, Berlin Wilhelmstr. 68, Room 136.

196 *Purzelbaum ins Leben. Erster Zeichenfarbfilm der DEFA.* In: Neues Deutschland No. 175, November 15, 1946.

With ***Purzelbaum*** almost ready for release, another former employee of Deutsche Zeichenfilm GmbH who was sentenced to slave labor in the Organization Todt had returned. In a letter dated August 3, 1946, this artist, Bernhard Klein, who was married to a Jewish wife, complained bitterly about his experiences under Karl Neumann and Gerhard Fieber. Klein had a background in theater and painting (the paintings of his older brother, César, were classified as *Entartete Kunst* - Degenerate Art and banned) but took an early interest in animated cartoons. He had decided to experiment with animation and produce a cartoon of his own [197]. In 1938, he came to the conclusion that it would be best for his wife and himself to leave Germany as soon as possible. He finally saw a chance to do so in 1941. To raise some money he tried to sell a cartoon film he had finished recently and found himself trapped in the network of animation under the swastika that was called Deutsche Zeichenfilm GmbH. In his letter he recalls the failure of that company:

In the meantime, prompted by Disney's **Snow White** *success story, German film industry had become wide-eyed. The Cultural Film Center arranged immediately that my film was accepted by Tobis and released successfully. Then, however, they launched their own production and followed my example, initially under the roof of Tobis, where still a certain artistic atmosphere dominated, later under the label "Deutsche Zeichenfilm G.mb.H." which was supervised by a scenario-wise completely obstinate chief dramaturge (Leberecht). At that place happened exactly what I had always feared. Advertising filmmakers and commercial artists were entrusted with the task which was tantamount to assigning poster artists to do a painting.*

Under these circumstances, I wasn't interested anymore to try to prevent the Zeichenfilm Company from having to make experiences the hard way. Anyway, the people in charge always knew better with the result that the Zeichenfilm Company, with a budget of RM 4.5 million, 100 employees plus 200 trainees, didn't achieve more than I did with a film of equal length but without any assistance.

There was no evidence at all that any of the five chief animators of Zeichenfilm Company was more skilled than others. They all were beginners compared to this

197 *Sonntagsabenteuer: Der treulose Wecker.*

artistic challenge and in some cases not artistically minded at all. If at all, they were appreciated for political reasons and political disposition. Two were foreigners, one a true anti-fascist, the other unpleasant and pendant with occasional anti-Semitic statements. The 5th, however, the artist ***Gerhard Fieber*** *fraternized with the National Socialists. He sympathized with the respective ideas of the shop steward, shared deliberately all victory-focused propaganda foolery and spread these delusional ideas. In several copies he made caricatures showing Jews marked with Jewish stars: a street scene populated by Stürmer types, the yellow star overemphasized, under the headline: "Es leuchten die Sterne" [The Stars Shine].* [198]

The Stars Shine was a popular song by Leo Leux.

Anti-semitic caricature by Gerhard Fieber.
Courtesy of J. P. Storm Collection

Bernhard Klein had already approached the trustee of Zeichenfilm GmbH, one Mr. Christensen who tried to appease him: "One day or other each of us had positive views." [199] These views concerned the Nazis.

198 Letter addressed to a Mr. Rosen in the collection of J. P. Storm.
199 Bundesarchiv: File memo Berlin, July 1, 1946 Sch/Ki.

Fieber who had heard about it seemed to lose the ground under his feet and preferred to leave Berlin as soon as possible and restart in the Western zones. He settled in Bad Sachsa where he was able to rent a spa hotel for cheap money - 1,100 Mark monthly: "*The whole giant hotel, they didn't have any spa guests after '48. So they were happy to rent it to us.*"[200]

There, during 1948-49, Fieber's EOS Film GmbH created the first hand-drawn animated feature film in Germany, a project Goebbels and Karl Neumann had always dreamt of, ***Tobias Knopp, Abenteuer eines Junggesellen*** (***Tobias Knopp, Adventures of a Bachelor***), from an original by Wilhelm Busch. *"But when it was released it had no chance to compete with Disney's* **Snow White** *and other animated features that finally were shown in Germany as ours was only black and white, the American films, however, produced in Technicolor. It was like a dwarf fighting the giants!"*

Although some reviewers criticized that Wilhelm Busch was presented like Disney's ***Mickey Mouse*** [201] the film turned out a huge flop.

Hitler's favorite ***Snow White***, however, was liked well enough by German post-war audiences to have several revivals - in spite of what some critics wrote:

The Americanization of a German fairy tale jars on my nerves. Snow White and her knight are drawn like characters from a friendship book of Grandma's time. Desperately little came to the mind of Walt Disney and his 570 animators.

We cannot stand to hear these familiar fairy tale characters sing with Broadway voices and to see the dwarfs as slapstick comedians. We expect the mood of a fairy tale and no kiddie's revue that is rather made for adults. [202]

Fieber withdrew to producing commercials for the German railway and later participated in supervising the animated ***Mainzelmännchen*** (***Little Mainz Men***) for ZDF (Second Channel TV), much to the dismay of their creator, Wolf Gerlach. Between both men it was hate right from the beginning.

---

200 Gerhard Fieber interviewed by J. P. Storm.

201 *Der Traum eines Kritikers Tobias-Knopp-Film in Hannover.* In: Kölner Rundschau, March 5, 1950.

202 R.K., *Disneys "Schneewittchen" / Im Astor.* In: Nachtexpress, Berlin/GDR, March 4, 1950.

Mr. Abracadabra

After the war there were not many heroes left. Hitler let them bleed to death at the front. There were, however, survival artists and roly-polys. One of the most beloved creatures in post-war Germany was "Dr." Helmut Schreiber. Schreiber was a renowned name in Nazi films. At Tobis Filmkunst, he produced Emil Jannings' ***Der Herrscher*** (***The Ruler***) and the anti-Semitic comedy ***Robert und Bertram*** (***Robert and Bertram***). In June 1942, he was promoted production head of Bavaria Studios in Munich. But only insiders knew him under the name Schreiber. The audience knew and loved him as Kalanag the Great Magician, the proverbial Mr. Abracadabra. One of his most famous stage tricks was to let a Volkswagen vanish. He didn't look exactly like a Houdini. He wasn't handsome at all. He looked the prototype of the German petit bourgeois, a bespectacled bureaucrat who personified the transition from German film to television. Not only did he appear with his acts of magic on the TV screen. If West German chancellor Konrad Adenauer would have succeeded with his plans for a Freies Fernsehen Gesellschaft, a Free TV Company: Deutschland Fernsehen GmbH controlled by the conservatives, Schreiber would have been in charge of entertainment. Adenauer's project failed, however, due to the intervention of the Federal Constitutional Court (although it was the start of Second Channel TV, later to become the home of Gerhard Fieber).

Schreiber had met Adolf Hitler on several occasions, was invited to Hitler's Berghof and performed magic for the "Führer" and his guests.

Kalanag would have been an ideal subject for a comedy along the lines of Helmut Dietl's 1992 ***Schtonk!*** which satirized one of the biggest German press scandals, the forged Hitler Diaries. And indeed I wrote a screenplay for a Berlin production company about Kalanag. Alas, there was no funding. Here is a fictitious scene from that film project with the Magician performing for Hitler at the Berghof right before WW2.

The Great Magician

Abracadabra, Herr Reichskanzler!

The Magician stands in front of the "Führer". The "Führer" is excited by the Magician's tricks and laughs about *Mister Abracadabra's* successful dispersal act. Hitler's Golden party badge and the Iron Cross are gone for the moment.

Hitler

If you could blow off my enemies that easily!

The Great Magician

Geschwindigkeit ist keine Hexerei, Herr Reichskanzler. Speed is no sorcery!

Hitler

Should I ever have to fight a war, everything must roll as fast as in your show.

The Great Magician

A Blitzkrieg, Herr Reichskanzler, exactly!

Hitler

Blitzkrieg. Sounds good. I have to remember that.

After the performance, the Magician is cock of the walk and acts the gallant.

Goebbels walks with a limp towards him.

Goebbels

[Rhenish German intonation]

You, Abracadabra, please be so kind and follow me.

The Great Magician

Of course, Herr Reich Minister. Love to, Herr Reich Minister.

Outside in the hall Goebbels speaks with menacing undertone.

Goebbels

The Führer *sends me. He enjoyed your performance. But now, as a matter of urgency, he likes to reclaim his Iron Cross and the Golden party badge.*

The Magician starts to sweat. His facial features leave the track. He loses his composure and begins to stutter.

The Great Magician

A-Aber Herr... Herr Reichsminister, I have only...

Goebbels

[gruff]

Pardon, you have only?

The Magician gets sticky.

The Great Magician

I've conjured everything back?

Goebbels

Conjured back?! A tinker's curse you have!

He signals an SS officer in black uniform

Goebbels

Search him!

The SS officer gropes the Magician from head to toe and pulls party badge and Iron Cross out of the Magician's pocket. As is generally known, man consists of more than 60 percent water, and this water streams out of the Magician until only a picture of misery remains.

Goebbels

Look at that, the Führer's decorations! So you wanted to make off with them or what?!

The Magician stutters ruefully something unintelligible.

Goebbels

Shut up! A cheap thief you are!

The Great Magician

No, no, no, I'm... I'm innocent! This must be... a misunderstanding, Herr... Herr Reichsminister.

Goebbels

[scolds]

Misunderstanding?! This is what they all claim!

[To the SS Officer]

Take the man away, Sturmbannführer! Get him to Dachau! They have their ways to make him talk there. Maybe he is a spy and attempted the Führer's life.

The Magician is in a cold sweat. Eva Braun appears and stops the SS man.

Eva Braun

[to the Magician]

Please perform some magic, lieber Meister...

The Great Magician

[struggles in the Sturmbannführer's clutch]

I'm... I'm very sorry. I can't. They take me to the next concentration camp.

Eva Braun

But that can wait a little, can't it?

She gives Goebbels a wink.

Eva Braun

You won't do any harm to our good Master, Herr Doktor, won't you?

Goebbels winks back.
Then he slaps the Magician's back.

Goebbels

[laughs]
Just a joke, Master, no more. Here we are among friends, aren't we? The Führer knows the score and has borrowed his decorations so that I *can conjure a little and play a prank. Wasn't I ... convincing?*

Goebbels looks triumphantly around fishing for applause

Goebbels

Now go ahead, perform a trick for Fräulein Braun.Don't be shy.

Slowly the Magician regains his composure. The SS officer looks disgrunted.

The Great Magician

[still a little nervous]
Abra- cadabra!

He holds an artificial floral bouquet in his slightly trembling hands.
Fräulein Braun is delighted.

Eva Braun

Isn't that lovely? How sweet! I have to show them to the Führer.

Goebbels

And please take the Führer's decorations, Fräulein Braun. Otherwise the Führer might think you really wanted to steal them, Master.

So far for fiction.

On December 24, 1963, television was going strong in Germany calling for the services of Helmut Schreiber. But Kalanag wasn't able to participate any more. He died on Christmas Eve.

At Second Channel TV, another former Nazi sympathizer stepped in, Herbert Reinecker, who had written the final editorial for the SS paper *Das schwarze Korps* on April 5, 1945: *We are facing the remarkable situation to realize that it is - maybe - possible to defeat us militarily but this will not change one iota of our belief in the rightness of our commission.* Herbert Reinecker became *the* expert for crime and detective stories at Second Channel TV. He penned endless episodes of murder & mayhem in Munich villas for ***Der Kommissar*** and ***Derrick***. In 1994, Reinecker was interviewed for a radio broadcast.

Interviewer: "How do you remove a tattoo?"

Reinecker: "That is completely unknown to me. I guess it's a painful procedure."

Then he understands. The interviewer adverted to Reinecker's SS blood group tattoo which he had asked an Austrian farmer's wife to remove right after the war. But the tattoo remained on Reinecker's upper arm - "and not only there". [203]

203 *Reineckerland: Der Schriftsteller Herbert Reinecker.* Munich: edition text + kritik, 2010.

The Treasure of Silver Lake: The Legacy of Spaetzle Westerns

In the 1960s, the German cinema struggled in its fight against television. Much of the old talent, numerous actors, directors and writers, like Reinecker, left the silver screen and prospered on the small TV screen. But the film producers still had a secret weapon: Karl May! He became West Germany's initiation to the way Hitler and the Nazis thought and felt.

Karl May was born on February 25, 1842, as fifth child of a family of poor weavers in a small village in Saxonia. Trained as a teacher, he came into conflict with the law from early on and was repeatedly jailed. His criminal record as a crook was considerable. May apologized, *There were all kinds of characters inside me, and they all wanted to be part of my worries, my work, my creativity, my writing and my composing.* This man sure had an inventive mind and a rich imagination, and in 1878 he became a freelance writer, famous for his travel accounts. In a later age, he began, a poor man's James Fenimore Cooper, to embellish his own biography and identify with his heroic characters such as Kara Ben Nemsi in the Orient and Old Shatterhand in the Wild West. When these characters took possession of him, he claimed to *be* these men. They became his alter ego and took over: May asked a studio photographer in Linz, Hitler's favorite city, to make portrait photos of him, dressed as Old Shatterhand. An impostor, a phony character, and a talented writer, all in one person.

More than 200 million copies of his books have been printed, a dimension otherwise associated with dictators or the founders of religions - or J. K. Rowling with her Harry Potter series. Half of the Karl May books printed were sold in German-speaking countries. He is virtually unknown in the English-speaking world, and only in Eastern Europe did he achieve a comparable degree of fame. The number of fans who remained loyal to him beyond their adolescent years is large, ranging from Albert Einstein to political activist Karl Liebknecht, Marxist philosopher Ernst Bloch and writer Martin Walser. [204]

Martin Walser, by the way, was the one who complained in Frankfurt on November 11, 1998, that Auschwitz was being used as a "moral club" to enforce

204 Jan Fleischhauer, *Germany's Best-Loved Cowboy: The Fantastical World of Cult Novelist Karl May.* SPIEGEL Online, March 30, 2012.

political correctness. No wonder, Hitler, too, adored Karl May. (As did in his youth Fritz Lang. And Thea von Harbou as a girl fell, in her own words, in love with Winnetou.) From youth on, the "Führer" had a lifelong fascination with May's work and kept the books at his Berghof near Berchtesgaden and even at his military resort Wolfsschanze: *On his bookshelf there are works of political science, some brochures and books about the breeding of sheep dogs and then - German boys, listen! then there are numerous volumes by - Karl May!* [205]

Patterns of the lives of Karl May and Hitler were similar. Both had penurious beginnings; both were confined in prison, and they experienced delusions of grandeur that were given expression in writing; both were neurasthenic, and, significantly, May was discredited completely before his death in 1912. [206] The reading experience didn't make Hitler a fascist. But Klaus Mann, Thomas Mann's unfortunate son, went so far as to say in American exile that the Third Reich was Karl May's ultimate triumph, the ghastly realization of his dreams:

The villains are shrewd and efficient: but definitely less so than Old Shatterhand, who always rushes into the picture, an experienced deus ex machina, *just in the nick of time - a fascinating blend of young Siegfried and Tom Mix: smart and blond, tough and charming, generous and swift, exceedingly attractive, fairly cultured, even scholarly, and a shade sadistic.* [...] *A whole generation grew brutish and run wild - partly through the evil influence of Karl May.* [207]

And this in spite of the fact that May was a declared pacifist and anti-racist. It is said that on March 22, 1912, Hitler, back then an unemployed amateur artist who painted postcards and watercolors, was among the listeners when May came to Vienna to talk about a kingdom of noble men. [208]

No wonder that even near the end Goebbels checked color film tests for a Karl May picture.

---

205 Robert Achenbach in: Sonntag-Morgenpost, Munich April 23, 1933.

206 R.G., *Karl May: Literary Bushranger.* In: The Argus Week-end Magazine.

207 Klaus Mann, *Karl May, Hitler's Literary Mentor.* In: The Kenyon Review, Autumn 1940, pp. 399.

208 *Empor ins Reich der Edelmenschen!* See also: Hans Christoph Buch, *Wie Karl May Adolf Hitler traf: Und andere wahre Geschichten.* Frankfurt: Eichborn, 2003 and Rainer Buck, *Karl May im Nationalsozialismus.* In: *Karl May: Der Winnetou-Autor und der christliche Glaube.* Moers: Joh. Brendow & Sohn, 2012.

The first movies made from May's work were Arabian adventures, featuring a young Béla Lugosi who had just fled from his native Hungary. Old Shatterhand and his noble Indian blood brother, the savage Apache chief Winnetou who would declare himself a Christian when the hand of a villain kills him, didn't come to the mind of German filmmakers before 1945 - only William (Wilhelm) Dieterle suggested it to Ufa as early as 1926 but then left Germany. Dieterle had the idea still in his luggage when he returned to Germany and worked for Artur Brauner on a remake of Joe May's ***Herrin der Welt*** (***Mistress of the World,*** 1960) with screenwriter Harald G. Petersson. Apparently, he suggested a May project to Brauner as well as Horst Wendlandt who had been production manager at Brauner's CCC Film Company and now was with Rialto Film.

Sixteen years after Hitler's suicide, the project took form when Preben Philipsen's Rialto Film and Horst Wendlandt signed a deal with West Germany's leading distribution company, Constantin Film, to produce Karl May's ***Der Schatz im Silbersee*** (***Treasure of Silver Lake***) written by Harald G. Petersson but with a different director, Dr. Harald Reinl.

Both Petersson and Reinl had a past in Nazi filmmaking: Petersson was a German-Swedish screenwriter, born on October 16, 1904, in Weimar. His film career began as press chief at Tobis Filmkunst. Petersson was married to actress Sybille Schmitz, star of the Nazi ***Titanic,*** and wrote two outspoken Nazi movies: ***Wetterleuchten um Barbara*** in 1940, with Austrians fighting for Hitler before the *Anschluss*, and the previous year ***Blutsbrüderschaft***, a comradeship not between a white hero and a savage but between two young men in World War 1. In the post-war period of the Weimar Republic, one of the blood brothers is sabotaging the Occupying Powers while the other has become the manager of a factory, unfortunately controlled by the British. But on September 1, 1939, both leave to serve their country again in WW2. Austrian-born Harald Reinl was a great skier when Arnold Fanck discovered him and used him as an extra in several of his movies. Soon he became the protégé of Leni Riefenstahl and assisted her on ***Tiefland*** (and maybe elsewhere too). Hubert Schonger, the well-known producer of fairy tales, granted Reinl the chance of his first feature film in 1949: ***Bergkristall***. Reinl was murdered by his third (alcoholic) wife, Czech actress Daniela Marie Delisová, on October 9, 1986, in his house on Teneriffa.

The Treasure of Silver Lake offered *a spectactular adventure in a spectacular setting* (a.k.a. not exactly Wild West but the wilderness of Yugoslavia). Strangely enough, Germans were out of the question to portray the two heroes. Ex-Tarzan Lex Barker was to play the Aryan prototype Old Shatterhand and nobody else than Christopher Lee, trying to escape the curse of Hammer's Dracula image (and British taxes), was screen-tested for the part of Winnetou, Shatterhand's Apache blood brother. Horst Wendlandt, the producer, was a little, aggressive, pushy man whom Lee, in the presence of Hammer expert Uwe Sommerlad, once pointed out disdainfully, *This man is a Nazi!* Wendlandt decided against Lee and favored an upcoming but rather inexperienced and vain French actor by the name of Pierre Brice to play the "Aryan" Indian.

Besides them, there was Erwin Lange, the explosives expert on ***Kolberg*** (who also lit Rühmann's ***Brandy Punch***), to handle rifles and pyrotechnics. In the cast they had Marianne Hoppe, Gustaf Gründgens' widow, both close to Hermann Göring, and Götz, the son of Heinrich George. In other entries of the series, Lex Barker was sometimes substituted by other English-speaking ex-stars, Stewart Granger and Rod Cameron.

Although released by Columbia Pictures abroad, ***Treasure of Silver Lake*** and its sequels are not widely known to American audiences. One who knew was Quentin Tarantino. As a tribute to Winnetou, he built a scene in ***Inglorious Basterds*** (2009) in which German soldiers are playing one who-am-I guessing game with the right answer: *Winnetou, Chief of the Apaches*!

As a matter of fact, realizing the success of European westerns, Constantin Film went on and co-produced Sergio Leone's ***Per un pugno di dollari*** (***For a Fistful of Dollars***) in Italy which was the beginning of Spaghetti or Italo westerns.

When the 1968 student revolt was at its height and with Winnetou no drawing card anymore (and New German Cinema was born), the traditional

German film industry answered with - ***The Brandy Punch***, a remake (1970, directed by Helmut Käutner and produced by Horst Wendlandt) as well as a series of only slightly disguised brandy punchers calling themselves ***Lümmel von der ersten Bank*** with Hansi Kraus as Pepe Nietnagel, king of pranksters, and his fight with old-style teachers.

Sexy Films: Count Porno and Herr Brummer

In the early 1960s, as we have noted somewhere else, producer Wolf C. Hartwig had offered a horrified Veit Harlan a *horror* picture ***Die Nackte und der Satan***, also known as ***Des Satans nackte Sklavin***, in America ***The Head***, to direct. The offer was beyond Harlan's belief. Of course he turned it down. Hartwig hired one of the émigré directors who had returned to Germany: Victor Trivas.

Some years later, when the traditional post-war film industry slowly died away, with no Old Shatterhand around to save it, the same Hartwig became famous for his ***School Girl Reports***. If Harlan would have lived long enough, maybe he would have been offered one of those too to direct. German film had sunk to the bottom.

During WW2, Hartwig had served as interpreter in the German headquarters in occupied Paris. He seemed to have been in the rear with the gear. After the war, he opened with his first wife a language school, then became an ironmonger before he founded Rapid Film. His first movie, of course, was devoted to Hitler and the Third Reich, the documentary ***Bis fünf nach zwölf - Adolf Hitler und das 3. Reich***. The film premiered on November 20, 1953, in Cologne, but shortly after it was banned. Even Chancellor Konrad Adenauer considered it "hidden propaganda for National Socialism and against the European Defense Community".

Among Hartwig's later ***Report*** actors was a little Italian by the name of Rinaldo Talamonti. We met him on several occasions and he allowed us a rare look behind the secret doors of German sex film production end of the 1960s and in the early 1970s.

Wanted: Nice and good-looking girls

preferably with acting talent, for parts in funny pictures.

In those days small ads like the above appeared in Munich papers. But it was not Hartwig who placed these ads but one of his competitors, Alois Brummer. Small in stature, perspiring, dumpy, a shrewd wheeler-deeler, a reincarnation of Weiss Ferdl, born 1926, Brummer served as a common soldier in WW2. After the war, he became a hauler in Ingolstadt but never dreamed to enter the movie business - until he accidentally inherited two cinemas from a debitor. Soon he opened his own distribution company, AB Film, and finally decided to become a producer, too.

And as he was the son of a farmer, he didn't use expensive regular film sets but farms and cow barns he found in the Bavarian villages around Munich. Even hay carts were used for nude love scenes. Of course he didn't tell the farmers that he produced sex films. He just told them that he shot funny pictures: *Heimatfilme* so to say, popular sentimental films in idealized regional settings.

The producer always arrived in his white Mercedes, had a bundle of banknotes in his trousers pocket and soon would contract with the respective farmers.If a farmer got wary and realized during shooting that amidst his cows some girls took off their clothes, his conscience was silenced by his being paid some more money. Afterwards the papist wife of the farmer, for any eventuality, would take care that the sullied location was radically purged by the village priest with pious blessing and holy water. The priest didn't ask questions although rumors spread like wildfire. Some small donation, a basket filled with eggs and a charitable break adjusted everything.

The girls got appointments to show up right on location. Of course not the cow barns were what they were shown first, but the film crew with the whole enchilada, the 35mm camera, the lighting equipment, and other ladies who acted dressed in front of this camera. When the aspirants had gazed enough in amazement without becoming suspicious, they were asked if they would take part or not. Of course most of them were more than willing. They had to sign a pre-formulated contract. Most didn't even bother to read what they signed on the hood of or inside the producer's Mercedes. The usual standard terms were changed to the detriment of the girls. Including all rights, they were given a shoddy payment of 50 Marks daily. The producer was in the clear.

After a while, it came to cinematic light that the girls were expected to undress to appear in this funnly, harmless *Heimatfilms*. For the extra service they were offered a higher rate. Girls who cast off their clothes got a daily rate of 100 Marks. The contracts, hastily signed, disappeared immediately in the briefcase of the location manager who signaled the producer with a vulpine look that the girl was caught in the trap. With a sanctimonious smile the female applicants were congratulated on their decision.

Often the girls brought along their girlfriends. When these realized where they had run aground, some friendships broke up.

All possibilities of a successful casting were exploited. Besides ads, some applicants were placed by shabby small agencies. The girls were regarded as nothing else than meat stock. They didn't have the slightest chance of a real, honest career, but they were good enough as cannon fodder for the wave of sex films. For some of the aspiring actresses their participation in such crap later became a calamity jobwise. Instead of reaching their dream destination nothing else remained than a sour aftertaste and bitterness. They were typecast, without any chance of getting parts in serious films.

Nevertheless, there even were mothers who sacrificed their innocent, naive daughters and brought them to the casting. These girls were expected to fulfill their mothers' lifelong dream and start a solid career as starlet.

Another trick was purposeful recruitement. The producer sent his sleuths onto Munich streets. They were lying in wait in front of schools, universities, bars, discos, public swimming pools, attended parties and so on. Where there was a chance to capture a lot of booty for the camera, they were lurking. Housewives were in demand, too, who wanted to bump up the meagre salary of their husbands or who felt bored and unsatisfied at home and were looking for an "adventure".

This way a file was compiled. It was worth a mint: contacts, addresses and phone numbers, horses for courses. Location and production managers kept the record and for some extra charge imparted their knowledge to other production companies.

On location, the girls were treated well and diplomatically. Important was to get them undressed voluntarily. The main problem concerning the girls were the million eyes of spectators watching with voyeuristic grin. The production tried its best to reduce the staff to a minimum: cameraman and assistant, director and assistant, one gaffer, a makeup man - no more than six persons who acted as professionally as possible.

If they found out that a girl was underage, she was substituted immediately to avoid trouble with government agencies and families. Many parents didn't know in what type of *schmuddelecke* their daughters had repaired to. These young girls didn't have much life experience.

The fees were paid off daily after shooting. This was psychologically effective because the banknotes were remedy for the wounds of the sensitive creatures. Shooting schedules lasted on average 25 days. Main parts were paid roughly 2,500 Marks.

How did Brummer enter production? In 1968, Günter Hendel, a bit player in TV films and series, approached Brummer who was only a distributor back then and showed him ***So viel nackte Zärtlichkeit*** (***So Much Naked Tenderness***), his first directorial assignment. Brummer wanted to know how much such a production would cost. Hendel answered, "About 400,000 Marks." Brummer looked heavy-hearted, "I don't have that much, not even half of that." But Hendel didn't give up. He showed Brummer a screenplay he had written titled ***Gelegenheit macht Triebe*** (***Opportunity Makes the Drive***). Brummer stopped him with a wave of his hand, "I don't read books! I give you all authority while shooting, and we decide about the definite title later." He was willing to scare up *half* the budget. Now another 200,000 Marks were needed to close the budget. Hendel persuaded an investor named Karl Muvick. Muvick cautioned Hendel against Brummer who, in his eyes, was no reliable partner. He insisted on bills of exchange. Only then production could start.

Doris Arden, an "actress" Hendel had brought into the show, insisted that her brother Pierre O. Pistek should be aboard, too. Pistek had no formal training but he was alert and very ambitious and besides that a gifted photographer. Hendel introduced him to the producer and got him a job. To Brummer he became stills photographer, janitor, butler, location manager in one person. Brummer who had definitely no taste even let Pistek select a black suite for the interior sets in his own villa in Munich Pasing.

Porno at that time was not allowed in German cinemas but by changing the film's title from ***Opportunities Make the Drive*** to ***Graf Porno und seine Mädchen*** (***Count Porno and His Girls***) Brummer lured three million "filmfans" into the theaters - in three months.

With hindsight, Brummer said he should have quit after that success but now that he had tasted blood, was hooked and thus needed Pierre Pistek. Pistek became Brummer's right-hand man. He was slim, pale, of medium size, dark blond, sideward parted, well-tended, with blue eyes behind yellowish Ray Ban glasses, state-of-the-art in those days. He wore tight light-colored jeans, a white or green Lacoste T-shirt, white moccasins or white sneakers.

The moment a girl came near to him he began to beam. The name of his girlfriend was Marion. She was pretty as a picture and sympathetic but they quareled all time because Pierre was such a womanizer. Enthusiastically, he photographed anything that happened on the set with his Rolex camera. Of course he caused non-stop trouble. But most often, Pierre managed to pull a Pinocchio and squirm free. Thus things were settled.

When the producer included him in his team, he extended his responsibility. Pistek was allowed to work on the screenplay and to sit down next to camera and read aloud the lines. That worked perfectly as they didn't use original soundtrack but shot silent and the rest was left to post-dubbing.

When Pierre was promoted to assistant director, a new stills photographer popped up. This man, one Alexander Kessler, was not very popular with the girls but he was a friend of the producer and even played the title role in one of his sex films, ***Dr. Fummel und seine Gespielinnen*** (***Dr. Fummel and His Playmates***). He used his camera in a pushy way because he was determined to get alluring erotic subjects for the posters.

"But how did *you* get involved in all of this?" I asked the chatty Rinaldo Talamonti who was born in August 1947 in San Benedetto del Tronto, Italy, and arrived with his parents in Munich in 1964. Rinaldo told me his story:

In 1969 I was a bloody amateur and stumbled just by accident into the production of a commercial. The people raised my hopes for a job in America but I was lovestruck and didn't want to leave Munich. Besides that, my father wanted me to learn German. Soon I heard that they were looking for a man of small stature for a movie. That was my first encounter with Günter Hendel.

5'2"? Bingo! When he saw me Günter jumped out of his armchair as if stung by an adder. His eyes shone. He extended his hand and said, "You are Harry Holst, private eye!!!" Mrs. Hendel served coffee while her husband explained the first scene of the film. A white Rolls Royce stops at a red traffic light. Looking through the car window, the audience thinks Harry Holst sits in the car but when the traffic light is green we see that Harry isn't in the car but next to it on a tiny bike. Hendel was the one to guffaw the most about his ideas which he considered brilliant. I didn't have a chance but to join in his laughter. Harry Holst, the inexperienced private eye, has set his mind on putting a stop to a bon vivant's activites. Hendel was going to play this bon vivant himself. That was the simple plot. We sipped our coffee. Then Hendel brought me immediately into the lion's den, the villa in Pasing where the producer lived and which he used, money-consciously, as film studio. When he opened the door, a perfumed whiff almost knocked me down.

In front of me, I saw a burly man in a white shirt, silk grey trousers, black slippers and with thin hair combed backwards. In his moon face I realized the flash of a gold tooth. He shook my hand. In the other hand he had a framed black and white photo which showed a rundown vagrant. The caption read: "He gave the highest discount." I didn't understand but Hendel whispered and explained I shouldn't be "too expensive" and shouldn't make "demands". The man who feared to transform into a beggar if he didn't save money was Alois Brummer, the producer. My contract was ready to sign. I needed the money. Our first child was born. So naively I signed.

No word about nudity. No word about porno. If anything was non-serious, it was Brummer's releasing title **Count Porno**. *There was only one pan shot with three nude girls under a shower. If the audience had expected sex orgies, these didn't happen.*

Brummer smelled more cash in the meantime. At once, he paid off the unbeloved Muvick and financed the next entries out of his own pocket. A sheer flood of telegrams burst into Brummer's office. Cinema owners in all of Germany comgratulated him and asked for more.

Using the pseudonym Sven Ole Larsen, Brummer himself wrote a new screenplay: **Eros Center Hamburg**, *an erotic crime story that played among pimps and prostitutes in the red light district of St. Pauli.*

I was supposed to play again on Hendel's side, this time an Italian who allegedly has murdered his girlfriend. For the first time on screen, I was publicly bad-mouthed Itaker *(goombah) and* Spaghettifresser *(dago). Pistek who crouched next to the camera fed me with my lines and I parroted them.*

While directing, Hendel liked to show the male actors how to get into a scene with a female partner. This gave him plenty of opportunity to fumble, fondle and kiss.

The market was starving for that kind of moronism. In 1973, Friedemann Hahn, an artist and poet, reviewed productions such as those of Brummer and called them "films like slaps in the face": *The laughter sticks already in the stomach if one should find it funny that, doing a side leap in the Eros Center, Baron von Schlecker gets a rap over the knuckles by Fiddling Moni.* [209]

And because something like this made the cash tills ring only and preferably in Germany, director Günter Hendel acted fast and did a ***Porno*** sequel in which he played the part tailor-made for him. In ***Graf Porno und seine liebesdurstigen Töchter*** (France: ***Les orgies du comte Porno***) *he was again "starring" as the buffoon Peter Garibaldus Porno von Geilsberg and obviously had a ball.*

Talamonti, *I felt like being on the beach of a tropical island, the spotlights heated the set by 40 degrees. I had overcome my inhibitions fast. Not only did I hop without a stitch on in front of the camera but made a contribution to help the girls overcome their inhibitions to strip, too. As born Arlecchino (Harlequin) I got the nickname "Mister Klamottini" (Klamotte = cheap farce).*

After the second ***Count Porno***, Brummer decided that he now knew enough about directing films and didn't need to pay a director but could handle these chores himself. So Hendel was on his own now - and failed.

209 *Kinos in der Kaiserstrasse.* In: Filmkritik 3/73, pp. 122-131.

Using the alias "Robert S. Gordon", Hendel wrote an erotic western[210] *for his own "Production Günter Hendel" titled* **Ein langer Ritt nach Eden (A Long Ride to Eden)** *and released by Bodo Gaus (Mercator Filmverleih). That was end of 1973. In America Günter would have been a cowboy - that's for sure - or at least a director of B pictures.*

If noticed at all, the reviews re: his last directorial effort that looked absolutely amateurish were disastrous. Ronald M. Hahn wrote: *A pathetically played, woefully directed mix of western and dirty joke sex.*

The products from the basement party room sauna in Brummer's Pasing villa didn't fare any better and were trashed likewise as incredibly naive, dirty stuff from Bavaria.

But who cared about the reviewers provided money was rolling in? *Pecunia non olet!*

With Brummer, teams and all male actors had to restrain themselves. He was angst-ridden that his house might be dismissively called a brothel. It should be no more than a cheap studio. Booze was strictly forbidden, smoking too. One who wouldn't observe the rules was fired immediately. The catering consisted of sausage, head cheese, hard rolls, and pretzels, and to drink only lemonade and water.

Good and professional actors and actresses weren't available for that kind of job. What remained was C grade at most. Well-known postwar actors took care to prevent from being confused with this type of production and kept a distance - in spite of the frustratingly low fees at the theater. I didn't bother about acting, at least not at that time, and didn't care that I was typecast in a genre that ranked lowest in high culture.

Later, when this wave of films had become mainstream, some more illustrious actresses and actors dared to participate. They jumped, so to speak, from the pan into the fire, I will say: out of personal financial calamities into an awkward situation damaging what was left of their reputation.

Undress, dress, again and again... There was no room for professional acting. Those who succeeded in turning a producer's or director's head did a small career leap but it was rather ephemeral.

210 Also published as paperback: Martin Kelter Verlag.

Rinaldo Talamonti, *Back in the 1970s, it was all the rave to smoke joints while the kids of the upper class inhaled their lines of coke. In the film industry it was not different. Many saw a chance to gain control that way of inhibitions and other problems. When almost everybody smoked - hippies, musicians, creative artists, even politicians - and cabaretist Wolfgang Neuss proclaimd that on German soil never more a joint should burn out, my curiosity won. But after awhile, I quit because I had no desire for such things.*

Around us blazed something like a cultural revolution: music, art, hippie and APO [extra-parliamentary opposition] protesters, sexual revolution - that was drowned in petit bourgeois consumption.

Time went by. Many of my film partners were drug-addicted. They didn't have the strength to get out and fell into a black hole of depression, frustration and hatred for their fate. Some even paid with their life. Police, prosecution and other public authorities tried to intervene, but most often their efforts came too late.

On the set, I tried to overact in my clownery. Sometimes my hokums fussed the others, but the girls laughed because I didn't make a grab at them as the others did. Brummer himself was reticent. He responded to the girls with his beaming gingerbread face, but when they talked, his expression changed from jolly to stern. Brummer had a secretary, an honest, funny person with a slight squint, a faithful soul behind tight breasts. She was convinced that some day Brummer would marry her, but he didn't. She gave everything for him, even placed her apartment at his disposal as location. Nevertheless, I got the impression that they were involved with each other. When Brummer later married the owner of a coffeehouse in Harlaching, his secretary was deeply hurt.

Brummer tried to convey to the girls in his robust, slightly nasal Bavarian dialect what it was all about. When he had no more arguments and began to feel uncomfortable in his skin, he abandoned the conversation abruptly, "Will you take part now? Yes, or no?"

As soon as his shrewd instinct sensed a certain disposition, he threw the female applicants in at the deep end and explained what came up to them, "We are making a funny sex film. We need a few girls who are willing to take off bra and panties and stand a little nude in front of the camera." He finished the sentence, "Well then, will you take part? You will have fun. We are like a family."

There was no problem to convince the girls to take off their bras. The slip was a bigger problem. There were complaints and trouble. Take for instance a bedroom scene: Who is going to bed to make love in panties? For the cameramen the panties offered technical problems of their own. How to avoid showing panties with a little streak? So they talked to the girls until they were softened up and willing. An additional blue banknote worked sometimes miracles.

Each minute cost money. Film stock was saved. Three rehearsals, at most two takes. So: hush! hush! The woman lay naked, you were atop, some petting, kissing... then expertly swinging between her legs without revealing genitalia and pubic hair.

The mating began either gently or in hectic rabbit speed.

The agitation in the bed at group sex was more than distressing. No trace of sex. But who cared? The audience wasn't that sophisticated. They just wanted to laugh, see some flesh and attractive girls.

Whether blond or brown, the girls looked terrific. The original hair color didn't matter when they were hired. But when there was a shortage of girls, they opened their bag of tricks and used wigs to disguise an actress and have one and the same girl in a dual role. That meant also: twice as much fee.

Most "actresses" who were pushed into such dual or even triple roles were office assistants or housewives. Enough make-up and wigs were available. Itinerary laborers preferred to see German blondies, if possible Valkyries. The main point was that the naked women could move naturally and pretend a natural moaning.

Not only the "actresses" were double, sometimes even the movies led a double life. Thanks to smart contracts that defined all rights in their interest, the producers were able to recycle and change the complete footage as the whim took them. AB Film (Brummer) or Dynamik Film (Gunter **Lass jucken Kumpel** *Otto) tattered two movies in a way that they got a third one without spending a dime. These financially successful manipulations inspired several producers to insert scenes with foreign actors which couldn't be done in this country for legal reasons.*

When the "actresses" saw themselves for the first time on the screen, they giggled while others were ashamed. I felt a little embarrassed. In the cinema I always sat in the last row next to the exit and left before the lights were turned on. I didn't want to be seen and recognized by the audience. Unconsciously, I realized that I was barking up the wrong tree but it was too late to pull out.

It was a long way down the ladder from Ernst Lubitsch and Fritz Lang to Veit Harlan and Harald Reinl to characters like Alois Brummer. Oddly, Brummer died on May 4, 1984, by falling from a ladder while doing a repair job on his roof. Talamonti claims that Brummser never touched a hammer in his life, because he was all thumbs.

Resurrection of the Dead, Part Two: Fritz Haarmann and Adolf Hitler

Besides Wolf C. Hartwig, there were the young filmmakers who tried to revive the reputation of Weimar Republic German Cinema in a cultural landscape stained by people like Alois Brummer. At least for a brief time, they changed the reputation of West German films. When German chancellor Willy Brandt spontaneously fell to his knees in 1970 in front of the Holocaust memorial in Warsaw, the world recognized that there was a different Germany and looked with interest what this country's artists, authors and filmmakers produced: Günter Grass, Volker Schlöndorff, or Alexander Kluge.

However:

Not in primitive sex films that were just a consequence of the miserable state of German filmmaking, but in films made by intellectuals the Nazi past overtook Germans again. No, not a war hero like Rommel, Hitler himself was in the air again. (Even in East German DEFA films Nazi topics, anti-Fascist of course, were on top. They even had an actor who specialized in playing Hitler, in fact one of the best: Fritz Diez.)

In 1973, a voluminous book was published that became an instant bestseller: Joachim C. Fest's work brought German Fascism exlusively down to one man - *Hitler.*

In 1977, the Berlin Film Festival screened the corresponding documentary: ***Hitler - Eine Karriere*** (***Hitler: A Career***) by Fest and Christian Herrendoerfer that made Hitler a star again on German screens, as he had been in ***Triumph of the Will.*** Consequently, many clips were taken from Riefenstahl's film. German audiences stormed into the cinemas to see the movie and wouldn't listen to the scattered voices of critics like Wim Wenders who saw it at the Berlinale and was aghast:

The handbill, filled with strong declarations, I had high expectations seeing the film. I read: "This film shows Hitler's time unprejudicedly, objectively and rationaly. It conveys the fascination of Hitler's career without giving in to the temptation to sink beneath the weight of it.

"This film doesn't manipulate our history. It doesn't glorify and idealize. It

explains." Why to defend something that hadn't been attacked yet?

My astonishment was justified as soon as the film began, and it grew into disbelieving bewilderment. When it was over, there was some brief applause, then the usually forceful festival audience skedaddled, puzzled and embarrassed. One made a joke, "That's Entertainment, Part 3", but it was no release.

Wenders felt obliged to talk about this *Unfilm,* misfilm, as one who made movies in Germany: *I speak up for all who in the past years, after a long blankness, began again to produce images and sounds in a country that is prepossessed with an abysmal distrust of images and sounds that tell about it, that on this account for 30 years anxiously absorbed all foreign images if only they distracted us from ourselves. I don't believe that anywhere there is such a loss of trust in the own images, the own stories and myths as with us. We, the directors of New German Cinema, have sensed this loss the plainest, considering the lack – the absence – of our own tradition, growing up fatherless, and we sensed it in the helplessness and the initial reserve of the viewers. Only slowly, this defensive attitude on one side and the lack of self-confidence crumbled away, and in a process that maybe might last years, a feeling is developing here again that images and sounds don't need to be imported but should tell about this country and could come from this country.*

There is good reason for this distrust for nowhere else images and voice were used so unscrupulously as in this country, never before and nowhere else were they so vulgarized for the transport of lies. And now there comes a film that, with unfathomable rashness, wants to sell these images as the crux of the matter and as "documentary footage", DOES SELL, and therefore, ONCE AGAIN, transports some lies.

The "career" Fest und Herrendoerfer are going to comprehend was made possible not least because there was a total control about any foot of film footage, because all images that exist of this man and his ideas were ingeniously made, skilfully selected and utilized purposefully. Because of this demagogically dealing with images, all who responsibly and competently had to do with images in Germany left this country. For their "comprehensive documentary" Fest and Herrendoerfer therefore only can refer, with few exceptions, to the images of fellow travelers, to the view of accomplices, propaganda stuff that is, the swinishest feet of film ever exposed.

All of this they absorb uncritically, don't draw the slightest consequences for their method of operating. They have the effrontery to write the introduction: "For this film no scene was reconstructed", smarten it even up at most, inflate and double the propaganda value occasionally and make themselves subsequently to instruments.

Once again: Because of these images which we are watching for two hours there was a hole of thirty to forty years in the cinematic culture of this country. Fest and Herrendoerfer tear it open again with a smile taking pride in their horrible discoveries. Against what is oozing out they are counterposing nothing else than a commentary. [...]

This film is fascinated by its own object, by the importance of that object in which it participates ("He proves the truth of the word that history sometimes likes to take shape in a SINGLE man."), so that this object takes over, becomes its own narrator. [211]

In 1940 a sentimental Hitler told Leni Riefenstahl, "*It would be marvelous if one could watch films from the past today, films about Frederic the Great, Napoleon and the historical events of ancient Greece.* [212] Fate provided enough film footage that showed him in the best light. Fest and Herrendoerfer had become fascinated by the memory of the "Führer", but not only them: some young German filmmakers were obsessed with Hitler as well. Hans Jürgen Syberberg, an eccentric outsider among Germany's young filmmakers, produced portraits of Alois Brummer (***Sex-Business - Made in Pasing***), Romy Schneider (***Romy, Portrait eines Gesichts***), King Ludwig (***Ludwig - Requiem für einen jungfräulichen König***), Karl May (***Karl May*** with Helmut Käutner in the title role and with Kristina Söderbaum) and ***Winifred Wagner und die Geschichte des Hauses Wahnfried***. Frau Wagner, direct quote: "*If Hitler would come through that door today, I would be as happy to see him here and have him here as ever...*" Finally, after these "finger exercises", Syberberg felt qualified enough to offer, the same year Fest's film was released, an almost Wagnerian ***Film aus Deutschland (a film from Germany)***: ***Hitler*** (world-wide title: ***Our***

211 Wim Wenders, *That's Entertainment: Hitler. Eine Polemik gegen Joachim C. Fests Film „Hitler - Eine Karriere"*. In: Die Zeit, August 5, 1977.

212 Leni Riefenstahl, *Memoiren*. p. 367.

Hitler) in four parts between 90 and 120 minutes each, produced for a low-budget of (estimated) one million Marks by Bernd Eichinger: *The critical reaction to this film has been very mixed. Syberberg met with almost universal rejection in Germany and with much, at times enthusiastic, acclaim outside Germany particularly in America and in France, where his film was hailed as* Faust, Part III. *In this country, Susan Sontag wrote a passionately partisan yet greatly illuminating essay about the film in* The New York Review of Books *(February 1980). She judged it a masterpiece of "unprecedented ambition."* [213]

Among Syberberg's fellow campaigners were some actors from Rainer Werner Fassbinder's cycle (Peter Kern, Peter Moland, or Harry Baer) and Fassbinder's former cameraman, Dietrich Lohmann. Although Fassbinder himself was absent, he, too, was interested in the movement of the Brownshirts. One night, Fassbinder, according to his final producer, Thomas Schühly, walked with him arm in arm along Paris' Avenue des Champs Elysées singing the Horst Wessel song. *He was no Fascist,* Schühly excused. *He was just interested, as a homosexual, in the male society of the SA.*

Actually, in the mid-1970s, Fassbinder was hooked by this episode of German history and was going to prepare a movie about an "important personality of the Third Reich". Kurt Raab, back then an adamant member of Fassbinder's clique, remembered: *He featured a philistine, similar to Heinrich Himmler, but he didn't intend a biopic. Instead he wanted to show how someone who had climbed to a position of power was able to extinguish human lives by just sitting behind his desk, and planned all those horrible things like a pedantic paper pusher, giving these orders without ever being confronted with reality but, as happened in Himmler's case, had to fetch up if he witnessed an execution. But as he* [Fassbinder] *ran short of time, he assigned me as screenwriter, and* [TV editor Peter] *Märthesheimer sent me a contract via Bavaria.* [214] But eventually, after some research had been done, the project fell through. Fassbinder himself stopped it on the grounds that he didn't want to provide "more ammunition

213 Hans R. Vaget, *Syberberg's "Our Hitler": Wagnerianism and Alienation.* In: The Massachusetts Review, Vol. 23, No. 4 (Winter, 1982), p. 593.

214 Kurt Raab/Karsten Peters, *Die Sehnsucht des Rainer Werner Fassbinder.* Munich: C. Bertelsmann Verlag GmbH, 1982, p. 286.

towards the topic of anti-Semitism". This had to do with Fassbinder's experiences concerning a play he had written in 1975, ***Der Müll, die Stadt und der Tod***, but the curtain never raised for this play during his lifetime as the "Jewish community, flexing its muscles for one of the first times since World War 2, blasted the piece for being anti-Semitic and managed to prevent its debut".[215]

Nevertheless, Fassbinder's name is associated with ***Die Ehe der Maria Braun*** which many people naively believed to be Eva Braun and with a Hitler film titled ***Adolf und Marlene*** which he didn't direct (director was Ulli Lommel) but which he produced. Kurt Raab, who liked to be compared to Peter Lorre because he had played serial killer Fritz Haarmann, the "Vampire of Hanover" in ***Zärtlichkeit der Wölfe*** (***Tenderness of the Wolves***) in 1973, was given the doubtful chance to play Hitler. There was an interesting observation once made by Klaus Mann, the son of Thomas: In 1932, he sat, by pure chance, next to Herr Hitler in the team room of the Munich Carlton Hotel. All of a sudden, he believed to recognize in Hitler's "pathological" physiognomy the features of Fritz Haarmann, a mass murderer who was executed in April 1925. Under such premises, ***Adolf und Marlene*** could have been an unusual picture but Lommel fabricated nothing else than a cheap farce, not the slightest the way Chaplin, Lubitsch or Monty Python (***Mr. Hilter***) did. We hear Raab (*sans* Hitler beard) barking, see him crawling on all fours or playing Battleship, listening to Wagner's music (***Rienzi***). We also see a group of soldierly male bodies and a choir of Hitler Youth singing *Guten Abend, gut' Nacht.* In between, Raab's Hitler longs for Marlene Dietrich and asks Goebbels (a miscast Lommel) to lure her back to Germany. This idea is based on facts: Ufa indeed tried to interest freshly baked Hollywood Marlene to do a few films in Germany again, for 100,000 Reichsmark per movie, but Marlene turned the Germans down. Margit Carstensen played Marlene.

Critic Wolfgang Limmer wrote that she tries honestly to live up to Marlene's

215 Christopher Lawton: *Controversial Fassbinder Play to Open After 20-Year Delay.* SPIEGEL Online, October 1, 2009.

singing voice, but in the end she radiates the sex appeal of a coat rack.[216]

All attempts to save the movie by re-editing failed. Neither is it an exploitation film, nor New German Cinema. Lommel called it a "Fantasy Trip into the Abyss of the Germanic horror soul" and ahead of its time: "For a German director at that time it was taboo to meet Hitler satirically."[217] Lommel decided to stop working in Germany and go to America where he was involved in B pictures like ***The Boogey Man, Olivia, Blood Suckers***, and ***Diary of a Cannibal.***

Fassbinder distanced himself from the movie, called it fascistic, but there was no way to cut out his minor acting part in the production. ***Adolf und Marlene*** is rarely seen and part of the Fassbinder Foundation's poison cabinet.

216 Wolfgang Limmer, *Romanze in Ulk.* In: DER SPIEGEL, No. 17/1977, April 18, 1977.

217 https://www.br.de/fernsehen/ard-alpha/sendungen/alpha-forum/ulli-lommel-gespraech100~attachment.pdf?.

I Aim at the Stars...

...was the title of a Charles H. Schneer/Friedrich A. Mainz co-production starring Curd Jürgens as Wernher von Braun. But more qualified to produce a biopic than Schneer, who usually was associated with stop-motion artist Ray Harryhausen, would have been Walt Disney.

His TV ambitions that contradicted the boycott policy of the established Hollywood producers "reunited" Disney with Germany, particularly with Nazi Germany's former rocket scientists. In charge of Disney's TV Nazi Rocket project was animator Ward Kimball:

At that time Walt Disney planned Disneyland and quasi as promotion for the various subject areas Adventureland, Frontierland, Fantasyland, and Tomorrowland he joined TV. Since I was interested in science fiction all along, Walt offered that I should produce some films on this topic. I said O.K. and got together with those German space experts like Wernher von Braun and Heinz Haber and made a series of films with them: **Man in Space, Tomorrow the Moon, Mars and Beyond, The Spy in the Sky**. *Back then the United States weren't that interested in space exploration, but that changed when the Russians launched their Sputnik. President Eisenhower even asked Walt Disney for a print of my first film* **Man in Space** *to show it to his generals. One has to imagine: I made a child-oriented film and then it was used by the military! When it was screened at a convention of rocket experts in Denmark, the Russians saw it and asked for a print, too. I called Walt but he strictly refused.* [218]

An estimated forty-two million viewers saw the first show, **Man in Space**, *when it premiered in March 1955. When the show was rerun just three months later in June 1955, supposedly President Eisenhower requested a copy of the television show to show the Pentagon. Shortly afterwards in July, President Eisenhower announced that the U.S. would launch a small unmanned earth-circling satellite as part of the U.S. participation in the International Geophysical Year.*

Though Ward Kimball frequently told this story (sometimes elaborating on

218 Interview with Ward Kimball on October 30, 1980 in: Strzyz, Klaus/Knigge, Andreas C., *Disney von innen. Gespräche über das Imperium der Maus.* Frankfurt/M.;Berlin: Ullstein, 1988, p. 157.

the confusion at the Disney switchboard when the President's office called with operators thinking it was a prank by animators) and definitely corresponded with von Braun indicating that Disney was planning to publicize this involvement when the show was scheduled to be rerun again in September, it is important to remember that neither the Office of the Historian at the Pentagon nor the archivists at the Eisenhower Library have been able to locate the documentation supporting Eisenhower's interest in the Disney film.

That doesn't mean that Kimball's story is untrue. It only means that supporting documentation has been elusive. One thing that cannot be denied is the huge impact the three Disney space oriented shows had on public opinion which obviously influenced the acceleration of effort on the U.S. space program. The films also influenced many people who later became aerospace engineers and even top NASA officials and had a significant cultural impact on the American space program, especially when the news articles half-seriously suggested that the United States should turn over the space program to Disney since Disney had a plan and a vision. [219]

In the United States von Braun's past was superseded. Wernher von Braun (1912-1977) had been a member of both the NSDAP and the SS. He was the organizing force behind Nazi Germany's V2 experiments. He was a modern-day Faust. On the radio one British comedian, Mort Sahl, added (when Schneer's ***I Aim at the Stars*** was premiered in London): *I aimed at the Stars – but sometimes hit London.* Disney, who had a good relationship with the Pentagon, joined forces with von Braun and made space travel popular for American tax payers:

Determinedly, Wernher von Braun became an advocate of the intensification of the arms race in the 1950s and speaks up publicly for a policy of strength, even for a preemptive strike against the Soviet Union. Even in 1953, his imagination surpasses everything that U.S. President Ronald Reagan later will shoot for under the abbreviation SDI. His ideas emanate almost one-on-one from his youth fantasy

219 Jim Korkis, *The Other Walt Disney Space Story.* JHM Jim Hill Media. September 14, 2003.

Lunetta: an artificial Earth's moon shaped as a wheel armed with atomic weapons orbiting the planet as "decisive weapon" and thus enforcing world peace.

Meanwhile to the public Braun presents himself a technically highly gifted dreamer. Thanks to magazine articles and TV interviews, he reaches and fascinates an audience of millions. He appears in Walt Disney's TV film **Man in Space** *and together with his colleague Willy Ley he even designs a rocket model for Disneyland. Amidst a technological race of systems with the Soviet Union, Wernher von Braun ingeniously transforms into an agent of an allegedly non-political dream of mankind: to set foot on the Moon.* [220]

These programs were influential in captivating the attention of the public, igniting the imagination of viewers, and shaping the culture with a desire and dream of space exploration. These programs were considered essential in moving the space program forward and are historic in their significance.

Years after these programs aired, Wernher von Braun invited his friend Walt and his associates to tour the NASA facilities across the country to talk about the possibility of a new project. In April 1965, Walt Disney accompanied by his brother Roy as well as several WED Enterprise personnel including Bill Bosche, Ken Peterson, John Hench, Claude Coats and Ken O'Connor visited the three space centers at Houston, Cape Kennedy and Huntsville, Alabama. As a sidenote here – Walt took time out between his looking around to fly a couple of simulators! These high-tech simulated flight missions were accomplished at NASA's manned spacecraft center at Houston. [...]

The Team Disney Tour in 1965 was von Braun's hope for a renewed public interest in the future of the Space Program at NASA. Walt was quoted as saying "If I can help through my TV shows… to wake people up to the fact we've got to keep exploring, I'll do it."

Wernher hoped that the tour would result in a Disney picture about manned space flight. While very much in favor and a huge fan of space, Walt's attention was

---

220 *Wernher von Braun: Auf der Seite der Sieger.* In: ZEIT Geschichte No. 3/2011, August 23, 2011.

focused on other projects. He was busy with EPCOT, Cal Arts, Mineral King and a handful of other things that took precedence over developing another space series.[221]

Instead of Walt, Stanley Kubrick would step in and do it for MGM in Great Britain – but without the assistance of von Braun. He hired team members of a Los Angeles-based company called Graphic Films that had made educational films for NASA. These team members were Douglas Trumbull and Con Pederson, and the film was called ***2001: A Space Odyssey***. The man behind Graphic Films was Lester Novros. He was a former Disney man, having worked on ***Snow White*** and the *Night on the Bald Mountain* segment of ***Fantasia***. The ingenious effects of ***2001*** inspired another filmmaker by the name of George Lucas.

Wernher von Braun, the mastermind, remained a man of WW2 – and what else was ***Star Wars*** in its original packing than WW2 in Outer Space? Many of the X-winged VFX elements we saw in 1977 on the screen were modeled frame by frame copying footage from dogfights taken from newsreels (that contained scenes from ***Front in the Sky***) and from ***The Dam Busters***, a 1955 British war film that described an air raid of Avro Lancaster Bombers against a dam which contained the Möhnesee (May 16/17, 1943). *...one of the key visions I had of the film when I started,* Lucas said, *was of a dogfight in outer space with spaceships - two ships flying through space shooting at each other. That was my original idea.*

To a World War II history buff, the iconic Millennium Falcon from **Star Wars** *resembles one of the best-known bombers of all time.*

The greenhouse cockpit configuration, along with the gun turrets, aboard the ship was lifted straight out of the blueprints for the Boeing B-29 Superfortress.

The Superfortress was a workhorse of the US Army Air Forces that was best known for dropping atomic bombs on the Japanese cities of Hiroshima and Nagasaki.

Star Wars *creator George Lucas is known to have studied 20 to 25 hours of footage from World War II dogfights while doing research for the film.* [...]

221 Jeff Dixon, *Walt Disney Reaching For The Stars...And Beyond!* August 9, 2014.

According to a 1997 interview with Willard Huyck, a screenwriter who is a friend of Lucas, footage of World War II dogfights was used as a placeholder before the special effects were edited into the original film. [222]

The shooting for the very first ***Star Wars,*** today ***Episode IV*** according to the gospel of the saga, took place in 1975, the year of the fall of Saigon that marked the end of the Vietnam War. On August 9, 1974, Richard M. Nixon had resigned and became immortal as the role model for the ***Star Wars*** Imperator who split family ties.

My colleague Robert Blalack and his optical printer were part of the original project. This is what he told me,

20th Century-Fox had no idea how much the **Star Wars** *never-been-done Visual Effects would cost. But Fox knew it had a contract with the Hollywood Unions that required every hour worked on Fox movies to be Union. After 40 hours, Time and ½. After 50 hours, Double Time or "Golden Time". After 60 hours, Triple Time. Each hour frosted with a 37% Pension, Welfare and Vacation surcharge.*

Fox's minimalist budget demanded the invention of a shell corporation, called Industrial Light & Magic, funded by Fox to function as the arms-length Non-Union Employer of the **Star Wars** *VFX workers. These non-Union VFX workers were to all be paid a fixed weekly "salary", a fraction of the 40 hour base pay of their Union counterparts. The* **Star Wars** *VFX work menu was for many a 6 day, 60 to 80 hour week, no Overtime, zero Union Pension and Welfare and Vacation pay.*

With the VFX projected to cost 300% less than if the horrid Union VFX workers did the movie, it was a Studio gamble worth a roll of the dice, even if it went over budget, which it did.

With experienced Union VFX workers out of the equation, the VFX labor pool was drawn from young artists and Vietnam vets infatuated with movies, with nothing to lose. None of the VFX crew had ever worked on a Visual Effects movie of this scale. Most had never worked on any Hollywood movie.

---

222 Alex Lockie, https://www.businessinsider.com/star-wars-world-war-ii-dog-fights-2-ww2-2015-12. December 18, 2015.

When **Star Wars** *started shooting its Live Action out of England, we started creating from scratch the photographic tools and processes of a revolutionary VFX studio, in an empty warehouse in Van Nuys, California.*

After 14 months, with 10 months to the finish line, the photographic VFX system we created had its wrinkles ironed out. 1 of 365 shots was finished. $1 million of the $1.6 million VFX budget was gone. Lucas and his VFX Supervisor Dykstra mix like a librarian and a Hells Angel. A Hatchet Man arrived on cue to fire Dykstra and discipline the too-arty non-Union crew. We tell Hatchet if Dykstra goes, we go. So Dykstra stays, while Hatchet Man plays combo marriage counselor and Consigliere.

Did Fox's hysteria about the movie's Over Budget, mixed with its terror that Universal made the Smart Choice [to turn the Lucas project down], convince it to give Lucas the Toy and Sequel rights in exchange for not killing the movie, but only if the filmmakers paid $2 for every $1 the movie was over budget from their share of any box-office profits?

George Lucas, inspired by Disney, old ***Flash Gordon*** serials, WW2, von Braun, Stanley Kubrick and NASA vision that had relapsed after the Moon landing in 1969, made millions just from the merchandise and consequently sold out to Disney in 2012 for $4 billion: *I felt that I really wanted to put the company somewhere in a larger entity which could protect it. Disney is a huge corporation. They have all kinds of capabilities and facilities, so that there's a lot of strength that is gained by this... I'm doing this so that the films will have a longer life, and so that more fans and people can enjoy them in the future. It's a very big universe I've created and there are a lot of stories that are sitting in there.* [223]

After closing the deal, Lucas seemed to have had seller's remorse. In an interview with Charlie Rose, Lucas did regret his decision, "I sold them to the white slavers that take these things, and..." Later he apologized for that comment, but he remained unhappy, particularly when Disney set his advice at naught concerning the finish of the trilogy: "They weren't that keen to have me involved anyway - but if I get in there, I'm just going to cause trouble, because they're not going to do what I want them to do. And I don't have the

223 Tech Crunch.

control to do that anymore, and all I would do is to muck everything up. And so I said, 'OK, I will go my way, and I'll let them go their way.'" [224]

Germany's answer to the initial success of ***Star Wars*** was ***The Boat*** (***Das Boot***), released to cinemas in 1981 and to TV (first in Britain) in 1984. The (contrary to ***Star Wars***' sci-fi fiction) WW2 "original" based on a book by art collector and WW2 participant Lothar-Günther Buchheim turned out to become Germany's biggest international success ever. It was quite an odyssey from beginning to the finished product:

Film rights for Buchheim's book were first purchased in the mid-1970s by American producers, who initially worked with Don Siegel and hoped to attract a star of the caliber of Robert Redford or Paul Newman. Throughout the 1970s Americans were heavily involved in a number of high profile projects about German experiences during the Third Reich and World War II (often with some input from German investors, creative or technical personnel). These projects included, most notably, **Cabaret** *(1972)* [...]; *the war epic* **A Bridge Too Far** *(1976), another big hit; and also, of course, the hugely successful and influential mini-series* **Holocaust** *(1978).* [225]

Lothar-Günther Buchheim's book about his "adventures" on ***The Boat*** sold almost two million copies worldwide. Buchheim, courted by the creme of German producers, Horst Wendlandt and Luggi Waldleitner, decided to sell the property in May 1975 to Bavaria:

*The Film people wanted to turn the big wheel and considered Buchheim's ideas obstructive. They found a partner in the United States who was willing to enter a really big production, they hired Hollywood director John Sturges (***The Magnificent Seven***) and screenwriter Ronald M. Cohen.* The U.S. partner's name was Edward R. Pressman (***Conan the Barbarian***) who got Sturges to direct the movie at Bavaria Studios in Munich, with a budget of $12 million, co-funded by German tax shelter company Geria which channeled money of German investors in order to generate tax savings rather than profits.

224 Charlie Rose, CBS News, December 2015.

225 Peter Kramer, *Das Boot- Probably the Biggest German Blockbuster of All Time.* October 8, 2017.

In the 1970s, ***Schulmädchen*** producer Wolf C. Hartwig had already hired two American directors, Sam Peckinpah and Andrew V. (son of Victor) McLaglen, to helm ***Steiner - Das Eiserne Kreuz I*** and ***II*** respectively. But the German partners, Bavaria head Helmut Jedele, chief dramaturge Dr. Helmut Krapp and most notably the strident Buchheim, weren't satisfied:

To please Hollywood taste the film had to take place two years after the actual events because America was supposed to have entered the war with brave soldiers fighting unsympathetic Nazis. [226] At the end, some American soldiers in distress at sea were killed by the crew of the Boat.

Buchheim raged and called the script *bullshit, such scenes I jerk in the morning 50 times.* He disliked the screenplay written by Cohen, a Jew, for being openly anti-German: The Germans would be depicted as blood drinkers. Sturges threw in the towel and backed out. Not until then, Don Siegel took care of the project, with a new writer, Dean Riesner, who as a child had been seen acting as a mischievous kid in Chaplin's ***The Pilgrim*** (1923) and, as an adult, had written two Clint Eastwood movies. Obviously he was Jewish too, so Buchheim disliked him right away.

There was only one to write the screenplay for a Buchheim movie and that was Buchheim himself. The project was postponed. After all, as war correspondent, he had been on such a U-boat: *I can bring aboard enough blood and shit, pus and urine. The Atlantic was the worst of all battlefields.* Buchheim was not unhappy that Sturges had to quit for other commitments: *That man would have made a submarine western.* In 1979, after spending $7 million on pre-production, Geria gave up and Bavaria was left the sole partner. Eventually they joined forces with Neue Constantin Film as German distributor and Mark Damon (PSO), who once was married to a German wife (actress Barbara Frey), for international sales for a reported $8 million. Instead of Sturges, Siegel or Sidney Pollack, they voted for a "hot" *German* TV director to helm the project. Who else should be around more qualified

226 Yves Buchheim/Franz Kotteder, *Buchheim: Künstler, Sammler, Despot - Das Leben meines Vaters.* Munich: Wilhelm Heyne Verlag/Random House GmbH, 2018.

to portray Nazi submariners and grind Nazisploitation than a non-Jewish German: Wolfgang Petersen (*1941 in Emden) who had studied at the German Film and Television Academy in West Berlin (although he didn't join his politicized fellow students like later RAF terrorist Holger Meins who renamed the film school Dziga Vertov Institute).

Any politics? No chance with Wolfgang Petersen! *Politics play only a marginal role in novel and film. When the captain and his officers complain about Nazi propaganda - as communicated to them via speeches broadcast on the radio - or about the measures taken by the German military high command - as relayed to them via radio messages - it is because of their stupidity and military ineffectiveness rather than their objectionable ideology or their warmongering; similarly, the young Nazi officer is merely a harmless figure of fun. As military professionals, the captain and his officers (excluding, of course, the young Nazi) are only interested in doing their job.* [227]

Bernd Eichinger, the young head of distributor Neue Constantin, was an avid reader of Marvel comic books and ***Perry Rhodan*** sci-fi pulps and was convinced that a movie like this could recoup its investment only internationally, never in Germany alone:

The basic idea alone is more than daring. A German production company, Bavaria, takes a late shot (never tried before) to break away from the arthouse ghetto and Fassbinder's ballad film manufacture with a completely German action movie and penetrate the international market where the real tough guys of the movie business compete: **Stars Wars** *and* **The Empire Strikes Back** *(stupendous visual effects),* **Jaws** *(underwater horror) and* **Apocalypse Now** *(bombs, corpses, mindless war).*

No other German film topic is that reminiscent of the global success stories in previous year's cinema than Buchheim's Atlantic terror mission: Men who venture out far away in a tight vehicle, not up to Outer Space, but to the unlike more dangerous oceans of world war. Men on a long cruise to the end of their mind (and their life) in the fashion of Francis Coppola's apocalyptic jungle trip in Vietnam.

"The U-boats were the first spaceships," says Wolfgang Petersen, the 39-year-

227 Ibid.

old director, who wrote the final draft. "But the spaceships of the cinema are figments of the imagination which buzz through science fiction fairy-tale realm. Our boat is up in the audience's grill that tight and authentically that it seems to take part of the trip. Our ideal conception is that the cinemas have to keep vomit bags available because the people get seasick during the storm sequences."

"We need spectacular images: the burning images when a tanker is hit and explodes. Or explosions of water bombs that fill the screen and look as if an atom bomb has been dropped," says Bernd Eichinger, 31, the boy wonder of German film distribution. [...]

Spectacular images, Eichinger explains, are indispensable if a movie should spark today's cinema audiences - and this consists of 90 pecent out of the 17- to 28-year-olds who are lusting for action and filled with a "certain appetite for destruction."[228]

The German reviewers were sparing with praise, but that had no influence on the box office receipts. Petersen was more interested in what the influential Jewish community in Los Angeles would say. He remembers that at the LA premiere there was applause when the first title read that of 40,000 German submariners in WW2 30,000 didn't return, but when the movie rolled, he says, the audience was spellbound, the picture was sold to and accepted by America and Petersen able to start a career as Hollywood director.

But it would need another filmmaker to climb Hollywood heights to propel the wave of sci-fi war movies to new SFX heights in 1996 with ***Independence Day***. While ***The Boat*** was produced, Roland Emmerich from Sindelfingen studied production design, then film directing at the Munich Film and TV School and tried his hand at low-budget fantasy filmmaking that was only lukewarmly received in his home country: ***Das Arche Noah Prinzip*** (***The Noah's Ark Principle,*** 1984, his graduation film), ***Joey*** (***Making Contact,*** 1985), ***Hollywood Monster*** (1987) and ***Moon 44*** (1990), all co-funded by his father, a factory owner (Solo Kleinmotoren GmbH). Critics called him "Spielbergle" (Little Spielberg). When he realized that a prophet

228 Wilhelm Bittorf, *Das Boot: Als Wahnsinn imponierend.* In: DER SPIEGEL No. 53/1980, December 29, 1980.

is not valid in his own country, he became a success in Hollywood by directing ***Universal Soldier*** (1992), ***Stargate*** (1994) and eventually ***Independence Day***. The blueprint for the latter was a movie Curt Siodmak had written for Charles H. Schneer and Ray Harryhausen in 1955-56: ***Earth vs. the Flying Saucers***. In both films a U.F.O. armada attacks Washington D.C., but while Harryhausen and Schneer have it only landing in front of the White House, Emmerich actually had it destroyed by the spaceship. No American filmmaker would have dared. Nope, they were too patriotic to commit such kind of "blasphemy". For this job a German was needed. Roland Emmerich had the guts to blow a scale model of the White House to pieces.

German special effects people were at hand to design and film the disaster and won an Academy Award for it. VFX supervisor Volker Engel worked closely with cinematographers Anna Foester and Philipp Timme. Timme, *The schedule for* **Independence Day** *provided for two takes for each scene that involved explosives. Consequently, two models were built for each of these scenes [as safety factor] - including the White House.* [...]

To capture the explosion from all conceivable angles we installed seven cameras with a frame rate between 300 and 120 frames per second. Except for the main camera, all other angles were planned in a way that no further postprocessing was necessary but that they could be used as plain in-camera effects. [...] *The lighting was finished the day before and when all cameras were ready for shooting, everything went by quite fast. The explosion lasted a few seconds and checking the image on the video monitors the result looked quite spectacular so that the whole set could be wrapped the same night.* [229]

The explosion of the White House in Emmerich's sci-fi pic and an air-liner that rammed an apartment tower in London in Jack Gold's ***The Medusa Touch*** (1978, based on a book by Peter Van Greenaway) might belong to the involuntary blueprints for 9/11.

I wondered how many terrorist attacks even in German film projects were suggested in 2001. Former Fassbinder author Peter Märthesheimer wrote a (never made) screenplay about a terrorist group adopting the ubiqui-

229 Lecture given in Cologne, November 28, 1997.

tous name of ***Mabuse*** and inducing lethal gas during a mass into the Cologne Cathedral to kill all believers. In another movie (***Der Zimmerspringbrunnen***) the Berlin TV Tower explodes in a dream sequence. Sad highlight was a German commercial screened only two days before 9/11 and then withdrawn from circulation. The spot opens in a sidewalk cafe in Manhattan. Above it, we recognize a skyscraper that resembles, with some imagination, a tower of the World Trade Center. A young couple is served red wine and coffee when the table begins to vibrate. Aircraft engines are roaring. Horrified, the guests look up. They see a passenger airplane crashing in broad daylight into the tower above them. People flee screaming while - cut - the passengers aboard the airplane are given a good shake. The plane penetrates the building like a gigantic arrow and we see a huge billboard with the phone number of the client. Everybody has a good laugh. No catastrophe, nobody is harmed or injured, no victims, no dead, just a spectacular special effect for entertainment's sake. We don't care what has happened aboard the plane: a terrorist attack? drunken pilots? a malfunction of the instruments?

In charge of the model work was SFX supervisor Joachim Grüninger, CEO of the Munich-based Magicon GmbH. Since the early days, Grüninger worked repeatedly with his friend Roland Emmerich (although he was not involved in ***Independence Day***). The spot was the brainchild of a Hamburg advertising agency that was commissioned by Telegate AG, a communication service provider founded in August 1996 by Dr. Klaus Harisch and Peter Wünsch.

Anja Meyer, in charge of Telegate's public relations, was aghast when she saw the real events of 9/11. She stormed into the office of her bosses, "I don't believe this. Turn on the TV. In New York somebody tries to imitate our spot."

Harisch and Wünsch watched the terrorist attacks with unbelieving eyes. Harisch's first thought: "Damn, we have to stop our spot! Immediately!!" No thought wasted on the victims, only damage control.

What was it what they wanted? Harisch didn't need long to answer the question.

"We wanted a real bombshell. Something that was outstanding and big. A Big Bang. Everyone should realize that with us a new era opened. So we announced a competition."

And indeed they got what they wanted.

One day Harald Prantner from the Hamburg agency McCann-Erickson came with his boards to Munich and pitched his idea: A large airplane, an Airbus or a Boeing, crashes through a skyscraper in Manhattan and destroys the phone number in question. In a second spot, a huge Godzilla should break through the same skyscraper.

Harisch said, "Okay, that's it. We'll do it. But only if you are going to party really hard. It must look big and authentic, like Hollywood."

Four months and a million mark budget later it looked real big. Like Hollywood. They had partied hard indeed. The Big Bang. "We watched it on the same TV set that we saw the horrible truth on September 11." [...]

Harisch was enthusiastic, "That's a real winner. Super. Terrific. Awesome. On air with it."

On September 9, the spot was aired the first time, on all German TV channels. On September 10, a second time. Then came September 11, the day even advertising stood still for a moment worldwide.

Ten years later Harald Prantner talked to Evelyn Roll, the only journalist who bothered to do some research on this:

"Yes, true, I got that stupid idea. It was my brainchild. That thing has left a big scar. It really made me sick." [...]

He still remembers that on September 11 he allowed himself for a few seconds the thought, "If we don't take it out, if we let it on air, everybody on the whole world will talk about Telegate." [...]

Then he says, "You know what really sent me into orbit? When we learned that the terrorists came from Hamburg. Do you understand? They were in this city. They didn't conspire in Kabul or in Mexico or whatever! No, it had to be Hamburg, the same city where we had planned our film."

Maybe they had the same idea at the same time:

The idea to destroy something really big to indicate that something new has to happen: Maybe these terrorists over there in Hamburg-Harburg sat one evening in their pantaloons and turbans on their carpet and thought the same thing: We need a Big Bang to destroy the Old and make room for something New. [230]

Or they read an outline accidentally provided by the nearby agency.

230 Evelyn Roll, „*Wir wollten einen Knalleffekt*". In: Süddeutsche Zeitung, May 17, 2010.

Maya the Bee and Hitler's Fork

Hitler's fascination with animation and cartoons continues in Germany to this day. Around the time Gerhard Fieber joined Second Channel TV and ***Mainzelmännchen***, a German comic book editor, in need of stories, purchased Franco-Belgian comic material. His name was Rolf Kauka and he was the first to publish ***Asterix*** (created in France in 1959) in his comic magazine *Lupo Modern* during the mid-1960s. But Kauka, an archconservative German national, not only renamed all the Gaul warrior characters in the first story, ***The Golden Sickle***: Asterix became Siggi, Obelix Babarras, Miraculix the druid Konradin, a homage to Konrad Adenauer, he bastardized all the dialogue too, and went so far to change the content of the stories. The village of the Gauls was renamed Bonnhalla (derived from Bonn, at that time West Germany's seat of government).

Asterix was originally a parody of the Boches, the Nazi troops who had occupied France like Julius Caesar and the Romans in the stories of ***Asterix***. This cunning little Gaul who developed super strength thanks to the druid's magic potion was a true French Résistance fighter, although artist Albert Uderzo denied this interpretation. Anyway, Kauka's version changed the plot. The Gauls were transformed into Germans, and in the Cold War the stories became a parody of Germany West and East. In their version of the Visigoths and Ostrogoths taken from the story ***Asterix and the Goths***, Kauka and his loyal assistant Peter Wiechmann went so far as to satirize the German Democratic Republik. Cholerik, for instance, the leader of the Ostrogoths, became comrade Hullberick (=Walter Ulbricht) in Kauka's Germanized draft. After awhile, the French creators, René Goscinny and Albert Uderzo, caught wind of Kauka's odd editing practices and they took legal action.

Albert Uderzo: *An acquaintance called and said I should read the [German] magazine* Bravo. *I got the issue at a kiosk in France. There was an article that called "my" characters Siggi and Babarras and termed them little Germans. I had the article translated and was aghast. The article complained that it was scandalous and tasteless to sell such stories with nationalist undertones to kids.* [...] *We asked the French consul to stop that. He said that he couldn't because that would have* *been a political intrusion. We thought that odd. It wasn't legal to bastardize our text. So we had our lawyer interdict that. I don't know Herr Kauka's intentions. He attacked me for a long time, invented stories that I had been a collaborator of the Germans during the war. At that time [when the Nazis occupied Paris], I was 14 years old. I guess he was a little crazy. But there are such people not only in Germany.* [231]

Kauka lost the license in 1966, which was in turn sold to Egmont Ehapa and became an instant hit with German comic readers - and cinemagoers who came in droves to see the Asterix animated films. The Asterix films, distributed by Jugendfilm, became a box office bonanza in West Germany. One, ***The Twelve Tasks of Asterix*** (***Les douze travaux d'Asterix/Asterix erobert Rom***), sold six million tickets. Finally, Jürgen Wohlrabe, the owner of Jugendfilm, felt strong enough to get the production control over from France to Berlin (probably for a lot of money) in the early 1990s. He had delusions of grandeur and produced ***Asterix in America*** to conquer the Disney-dominated market in the United States - but almost no American wanted to see it as the Goscinny-Uderzo comics were virtually unknown in the United States. Wohlrabe failed in an even more spectacular way than Karl Neumann of Deutsche Zeichenfilm GmbH. Wohlrabe died the year after his big fiasco.

In the early 1940s, high on Karl Neumann's wish list for Deutsche Zeichenfilm GmbH was a character named *Maya the Bee*. He and Gerhard Fieber went to Lake Starnberg to meet with Maya's creator, writer Waldemar Bonsels, and purchase an option. Nobody else than Thea von Harbou was commissioned to write a screenplay. Waldemar Bonsels' adventures of Maya the Bee, *Die Biene Maja und ihre Abenteuer*, was first published in 1912, a partly brutal, social Darwinist initiation tale that took place among insects. The book became a success with German soldiers in WW1. It didn't take long until Little Maya in her brave fight against the hornet enemies was as famous (and certainly more popular) than the Kaiser, Hindenburg and Ludendorff together.

---

231 *Albert Uderzo, "Die Leser haben Asterix am Leben erhalten"* In: Die Welt, October 21, 2013.

In 1951, one year before his death, Bonsels wrote to his American publisher: *As a matter of importance, the great success story of the book began in the war year 1915 with the soldiers in action. To these men who spent their life between fight, death and horror the book was a reminder of* Heimat *[home].*

Some time later, Bonsels' widow Rose-Marie tried to interest Walt Disney in the property but she wasn't successful. Maybe Disney knew that Bonsels had sympathized with Hitler and the Nazis and had anti-Semitic feelings.

In the early 1970s, Gerhard Fieber and colleagues traveled to Tokyo and met Isao Takahata who displayed interest in producing the ***Mainzelmännchen*** for little money in Japan. He even cited a poem by Heinrich Heine in German language to show how honored he felt by the offer. But at the last moment the powers at Second Channel TV got cold feet because they feared the Nippon-produced ***Little Mainz Men*** might look too Asian.

But with *Maya the Bee* there was no objection. *Maya* became a favorite project of TV editor Josef Göhlen and his mastermind, German media mogul Leo Kirch. They ordered two seasons of 52 episodes each of an animated ***Maya the Bee*** series produced by Zuiyo Enterprise (later renamed Nippon Animation). The characters were designed by former Hanna-Barbera stalwart Marty Murphy. Bonsels' name and all nationalist touches of the original book were omitted. Bonsels' brainchild was whitewashed.

In 2013, Second Channel TV aired new 3D-made episodes, and in addition two feature films were made for the cinema. When I talked in a radio broadcast about the brownish, nationalist background of the original bee I reaped a shitstorm of protest.

- Hitler ate his soup with a spoon. The spoon should be banned as nationalist symbol of a brown past!!

- Because Herr Goebbels produced "Heile-Welt-Filme" for his kids, we shouldn't be allowed to see them? Why? What will happen?

- Here they are again, our pseudo-submissive, dismayed virtuosos who in the moral self-righteousness of a priestly caste see the Antichrist even in **Maya the Bee**.

The Resurrection of the Dead, Part Three: Look Who's Back

The one person that had made Hitler "acceptable" again, focusing on the person and not the system, rendering the man almost god-like, was Joachim Clemens Fest with his voluminous biography which reviewers called a "towering achievement, a compelling story told in a way only a German could tell it". We have mentioned his *magnum opus* and the film documentary based on it.

From the introduction of the English-language translation published by Harcourt, Inc. in 1974:

History records no phenomenon like him. Ought we to call him "great"? No one evoked so much rejoicing, hysteria, and expectation of salvation as he; no one so much hate. No one else produced, in a solitary course lasting only a few years, such incredible accelerations in the pace of history. No one else so changed the state of the world and left behind such a wake of ruins as he did. It took a coalition of almost all the world powers to wipe him from the face of the earth in a war lasting nearly six years, to kill him - to quote an army officer of the German resistance - "like a mad dog."

Hitler's peculiar greatness is essentially linked to the quality of excess. It was a tremendous eruption of energy that shattered all existing standards. Granted, gigantic scale is not necessarily equivalent to historic greatness; there is power in triviality also. But he was not only gigantic and not only trivial. The eruption he unleashed was stamped throughout almost every one of its stages, down to the weeks of final collapse, by his guiding will. [...] *In fact, to a virtually unprecedented degree, he created everything out of himself and was himself everything at once: his own teacher, organizer of a party and author of its ideology, tactician and demagogic savior, leader, statesman, and for a decade the "axis" of the world.* [232]

Fest is using an accumulation of superlatives to describe this mass murderer and war criminal such as: *tremendous eruption of energy - gigantic scale - guiding will - savior - "axis" of the world.*

Fest was born on December 8, 1926, in Berlin Karlshorst as second son

232 Joachim Fest, *Hitler.* Translated by Ralph Manheim. Orlando, Florida: Harcourt, Inc., 1974, p. 3.

of a school rector, a typical member of the educated classes, a Catholic who steadfastly refused to join the NSDAP. After the war which he experienced as anti-aircraft auxiliary, the teacher's son worked as a journalist and, against his father's advice, became fascinated with personalities who formed and defined the Third Reich. Besides his ***Hitler*** book, he supported Albert Speer in editing his biography. He seemed to have been that fascinated by Hitler and Speer that he turned into their literary high priest. (Secretly dreaming maybe that a tiny bit of Hitler's infamous fame might leap to him, the chronicler of the brown "Savior".)

Roughly three decades after Fest's film ***Hitler: A Career*** that used only documentary footage, notably made by Leni Riefenstahl and newsreel cameramen to render an image of Hitler that he would have liked himself, Bernd Eichinger, the producer behind Syberberg's ***Hitler: A Film from Germany*** and distributor of ***The Boat***, tried his hand at scriptwriting and based another production on Fest's writings and the memories of Hitler's former secretary, Traudl Junge: ***Der Untergang*** (***The Downfall***), however, was a feature film, not a documentary, recalling the last 10 days in the Führer Bunker.

Bernd Eichinger was interviewed by *Rheinische Post*, a local paper from the Lower Rhine Valley, and asked why he wanted to retell this gloomy chapter of history.

Eichinger answered, *It is much more than a gloomy chapter. It is the most dramatic part of German history and as that something that concerns us all. My parents have experienced the war. I myself was born right after the war and have experienced vividly the effects. So I began to busy myself with the German history and especially NS history. For 20 years, I'm doing intense reading on this period.*

Joachim C. Fest's book ***The Downfall*** became Eichinger's guideline: *Fest, so to speak, handed me the dramaturgic key to write the screenplay. In the book he not only observes the final days of Hitler but the collapse of the whole system. In these twelve days one could observe all the mechanisms of the NS regime as if in a nutshell, and this in an intensified form because events at the end of the war did dramatize once more.*

About the biggest challenge:

To do what no one has dared since: to portray the personalities who have shaped the NS regime in great parts as three-dimensional characters. And with it break with previous demonization and break a taboo. The objective was not to deliver a template but to penetrate the personalities. And win insights which, I guess, are very important.

One shouldn't regard the evil as an abstract mass which takes on a life of its own and then affects the people but should understand that these are people who have their own emotions with whom people can identify in case of doubt to a certain degree. [233]

Eichinger, who was quite simple-minded, a Karl May and Marvel comics devotee, wanted to show Hitler the human and so he begins his film treatment not in the bunker in 1945 but with the introduction of a young lady who applies for a job as Hitler's secretary in the Wolfsschanze. Traudl Junge is pretty nervous and in a typewriting test makes many mistakes but Hitler consoles her because he likes her: a nice, old gentleman, not evil at all, the human touch of the monster: the fatalism of evil. As a German, you would like to become his friend.

...if the film has one value, Eichinger said, *it is the fact that it contains no judgement.* No judgement concerning the crimes: Sympathy for the Devil - to quote the Rolling Stones. The lesson is clear: Hitler was no beast.

The holocaust doesn't fit in that grandfatherly image of this Film-"Führer" and is referred to only briefly. Otherwise, the dictator is portrayed as a soft-spoken dreamer with a human side who enjoys chocolate cake: no antihero but a negative hero, anyway, a hero.

A short time before Mel Gibson's ***The Passion of Christ*** hit the cinemas, Eichinger produced a sort of ***The Passion of Adolf Hitler***.

Henry Hübchen, former GDR actor, took a mischievous pleasure in his acceptance speech at Deutscher Filmpreis (German Film Award) in July

233 *Bernd Eichinger: "Ich will keine Schablonen"*. In: Rheinische Post, September 14, 2004.

2005 that he, a little Jew, won as best actor and not Hitler who was also nominated in the person of actor Bruno Ganz.

When I was in China, I saw a shop that sold Third Reich memorabilia. And there were photos of the real Hitler right beside Bruno Ganz as Hitler in Eichinger's movie that was directed by Oliver Hirschbiegel and seen in the cinemas by five million Germans. Hirschbiegel, "*Bad people do not walk around with claws like vicious monsters, even though it might be comforting to think so. Everyone intelligent knows that evil comes along with a smiling face.*"

Originally, since the 1980s, Eichinger was even more interested in the ***Nibelungen***. In a way, he was interested in Hitler because of the ***Nibelungen***. When Fritz Lang returned to directing in Germany again, Berlin-based producer Artur Brauner, a Polish Jew who escaped the Holocaust, immediately offered him a remake of the ***Nibelungs*** in 1959. Lang turned this offer down ("That's impossible today"), and instead made a remake of ***The Indian Tomb*** which proved impossible as well. But Brauner didn't give up the plan to produce a monumental remake of one of Hitler's favorite movies, actually a Nazi movie. He ignored the warnings of film critics and contacted the Allensbach Institute for Public Opinion Research. The poll attested that at least every third federal citizen would like to watch such a remake. The following years Brauner toyed with a lot of casting ideas: Marianne Koch or Romy Schneider as Kriemhild; Dieter Borsche, Walter Reyer, Claus Holm or Will Quadflieg as her brother, Burgundians' King Gunther; Brunhild, Gunther's love affair, to be played by Barbara Rütting, Eva Bartok or Cuban actress Chelo Alonso; the part of Siegfried's sworn enemy, grim Hagen, offered to Gert (***Goldfinger***) Fröbe and as Siegfried, the hero, Jerome Courtland, who after some parts in the ***Disneyland*** series was stranded in Germany where Kirk Douglas' Bryna Productions shot the TV series ***Tales of the Vikings*** in 1959. But the distributors protested: A German hero had to be played by a genuine German, an Aryan so to speak, and not an American. Brauner was desperate, "There is no Siegfried here anymore! Give me a German Siegfried and I will start." Years went by, and eventually Brauner found a Germanic hero that pleased Germany's biggest distributor, Constantin Film, that also released the Karl May westerns with Lex Barker and Pierre Brice: an ersatz-Johnny Weissmuller, Uwe Beyer, a tall (6'3") German track and field athlete and hammer thrower, who had enough muscle at his command but not enough brain to act out the demanding part. His father, Erich Beyer, by the way, had failed to qualify for Hitler's Olympic Games 1936 as a shot putter. Nazi film-schooled Gerhard Menzel, who after the war wrote West Germany's first scandalous movie, ***Die Sünderin*** (***The Sinner***) that aroused the protest of the Catholic Church organized by Chaplain Carl Klinkhammer, was hired to write the screenplay, but Brauner was not satisfied because Menzel saw the dragon not larger than a lizard from the zoo. Anyway, Menzel passed away in 1966 and Brauner decided to hire Karl May (and Nazi film) veteran Harald G. Petersson and with him two other May experts, director Harald Reinl and cinematographer Ernst Wilhelm Kalinke.

The rest of the cast wasn't that spectacular anymore but at least more competent than the hammer thrower: Karin Dor, back then Reinl's wife, played Brunhild, Maria Marlow was seen as Kriemhild, Rolf Henniger as Gunther, and Herbert Lom as Etzel/Attila, King of the Huns, who fulfills the revenge of Kriemhild, widow of Siegfried slain by another Siegfried, in this case actor Siegfried Wischnewsky who played Hagen. In 1966 and 1967, the two parts actually made their money - despite all the negative reviews. DER SPIEGEL, for instance, called the production *childish hero cinema: Siegfried demonstrates his muscles, a hydraulically operated dragon chuffs fire from its nozzles, ladies in glossy paper Gothic make faces and Burgundy's unloquacious veterans' association looks solemnly around.* [234]

Since he attended film school in Munich, Bernd Eichinger's pet project was a 2nd remake of the ***Nibelungs*** and, becoming the head of the New Constantin Film that was established after the bankruptcy of the old company, followed that vain dream until his premature death in 2011: his first script titled ***The Morning of Valhalla***, the final draft ***Wrath.*** Director Tom

234 *Leichen unter Eichen.* In: DER SPIEGEL, 52/1966, December 19, 1966.

Tykwer who had read it, *There he had picked a sandtrap as big as a swimming pool. If he would have made that movie, the critics would have crucified him.* [235]

Some New German Hitler Devotion rose indeed at the time Eichinger had reached his peak (and after his sudden death) in a 3D-animated cartoon that showed Walter Moers' caricature of Adolf singing in the bathtub (the video clip ***Der Bonker*** was an instant hit on the internet with millions of clicks in 2006) and in a ***Borat***-inspired satire: ***Er ist wieder da*** (***Look Who's Back***, 2015) based on a bestselling book by Timur Vermes. Hitler awakes from a coma on the site of his former bunker and finds himself in the present.

"Our idea was to find out how people react to Hitler today, and to his ideas and to ask does he have a chance nowadays," director David Wnendt told the Guardian. His conclusion? "Unfortunately, yes."

He said the film's main aim was to make people laugh. "Germans should be able to laugh at Hitler, rather than viewing him as monster because that relieves him of responsibility for his deeds and diverts attention from his guilt for the Holocaust," Wnendt said.

"But it should be the type of laugh that catches in your throat and you're almost ashamed when you realise what you're doing."

Wnendt said his travels around Germany with [Oliver] Masucci as Hitler - everywhere from the North Sea island of Sylt, a holiday location for wealthy Germans, to small towns in Bavaria where Masucci posed as a postcard painter in a nod to Hitler's failed attempts at an artistic career - revealed "a feeling of deep discontent in the population, where people of every social status demonstrated how they were against foreigners and fearful of Islamisation".

The film's release at a time when the country is locked in a fierce debate over the mass arrival of refugees and whether it serves as an opportunity for Germany or a threat, could hardly be more timely. The film includes footage of Pegida demonstrators holding anti-foreigner placards, as well as news reels showing recent arson attacks on asylum-seekers' homes. [236]

---

235 Süddeutsche Zeitung, September 5, 2012.

236 *David Wnendt on filming Look Who's Back: 'Our idea was to see how people react to Hitler'.* In: The Guardian, October 6, 2015.

Reviews like these convey the impression that ***Look Who's Back*** is basically ***Candid Camera*** with actor Masucci substituting for Hitler. But actually most scenes depict a typical German comedy with Hitler turned into a popular TV star, something already tried in a virtually unknown paperback from 1987: *Fernsehen wie es jeder hasst (Television as Anybody Hates It)* with a chapter devoted to an old Hitler as guest of honor in a popular German talk show hosted by Joachim Fuchsberger.

In the meantime there was a new part for Oliver Masucci. Directed by Oskar Roehler who describes himself as politically more right-wing, he stars as the late director Rainer Werner Fassbinder in ***Enfant Terrible***. When he had seen ***Jew Suss*** for the first time, Roehler had decided on the spot to make a film about the shooting of this Nazi production with Tobias Moretti as Ferdinand Marian and Justus von Dohnányi as Veit Harlan: ***Jud Süss - Film ohne Gewissen*** (***Jew Suss: Rise and Fall***, 2010).

In the long run, Old and New German cinema had come to terms.

At its premiere at the Berlin Film Festival in February 2010, Roehler's account of ***Jew Suss*** was poorly received and booed. Actor Moritz Bleibtreu who played Joseph Goebbels tried to defend the movie, "*It's about time we Germans were able to live with our history in a freer way, so that we can emancipate from it to some extent.*"

Sometimes actors should keep their mouth shut.

Why Sky Sharks Love to Fuck Göhte

Director John Landis was rather annoyed when he attended a small film festival in Braunschweig and met the lowest of the low budget filmmakers, a guy by the name of Marc Fehse who tried to get on the bandwagon of ***Sharknado*** and ***Iron Sky*** and combine the idea of flying sharks with German history and Nazis - ***Sky Sharks***:

A team of Arctic geologists stumble across an abandoned laboratory in which the Nazis developed an incredible and brutal secret weapon during the final months of WW2.

Deep in the ice, the team accidentally awakes a deadly army of flying zombie sharks ridden by genetically mutated, undead super-humans, who are unleashed into the skies, wreaking their bloodthirsty revenge on any aircraft that takes to the air.

An elite task force is assembled to take on this deadly threat and stop the Sky Sharks from conquering the air, but as time runs out, the task force realises they will have to fight fire with fire, and the stage is set for the greatest flying super-mutant zombie shark air battle the world has ever seen... [237]

Whoever was available for a brief cameo (and had something of a name) was written in by Marc and his brother Carsten Fehse:

With **Sky Sharks** *it is our intent to create the ultimate cult movie - unlike any seen before, that will capture the hearts, mind, and souls of genre film fans around the world. Additionally, Germany in the early 1920s was the cradle of horror films, but over the decades it has passed into oblivion. Today it's carving out a miserable existence. Our hope with* **Sky Sharks** *is to not only make a great horror film, but to help put Germany back on the horror-making map.* [...]

We've carefully crafted some great rewards for you burgeoning **Sky Sharks** *fans! From the standard t-shirts and blu-rays, to your chance to die on screen at the hands of a Nazi Zombie, we have something for everyone at every price point. And of course, every dollar earned will go up on screen to make* **Sky Sharks** *the best Flying Shark/Nazi Zombie movie you've ever seen!*

237 https://moviesandmania.com > 2015/01/23 > sky-sharks-2016-german-comedy-action-horror-movie-by-marc-fehse-cast-plot-trailer/.

That is provided you participate with a few bucks in the Fehse Brothers' Crowdfunding campaign because:

To shoot a film independently is getting more and more difficult. Raising the money is always a challenge due to the risks in the marketplace and the growing swell of piracy. Very rarely will a distributor take a chance and pay for an independent film in advance. [...] *So by contributing to* **Sky Sharks** *you're actually helping us twofold. We also want to emphasize the positive impact your support has on our production, driving us to creative heights. The trust you put in us will be paid back, by giving you a never-before-seen piece of movie madness, murder and mayhem.* [238]

The minimum investment: 5 Euro! (*We'll also post some exclusive set photos for you.*)

While Fehse compiled his film over the years, Martin Moszkowicz, who survived Bernd Eichinger, and Constantin Film were instrumental in reviving ***The Brandy Punch*** for a new audience: ***Fack Ju Göhte*** (***Suck Me Shakespeer***) was made by Turkish-German director Bora Dagtekin. Zeki Müller, an ex-con who was in jail for 13 months and barely can spell his name, lands a position at Goethe Comprehensive School that happens to sit over the spot where money from one of his robberies was stashed. Just by the way, he is being promoted substitute teacher. As such he tames the rather stupid teenage monster pupils introducing them to "real life". The picture, a smash hit in Germany, making $9 million at the box office, the best score for a German film in 2013, so far spawned two sequels and was mainly intended for morons. Nevertheless, Elyas M'Barek who plays Zeki was amused, *It happened that we had to interrupt shooting because of fits of laughter. I witnessed that only with the* **Fack ju Göthe** *films that even cameramen and gaffers collapsed with laughter.* [239]

A similar situation aroused during the shooting of the original ***Feuerzangenbowle*** in 1944 as a German newsreel reveals.

Oddly enough, a German Supreme Court denied Heinz Rühmann's authorship and the entitlement of his heirs to royalties still made by ***Feuerzangenbowle*** on TV and via the vast number of Blu-ray sales. They

238 Kickstarter.

239 www.goldenekamera.de

claimed that Rühmann's assistant Helmut Weiss, who was given the chance to direct the movie (but with producer Rühmann, credited *künstlerischer Gesamtleiter* planning every detail in advance), was the sole author: *In consideration of all circumstances it is not sufficiently evident that Heinz Rühmann had creatively contributed at least marginally to the picture* **Die Feuerzangenbowle**.

Brandy Punch (Die Feuerzangenbowle).
Courtesy of Jens Geutebrück, Coronaretro Archives

APPENDIX

Film Chronology 1933-1945

1933

January 30: Reich President Paul von Hindenburg appoints Adolf Hitler as Reich Chancellor.

January 31: The U-boat drama ***Morgenrot (Dawn)*** directed by Gustav Ucicky is premiered at Berlin's Ufa Palace at the Zoo in the presence of Adolf Hitler and Ufa chief Alfred Hugenberg.

February 3: ***Der Choral von Leuthen*** (***The Anthem of Leuthen***) with Otto Gebühr as King Frederick II.

February 27: Reichstag fire.

March 13: Dr. Joseph Goebbels is named Minister of Public Enlightenment and Propaganda.

March 28: Goebbels speaks to the leaders of the German film industry at the Hotel Kaiserhof in Berlin.

April: Official boycott of Jewish shops.

May 10: Nazi book burning in the square at the State Opera in Berlin. Joseph Goebbels speaks, "The era of extreme Jewish intellectualism is now at an end. [...] The future German man will not just be a man of books, but a man of character."

Spring: Ufa decides to lay off its Jewish employees.

June 1: Filmkreditbank is established, a special bank commissioned to fund the film industry.

June 14: ***S.A.-Mann Brandt*** (***Storm Trooper Brandt***) by Franz Seitz. Goebbels' diary [240]: *Not as bad as I feared.*

June 28: The "reliability clause" to further the "Aryanization" of German film. It is decreed that everyone involved in the production of a German film must be of German descent and hold German citizenship. This leads to an exodus of Jewish artists.

July 14: The Reich Chamber of Film (Reichsfilmkammer) is established and becomes one of the key implements of control for National-Socialist film policy.

August 30: Deutsche Universal releases Arnold Fanck's ***SOS Eisberg*** starring Leni Riefenstahl and flying ace Ernst Udet. In the United States an American version is compiled by Tay Garnett.

September 12: ***Hitlerjunge Quex: Ein Film vom Opfergeist der deutschen Jugend*** (***Hitler Youth Quex***) is premiered in Munich in the presence of the "Führer".

September 29: ***Ein Unsichtbarer geht durch die Stadt*** (***An Invisible Man Walks the City***), sci-fi by Harry Piel.

December 1: ***Der Sieg des Glaubens*** (***The Victory of Faith***), the 1933 party rally filmed by Leni Riefenstahl.

King Kong released as ***Die Fabel von King Kong - Ein amerikanischer Trick- und Sensationsfilm*** (***The Tale of King Kong: An American Trick and Sensationalist Film***).

December 8: ***Flüchtlinge*** (***Refugees***) by Gustav Ucicky: Hans Albers leads a group of 40 German refugees out of the hell of Chinese Civil War in 1928. Their most pertinacious pursuer is a Soviet commissar.

240 June 14, 1933.

December 13: ***Hans Westmar,*** originally titled ***Horst Wessel***, based on a book by Hanns Heinz Ewers.

1934

February 13: ***So ein Flegel*** (***Such a Boor***), first film adaptation of Heinrich Spoerl's ***Feuerzangenbowle*** with Heinz Rühmann. Directed by Robert Adolf Stemmle.

February 20: ***Stosstrupp 1917*** (***Shock Troop 1917***) by Hans Zöberlein and Ludwig Schmid-Wildy.

March 9: ***Die Welt ohne Maske*** (***The World without Mask***) by Harry Piel.

March 29: ***Gold***, sci-fi with Hans Albers.

June 30: Night of the Long Knives: Ernst Röhm, his SA leaders and other "undesirables" are eliminated by Hitler and his regime.

July 26: ***Ein Mann will nach Deutschland*** (***A Man Wants to Get to Germany***), a nationalist drama directed by Paul Wegener: In 1914, German war volunteers battle their way back from abroad.

September 6: Luis Trenker, pauperized in New York, returns to his German soil as ***Der verlorene Sohn*** (***The Prodigal Son***).

November 2: ***Die Reiter von Deutsch-Ostafrika*** (***The Riders of German East-Africa***) by Herbert Selpin.

1935

January 29: ***Der alte und der junge König*** (***The Old and the Young King***) with Emil Jannings.

March 22: ***Hundert Tage (Hundred Days***), an Italo-German co-production based on a play by Benito Mussolini. Starring Werner Krauss as Napoleon Bonaparte.

March 28: ***Triumph des Willens*** (***Triumph of the Will***), the 1934 Nuremberg party rally recorded by Leni Riefenstahl.

July 18: ***Amphitryon - Aus den Wolken kommt das Glück*** (***Amphitryon: Happiness from the Clouds***), a confusion comedy with Greek gods among mortals: Willy Fritsch and Paul Kemp in dual roles.

September 15: Promulgation of the Nuremberg Laws relegates Jews to a separate second-class status, prohibits intermarriage and sexual relations with Germans.

November 19: ***Friesennot*** **(*Frisions in Distress*):** Germans' fate on Russian soil, co-written by Reich film dramaturge Willi Krause (using the nom de plume Peter Hagen).

December 30: ***Tag der Freiheit! Unsere Wehrmacht*** (***Day of Freedom! Our Armed Forces***) by Leni Riefenstahl.

1936

January 23: ***Traumulus*** with Emil Jannings.

February 20: ***Durch die Wüste*** (***Across the Desert***) based on a book by Karl May.

July 21: ***Der Kaiser von Kalifornien*** (***The Emperor of California***): Luis Trenker as Johann August Suter.

October 9: ***Wenn wir alle Engel wären*** (***If We All Were Angels***) written by Heinrich Spoerl and directed by Carl Froelich, with Heinz Rühmann.

1937

January 5: ***Weisse Sklaven*** (***White Slaves***), anti-Soviet propaganda.

February 8: ***Fridericus*** with Otto Gebühr in the title role.

March 17: ***Der Herrscher*** (***The Ruler***) with Emil Jannings, directed by Veit Harlan.

March 18: Hugenberg is forced to sell his Ufa shares for Reichsmark 21.25 million to Cautio Treuhand GmbH, a semigovernmental holding company controlled by Max Winkler (and Joseph Goebbels). Ludwig Klitzsch remains at his post as general manager, Carl Opitz in charge of public relations.

March 23: ***Die Tochter des Samurai*** (***Atarashiki tsuchi/A Daughter of the Samurai***), a German-Japanese co-production by Arnold Fanck.

March 24: ***Condottieri*** produced by Luis Trenker for Benito Mussolini infuriated Goebbels because Trenker made some extras who were members of the SS Leibstandarte "Adolf Hitler" prostrate before the Pope.

April 9: ***Gordian, der Tyrann*** (***Gordian the Tyrant***) with Hitler favorite Weiss Ferdl.

August 31: ***Zu neuen Ufern (Life Begins Anew/To New Shores***) by Detlef Sierck [a.k.a. Douglas Sirk], with Zarah Leander.

September 24: ***Patrioten*** (***Patriots***) by Karl Ritter.

October 13: ***Der Mustergatte*** (***Model Husband***) with Heinz Rühmann.

October 19: ***Der zerbrochene Krug*** (***The Broken Jug***) with Emil Jannings.

November 10: ***Der Lachdoktor*** (***The Laugh Doctor***) with Weiss Ferdl.

December 18: ***La Habanera*** with Zarah Leander, again directed by Detlef Sierck.

1938

January 6: ***Der Berg ruft!*** (***The Mountain Calls***) by Luis Trenker.

January 11: ***Urlaub auf Ehrenwort*** (***Leave on Word of Honor***) by Karl Ritter.

January 28: ***Das indische Grabmal*** (***The Indian Tomb***), remake of the Joe May movie by Richard Eichberg.

February 11: ***Der Tiger von Eschnapur***, sequel to ***Indian Tomb***.

March 13: Annexation of Austria to the "Greater German Reich".

April 20: Leni Riefenstahl's film document about the 1936 Berlin ***Olympia*** in two parts: ***Fest der Völker*** (***Festival of Nations***) and ***Fest der Schönheit*** (***Festival of Beauty***).

June 25: ***Heimat*** (***Homeland***) with Zarah Leander premiered in Danzig.

July 1: ***Fahrendes Volk*** (***Traveling People***), a French-German co-production by Jacques Feyder.

September 30: Munich Conference.

November 9-10: Reichskristallnacht (Night of Broken Glass).

December 22: ***Pour le Mérite*** by Karl Ritter.

1939

January 30: At the Reichstag, Adolf Hitler predicts "the annihilation of the Jewish race in Europe" in case of a war.

January 31: ***Das unsterbliche Herz*** (***The Immortal Heart***) by Veit Harlan based on a play by Harlan's father Walter, starring Heinrich George, Kristina Söderbaum and Paul Wegener.

February 21: ***Bel Ami*** by Willi Forst. Music and songs by Theo Mackeben.

July 7: ***Robert und Bertram***, comedy with an anti-Semitic episode attached.

August 15: ***Es war eine rauschende Ballnacht*** (***It Was a Gay Ballnight***) with Zarah Leander.

August 23: German-Soviet Non-aggression Pact signed in Moscow.

September 1: Hitler invades Poland: World War 2.

September 26: ***Robert Koch, der Bekämpfer des Todes***, a German genius film with Emil Jannings seeking a cure for a tuberculosis epidemic.

October 16: ***Leinen aus Irland*** (***Linen from Ireland***): co-production between German Bavaria and Austrian Wien Film - anti-Semitic, anti-British.

October 26: ***D III 88*** by Herbert Maisch and Hans Bertram.

1940

February 8: ***Feldzug in Polen*** (***The Campaign in Poland***), propaganda documentary by Fritz Hippler.

March 5: ***Der Feuerteufel*** (***The Fire Devil***)***:*** Luis Trenker as Valentin Sturmegger, a Tyrolean freedom fighter, versus Napoleon.

April 4: ***Feuertaufe*** (***Baptism by Fire***)***:*** Hans Bertram's propaganda documentary shows the destruction of Polish cities by Hermann Göring's Luftwaffe.

April 24: ***Der Fuchs von Glenarvon*** (***The Fox of Glenarvon***)***:*** anti-British, pro-Irish. Directed by Max Wilhelm "Axel" Kimmich, Goebbels' brother-in-law.

Der Postmeister (***The Postmaster/The Station Master***), directed by Gustav Ucicky and based on a short story by Alexander Pushkin, with Heinrich George.

May 10: Blitzkrieg on Holland, Belgium, and France launched.

June 22: France surrenders to Nazi Germany.

July 17: ***Die Rothschilds - Aktien auf Waterloo*** (***The Rothschilds' Shares in Waterloo***), anti-Semitic family saga.

September: Battle of Britain.

September 24: ***Jud Süss*** (***Jew Suss***) by Veit Harlan with Ferdinand Marian.

November 1: ***Das Herz der Königin*** (***The Heart of a Queen***), Carl Froelich's anti-British drama with Zarah Leander as Mary, Queen of Scots.

November 13: ***Friedrich Schiller - Triumph eines Genies***, genius picture with Horst Caspar and Heinrich George.

November 28: ***Der ewige Jude*** (***The Eternal Jew***): anti-Semitic propaganda by Fritz Hippler.

December 6: ***Bismarck*** with Paul Hartmann as Otto von Bismarck.

December 30: ***Wunschkonzert*** (***Request Concert***) with Ilse Werner and Carl Raddatz and cameos by Heinz Rühmann, Paul Hörbiger, Hans Brausewetter, Weiss Ferdl, and Marika Rökk.

1941

January 3: ***Blutsbrüderschaft*** (***Blood Brotherhood***) written by Harald G. Petersson.

February 17: ***Mein Leben für Irland*** (***My Life for Ireland***), anti-British, pro-Irish propaganda by Max W. Kimmich.

February 28: ***Kampfgeschwader Lützow*** (***Fighting Squadron Lützow***) by Hans Bertram.

March 21: ***Über alles in der Welt*** (***Above All Else in the World***) by Karl Ritter.

Carl Peters: anti-British propaganda with Hans Albers.

March 23: ***Sieg im Westen*** (***Victory in the West***) by Fritz Hippler.

April 4: ***Ohm Krüger*** (***Uncle Kruger***), anti-British propaganda with Emil Jannings as Paul Kruger.

May 9: ***U-Boote westwärts*** (***U-Boat, Course-West!***) directed by Günther Rittau who was a cinematographer involved in the productions of ***Die Nibelungen, Metropolis, Der blaue Engel***, and ***F.P.1 antwortet nicht***.

May 30: ***...reitet für Deutschland*** (***Riding for Germany***) with Willy Birgel as triumphant German dressage rider.

June 22: Operation Barbarossa: German invasion of the Soviet Union.

July 31: Formal order for the planning of a coordinated "Final Solution of the Jewish problem in Europe" signed by Hermann Göring.

August 1: ***Der Gasmann*** (***The Gas Meter Reader***), comedy with Heinz Rühmann.

August 7: Deutsche Zeichenfilm GmbH. General Manager: Karl Neumann.

August 29: ***Ich klage an*** (***I Accuse***): pro-euthanasia propaganda by Wolfgang Liebeneiner, commissioned by suggestion of Dr. Karl Brandt, who headed the Nazis' euthanasia program together with Philipp Bouhler.

October 10: ***Heimkehr*** (***Homecoming***): "Film of the Nation" by Gustav Ucicky: German minority oppressed by Polish majority right before WW2. With Paula Wessely and her husband, Attila Hörbiger.

October 1: ***Frauen sind doch bessere Diplomaten*** (***Women Are the Better Diplomats***) with Marika Rökk in Germany's first feature film in the Agfacolor process.

December 7: Pearl Harbor.

December 11: Nazi Germany declares war against the United States.

December 16: ***Quax der Bruchpilot*** (***Quax the Crash Pilot***) with Heinz Rühmann.

1942

January 20: Wannsee Conference in preparation of the "Final Solution".

February 20: ***Himmelhunde*** (***Sky Dogs***): Hitler Youth learn to build and fly gliders.

March 3: ***Der grosse König*** (***The Great King***) by Veit Harlan with Otto Gebühr once again as Fridericus.

June 12: ***Die grosse Liebe*** (***The Great Love***) with Zarah Leander.

August 12: ***G.P.U.*** (***The Red Terror***), anti-Soviet propaganda by Karl Ritter.

September 3: Veit Harlan's blood and soil drama ***Die goldene Stadt*** (***The Golden City***) premiered at the Venice Film Festival.

October 6: ***Die Entlassung*** (***Bismarck's Dismissal***) with Emil Jannings as Bismarck and Werner Hinz as young Wilhelm II.

October 8: ***Wir machen Musik*** (***Vive la musique***) with Ilse Werner and Viktor de Kowa.

1943

January 31: Stalingrad: the surrender of the 6th Army under Friedrich Paulus.

March 3: ***Damals*** (***At that Time***): melodrama with Zarah Leander.

March 3: ***Münchhausen***, Ufa's 25th anniversary film with Hans Albers riding the cannonball in Agfacolor.

March 12: ***Paracelsus*** by Georg Wilhelm Pabst with Werner Krauss as genius physician-alchemist.

June 8: ***Ich vertraue dir meine Frau an*** (***I Trust You with My Wife***) with Heinz Rühmann.

June 25: ***Romanze in Moll*** (***Romance in a Minor Key***) by Helmut Käutner with Marianne Hoppe.

July 30: ***Das Bad auf der Tenne*** produced in color by Jürgen Clausen.

September 29: Karl Ritter and a film crew and cast of 43 men depart Berlin for the USSR, to film the Eastern Front footage for the Luftwaffe feature film ***Besatzung Dora***. The film release is banned after Stalingrad, in March 1943.

October 5: ***Der weisse Traum*** (***The White Dream***) by Géza von Cziffra.

November 11: ***Titanic*** premiered in Paris but banned in the German Reich.

December 8: ***Immensee*** by Veit Harlan, Kristina Söderbaum in Agfacolor.

Annual ticket sales shoot from RM 624 million in 1939 to RM 1.1 billion in 1943. Germany controls 8,600 cinemas at home and in the occupied countries and territories.

1944

January 28: ***Die Feuerzangenbowle*** (***The Brandy Punch***) by Heinz Rühmann.

May 24: ***Junge Adler*** (***Young Eagles***) by Alfred Weidenmann (co-written by Herbert Reinecker) with a young Hardy Krüger as one of the boys working in an aircraft factory.

June 6: D-Day.

July 20: Attempt to assassinate Hitler fails.

August 25: ***Frau meiner Träume*** (***Woman of My Dreams***): Marika Rökk once again in Agfacolor.

December: Veit Harlan's ***Opfergang*** (***The Great Sacrifice***) in Agfacolor.

Battle of the Bulge.

1945

January 30: ***Kolberg*** by Veit Harlan in Agfacolor.

April 30: Two newlyweds, Hitler and his wife Eva née Braun, commit suicide in the Berlin bunker.

May 1: Joseph Goebbels kills himself and his family.

May 7: Unconditional surrender of all German forces.

Short Biographies

Wartime and Post-war Filmmakers, Writers, Technicians, and Actors: Émigrés, Nazi Filmmakers and Film People involved in NS topics before, during and after the war.

HANS BERTRAM [Writer and Filmmaker]

Born on February 26, 1906, in Remscheid. Studied ship building and aircraft construction at Technische Hochschule in Munich. Apprenticeship at Blohm & Voss, a Hamburg shipyard, and at aircraft factory Bäumer. In 1927 went to China and for six years became a consultant to Chinese aviation authorities. With the Nazis' seizure to power former air ace Bertram returned to Germany where he published a best-selling book: ***Flug in die Hölle*** (***Flight to Hell***). Directed the propaganda documentary ***Feuertaufe*** (***Baptism of Fire***) about the German invasion in Poland and wrote the screenplays for a number of Tobis productions: ***D III 88*** (1939); ***Der Fuchs von Glenarvon*** (***The Fox of Glenarvon,*** 1939-40); ***Kampfgeschwader Lützow*** (***Fighting Squadron Lützow,*** 1940). Wounded in the right eye during the shooting of one of his films, Bertram incurred Goebbels' wrath and was excluded from the Reich Chamber of Culture (Reichskulturkammer) in October 1942 for alleged false statements and slander. Died on January 8, 1993, in Munich.

PETER PAUL BRAUER [Producer and Director]

Born on May 16, 1899, in Wuppertal-Elberfeld. His film career started in the Netherlands in 1928. The same year he returned to Germany and made some short films. Sympathized with NSDAP. When he was promoted to production chief of Terra Filmkunst, he helped to get ***Jud Süss*** (***Jew Suss***) on the screen which he hoped to direct (but Goebbels decided in favor of Veit Harlan). By colleagues he was feared as informer and denunciator. After the war, his company Capitol Film produced a middlebrow music comedy by Wolfgang Liebeneiner: ***Das tanzende Herz*** (***The Dancing Heart***, 1953). Died on April 28, 1959, in Berlin.

ARTUR BRAUNER [Producer]

Born Abraham Brauner on August 1, 1918, in Lódz as son of a Jewish wood wholesaler. Film fan from childhood. Studied at the polytechnic until the German invasion of Poland. Forty-nine of his relatives were killed in the holocaust. Three of his four siblings settled in Israel. After the war, Brauner thought about leaving Germany and going to the United States, but he remained and applied for a film license. On September 16, 1946, he founded CCC Central Cinema Company Film Gesellschaft in Berlin. In 1949, he built his own studios on the site of a former poison gas factory. There he produced films with former émigrés like Fritz Lang, Robert Siodmak, Gottfried (son of Max) Reinhardt; lots of entertainment films with old NS film alumni including Wolfgang Liebeneiner (***Auf Wiedersehen, Franziska***!), Veit Harlan's collaborator Alfred Braun, Heinz Rühmann, Lil Dagover, Olga Tschechowa, Carl Boese, Arthur Maria Rabenalt, Josef von Báky, Herbert Reinecker, Walter Wischniewsky (the editor of the anti-Semitic ***Rothschilds***, ***Münchhausen*** and ***Junge Adler***), and cinematographer Fritz Arno Wagner who died after a fall from a camera car during a CCC production in 1958. Besides some Karl May and Bryan Edgar Wallace films and a ***Dr. Mabuse*** series, he tried his hand at bigger projects: as producer of a remake of ***Die Nibelungen*** and ***Kampf um Rom*** (***The Last Roman***, with Laurence Harvey and Orson Welles) or as co-producer of ***Genghis Khan*** (with Omar Sharif and Stephen Boyd). In later years turned to political topics that dealt with the time of National Socialism and the holocaust like ***Eine Liebe in Deutschland*** (***A Love in Germany***) by Rolf Hochhuth (novel) and Andrzej Wajda (director), ***Hitlerjunge Salomon*** (***Europa Europa***) and ***Babij Jar***. Brauner died on July 7, 2019, at age 100 in Berlin (owing a reported €43 million to the German Tax Office).

CLAUS CLAUSEN [Actor]

Born on August 15, 1899, in Eisenach. Soldier in World War 1. After matriculation in 1920, he became a member of Weimar National Theater. In 1929 film debut in the patriotic ***Scapa Flow,*** followed by parts in Georg Wilhelm Pabst's ***Westfront 1918*** (1930), ***Cyankali*** (1930) by leftist writer Friedrich Wolf, and Luis Trenker's ***Berge in Flammen*** (***The Doomed Battalion***, 1931). From 1933-45, Clausen was a well-known face in nationalist films: ***Hitlerjunge Quex*** (1933, as Hitler Youth leader)***; Rivalen der Luft*** (***Rivals of the Air,*** 1933)***; Der alte und der junge König*** (***The Old and the Young King,*** 1934)***;*** Luis Trenker's ***Der Feuerteufel*** (***The Fire Devil,*** 1940); ***Mein Leben für Irland*** (***My Life for Ireland,*** 1940)***; Der grosse König*** (***The Great King,*** 1941-42)***; Kolberg*** (1943-44). In an American Cold War film, ***The Devil Makes Three*** (1952), Clausen played a fanatical old Nazi, who intends to build up a new fascist organization in the American zone. After the war, he focused on stage work in Bochum, Bonn, Wunsiedel, Wuppertal and Essen. Clausen died on November 25, 1989, in Essen.

EWALD von DEMANDOWSKY [Producer]

Born on October 21, 1906, in Berlin. Bank apprenticeship. NSDAP member since 1930. Supporting roles at Berlin theaters, secretary in a publishing house. *Along with Fritz Hippler, Ewald von Demandowsky, editor of the* Völkischer Beobachter *until 1937, then Reichsfilmdramaturg until 1939, crops up most frequently as the most important colleague and regular attendee at Goebbels' countless discussions in the most intimate circle. Born in 1906, he was the first party man in the post of production chief. In that capacity he directed Tobis Filmkunst from 1939 to 1945. At first Demandowsky was not able to deliver what the minister had expected from him in terms of political dynamism and acquiescence.... the production chief even wanted to abandon the super-expensive anti-British propaganda film* **Ohm Krüger** *that Goebbels had demanded. Such weakness and other 'mishaps' in film planning even brought Goebbels, in June 1940, to threaten Demandowsky with being called up into the Wehrmacht. But from mid-1940 Tobis developed and came to be the film studio with the highest proportion of political and 'national' material and war films.* [241] On February 28, 1944, Goebbels' diary entry read: *He [Demandowsky] is the actual Nazi among our production chiefs.* Up-and-coming film star Hildegard Knef was Demandowsky's mistress and was suspected to have him denounced to the American forces after the war. He was passed to the Soviets and shot in Berlin Lichtenberg on October 7, 1946.

FELIX von ECKARDT [Journalist and Screenwriter]

Born on June 18, 1903, in Berlin. Worked as journalist for Munich and Berlin newspapers. Thanks to director Fritz Wendhausen got screenwriting assignments during the Nazi time. Besides comedies, musicals and detective stories he wrote the screenplays for some nationalist propaganda films: ***Kopf hoch, Johannes*** (***Chin up, Johannes!,*** 1941); ***Menschen im Sturm*** (***People in the Storm,*** 1941) which justified the invasion of Slovenia; ***Die Entlassung*** (***Bismarck's Dismissal,*** 1942). In February 1952, West German chancellor Dr. Konrad Adenauer appointed Eckardt head of the Press and Information Office of Federal German government and government spokesman. Member of Bundestag parliament from 1961 to 1972. Died on May 11, 1979, on the Isle of Capri, Italy.

HANNS ECKELKAMP [Cinema Owner, Distributor and Producer]

Born on February 28, 1927, in Münster. Impressed by Ewald Balser in his screen appearance as ***Ewiger Rembrandt*** (***Immortal Rembrandt***), he transformed the huge restaurant of his father into a cinema (Gertrudenhof) and later built a

241 Felix Moeller, *The Film Minister*, p. 59.

movie theater chain in Duisburg. In 1959 founded the Atlas film distribution company, an art house releasing company, which emerged from Donau-Film-Nordwest. Re-released a series of German films: ***Das Cabinet des Dr. Caligari*** (***The Cabinet of Dr. Caligari***), ***Der müde Tod*** (***Destiny***), ***Dr. Mabuse der Spieler*** (***Dr. Mabuse the Gambler***), ***Nosferatu***, ***Der letzte Mann*** (***The Last Laugh***), ***Der blaue Engel*** (***The Blue Angel***), ***Quax der Bruchpilot*** (***Quax the Crash Pilot***), ***Die goldene Stadt*** (***The Golden City***), ***Münchhausen***, ***Die Feuerzangenbowle*** (***The Brandy Punch***) and ***Kolberg*** which was supposed to open a series of NS propaganda films. In late 1966, Atlas went into receivership but Eckelkamp was able to continue with 16mm film distribution and VHS cassettes, in between co-producing Fassbinder's ***Die Ehe der Maria Braun*** and ***Adolf und Marlene***.

BERND EICHINGER [Producer, Distributor, Director]

Born on April 11, 1949, in Neuburg/Danube as son of Manfred Eichinger, a country doctor, and his wife Ingeborg, a teacher. Attended Munich Film and Television Academy. Professionally began to work with Hans Jürgen Syberberg as production manager (***Karl May***) and producer (***Hitler, ein Film aus Deutschland***). 1979 CEO of Neue Constantin Film which was built on the ruins of the bankrupt original Constantin: ***Das Boot*** (***The Boat***), ***Christiane F. - Wir Kinder vom Bahnhof Zoo*** (***We Children from Bahnhof Zoo***), ***Die unendliche Geschichte*** (***The Neverending Story***), ***Der Name der Rose*** (***The Name of the Rose***), ***Das Mädchen Rosemarie*** (***A Girl Called Rosemary***), ***Werner - Beinhart!***, ***Resident Evil***, ***Fantastic Four***, ***Der Baader Meinhof Komplex*** (***The Baader Meinhof Complex***), ***Der Untergang*** (***The Downfall***) which he adapted from a book by Joachim C. Fest. Eichinger died on January 24, 2011, in Los Angeles. Right before he might have learned about some changes in his professional life. But that's all speculation.

HANS ERTL [Alpinist, Documentarist and Cameraman]

Born on February 21, 1908, in Munich. Worked with Arnold Fanck (***SOS Iceberg***), Luis Trenker (***Liebesbriefe aus dem Engadin***), and Leni Riefenstahl

(***Tag der Freiheit*** and the ***Olympia*** films). For the propaganda documentary ***Sieg im Westen*** (***Victory in the West***) he shot a sequence of a sapper who, under heavy fire, jumped into the Marne, grabbed a rope and pulled a rubber boat across the river. Newsreel cameraman who became Erwin Rommel's favorite cinematographer. After the war involved in film expeditions that led him up to ***Nanga Parbat*** and to South America (***Hito-Hito***), where he finally settled. His daughter, Monika Ertl, ended up as a terrorist, known as Che Guevara's avenger. Ertl died on October, 23, 2000, in Chiquitania, Santa Cruz, Bolivia.

RAINER WERNER FASSBINDER [Director, Writer]

Born on May 31, 1945, in Bad Wörishofen, Bavaria. Autodidact. His mantra: *Making many films so that my life will become a movie too.* Up to his death made 40 films ***(Die Ehe der Maria Braun, Lilli Marleen, Die Sehnsucht der Veronika Voss*** and the TV series ***Berlin Alexanderplatz)*** and wrote 24 plays, among them the anti-Semitic *Der Müll, die Stadt und der Tod* which premiered posthumously in 2009 but was filmed already by Daniel Schmid under the title ***Schatten der Engel***. Fassbinder might have been called an alcoholic and was certainly drug-addicted. Hie died on June 10, 1982, in Munich. He left a number of film projects unfinished: George Orwell's ***1984***; ***Rosa Luxemburg*** with Jane Fonda; a remake of Veit Harlan's ***Immensee*** with Romy Schneider.

GERHARD FIEBER [Animator]

Born on October 20, 1916, in Berlin Treptow as Gerhard Willi Otto Fieber. Attended Rütli School in Berlin-Neukölln; later, between 1930 and 1936, art school and Academy of Arts in Berlin, a graphic design school and *Volkshochschule* [community college]. In 1930 started work at the publicity department of Ufa and did humorous drawings for the press. Until 1937 also worked in a department store of Rudolf Karstadt chain. In the 1930s became associated with animator Wolfgang Kaskeline. One-year contract with Epoche Werbefilm A.G. In 1938 illustrator for Berlin Lewilbo Advertising. In late 1940 changed to Ufa and assisted Kurt Stordel on Ufa's animation project ***Quick macht Hochzeit*** (***Quick Marries***), which wasn't finished. On

August 20, 1941, signed with Deutsche Zeichenfilm GmbH where the typical ticket-puncher became animation director. For a brief time worked for DEFA. In 1948 founded EOS-Film in Bad Sachsa and did a feature-length Wilhelm Busch cartoon, ***Tobias Knopp – Abenteuer eines Junggesellen*** in 1948-49. Later, after joining forces with producer Franz Thies, was involved in television and ***Mainzelmännchen*** (***Little Mainz Men***) spots for Second Channel TV. Celebrating his 90th birthday, Wolfgang Dresler interviewed Fieber for a DVD ***Trickfilm-Fieber - Der Zeichentrick-Pionier Gerhard Fieber***. Died on January 6, 2013, in Walluf, Hesse.

HANS FISCHERKOESEN [Animator]

Born Hans Fischer on May 18, 1896, in Kösen, near Naumburg, at the River Saale in Saxonia. Later renamed himself after his birth town. The son of an entrepreneur dealing in building material began to draw while still a child, plagued by asthma. Later, for three years, he and his equally gifted sister Leni attended Academy of Graphic Arts in Leipzig. During World War 1 worked in army hospitals near the front line. First experiments in animation, since 1916 or '17, resulted in a short, ***Das Loch im Westen*** (***The Hole in the West***), which exposed the War Profiteer as the true cause of war. A few years later in 1921, he made his first animated commercial, ***Bummel-Petrus*** (***Strolling Peter***), for a Leipzig shoe factory, Nordheimer. Signed a joint venture with producer Julius Pinschewer in 1923. In 1927, Fischer-Kösen-Film released its output to Ufa through Epoche Reklamegesellschaft mbH [Werbekunst Epoche G.m.b.H.] and finally moved its activities to Berlin Charlottenburg. In the early 1930s, after doing some work for Tolirag [Ton-Lichtbild-Reklame A.G.], Fischerkoesen joined Ufa Werbefilm. In 1939 became independent, founded his own company, Fischerkoesen-Film-Studio, and moved to Potsdam, near Ufa Studios Babelsberg. Besides commercials and advertising films, contributed animated sequences to culture films and produced military training films for OKW [Army High Command] and Mars-Film GmbH. Famous for his technically superior trio of Agfacolor shorts: ***Verwitterte Melodie, Der Schneemann, Das dumme***

Gänslein - Weather-Beaten Melody (1942-43), ***The Snowman*** and ***The Silly Goose*** (both 1944), which Dr. Goebbels (and his children) liked so much. In 1945, his studio facilities were confiscated by the Red Army. Fischerkoesen was arrested and interned at Sachsenhausen concentration camp for three years as a possible Nazi collaborator. When released in 1949, he moved his operations to the French zone, first to Castle Marienfels near Remagen, then to Bad Godesberg-Mehlem, where he established himself as Germany's leading producer of animated commercials. For West German television [Hessischer Rundfunk] he created the popular character of ***Onkel Otto***. By 1956, he had won major prizes at various commercial film festivals: Rome, Milan (three times), Venice, Monte Carlo, and Cannes. Fischerkoesen died on April 23, 1973, in Mehlem. His original studio had closed a year earlier, but his son, Dr. Hans Michael Fischerkoesen, reorganized the company and continued the work.

Original cel from *Verwitterte Melodie (Weather-Beaten Melody)* by Fischerkoesen.
Courtesy of J. P. Storm Collection

CARL FROELICH [Director]

Born on September 5, 1875, in Berlin. Cameraman and constructor of cinematographic equipment for German film pioneer Oskar Messter. In 1913 debuted as film director with composer Giuseppe Becce starring as ***Richard Wagner***. Often worked with actress Henny Porten. In 1933 became a member of NSDAP, in 1934 made ***Ich für dich, du für mich*** for the Reich Propaganda Directorate of the NSDAP, in 1937 was appointed professor and in 1939 president of Reichskulturkammer [Reich Chamber of Culture]. Directed Emil Jannings in ***Traumulus*** (***The Dreamer***), Heinz Rühmann in the Goebbels-favorite ***Wenn wir alle Engel wären*** (***If We All Were Angels***) and ***Der Gasmann*** (***The Gas Meter Reader***), Zarah Leander in ***Heimat*** (***Homeland***) and the anti-British ***Das Herz der Königin*** (***The Heart of the Queen***), Heinrich George and Paul Wegener in ***Hochzeit auf Bärenhof*** (***Wedding in Barenhof***), Henny Porten and Marianne Simson ***in Familie Buchholz*** (***The Buchholz Family***). All in all, Carl Froelich made 77 films. De-Nazified in 1948. Froelich died on February 12, 1953, in Berlin.

GEORGE FROESCHEL [Screenwriter]

Born on March 8, 1891, in Vienna as son of a banker. Doctor of Laws. War reports for the k.u.k. army. In 1918 became novelist. Some of his stories were made into films. Because the film version of his novel ***Die Geliebte Roswolskys*** (***Roswolsky's Mistress***) was quite successful in Ufa cinemas, he got a job at Ufa as dramaturge from 1922 to 1924. Editor at Ullstein Publishing House. In 1936 Froeschel left Germany. In 1939 screenwriter at MGM. Academy Award for co-scripting ***Mrs. Miniver***. Last film (for producer Charles H. Schneer): ***I Aim at the Stars*** with Curd Jurgens as Wernher von Braun. Died on November 22, 1979, in Los Angeles.

OTTO GEBÜHR [Actor]

Born on May 29, 1877, in Kettwig Ruhr (today Essen Kettwig). After a commercial apprenticeship in Cologne, Gebühr joined a traveling theater. In 1898 became a member of the Royal Court Theater in Dresden. Since

1909 in Berlin at Lessing Theater, Theater Königgrätzer Strasse, and finally Deutsches Theater under Max Reinhardt. War volunteer in World War 1. His film career was supported by Paul Wegener. Gebühr was in Wegener's ***Der Golem wie er in die Welt kam.*** As King Friedrich II (1712-1786), he appeared for the first time in Carl Boese's ***Die Tänzerin Barberina*** and from then on starred, between 1920 and 1942, in a dozen films as The Old Fritz. When Veit Harlan tried to recast the part of Fridericus in ***Der grosse König*** (***The Great King***) with Werner Krauss, a better actor, Hitler intervened and said that Germany owed the part of Fridericus to Gebühr. After World War 2 the Allied Forces issued a stage ban until his denazification in 1947. Worked again with Veit Harlan (***Die Gefangene des Maharadscha, Die blaue Stunde***), Gerhard Lamprecht and shared a scene with Gene Kelly in MGM's ***The Devil Makes Three:*** "The house is kaput. I can't help you, Captain Elliot". Final film part as Jakob, an old gardener, besides young Christine Kaufmann in ***Rosen Resli.*** Died on March 13, 1954 in Wiesbaden.

FRITZ GENSCHOW [Actor and Director]

Born on May 15, 1905, in Berlin. Stage debut in 1924. In 1927 under Erwin Piscator at Theater am Nollendorfplatz in Berlin. With his wife, Renée Stobrawa, Genschow founded a children's theater. Opportunistic wryneck who changed sides from left to right when the Nazis came to power. Screen acting in ***Morgenrot*** (***Dawn***, 1932-33); ***Flüchtlinge*** (***Refugees***, 1933); ***Hundert Tage*** (***Hundred Days***, 1934); ***Ein Volksfeind*** (***An Enemy of the People***, 1937); ***13 Mann und eine Kanone*** (***13 Men and One Gun***, 1938); ***Drei Unteroffiziere*** (***Three Non-Coms***, 1938); ***Zwielicht*** (***Twilight***, 1940); ***Friedrich Schiller - Triumph eines Genies*** (1940); ***Titanic*** (1942). After the war, he was engaged in children's programs at RIAS radio broadcast in the American zone (featured as "Uncle Tobias") and continued to produce fairy tales for the screen securing the services of cinematographer Gerhard Huttula: ***Rotkäppchen; Frau Holle; Der Struwwelpeter; Aschenputtel; Dornröschen; Tischlein deck dich; Die Gänsemagd.*** Some of these children's films, with voiceover narration, were even shown in the United States: Genschow died on June 21, 1977, in Berlin.

HEINRICH GEORGE [Actor]

Born on October 9, 1893, in Stettin (now Szczecin, Poland) as Georg August Friedrich Hermann Schulz. George was one of Germany's leading stage and film actors. Before the Nazis came to power, George was active in the pro-communist *Revolutionäre Gewerkschaftsopposition (Revolutionary union opposition).* One of the stars of Fritz Lang's ***Metropolis*** (his brother Rudi George was the production manager on that movie and got him the part). After 1933, he made an about-face and appeared in the worst propaganda movies the brown regime produced: ***Hitlerjunge Quex*** (***Hitler Youth Quex,*** 1933); ***Reifende Jugend*** (***Ripening Youth,*** 1933); ***Unternehmen Michael*** (***Operation Michael,*** 1937); ***Ein Volksfeind*** (***An Enemy of the People,*** 1937); ***Sensationsprozess Casilla*** (1939); ***Jud Süss*** (***Jew Suss,*** 1940); ***Friedrich Schiller - Triumph eines Genies*** (1940); ***Wien 1910*** (***Vienna 1910,*** 1942); ***Kolberg*** (1943-44) and in Wolfgang Liebeneiner's lost ***Das Leben geht weiter*** (***Life Goes On***) project. Manager of the Schiller Theater in Berlin and a drinking buddy of Hermann Göring. Denounced by a former colleague, George died on September 25, 1946, in Sachsenhausen, a former Nazi concentration camp then occupied by the Soviets, where he fell ill with appendicitis. Father of Götz and Jan George. Götz George became a famous German TV star, Jan George acted in several projects directed by Rainer Werner Fassbinder.

PAUL JOSEPH GOEBBELS [Politician, National Socialist Film Minister]

Born on October, 29, 1897, in Rheydt. His parents hoped he would become a Catholic priest. Obtained Doctor of Philosphy degree from the University of Heidelberg in 1921 with a thesis on author *Wilhelm von Schütz* (1776-1847) and the same year published a little-read semi-autobiographical novel, *Michael.* In 1924 became attracted to National Socialism. Since October 1926 NSDAP Gauleiter in Berlin. In 1928 Member of the Reichstag. In December 1930 organized riots against Carl Laemmle's production of Erich Maria Remarque's ***All Quiet on the Western Front.*** On March 14, 1933, was appointed Reich Minister of Public Enlightenment and Propaganda.

As such became known as "Film Minister" and had affairs with actresses, including Lída Baarová. Nicknamed: "Der Bock von Babelsberg" (The Buck of Babelsberg). Interfered with productions, writing and casting of films and censorship of the German newsreel. On February 18, 1943, speaking at the Sportpalast in Berlin, he postulated total war. Before he committed suicide, Hitler appointed his faithful vassal Reich Chancellor but Goebbels saw no chance. One day later, May 1, 1945, Goebbels killed his children and departed this life together with his wife Magda.

THEA GABRIELE VON HARBOU [Screenwriter]

Born on December 27, 1888, in Döhlau-Tauperlitz as daughter of a senior forestry official. In her youth was an enthusiastic Karl May fan and began to write animal stories and little poems. In 1905, her first novel, *Wenn's Morgen wird*, was serialized in Deutsche Zeitung Berlin. She tried herself as an actress. In Aachen she met and married her colleague, Rudolf Klein-Rogge, in September 1914. In 1917, the couple went to Berlin. Thea had abandoned acting and focused completely on writing. In Berlin she wrote ***Das indische Grabmal*** (***The Indian Tomb***) which was turned into a movie by Joe May. While working for May, she met Fritz Lang and fell in love with him. Klein-Rogge and Harbou divorced, but Harbou would care that her former husband would be in any of her upcoming films with Lang: ***Das wandernde Bild*** (***The Wandering Image***)***; Der müde Tod*** (***Destiny***)***; Dr. Mabuse, der Spieler*** (***Dr. Mabuse the Gambler***)***; Die Nibelungen*** (***The Nibelungs***)***; Metropolis; Spione*** (***Spies***)***; Das Testament des Dr. Mabuse*** (***The Testament of Dr. Mabuse***). In 1933, after her divorce from Lang, she directed two pictures herself: ***Elisabeth und der Narr*** (***Elisabeth and the Jester***) and ***Hanneles Himmelfahrt.*** NSDAP member. She falls for anything Joseph Goebbels' propaganda spreads, Curt Riess wrote. Harbou was involved in writing or co-writing some of the biggest NS films: ***Der alte und der junge König*** (***The Old and the Young King***)***; Der Herrscher*** (***The Ruler/The Sovereign***)***; Der zerbrochene Krug*** (***The Broken Jug***)***;*** Veit Harlan's ***Jugend*** (***Youth***); ***Kolberg*** (uncredited); ***Das Leben geht weiter***

(***Life Goes On***). Died on July 1, 1954, in Berlin after a serious fall by leaving the Delphi Film Theater watching a reissue of ***Der müde Tod***.

VEIT HARLAN [Actor and Director]

Born on September 22, 1899, in Berlin *Veit Harlan was the director Goebbels would have liked to be. That he made almost no movie without Goebbels' interference, speaks all the more for the high reputation which he enjoyed with the Propaganda Minister. The Harlan films were that clear to Goebbels that he controlled them more intensely.* [242] Veit's father Walter Harlan was a playwright and actively involved in literary circles, presiding over the Association of German Stage Writers and Stage Composers. His mother, Adele Harlan, was born a Boothy. Veit Harlan was trained at the Max Reinhardt seminary. First stage part as sixteen year old in Berlin's Luisen Theater. End of 1916 enlisted as a war volunteer. Three years later he returned to the stage. First movie part in 1927. In 1931 had parts in ***Gefahren der Liebe*** (***Dangers of Love***), a sexual enlightenment movie, and in ***Yorck*** by Gustav Ucicky, a glorification of Prussian militarism. In 1932 in ***Der Choral von Leuthen*** (***The Anthem of Leuthen***) with Otto Gebühr as Fridericus Rex. On April 20, 1933, on the occasion of the "Führer's" birthday, he appeared as Friedrich Thiemann in Hanns Johst's staging of the infamous *Schlageter* play in which he issued the notorious line, "When I hear of culture, I release the safety catch of my Browning." Besides starring in pictures like ***Flüchtlinge (Refugees)***, ***Mein Leben für Isabell (My Life for Isabell)*** or ***Das Mädchen Johanna (Joan the Maid)*** with an all-star cast directed by Gustav Ucicky, Ufa's version of Jeanne d'Arc, Harlan found time to dub American movie actors such as Paul Muni, a Jew, in the German version of ***I Was a Fugitive from a Chain Gang***. In 1934, Harlan debuted as film director with the comedy ***Krach im Hinterhaus*** (***Trouble Backstairs***). In 1937, at Tobis, he directed ***Kreutzersonate*** and the same year Emil Jannings in ***Der Herrscher*** (***The Ruler/The Sovereign***) which brought him to the attention of Hitler and Goebbels. Consequently, he was chosen to become *the* Nazi film director:

242 Frank Noack, *Veit Harlan*.

Jud Süss (***Jew Suss***), ***Der grosse König*** (***The Great King***), the anti-Czech ***Die goldene Stadt*** (***The Golden City***), and ***Kolberg.*** Harlan was married three times: to Jewish actress Dora Gerson (who was gassed in Auschwitz), actress-to-turned-post-war politician Hilde Körber, and Kristina Söderbaum who starred in most of his Nazi films. On April 13, 1964, Veit Harlan died on the Isle of Capri surrounded by his family.

FRITZ HIPPLER [SS Obersturmbannführer and Reichsfilm Intendant]

Born on August 17, 1909, in Berlin. Studied sociology and law in Heidelberg. Joined NSDAP in 1927. In August 1936 entered the newsreel division of the Ministry of Public Enlightenment and Propaganda assisting Hans Weidemann until he was appointed Weidemann's successor as director of the German Newsreel office in January 1939. In 1939-40 compiled and supervised the notorious propaganda documentaries ***Feldzug in Polen*** (***Campaign in Poland***), ***Sieg im Westen*** (***Victory in the West***) and ***Der ewige Jude*** (***The Eternal Jew***). In February 1942, he was appointed Reichsfilm Intendant. But Goebbels became dissatisfied with Hippler ("incompetence, 'mishaps', alcoholism and family problems") and released him from his post in 1943. Hippler worked as a travel agent in Berchtesgaden where he died on May 22, 2002.

EMIL JANNINGS [Actor]

Born Theodor Friedrich Emil Janenz on July 23, 1884, in Rorschach, Switzerland, son of an American merchant from St. Louis and a German mother with Jewish-Russian roots. Because his mother forbade him to fulfill his dream and become an actor, Jannings went to sea before his mother allowed him an acting traineeship at the town state theater in Görlitz. Worked with theater companies in Bremen, Nuremberg, Leipzig, Königsberg and Glogau before joining Max Reinhardt and Deutsches Theater in the German capital. Breakthrough in 1918 as Judge Adam in Kleist's ***Der zerbrochene Krug*** (***The Broken Jug***) which, filmed in 1936, was one of Hitler's favorite movies. In films as early as 1914, his favorite screen directors were Ernst Lubitsch (***Die***

Augen der Mumie Ma/The Eyes of the Mummy as Radu, an Arab; ***Madame DuBarry*** as Louis XV; ***Anna Boleyn*** as Henry VIII; ***Kohlhiesels Töchter/ Kohlhiesel's Daughters*** as Peter Xaver) and Friedrich Wilhelm Murnau (***Der letzte Mann/The Last Laugh*** as hotel porter; ***Tartüff*** in the title role; ***Faust*** as Mephisto). In 1927 signed with Paramount and, in 1929, won the first Best Actor Oscar for his work in ***The Way of All Flesh*** and ***The Last Command.*** With the advent of sound, he returned to Germany and, directed by Josef von Sternberg from Hollywood, appeared in ***Der blaue Engel*** (***The Blue Angel***) at Ufa Studios in Neubabelsberg, a movie which, in turn, made his partner Marlene Dietrich a star. While Marlene followed Sternberg to Hollywood, Jannings remained and became the Nazis' highest-paid prestige star: ***Der alte und der junge König*** (***The Old and the Young King***); ***Der Herrscher*** (***The Ruler/ The Sovereign***), ***Robert Koch, Ohm Krüger*** (***Uncle Kruger***), ***Die Entlassung*** (***Bismarck's Dismissal***). Was in charge of his own production group and member of the Board of Directors of Tobis Film Company. After the war, his dreams of a comeback were in vain. Died on January 2, 1950, aged 65, in Strobl, Austria, from liver cancer.

Emil Jannings in *The Old and the Young King*.
Courtesy of Jens Geutebrück, Coronaretro Archives

LUDWIG KLITZSCH [General Manager]

Born on September 16, 1881, in Halle/Saale. Director of *Illustrirte Zeitung* Leipzig. On November 19, 1916, founded with Krupp manager Alfred Hugenberg Deutsche Lichtbild-Gesellschaft (DEULIG), a film company close to the state and German propaganda activities. Hugenberg, on his way to becoming Germany's press czar, made Klitzsch general manager of the Scherl Publishing House and finally of Ufa Universum Film Aktiengesellschaft. He remained head of Ufa until 1945. Klitzsch died on January 7, 1954, in Bad Wiessee.

GUIDO FRIEDRICH KNOPP [TV editor]

Born on January 29, 1948, in Treysa, Hesse. Studied history, political science and journalism. One of his teachers was Hitler biographer Werner Maser. PhD. Editor, *Frankfurter Allgemeine Zeitung*. In charge of foreign department, *Welt am Sonntag*. In 1978 joined ZDF Zweites Deutsches Fernsehen (Second Channel TV) in Mainz where he became known for formats like ***Damals*** and ***History***. Produced an endless stream of TV documentaries about Hitler and the Third Reich: ***Das Urteil von Nürnberg*** (1986); ***Der verdammte Krieg - Das Unternehmen Barbarossa*** (6 parts, 1991); ***Das Ende 1945*** (1995); ***Hitler - Eine Bilanz*** (1995); ***Hitlers Helfer*** (1996); ***Hitlers Helfer II*** (1998); ***Hitlers Krieger*** (1998); ***Hitlers Kinder*** (5 parts, 2000); ***Holokaust*** (2000); ***Hitlers Frauen und Marlene*** (2001); ***Die SS - Eine Warnung der Geschichte*** (6 parts, 2002); ***Sie wollten Hitler töten*** (2004); ***Hitlers Manager*** (5 parts, 2004); ***Die Wehrmacht*** (2007).

PAUL KOHNER [Producer-turned-Agent]

Born to a Jewish family on May 29, 1902, in Teplitz-Schönau, Austria-Hungary (now Teplice, Czech Republic). His father, Julius "Kino" Kohner, was the manager of the local film theater and editor of a film trade paper. During an interview in 1920, Kohner met Carl Laemmle who became his mentor. Paul's career at Universal Pictures headquarters in New York City began as an office errand boy. Some time later, he went to Hollywood to work at Universal City as production supervisor and casting director. In the late 1920s, Laemmle promoted Kohner head of Universal's European division which was based in Berlin. Kohner supervised the German release of ***All Quiet on the Western Front*** which was sabotaged by the Nazis, the productions of Luis Trenker's ***Berge in Flammen*** (***The Doomed Battalion***) and ***Der Rebell*** (***The Rebel***), Arnold Fanck's ***S.O.S. Iceberg*** and Fritz Lang's ***Testament des Dr. Mabuse*** (***Testament of Dr. Mabuse***). When the Laemmles were ousted out of their company, Kohner established one of Hollywood's leading talent agencies representing Marlene Dietrich, Billy Wilder, Erich von Stroheim, Ingmar Bergman, John Huston, and Klaus Kinski. In 1938, Kohner was co-founder of the European Film Fund that supported émigrés. Kohner, who was married to actress Lupita Tovar, died on March 16, 1988, of a heart attack in Los Angeles.

WERNER KRAUSS [Actor]

Born Werner Johannes Krauss on June 23, 1884, in Gestungshausen near Coburg. First stage experience as an extra. Regular stage parts in traveling and city theaters since 1902: in Guben, Magdeburg, Bromberg, Aachen, Nuremberg, Munich and, since 1913, in Berlin. Film parts since 1916 (***Hoffmanns Erzählungen/Tales of Hoffmann***). Won world fame in the expressionist ***Das Cabinet des Dr. Caligari*** (***The Cabinet of Dr. Caligari***) in 1920. His illustrious career was overshadowed by his stage appearance as Shylock in *The Merchant of Venice* and Veit Harlan's ***Jud Süss*** (***Jew Suss***), playing not only the title character's aide and secretary Levy but three other small Jewish parts, including that of Rabbi Loew: *It shall be shown how all these different temperaments and characters, the faithful patriarch, the cunning impostor, the haggling merchant, after all originated from the same roots.* Krauss' NS documentation listed him as "*deutschblütig*" (of German blood). In fact, after his appearance in ***Jew Suss***, Krauss asked Goebbels to announce publicly that he was not Jewish but a loyal "Aryan" merely playing a part as an actor in the service of the state. Krauss died on October 20, 1959, in Vienna.

Werner Krauss (left) with Ferdinand Marian in *Jew Suss*.
Courtesy of Jens Geutebrück, Coronaretro Archives

ILSE KUBASCHEWSKI [Distributor, Producer]

Born Ilse Kramp on August 18, 1907, in Berlin. In 1931 began as shorthand typist and dispatcher at Siegel Monopolfilm, a distribution company. In 1938 companion in a Berlin cinema. Married an Ufa employee, Hans Wilhelm Kubaschewski. In 1945, together with a partner, later producer Luggi Waldleitner, acquired a cinema in Oberstdorf, Bavaria. In 1949 founded Gloria Film GmbH, a releasing company that distributed Herbert J. Yates' Republic pictures. She produced and distributed ***Die Trapp Familie*** (***The Trapp Family***) and Fritz Lang's post-war ***Das indische Grabmal*** (***The Indian Tomb***). Almost released Veit Harlan's ***Kolberg*** a few years after the war and handled several post-war projects of this director: ***Sterne über Colombo*** (***Stars over Colombo***);

Die Gefangene des Maharadscha (***Circus Girl***); ***Verrat an Deutschland; Die blonde Frau des Maharadscha*** (***The Maharajah's Blonde***). Kubaschewski's production manager was Walter Traut who had worked with Arnold Fanck and with Leni Riefenstahl on all her National Socialist films. Retired from film production and distribution in 1974, only controlling the Gloria Palace in Munich. Kubaschewski died on October 30, 2001, in Munich.

FRITZ LANG [Director]

Born Friedrich Christian Anton Lang on December 5, 1890, in Vienna as son of architect Anton Lang and his wife Pauline Lang née Schlesinger. Briefly attended the Technical University of Vienna and studied civil engineering until he decided in favor of art and left Vienna to travel around the world. In World War 1, Lang served in the Austrian army. Wounded three times, he began to write film exposés and scenarios and send them to Berlin producers. When he came to Berlin, he worked for Joe May and Erich Pommer of Decla (a company that was absorbed by Ufa) who eventually promoted him director. In Germany directed: ***Dr. Mabuse, der Spieler*** (***Dr. Mabuse, the Gambler***); ***Die Nibelungen; Metropolis; Spione*** (***Spies***); ***Frau im Mond*** (***Woman in the Moon/ By Rocket to the Moon***); ***M; Das Testament des Dr. Mabuse*** (***The Testament of Dr. Mabuse***). While working in Germany, Lang was more right than left wing and sympathized with the Nazis. But the story that he met Goebbels who offered him the job of head of the German film industry or, rather, German Cinema Institute is not true. Anyway, Lang left Germany to do a movie for Erich Pommer and Fox, ***Liliom***, in Paris and, with a Hollywood contract in his pocket, left Europe in mid-1934. In Hollywood he made westerns, thrillers and the anti-Fascist ***Hangmen Also Die.*** His temporary return to Germany in the late 1950s and work for Berlin film producer Artur Brauner was less successful and turned out aesthetically backward achievements. His final project for Brauner titled ***...und morgen: Mord!*** (***...and tomorrow: Murder***) remained unrealized: A series of rape murders lead the police to a respected member of the community. In 1963, Lang was seen as actor (playing himself) in Jean-Luc Godard's ***Le Mépris***, a living legend besides

Brigitte Bardot, Michel Piccoli and Jack Palance. Fritz Lang died on August 2, 1976, in Beverly Hills.

Fritz Lang's Die Nibelungen.
Courtesy of Jens Geutebrück, Coronaretro Archives

ZARAH LEANDER [Actress]

Born Sara Stina Hedberg on March 15, 1907 in Karlstad, Sweden. Thanks to a German nanny and a German piano teacher, she learnt the German language from early childhood on. Stage career began in Sweden, breakthrough for her contralto voice in Vienna in the operetta *Axel an der Himmelstür* at the Theater an der Wien. On October 28, 1936, Leander signed with Ufa and for the next years became Germany's leading female film star. On October 6, 1937, Goebbels wrote in his diary: *The box-office receipts with her are enormous.* And even Hitler asked his shepherd's dog "to sing like Zarah Leander". Films: ***Premiere; Zu neuen Ufern (Life Begins Anew/To New Shores); La Habanera; Heimat; Der Blaufuchs (The Blue Fox); Es war eine rauschende Ballnacht (It Was a Gay Ballnight); Das Lied der Wüste (The Desert Song); Das Herz der Königin (The Heart of the Queen); Der Weg ins Freie (The Way to Freedom);***

***Die grosse Liebe* (*The Great Love*); *Damals* (*At That Time*).** On November 10, 1942, she left Germany and returned to Sweden. After the war stage appearances and some more films and TV shows in West Germany. Died on June 23, 1981 in Stockholm.

WOLFGANG LIEBENEINER [Director]

Born on October 6, 1905, in Liebau. Studied philosophy, Germanic philology and history in Germany and Austria. Debuted on the stage in 1928 in Munich under Otto Falckenberg. Under Goebbels he carved out a stunning career. In 1936, Liebeneiner was appointed Staatsschauspieler (State's Actor), in 1937 member of the Board of Terra Filmkunst, in 1938 head of the artistic faculty of Babelsberg Film Academy, in 1939 head of Fachschaft Film at Reichsfilmkammer. In 1940 directed ***Bismarck***, in 1941 the pro-euthanasia film ***Ich klage an*** (***I Accuse***) with Heidemarie Hatheyer, in 1942 ***Die Entlassung*** (***Bismarck's Dismissal***). In 1943, along with Veit Harlan, he was appointed professor by his mentor Goebbels and put in charge of production at Ufa Filmkunst. In 1944 supervised postproduction and editing of Harlan's ***Kolberg***. In 1945 ***Das Leben geht weiter*** (***Life Goes On***) directed by Liebeneiner was left unfinished. His career continued in West German film and television as if nothing had happened. Liebeneiner died on November 28, 1987, in Vienna.

PETER LORRE [Actor]

Born László Löwenstein on June 26, 1904, in the Hungarian town of Rósahegy (Rosenberg) in Liptó County, son of Alajos Löwenstein and his wife Elvira. His mother died when László was four years old. Acting career started in Vienna when he was 17 years old. He was seen on the stage in Breslau and Zurich before he came to Berlin and worked with playwright Bert Brecht. In 1931, Fritz Lang cast him in his first talkie ***M*** as child murderer Hans Beckert. In 1933, Lorre went to Paris and then to London where Hitchcock used him in ***The Man Who Knew Too Much*** (1934) and later in ***Secret Agent*** (1936). Arrived in Hollywood in 1935. Starred in Columbia's adaptation of

Dostoyevsky's ***Crime and Punishment*** directed by Josef von Sternberg and at MGM in the horror picture ***Mad Love*** directed by cinematographer Karl Freund. At Twentieth Century-Fox starred in a series of ***Mr. Moto*** films, at Warner Bros.-First National Studios became a regular in Humphrey Bogart movies (***The Maltese Falcon; Casablanca; Passage to Marseille***). His attempt at a comeback in Germany by directing and starring in ***Der Verlorene*** (***The Lost One***, 1951) failed. He didn't follow an invitation by Brecht to join him in East Berlin and returned to the States. Walt Disney restored Lorre's market value with a meaty supporting part in ***20,000 Leagues Under the Sea*** (1954). The end came with Irwin Allen productions, Roger Corman's AIPoe films, and Jerry Lewis ***(The Patsy).*** Lorre died on March 23, 1964, from a stroke.

FERDINAND MARIAN [Actor]

Born Ferdinand Heinrich Johann Haschkowetz on August 14, 1902, in Vienna. Left home as a 17-year old. Used his father's ties who was an actor in order to build a stage career in Graz. In the beginning appeared by using his father's stage-name Fritz, then as Ferdinand Marian. In 1927 moved to Germany and appeared on stages in Trier, Aachen, Mönchengladbach, Odenkirchen, Viersen and Rheydt, birth town of Joseph Goebbels, then to Hamburg. In Munich, in 1933, in Kurt Bernhardt's ***Der Tunnel*** (***The Tunnel***), played an agent provocateur. In 1939 was Zarah Leander's male partner in ***La Habanera***. On the stage he had already experience with Jewish parts, playing Ahasver. End of 1939, a Jewish film part sealed his fate: ***Jud Süss*** (***Jew Süss***). In ***Ohm Krüger*** (***Uncle Kruger***) he played Cecil Rhodes, in ***Münchhausen*** Cagliostro the magician who knows the secret of eternal life. His last film part was in the unfinished ***Die Nacht der Zwölf*** (***The Night of the Twelve***) in which he appeared as an obviously Jewish women's killer. Marian died on August 9, 1946, near Dürneck. The authorities registered his death as car accident.

JOE MAY [Director]

Born Joseph Otto Mandel on November 7, 1880, in Vienna. In his prime one of Germany's most prominent filmmakers. Began as stage director. In 1902, married actress Mia May (born Hermine Pfleger) and took his stage name from her. In movies since 1914 directing detective Stuart Webbs and Sherlock Holmes stories. In 1915 founded May Film GmbH. Director: ***Hilde Warren und der Tod*** (***Hilde Warren and Death***) written by Fritz Lang; the serial ***Herrin der Welt*** (***Mistress of the World***, 1919-20); the 2-part ***Das Indische Grabmal*** (***The Indian Tomb***). Later joined Ufa Studios where he directed ***Heimkehr*** (***Homecoming***, 1928) and ***Asphalt*** (1929), both starring Gustav Fröhlich, and produced Kurt Bernhardt's ***Die letzte Kompagnie*** (***The Last Company***, 1930) with Conrad Veidt. In 1933, he and his wife Mia left Germany and settled in the United States. At Warner Bros. directed Kay Francis, Ian Hunter and Basil Rathbone in ***Confession*** (1937) and made a number of films at Universal, such as ***The Invisible Man Returns*** and ***The House of the Seven Gables***, both with Vincent Price. From the major studios his way went to the bottom of Poverty Row. His last picture was ***Johnny Doesn't Live Here Any More*** (1944) for the King Bros. a Monogram release. Out of luck for the rest of his life. Died on April 29, 1954, in Hollywood after long illness.

KARL NEUMANN [Producer]

Although Neumann was no artist and not even a production professional, for a few years he became a seminal force in German cartoon film manufacture. Karl Albrecht Wolfgang Neumann was born on June 14, 1900, in Koeslin, the son of teacher Karl Neumann. In 1907, he attended primary and middle school in Koeslin, then from 1911 to 1919 the gymnasium. In the following decade he worked as clerk and proxy mainly for sausage and meat factories. In spring 1931 joined NSDAP, membership no. 567 908. On October 31, 1931, having lost his job, he worked on a voluntary basis for Gau administration Pomerania. On January 20, 1932, Neumann was promoted Deputy Gau Propaganda Chief, then Gau Propaganda and news service head, on June 1, 1932, full-time Gau Propaganda chief. On October 15, 1934, he became referee in the Reich Ministry of Public Enlightenment and Propaganda: "*Ich gelobe: Ich werde dem Führer des Deutschen Reiches und Volkes, Adolf*

Hitler, treu und gehorsam sein und meine Dienstobliegenheiten gewissenhaft und uneigennützig erfüllen." On April 12, 1938, Neumann was promoted *Oberregierungsrat* [Councillor]. One year later, Leopold Gutterer suggested to promote him. Neumann became Gutterer's deputy and Ministerialrat [undersecretary]. On October 1, 1939, Neumann changed to a position in Deutsche Propagandaatelier GmbH. Soon Goebbels took notice of him and assigned Neumann with the reorganization of cultural film production. Pleased with Neumann's work, Goebbels eventually put him in charge of Deutsche Zeichenfilm GmbH. In June 1945, the former Nazi functionary found his death in a Soviet camp hanged in a toilet.

A young Karl Neumann.
Courtesy of J. P. Storm Collection

GEORG WILHELM PABST [Director]

Born on August 25, 1885, in Raudnitz, Bohemia. Raised in Vienna. In 1901 took acting lessons. In 1912 stage directing debut at Deutsches Volkstheater in New York. When he returned to Austria at the beginning of World War 1, he was interned in France as enemy alien. During internship organized a camp theater. In 1919 back to Vienna where he became director of an avant-garde theater. In 1921 entered into a partnership with German director Carl Froelich. First big success as filmmaker directing Greta Garbo in her only German film, ***Die freudlose Gasse*** (***The Joyless Street***), in 1925. Garbo's partners were Asta Nielsen and Werner Krauss. Silents: ***Geheimnisse einer Seele*** (***Secrets of a Soul***), a psychoanalytical chamber play with Werner Krauss; ***Man spielt nicht mit der Liebe*** (***Don't Play with Love***); ***Die Liebe der Jeanne Ney*** (***The Love of Jeanne Ney***); ***Abwege*** (***The Devious Path***); ***Die Büchse der Pandora*** (***Pandora's Box***) and ***Tagebuch einer Verlorenen*** (***Diary of a Lost Girl***), both with Louise Brooks; ***Die weisse Hölle vom Piz Palü*** (***White Hell of Pitz Palu***), co-directing Leni Riefenstahl with Arnold Fanck. Early talkies included the anti-war film ***Westfront 1918*** and a film version of Bert Brecht's ***Die 3 Groschen-Oper*** (***The Three Penny Opera***). When Hitler became Reich Chancellor, Pabst was in France shooting ***Don Quichotte*** and decided not to return to Germany. In October 1933, he tried his luck in Hollywood where he made only one movie (for Warner Bros.), ***A Modern Hero*** based on a novel by Louis Bromfield, with Richard Barthelmess. Disappointed with the standardized Hollywood production methods, Pabst returned to France. Eventually, he decided to go back to the United States, but during a farewell visit at his mother's place in Austria he was surprised by the outbreak of World War 2. Unable to leave, Pabst continued filmmaking in Germany and was criticized by other émigrés as an opportunist. Made two big films for Bavaria and the Nazi regime: ***Komödianten*** (***Comedians***) and the genius picture ***Paracelsus*** with Werner Krauss. Leni Riefenstahl tried to get him co-directing her ***Tiefland*** project but after a brief time their collaboration ended in dispute and quarrel. In 1948, émigré Ernst Deutsch was honored with an award as best actor in Pabst's ***Der Prozess*** (***The Process***) in Venice. Pabst tried to launch a huge ***Ulysses*** project in Italy, but his concept wasn't realized. Instead the production company, Lux Ponti-DeLaurentiis, hired an Italian director, Mario Camerini, and made the Technicolor film with Kirk Douglas and Silvana Mangano. Two of his post-war films were quite successful, ***Der letzte Akt*** (U.S.: ***The Last Ten Days*** released by Columbia Pictures) with Albin Skoda as Adolf Hitler and Oskar Werner, and the resistance drama ***Es geschah am 20. Juli*** (***It Happened on July 20th***) with Bernhard Wicki as Stauffenberg. Pabst's final film, his only one in color, ***Durch die Wälder, durch die Auen*** (***Through the Forests and Through the Trees***), was a biopic devoted to the life of composer Carl Maria von Weber (played by Peter Arens). In 1957, Pabst was diagnosed Parkinson's disease and had to give up filmmaking. He died on May 29, 1967, in Vienna.

HARALD G[IERTZ] PETERSSON [Screenwriter]

Born on October 16, 1904, in Weimar. Son of a Swedish father and a German mother. When his book *Herz ist Trumpf* was filmed in 1934, he entered the film industry. In the 1930s Tobis press chief. Wrote ***Die Nacht der Entscheidung*** (***The Night of Decision***) and ***Die fromme Lüge*** (***The Pious Lie,*** 1938) with Pola Negri, ***Blutsbrüderschaft*** (***Blood Brotherhood,*** 1939), ***Wetterleuchten um Barbara*** (1940) and ***Der Verteidiger hat das Wort*** (***Address by Counsel,*** 1943) with Heinrich George. After the war, working for Horst Wendlandt and Constantin Film, was involved in a series of Edgar Wallace and Karl May films and in Artur Brauner's remake of ***Die Nibelungen***. Was married to the star of Herbert Selpin's ***Titanic***, Sybille Schmitz. Died on July 8, 1977, in Berlin.

CARL RADDATZ [Actor]

Leading heroic man in NS movies. Born on March 13, 1912, in Mannheim. Private actors' training with Willy Birgel in 1930-31. In 1937 won a film contract with Ufa: ***Urlaub auf Ehrenwort*** (***Leave on Word of Honor,*** 1937); ***Wunschkonzert*** (***Request Concert,*** 1940); ***Zwielicht*** (***Twilight,*** 1940); ***Über alles in der Welt*** (***Above Else in the World,*** 1940); ***Stukas*** (1940); ***Heimkehr***

(***Homecoming***, 1941); ***Immensee*** (1943); ***Opfergang*** (***The Great Sacrifice***, 1944); ***Unter den Brücken*** (***Under the Bridges***, 1945). After the war dubbed American stars like Kirk Douglas, Burt Lancaster, Lee Marvin, and Robert Taylor. Died on May 19, 2004, in Berlin.

HERBERT REINECKER [Screenwriter/TV Writer]

Born on December 24, 1914, in Hagen. Career started as NS journalist. Member of the SS since 1940. Editor of the Hitler Youth magazine *Jungvolk*. War reporter. Authored National Socialist pamphlets like *Das Dorf bei Odessa (The Village near Odessa)*, published in 1942. In 1943 joined Alfred Weidenmann in producing ***Junge Adler*** (***Young Eagles***). The two would join forces again in 1956 making ***Der Stern von Afrika*** (***The Star of Africa***), a biopic of WW2 fighter ace Hans-Joachim Marseille who died in 1942 (played by Joachim Hansen). In the 1960s, working for Munich producer Helmut Ringelmann, Reinecker became the most prolific writer of TV crime series like ***Der Kommissar*** with Erik Ode and ***Derrick*** with Horst Tappert. Died on January 27, 2007, in Kampfenhausen, Lake Starnberg, Bavaria.

HARALD REINL [Director]

Born on July 8, 1908, in Bad Ischl, Austria. The dedicated skier was used by Arnold Fanck in one of his alpine films and was hired by Leni Riefenstahl to assist her in the making of ***Tiefland*** (***Lowlands***). After the war got a chance to direct his first feature film for producer Hubert Schonger: ***Bergkristall***. In 1955 he directed ***Solange du lebst*** (***As Long As You Live***) that glorified Legion Condor with a love story against the background of the Spanish Civil War: Marianne Koch played a Franco sympathizer who hides a crashed German pilot (Adrian Hoven). Two other war films followed: ***Die grünen Teufel von Monte Cassino*** (***The Green Devils of Monte Cassino***) and ***U 47 - Kapitänleutnant Prien*** (***U-47 Lt. Commander Prien***). In the 1950s to early 1970s Reinl helped to create some of the most successful German film waves: Ludwig Ganghofer and *Heimatfilme*, Edgar Wallace, Karl May, Jerry Cotton, Erich von Däniken (***Erinnerungen an die Zukunft/Chariots of the***

Gods). Artur Brauner hired him to direct his two-part ***Nibelungen*** remake. Then, however, he wasn't able to keep pace with new developments on screen. He was stabbed to death during a quarrel on October 9, 1986, in Puerto de la Cruz, Teneriffa, by his third wife, former Czech actress Daniela Marie Delisová, who was an alcoholic.

EUGEN REX [Actor]

Born on July 8, 1884, in Berlin. Stage debut in 1905. Since 1918 acting in films: ***Die Dame, der Teufel und die Probiermamsell*** (***The Lady, the Devil and the Mannequin***, 1918); ***Ferdinand Lassalle*** (1918); ***Der brennende Acker*** (***The Burning Soil,*** 1921-22, director: F. W. Murnau); ***Die zwölfte Stunde (The Twelfth Hour,*** sound film version of ***Nosferatu); Der Hauptmann von Köpenick*** (***The Captain of Köpenick***, 1931); ***Der Kongress tanzt*** (***The Congress Dances,*** 1931); ***Schwarzwaldmädel*** (***Black Forest Girl,*** 1933); ***Ein Unsichtbarer geht durch die Stadt*** (***An Invisible Man Walks the City,*** 1933); Svend Noldan's ***Was ist die Welt?*** (1933, as narrator); ***Konjunkturritter*** (***Prosperity Crooks***, 1933-34); ***Der alte und der junge König (The Old and the Young King,*** 1934-35); ***Die Rothschilds. Aktien auf Waterloo*** (1940). Member of NSDAP since 1933. Functionary, stage and film. Died on February 21, 1943, in Berlin.

MARIKA RÖKK [Actress and Dancer]

Born Marie Karoline Rökk on November 3, 1913, in Cairo, daughter of a Hungarian architect and building contractor. Raised in Budapest. Dancing lessons. Appeared on the stage of the Moulin Rouge in Paris and on Broadway in New York City, in Monte Carlo, Cannes, and London. First film in Britain in 1930. In 1934 signed with Ufa and became a faithful servant of the Cinema of the Third Reich. Her favorite director became her husband, Georg Jacoby (they married in 1940): ***Eine Nacht im Mai*** (***A Night in May***)***; Kora Terry***; the Agfacolor productions ***Frauen sind doch bessere Diplomaten*** (***Women Are the Better Diplomats***) and ***Frau meiner Träume*** (***Woman of My Dreams***). When Jewish producer Alfred Zeisler and his wife, Lien Deyers, had to leave Germany, Marika Rökk acquired their villa in Potsdam Babelsberg. Zeisler died in 1985 but didn't see a dime. Instead, Rökk hired a lawyer to prevent the Jewish Claims Conference from inheriting the building. Rökk, still active in films and on TV until her demise, died on May 16, 2004, in Baden, Lower Austria.

HEINRICH ROELLENBLEG [Newsreel editor]

Born on May 13, 1901. Career began at Tobis Melofilm. Editor-in-chief of ***Emelka Wochenschau, Ufa Wochenschau*** and since September 4, 1940, of the German Wartime Newsreel ***Deutsche Wochenschau*** (until he fell into disgrace with Goebbels). After the war became chief executive of ***Neue Deutsche Wochenschau*** (***New German Newsreel***). Helped to produce ***Das war unser Rommel*** and ***So war der deutsche Landser.*** Died on February 2, 1963.

HEINZ RÜHMANN [Actor]

Born Heinrich Wilhelm Rühmann on March 7, 1902, in Essen. First "appearances" as little boy in the station restaurant of his parents. In March 1915, his parents filed for divorce. Hermann Rühmann went to Berlin where he committed, as they say, suicide. In 1916, the rest of the family settled in Munich. Acting lessons with Friedrich Basil, the same actor who trained Adolf Hitler. Rühmann's stage career began in Breslau (today Wroclaw), followed by Hanover and Bremen where he was seen for the first time in the comedy *Der Mustergatte (Model Husband).* In 1924, in Munich, married a Jewish actress, Maria Bernheim, who gave up her career for him and became his personal director. In Berlin quite successful on stage in *Der Mustergatte* and *Charleys Tante (Charley's Aunt),* he was hired by Ufa producer Erich Pommer: ***Die Drei von der Tankstelle*** (***Three from the Filling Station***); Robert Siodmak's ***Der Mann, der seinen Mörder sucht*** (***Looking for His Murderer***) co-written by Siodmak's brother Curt; ***Bomben auf Monte Carlo*** (***The Bombardment of Monte Carlo***). Hitler and Goebbels cherished Heinz Rühmann. Goebbels liked him in Carl Froelich's ***Wenn wir alle Engel wären*** (***If We All Were Angels***). In the 1940s, Rühmann was granted his own production unit at Terra Film Company located at Babelsberg Studios: ***Kleider machen Leute***

(***Clothes Make the Man***); ***Der Gasmann*** (***The Gas Meter Reader***); ***Quax, der Bruchpilot*** (***Quax the Crash Pilot***); ***Ich vertraue Dir meine Frau an*** (***I Entrust You with My Wife***); ***Die Feuerzangenbowle*** (***The Brandy Punch***). After the war faced bankruptcy with his own film company Comedia. Years went by until he became successful again: ***Auf der Reeperbahn nachts um halb eins; Charleys Tante*** (***Charley's Aunt***); ***Der Hauptmann von Köpenick*** (***The Captain of Köpenick***); ***Es geschah am hellichten Tag*** (***It Happened in Broad Daylight***); ***Der brave Soldat Schweijk*** (***The Good Soldier Schweik***) and three ***Father Brown*** films. In 1956, directed by Stanley Kramer, he was seen as a Jew in an American movie, ***Ship of Fools.*** Rühmann died on October 3, 1994, in Aufkirchen, Lake Starnberg.

HANS ADALBERT [von] SCHLETTOW [Actor]

Born Hans Adalbert Droescher on June 11, 1888, in Frankfurt/Main. Began as an actor trainee at Schauspielhaus Frankfurt in 1908. First screen appearance in 1916. On the silent screen his tall appearance left an impact as Hagen von Tronje in Fritz Lang's 2-part ***Nibelungen***. Made quite a career as supporting actor in NS films: ***Der Choral von Leuthen*** (***The Anthem of Leuthen,*** 1933); ***Hundert Tage*** (***Hundred Days,*** 1934); ***Mit versiegelter Order*** (***Under Sealed Orders,*** 1938); ***Kongo Express*** (1939); ***Die Geierwally*** (***Wally of the Vultures,*** 1940); the anti-Semitic ***Die Rothschilds*** (1940); ***Wunschkonzert*** (***Request Concert,*** 1940); ***Ohm Krüger*** (***Uncle Kruger,*** 1940) as Boer commander de Wett; ***Heimaterde*** (1941). Feared by his colleagus as an eager informer and denunciator. Made it onto Goebbels *Gottbegnadetenliste* of actors who wouldn't be conscripted. Died during the Battle of Berlin, the same day as his "Führer", on April 30, 1945.

"DR." HELMUT EWALD SCHREIBER [Producer and Conjuror]

Born on January 23, 1903, in Backnang as son of a factory owner. Studied philosophy in Munich. In 1926 joined the Berlin film industry as production manager. Member of the NSDAP since 1933. Thanks to his good ties with the Minister of Public Enlightenment and Propaganda, Joseph Goebbels, he was promoted head of a production unit at Tobis: ***Das Schloss in Flandern*** (***The Castle in Flanders***); ***Truxa; Der Herrscher*** (***The Ruler/The Sovereign***). In 1942 production chief of Bavaria in Munich. A friend of Hitler's personal adjutant, Julius Schaub, and Berlin's police director, Wolf-Heinrich Graf von Helldorf. After the war, he was supposed to become entertainment director of Deutschland Fernsehen GmbH, a television company planned by West German chancellor Konrad Adenauer. To the public Schreiber was better known as Kalanag, a famous stage magician who even appeared at Hitler's Berghof. Died on December 24, 1963, in Gaildorf.

NORBERT SCHULTZE [Composer]

Born on January 26, 1911, in Braunschweig. His hits were *Lili Marleen* and *Bomben auf Engelland.* Film scores include ***Feuertaufe*** (***Baptism by Fire***, 1939); ***Bismarck*** (1940); ***Kampfgeschwader Lützow*** (***Fighting Squadron Lützow***, 1940); ***Ich klage an*** (***I Accuse***, 1941); ***Kolberg*** (1943-44) and the unfinished ***Das Leben geht weiter*** (***Life Goes On***, 1944-45). After the war, Schultze was involved in two war films: ***U 47 - Kapitänleutnant Prien*** (***U-47 Lt. Commander Prien***, 1958) and ***Soldatensender Calais*** (***Headquarters State Secret***, 1960). With his sons Kristian and Norbert Jr. produced a color ***Max & Moritz*** in 1956, adapted from Wilhelm Busch. Died on October 14, 2002, in Bad Tölz, Bavaria.

HERBERT SELPIN [Director]

Born on May 29, 1904, in Berlin. Medical studies, then various jobs. Internship at Ufa. Worked on the set of F. W. Murnau's ***Faust***. Directorial debut in 1932: ***Chauffeur Antoinette***. NSDAP member since 1934. Directed several films with Hans Albers. During the making of ***Titanic*** (1942), having made some antimilitaristic remarks, was denounced by his own friend, screenwriter Walter Zerlett-Olfenius. He was arrested and committed suicide in his cell on August 1, 1942.

CURT SIODMAK [Writer]

Born on August 10, 1902, in Dresden as son of Jewish merchant Ignatz Siodmak and his wife Rosa Philippine née Blum. Curt studied physics, mathematics and engineering in Dresden, Berlin, Stuttgart and Zurich where he married Baronesse Henrietta Erna de Perrot. He began to write short stories and work as a journalist. Joined his older brother Robert in making ***Menschen am Sonntag*** (***People on Sunday***) in 1929 and followed him and Billy Wilder to Ufa: ***Der Mann, der seinen Mörder sucht*** (***Looking for his Murderer,*** 1931). His final sale to Ufa was ***F.P. 1 antwortet nicht (F.P. 1 Doesn't Answer)*** in 1932, made from his novel. Left Germany in 1933 and worked in France and England before he came to the United States in 1937, trying his luck at Paramount Studios. Joe May got him a job as co-writer on ***The Invisible Man Returns*** in 1939 at Universal City. For years to come Siodmak became the main supplier of screenplays for Universal Horrors: ***Black Friday; Invisible Woman; The Wolf Man; The Invisible Agent; Son of Dracula: Frankenstein Meets the Wolf Man; House of Frankenstein.*** In 1942 his novel ***Donovan's Brain*** was published. It was filmed three times. In the 1950s, Curt Siodmak directed some B movies: ***Bride of the Gorilla; Curucu, Beast of the Amazon; Love Slaves of the Amazons; Tales of Frankenstein*** (pilot for a planned Hammer/Screen Gems series). Curt Siodmak died on September 2, 2000, at his home in Three Rivers, California, from cancer at age 98.

ROBERT SIODMAK [Director]

Born August 8, 1900, in Dresden, the older brother of screenwriter Curt Siodmak. Robert Siodmak began in the industry by recutting silent films for his cousin, producer Seymour Nebenzal. In 1929, he co-directed ***Menschen am Sonntag*** (***People on Sunday***), a forerunner of the post-war neorealist films, with Curt, Billy Wilder, Edgar Ulmer, and cameraman Eugen Schüfftan. Established himself as director at Ufa Studios. Left Germany in 1933 and made his best films in France: ***La crise est finié; La Vie parisienne; Mollenard.*** In 1939, in Hollywood, directed a number of B pictures for Paramount (Siodmak called it *Paramount shit*), then better films at other studios such as

The Spiral Staircase for RKO and ***The Great Sinner*** at MGM. Several pictures at Universal: ***Son of Dracula; Cobra Woman; Phantom Lady; The Suspect*** (with Charles Laughton) and the highly-acclaimed dark noir thriller ***The Killers*** with Burt Lancaster in his film debut. In 1954 decided to return to Europe where he ended up wasting his talents and making Karl May films (***Der Schut***) and the untimely epic ***Kampf um Rom*** for producer Artur Brauner. Siodmak died on March 10, 1973, of a heart attack in Locarno, seven weeks after the death of his wife.

KRISTINA SÖDERBAUM [Actress]

Born on September 5, 1912, in Stockholm, the third of four children of Dr. Henrik Gustav Söderbaum, President of the Royal Swedish Academy of Sciences and Chairman of the committee that awarded the Nobel Prize in 1901. A movie buff from youth, Söderbaum learned the German language by watching films starring the great Elisabeth Bergner. Her favorite directors were Ernst Lubitsch, Carl Froelich, and G. W. Pabst. After the death of her parents, Kristina left for Berlin in September 1934, with the objective to make a career in German studios. The Swedish film industry at that time was in turmoil, not capable of holding talents such as Ingrid Bergman or Zarah Leander. She took speech lessons with Margarethe Wellhoener. First small screen part in Erich Waschneck's ***Onkel Bräsig (Uncle Stolid***) in 1936. The same year met Veit Harlan whose second marriage to actress Hilde Körber existed only on paper. Got a part in Harlan's ***Jugend*** (***Youth***). Harlan and Söderbaum got married in 1939. Henceforth, Söderbaum became Harlan's female star: ***Jud Süss*** (***Jew Suss,*** 1939-40); ***Die goldene Stadt*** (***The Golden City,*** 1941-42)***; Der grosse König*** (***The Great King,*** 1941-42)***; Immensee; Opfergang*** (***The Great Sacrifice***); ***Kolberg*** (1943-44). Some postwar films, still directed by Veit Harlan. After the death of her husband, Söderbaum became a portrait and fashion photographer. Died on February 12, 2001, in Hitzacker, Nether Saxonia, after a long illness.

HANS STEINHOFF [Director]

Born as Johannes Reiter on March 10, 1882, in Marienberg. In 1933 directed ***Hitlerjunge Quex*** (***Hitler Youth Quex***) and ***Mutter und Kind*** (***Mother and Child***), in 1937 ***Ein Volksfeind*** (***An Enemy of the People***), in 1940 Emil Jannings in ***Ohm Krüger*** (***Uncle Kruger***). Allegedly died during the last weeks of the war when he tried to flee the set of an unfinished mystery movie produced in color at Barrandov Studios in Prague starring Hans Albers and Ferdinand Marian, ***Shiva und die Galgenblume*** (***Shiva and the Gallows Flower***). With the Soviet troops virtually on the outskirts of the city, Steinhoff closed the set and had two SS men escort him to a waiting plane. The plane never got to Berlin but was shot down by Soviet Forces at Glienig near Luckenwalde on April 20, 1945. Three crew and seventeen passengers were on board. Only two survived. Later, there were unfounded rumors that Steinhoff had escaped the crash and (contemporaneously) the Third Reich with false papers.

LUIS TRENKER

Born Alois Franz Trenker on October 4, 1892, in St. Ulrich, Tyrol, as son of a wood-carver and painter. Studied at Technical University in Vienna. Architect. WW1 participant. At the end of the war First Lieutenant. Arnold Fanck hired him as alpine guide for ***Berg des Schicksals*** (***Mountain of Destiny***) in 1924 but then made him the male star as he realized that the actor originally chosen couldn't climb. Trenker had a brief affair with Leni Riefenstahl during the production of ***Der heilige Berg*** (***The Holy Mountain***, 1926). First directorial assignment: ***Der Kampf ums Matterhorn*** (***Fight for the Matterhorn***, 1928). Carl Laemmle's Universal gave him the chance to direct two successful films that were quite popular with the Nazis: ***Berge in Flammen*** (***The Doomed Battalion***, 1931) and ***Der Rebell*** (***The Rebel***, 1932). Became a Nazi favorite. Member of the NSDAP in 1940. However, when he voted, a born South Tyrolean, for Italian nationality, Goebbels held that against him: *I report the case of Trenker to the Führer. This Schweinestück [swine] didn't vote in South Tyrol for us. Delay, being friendly but otherwise dump him.*

[243] Trenker tried to correct his "mistake", to no avail. Between 1941 and 1945 he got only one film assignment: a second lead in the propaganda picture ***Germanin*** (1943). As Italian citizen Trenker was saved from denazification. In 1946 tried to make some money by selling the "diaries" of Eva Braun that turned out forgeries. Trenker claimed that the notes were published against his will. He produced some more movies and got his own TV show ***Luis Trenker erzählt*** in 1959. Trenker died on April 12, 1990, in Bozen.

GUSTAV UCICKY [Director]

Born on July 6, 1899 in Vienna. Son of artist Gustav Klimt. Entered the film industry as cameraman in 1920 and turned to film directing in Austria in 1925. Coming to Germany three years later, he made nationalist films at Ufa even before the Nazis' seizure of power: ***Das Flötenkonzert von Sanssouci*** (***The Flute Concert of Sans-Souci,*** 1930) starring Otto Gebühr as Fridericus Rex; ***Yorck*** (1931) with Veit Harlan in the supporting cast; the submarine epic ***Morgenrot*** (***Dawn,*** 1932). His first film under the swastika was ***Flüchtlinge*** (***Refugees,*** 1933) and his Emil Jannings picture ***Der zerbrochene Krug*** (***The Broken Jug***) belonged to Hitler's favorite films. For his 1939 ***Mutterliebe*** (***A Mother's Love***) that postulated a model of femininity of serving wives and waiting mothers at the beginning of WW2 an enormous propaganda campaign was mounted. In 1941 Ucicky directed the anti-Polish ***Heimkehr*** (***Homecoming***) with Paula Wessely. Ucicky died on April 27, 1961, in Hamburg.

PAUL WEGENER [Actor and Director]

Born on December 11, 1874, in Arnoldsdorf (later Jarantowice, Poland). Breaking off his law studies, Wegener fulfilled his dream and became a stage actor in 1895, in films since 1912 and one of the most prominent actors and originators of fantastic fairy tales: ***Der Student von Prag (The Student of Prague,*** 1913) written by his friend, Hanns Heinz Ewers; ***Der Golem*** (***The Golem,*** 1914); ***Der Yoghi; Rübezahls Hochzeit*** (***Old Nip's Wedding***); ***Hans***

243 Goebbels Diary Entry, March 5, 1940.

Trutz im Schlaraffenland; Der Rattenfänger (***The Pied Piper of Hamelin***); ***Der Golem, wie er die Welt kam; Lebende Buddhas*** (***Living Buddhas***); ***The Magician*** (directed in Nice by Rex Ingram) as sort of Aleister Crowley, ***Ramper der Tiermensch*** (***The Strange Case of Captain Ramper***). With the Nazis coming to power he tried to arrange with them: ***Hans Westmar - Einer von vielen*** (***Hans Westmar, One of Many***, 1933); directed ***Ein Mann will nach Deutschland*** (***A Man Wants to Get to Germany***, 1934); ***Mein Leben für Irland*** (***My Life for Ireland***, 1940); ***Der grosse König*** (***The Great King***, 1941-42); ***Kolberg*** (1943-44). Was supposed to appear in Harlan's final anti-Semitic film project, ***Der Kaufmann von Venedig*** (***The Merchant of Venice***), with Werner Krauss. In 1945, Wegener who was Buddhist emersed himself in democratic activities, became President of the *Kammer der Kulturschaffenden* and impressed on the stage of Deutsches Theater as *Nathan der Weise (Nathan the Wise)*. Died on September 13, 1948, in Berlin Wilmersdorf.

ALFRED WEIDENMANN [Director]

Born on May 10, 1916, in Stuttgart, son of an industrialist. In 1936, at a competition for 16 mm film amateurs, he won the first prize for a children's movie. After studying three semesters art history, he became a journalist and traveled for two Stuttgart newspapers. Shortly after, he joined NS Reichsjugendführung (RJF, Reich Youth Leadership) and reported about rght-wing countries. In 1938-40 edited a 13-volume book series ***Bücher der Jugend*** (***Books of the Youth***). After war began, Weidenmann produced short films for RJF. His youth novel, ***Jakko***, was made into a Tobis movie by Fritz Peter Buch in 1941. In 1942, he directed his first feature film for Reichspropagandaleitung, ***Hände hoch!*** (***Hands up!***) and a Hitler Youth film, ***Junges Europa*** (***Young Europe***). In 1943-44, made ***Junge Adler*** (***Young Eagles***) with his writing comrade Herbert Reinecker, discovering 15-year old Hardy Krüger, a pupil of the Adolf Hitler Schools. After the war, Weidenmann and Reinecker continued their collaboration on ***Canaris*** (1954) and ***Der Stern von Afrika*** (***The Star of Africa***, 1956) and episodes of TV crime series. Weidenmann died on June 9, 2000, in Zurich.

HORST WENDLANDT

Born Horst Otto Grigori Gubanov on March 15, 1922, in Criewen/Schwedt as son of a Russian farmhand and a German mother. Adopted by his mother's sister whose name he bore. In 1939 apprenticeship at Tobis-Tonbild-Syndikat, in 1941 cashier for that company who cashed out the pay to the film units. In 1944 war volunteer at Luftwaffe. After the war worked as production manager for various companies, among them Artur Brauner and CCC. Danish film entrepreneur Preben Philipsen hired him as producer for his Rialto Films. Wendlandt produced some of the most successful movies of the 1960s: Edgar Wallace and Karl May. Because nobody would distribute the Chaplin re-releases he had bought for the German territory, he founded his own distribution company, Tobis Film, in 1971. Mainly produced surefire films with comedian Otto Waalkes, Loriot (Vicco von Bülow), Rainer Werner Fassbinder, Bud Spencer and was one of the first to put in money for the German distribution rights of Francis Coppola's ***Apocalypse Now***. Died on August 30, 2002, in Berlin.

BILLY WILDER [Director]

Born Samuel Wilder on June 22, 1906, in Sucha Beskidzka. As a journalist Wilder came to Berlin and got in touch with movie people who produced ***Menschen am Sonntag*** (***People on Sunday***). Continued his screenwriting career in Germany with ***Emil und die Detektive*** (***Emil and the Detectives***) and ***Ein blonder Traum*** (***A Blonde Dream***). Emigrating to the United States, he worked with Ernst Lubitsch whom he adored: ***Bluebeard's Eighth Wife, Ninotchka.*** Became one of Hollywood's top directors: directing Ray Milland in ***Lost Weekend***, Fred MacMurray and Barbara Stanwyck in ***Double Indemnity***, William Holden, Erich von Stroheim and Gloria Swanson in ***Sunset Boulevard***, Kirk Douglas in ***Ace in the Hole***, Marlene Dietrich in ***A Foreign Affair*** and ***Witness for the Prosecution,*** Audrey Hepburn in ***Sabrina,*** Marilyn Monroe in ***The 7th Year Itch*** and ***Some Like it Hot,*** Shirley MacLaine and Jack Lemmon in ***The Apartment*** and ***Irma la Douce***. Won a total of six

Academy Awards. Apparently the most successful among Germany's film émigrés. Wilder died on March 27, 2002, in Los Angeles.

HERBERT WINDT [Composer]

Born on September 15, 1894, in Senftenberg. War volunteer in 1914, severely wounded at Verdun in 1917, his face distorted, his left eye lost. NSDAP member since November 1931. Composed the national tunes for Gustav Ucicky's ***Morgenrot*** (***Dawn***) in 1932. For Leni Riefenstahl's Party Rally ***Triumph des Willens*** (***Triumph of the Will***) he added studio-recorded march music to the actual sound in order to enhance the vitality of the images and the dynamic editing. Windt's scores accompanied Riefenstahl's films (***Sieg des Glaubens; Olympia; Tiefland***) as well as those of Karl Ritter: ***Unternehmen Michael*** (***Operation Michael,*** 1937); ***Pour le Mérite*** (1938); ***Im Kampf gegen den Weltfeind*** (***In Battle Versus the Enemy of the World,*** 1939); ***Legion Condor*** (1939); ***Kadetten*** (***Cadets,*** 1939); ***Über alles in der Welt*** (***Above All Else in the World,*** 1940-41); ***Stukas*** (1941); ***G.P.U.*** (1941-42); ***Besatzung Dora*** (***The Crew of the Dora,*** 1942-43). In West-German post-war cinema, Windt's scores illustrated two so-called anti-war movies: ***Heldentum nach Ladenschluss*** (1955) and the Stalingrad epic ***Hunde, wollt ihr ewig leben?*** (***Stalingrad: Dogs, Do You Want to Live Forever?***, 1958-59). Windt died on November 23, 1965, in Deisenhofen near Munich.

MAX WINKLER

Born on September 7, 1875, in Karrasch, West Prussia, as son of teacher Julius Winkler. In 1891 started at Reichspost. In November 1919 became Mayor of Graudenz. In January 1919, as Member of Deutsche Demokratische Partei (DDP), delegate of the Prussian Country Assembly. His career as Reich trustee and business consultant began in 1920. In 1929, Winkler founded Cautio Treuhand GmbH and focuses on the German press. Winkler wasn't sympathizing with the National Socialists and his apartment was twice searched. He tried to correct that and was willing to change sides as soon as possible. He got in touch with Hans Heinrich Lammers, chief of the

Reich Chancellery, and Walter Funk and henceforth was instrumental in nationalizing the German press and film industry. This made him one of the most important confidants of Goebbels. After the war, Winkler was in custody for several years. He was a witness at the Nuremberg Trial and at the Wilhelmstrasse Trial, helped to decartalize Ufa and acted again as business consultant (thanks to his strong ties to Ludwig Erhard, West Germany's Minister of Economic Affairs). He died on October 12, 1961, in Düsseldorf.

WOLFGANG ZELLER [Composer]

Born on September 12, 1893, in Biesenrode in the South Harz as son of a clergyman. Violin lessons with Felix Berger, studied composition with Jean Paul Ertel. As soldier in World War 1, October 1914-November 1918. Violin player in the orchestra of Volksbühne Berlin, then conductor and composer. Started in the movies with film music for silents: Lupu Pick's ***Der Dummkopf***; Lotte Reiniger's feature-length silhouette film ***Die Abenteuer des Prinzen Achmed*** (***The Adventures of Prince Ahmed***), Hans Kyser's ***Luther - Ein Film der deutschen Reformation***. Scored Carl Theodor Dreyer's ***Vampyr*** and G. W. Pabst's ***Die Herrin von Atlantis*** (***The Mistress of Atlantis***). Although no party member of NSDAP, Zeller's most active years were those composing Nazi film scores for Emil Jannings, Veit Harlan and others: ***Ewiger Wald*** (***Eternal Forest***); ***Der alte und der junge König*** (***The Old and the Young King***); ***Der Herrscher*** (***The Ruler/The Sovereign***); ***Der zerbrochene Krug*** (***The Broken Jug***); ***Robert Koch, der Bekämpfer des Todes; Der Gouverneur*** (***The Governor***); ***Jud Süss*** (***Jew Suss***); ***Andreas Schlüter; Immensee.*** After the war scored anti-Fascist films: ***Ehe im Schatten*** (***Marriage in the Shadows***); ***Morituri*** (one of Artur Brauner's first productions); ***Grube Morgenrot*** and Bernhard Grzimek's African documentary ***Serengeti darf nicht sterben*** (***Serengeti***). Zeller was a member of Christian Peace Conference. Died on January 11, 1967, in Berlin.

Bibliography

Agde, Günter, *Flimmernde Versprechen. Geschichte des deutschen Werbefilms im Kino seit 1897.* Berlin: Verlag Das Neue Berlin, 1998.

Albrecht, Gerd, *Nationalsozialistische Filmpolitik. Eine soziologische Untersuchung über die Spielfilme im Dritten Reich.* Stuttgart: Ferdinand Enke Verlag, 1969.

Alt, Dirk, *"Der Farbfilm marschiert!". Frühe Farbfilmverfahren und NS-Propaganda 1933-1945.* Munich: Belleville, 2013.

Alt, Dirk, *The Dictator as Spectator. Feature Film Screenings before Adolf Hitler, 1933-1939.* In: Historical Journal of Film, Radio and Television No. 03/September 2015, pp. 420-437.

Aurich, Rolf/Beckenbach, Niels/Jacobsen, Wolfgang (ed.), *Reineckerland: Der Schriftsteller Herbert Reinecker.* Munich: edition text + kritik, 2010.

Aurich, Rolf, *Kalanag. Die kontrollierten Illusionen des Helmut Schreiber.* Berlin: Verbrecher Verlag, 2016.

Baarová, Lída, *Die süße Bitterkeit meines Lebens.* Koblenz, 2001.

Bach, Steven, *Leni: The Life and Work of Leni Riefenstahl.* London, 2007.

Baird, Jay W., *To Die for Germany: Heroes in the Nazi Pantheon.* Bloomington, Indiana: Indiana University Press, 1992.

Bauer, Alfred, *Deutscher Spielfilm Almanach 1929-1950.* Berlin: Filmblätter-Verlag, 1950. Reissued Munich: Filmladen Christoph Winterberg, 1976.

Beer, Hester, *Dismantling the Dream Factory: Gender, German Cinema, and the Postwar Quest for a New Film Language.* New York and Oxford: Berghahn Books, 2009.

Beyer, Friedemann, *Der Fall Selpin. Chronik einer Denunziation.* Munich: Collection Rolf Heyne, 2011.

Beyer, Friedemann/Koshofer, Gert/Krüger, Michael, *Ufa in Farbe. Technik, Politik und Starkult zwischen 1936 und 1945.* Munich: Rolf Heyne Collection, 2010.

Biddiscombe, Perry, *The Last Nazis: SS Werewolf Guerilla Resistance in Europe 1944-1947.* Stroud, Gloucestershire: The History Press, Ltd., 2004.

Billy Wilder. Eine Nahaufnahme von Hellmuth Karasek. Hamburg: Hoffmann und Campe, 1992.

Blumenberg, Hans C., *Das Leben geht weiter. Der letzte Film des Dritten Reichs.* Stuttgart: J.B. Metzler Verlag, 1993.

Bock, Hans-Michael (ed.), *CineGraph: Lexikon zum deutschsprachigen Film.* Munich: edition text + kritik, 1984 -

Bock, Hans-Michael/Lenssen, Claudia (eds.)., *Joe May: Regisseur und Produzent.* Munich: edition text + kritik, 1991.

Bock, Hans-Michael/Töteberg, Michael, *Das Ufa-Buch.* Frankfurt am Main: Zweitausendeins, 1992.

Bock, Hans-Michael/Distelmeyer, Jan/Schöning, Jörg (eds.), *Filmpionier und Mogul. Das Imperium des Joe May.* Munich: edition text + kritik, 2019.

Brandt, Hans-Jürgen, *Untersuchungen zum Dokumentarfilm des Dritten Reiches am Beispiel von drei Regisseuren: Hippler, Noldan und Junghans.* Diss. phil. Frankfurt/Main: Johann Wolfgang von Goethe Universität, 1985.

Brodnitz, Hanns, *Kino intim. Eine vergessene Biographie.* Teetz: Hentrich und Hentrich Verlag, 2005.

Buchheim, Yves/Kotteder,Franz, *Buchheim: Künstler, Sammler, Despot - Das Leben meines Vaters.* Munich: Wilhelm Heyne Verlag/Verlagsgruppe Random House GmbH, 2018.

Bundesarchiv/Filmarchiv, *Bestandsnachweis: Deutsche Trickfilme (1909-1945).* Compiled by Manfred Lichtenstein. Edited by Doris Hackbarth. Berlin: 1998.

Cziffra, Géza von, *Es war einmal eine rauschende Ballnacht - Eine Sittengeschichte des deutschen Films.* Munich and Berlin: Herbig, 1985.

Dahlke, Günther/Karl, Günter (eds.)., *Deutsche Spielfilme von den Anfängen bis 1933. Ein Filmführer.* Berlin/GDR: Henschelverlag Kunst und Gesellschaft, 1988.

Doherty, Thomas, *Hollywood and Hitler 1933-1939.* New York: Columbia University Press, 2013.

Döhring, Herbert, *Hitlers Hausverwalter.* Bochum: ZeitReisen Verlag, 2013.

Drewniak, Bogusław, *Der deutsche Film 1938-1945. Ein Gesamtüberblick.* Düsseldorf: Droste, 1987.

Ewers, Hanns Heinz, *Horst Wessel. Ein deutsches Schicksal.* Stuttgart/Berlin: Cotta'sche Buchhandlung Nachfolger, 1932.

Feilitzsch, Hanna von, *Mädchen mit Beziehungen. Das Leben der Margarete Slezak.* Rottach-Egern. Feilitzsch-Verlag, 2014.

Fest, Joachim, *Hitler.* Translated by Ralph Manheim. Orlando, Florida: Harcourt, Inc., 1974.

Fiebing, Malte, *Titanic (1943): Die Nazis und das berühmteste Schiff der Welt.* Norderstedt: Books on Demand GmbH, 2012.

Filmblatt. Edited by CineGraph Babelsberg, Berlin-Brandenburgisches Centrum für Filmforschung e.V., 1996-

Fraenkel, Heinrich, *Unsterblicher Film.* 1: *Die grosse Chronik von der Laterna Magica bis zum Tonfilm.* Munich: Kindler Verlag, 1956. 2: *Die grosse Chronik vom ersten Ton bis zur farbigen Breitwand.* Munich: Kindler Verlag, 1957.

Fröhlich, Elke (ed.), *Die Tagebücher von Joseph Goebbels. Sämtliche Fragmente.* Munich-New York-London-Paris: K.G. Saur, 1987-

Garden, Ian, *The Third Reich's Celluloid War: Propaganda in Nazi Feature Films, Documentaries and Television.* The History Press, 2016.

Gehrke, Ulrich, *Veit Harlan und der Kolberg-Film. Filmregie zwischen Geschichte, NS-Propaganda und Vergangenheitsbewältigung.* Hamburg: Author's Edition, 2011.

Giesen, Rolf, *Nazi Propaganda Films: A History and Filmography.* Jefferson, North Carolina, and London: McFarland & Company, Inc., 2003.

Giesen, Rolf/Hobsch, Manfred, *Hitlerjunge Quex, Jud Süss und Kolberg. Die Propagandafilme des Dritten Reiches.* Berlin: Schwarzkopf & Schwarzkopf, 2005.

Giesen, Rolf/Storm, J.P., *Animation Under the Swastika: A History of Trickfilm in Nazi Germany, 1933-1945.* Jefferson, North Carolina: McFarland & Company, Inc., 2012.

Giesen, Rolf, *Bienenstich und Hakenkreuz. Zeichentrick aus Dachau – die Deutsche Zeichenfilm GmbH.* Frankenthal: Mühlbeyer Filmbuchverlag, 2020.

Gillespie, William, *Karl Ritter – His Life and 'Zeitfilms' under National Socialism.* 2nd edition. Potts Point: German Films Dot Net, 2014.

Gladitz, Nina, *Leni Riefenstahl. Karriere einer Täterin.* Zurich: Orell Füssli AG Verlag, 2020.

Grob, Norbert, *Fritz Lang: "Ich bin ein Augenmensch".* Berlin: Ullstein Buchverlage GmbH, 2014.

Hanfstaengl, Ernst, *Zwischen Weißem und Braunem Haus.* Munich, 1970.

Harlan, Veit, *Im Schatten meiner Filme. Selbstbiographie.* Edited by Hans-Carl Opfermann. Gütersloh: Sigbert Mohn Verlag, 1966.

Haus der Geschichte Baden-Württemberg, *'Jud Süss': Propagandafilm im NS-Staat.* Stuttgart, 2007.

Helker, Renata, *Carl Raddatz 1912-2004.* Munich: belleville, 2018.

Herzberg, Bob, *The Third Reich on Screen, 1929-2015.* Jefferson, North Carolina: McFarland & Company, Inc., Publishers, 2015.

Higham, Charles, *Errol Flynn: The Untold Story.* New York: HarperCollins Publishers, 1980.

Hinton, David B., *The Films of Leni Riefenstahl.* Second edition. Filmmakers, No. 29, Metuchen, N.J., & London: The Scarecrow Press, Inc., 1991.

Hippler, Fritz, *Die Verstrickung.* Düsseldorf: Verlag Mehr Wissen, 1981.

Hobsch, Manfred, *Film im 'Dritten Reich' - Alle deutschen Spielfilme von 1933 bis 1945.* Berlin: Schwarzkopf & Schwarzkopf, 2010.

Hoffmann, Hilmar, *"Und die Fahne führt uns in die Ewigkeit": Propaganda im NS-Film.* Frankfurt/Main: Fischer Taschenbuch Verlag, 1988. English translation by John A. Broadwin and V. R. Berghahn, *The Triumph of Propaganda: Film and National Socialism 1933-1945.* Providence and Oxford: Berghahn Books, Inc., 1996.

Hollaender, Friedrich, *Those Torn from Earth.* New York: Liveright, 1941. German translation by Stefan Weidle, *Menschliches Treibgut.* Bonn: Weidle Verlag, 1995.

Hollstein, Dorothea, *Antisemitische Filmpropaganda. Die Darstellung der Juden im nationalsozialistischen Spielfilm.* München-Pullach/Berlin: Verlag Dokumentation, 1971.

Holtz, Reinhold Johann, *Die Phänomenologie und Psychologie des Trickfilms: Analytische Untersuchungen über die phänomenologischen, psychologischen und künstlerischen Strukturen der Trickfilmgruppe.* Dissertation. Hamburg: Philosophische Fakultät der Universität Hamburg, 1940.

Hull, David Stewart, *Film in the Third Reich: A Study of the German Cinema 1933-1945.* Berkeley and Los Angeles: University of California Press, 1969. Reprint New York, Simon and Schuster, 1973.

Jacobsen, Wolfgang (ed.), *Babelsberg. Das Filmstudio.* Berlin: Argon Verlag, 1994.

Junge, Traudl/Müller, Melissa, *Bis zur letzten Stunde. Hitlers Sekretärin erzählt ihr Leben.* Munich: List, 2003.

Kater, Michael H., *Review: Film as an Object of Reflection in the Goebbels Diaries: Series II (1941-1945).* In: Central European History, Vol. 33, No. 3 (2000), pp. 391-414.

Keiner, Reinhold, *Thea von Harbou und der deutsche Film bis 1933.* Hildesheim: Georg Olms Verlag, 1984.

Kinkel, Lutz, *Die Scheinwerferin. Leni Riefenstahl und das "Dritte Reich".* Hamburg/Vienna: Europa Verlag, 2002.

Knilli, Friedrich, *Ich war Jud Süss. Die Geschichte des Filmstars Ferdinand Marian.* Foreword by Alphons Silbermann. Berlin: Henschel Verlag, 2000.

Körner, Torsten, *Ein guter Freund - Heinz Rühmann Biographie.* Berlin: Aufbau Verlag, 2001.

Koop, Volker, *Warum Hitler King Kong liebte, aber den Deutschen Micky Maus verbot: die geheimen Lieblingsfilme der Nazi-Elite.* Berlin: be.bra Verlag, 2015.

Kracauer, Siegfried, *From Caligari to Hitler: A Psychological Study of German Film.* Princeton, NJ: Princeton University Press, 1947.

Krauss, Werner, *Das Schauspiel meines Lebens.* Hamburg: Goverts Verlag, 1958.

Kreimeier, Klaus, *Die Ufa-Story. Geschichte eines Filmkonzerns.* Munich: Hanser, 1995. English edition: *The Ufa Story: A History of Germany's Greatest Film Company, 1918-1945.* Translated by Robert Kimber and Rita Kimber. Berkeley: University of California Press, 1999.

Laqua, Carsten, *Wie Micky unter die Nazis fiel: Walt Disney und Deutschland.* Reinbek: Rowohlt, 1992.

Leiser, Erwin, *'Deutschland erwache!' Propaganda im Film des Dritten Reichs.* Reinbek/Hamburg: Rowohlt, 1969.

Longerich, Peter, *Goebbels. Biographie.* Munich: Siedler, 2010.

Magilow, Daniel H./Vander, Kristin T./Bridges, Elizabeth (eds.), *Nazisploitation! The Nazi Image in Low-Brow Cinema and Culture.* New York: The Continuum International Publishing Group, 2012.

Manvell, Roger/Fraenkel, Heinrich, *Doctor Goebbels: His Life and Death.* London: Pen & Sword Books Ltd., 2010.

McElhaney, Joe, *A Companion to Fritz Lang.* Malden, MA: John Wiley & Sons, Inc., 2015.

McGilligan, Patrick, *Fritz Lang: The Nature of the Beast.* University of Minnesota Press, 1997.

Moeller, Felix, *The Film Minister: Goebbels and the Cinema in the Third Reich.* Stuttgart and Fellbach: Edition Axel Menges, 2001.

Moritz, William, *Resistance and Subversion in Animated Films of The Nazi Era: the Case of Hans Fischerkoesen.* In: Animation Journal #1. Fall 1992.

Niven, Bill, *Hitler and Film: The Führer's Hidden Passion.* New Haven and London: Yale University Press, 2018.

Noack, Frank, *Veit Harlan. "Des Teufels Regisseur".* Munich: belleville, 2000.

Noack, Frank, *Veit Harlan: The Life and Work of a Nazi Filmmaker.* Lexington, Kentucky: The University Press of Kentucky, 2016.

Ode, Erik, *Der Kommissar und ich: Die Erik Ode Story.* Starnberg: Verlag R. S. Schulz, 1972.

Ohmann, Oliver, *Heinz Rühmann und "Die Feuerzangenbowle".* Leipzig: Lehmstedt Verlag, 2010.

Prainsack, Hemma Marlene, *"So sank die Titantic. Antibritische Propaganda im nationalsozialistischen Spielfilm."* Diploma thesis. Vienna: Theater-, Film- und Medienwissenschaft, 2013.

Prinzler, Hans Helmut, *Chronik des deutschen Films 1895-1994* Stuttgart: J. B. Metzler, 1995.

Raab, Kurt/Peters, Karsten, *Die Sehnsucht des Rainer Werner Fassbinder.* Munich: C. Bertelsmann Verlag GmbH, 1982.

Rabinbach, Anson/Gilman, Sander L. (eds.), *The Third Reich Sourcebook.* Berkeley/Los Angeles/London: University of California Press, 2013.

Reinecker, Herbert, *Ein Zeitbericht unter Zuhilfenahme des eigenen Lebenslaufs.* Erlangen-Bonn-Vienna: Verlag Dr. Dietmar Straube GmbH, 1990.

Rentschler, Eric, *The Ministry of Illusion: Nazi Cinema and Its Afterlife.* Cambridge, Massachusetts/London: Harvard University Press, 1996.

Riefenstahl, Leni (and Jaeger, Ernst), *Hinter den Kulissen des Reichsparteitagsfilms.* Munich: Zentralverlag der NSDAP/Franz Eher Verlag, 1935.

Riefenstahl, Leni, *Memoiren.* Munich/Hamburg: Albrecht Knaus Verlag, 1987. English: *A Memoir.* New York: St. Martin's Press.

Riess, Curt, *Das gab's nur einmal. Das Buch der schönsten Filme unseres Lebens.* Hamburg: Verlag der Sternbücher, 1956.

Rodman, Howard A., *Destiny Express.* New York City: Atheneum Books, 1990.

Roffat, Sébastien, *Animation et propaganda des dessins animés pendant la Seconde Guerre mondiale.* Paris-Budapest-Torino: L'Harmattan, 2005.

Ross, Steven J., *Hitler in Los Angeles: How Jews Foiled Nazi Plots against Hollywood and America.* New York: Bloomsbury, 2017.

Rühmann, Heinz, *Das war's. Erinnerungen.* Berlin; Vienna; Frankfurt/Main: Ullstein, 1982.

Sackett, Robert Eben, *Popular Entertainment, Class, and Politics in Munich, 1900-1923.* Cambridge, Massachusetts and London, England: Harvard University Press, 1982.

Schmid, Antonia, *Ikonologie der "Volksgemeinschaft". 'Deutsche' und das 'Jüdische' im Film der Berliner Republik.* Göttingen: Wallstein Verlag, 2019.

Seidl, Ernst (ed.), *"Jud Süss" - Propagandafilm im NS-Staat.* Stuttgart: Haus der Geschichte, 2007.

Siemens, Daniel, *The Making of a Nazi Hero: The Murder and Myth of Horst Wessel.* Translated by David Burnett. London and New York: I.B. Tauris & Co. Ltd., 2009.

Söderbaum, Kristina, *Nichts bleibt immer so. Erinnerungen.* Munich: F. A. Herbig Verlagsbuchhandlung, 1992.

Storm, J. P./Dressler, M., *Im Reiche der Micky Maus. Walt Disney in Deutschland 1927-1945.* Exhibition at Filmmuseum Potsdam. Berlin: Hentschel Verlag GmbH, 1991.

Strzelczyk, Florentine, *Motors and Machines, Robots and Rockets: Harry Piel and Sci-Fi Film in the Third Reich.* In: German Studies Review, Vol. 27, No. 3 (Oct. 2004), pp. 543-561. Published by The John Hopkins University Press on behalf of the German Studies Association.

Theuerkauf, Holger, *Goebbels' Filmerbe. Das Geschäft mit unveröffentlichten Ufa-Filmen.* Berlin: Ullstein, 1998.

Theweleit, Klaus, *Männerphantasien.* 2 volumes. Frankfurt/Main: Verlag Roter Stern, 1977.

Urwand, Ben, *The Collaboration: Hollywood's Pact with Hitler.* Cambridge, Massachusetts: Harvard University Press, 2003.

Trimborn, Jürgen, *Leni Riefenstahl: A Life.* Translated by Edna McCown. New York: Faber & Faber, 2008.

Walsh, Mary Williams, *Hollywood on the Rhine.* In: Los Angeles Times, July 16, 1995.

Watson, Robert P., *Titanic: The Incredible Untold Story of a Doomed Ship in World War II.* Philadelphia: DaCapo Press, 2016.

Westemeier, Jens (ed.), *"So war der deutsche Landser..." Das populäre Bild der Wehrmacht.* Paderborn: Ferdinand Schöningh, 2019.

Wetzel, Kraft/Hagemann, Peter A. (eds.), *Zensur - Verbotene deutsche Filme 1933-1945.* Berlin: Verlag Volker Spiess, 1978.

Wieland, Karin, *Dietrich & Riefenstahl - Der Traum von der neuen Frau.* Munich: Hanser, 2011.

Wulf, Joseph, *Theater und Film im Dritten Reich. Eine Dokumentation.* Gütersloh: Sigbert Mohn Verlag, 1964.

Youngkin, Stephen D., *The Lost One: A Life of Peter Lorre.* Lexington, Kentucky: The University Press of Kentucky, 2005.

Index

Persons

Film Titles

www.ingramcontent.com/pod-product-compliance
Lightning Source LLC
LaVergne TN
LVHW010555100826
845148LV00014B/2731

* 9 7 8 1 6 2 9 3 3 6 2 9 9 *